A
Clash of Empires

The South Wales Borderers at Tsingtao, 1914

John Dixon

bridge
books
Wrexham

A Clash of Empires
The South Wales Borderers at Tsingtao, 1914
First published in Wales in 2008
by
BRIDGE BOOKS
61 Park Avenue
Wrexham
LL12 7AW

A CIP entry for this book is avialable from the British Library

ISBN 978-1-84494-052-3

www.bridgebooks.co.uk

Printed and bound
by
Cromwell Press
Trowbridge

Contents

List of Maps

Foreword

by

Brigadier Sir Nicholas Somerville, CBE

I am sure that this history of the Battle of Tsingtao will be a valuable addition to the records of the Regimental Museum of the Royal Regiment of Wales and will be of special interest to all those who have served with, or who have family connections with, the Second Battalion the South Wales Borderers (XXIVth Regiment).

'Tsingtao' is a completely unique, and comparatively unknown, Battle Honour. Those with an interest in military history will be intrigued to know more about it. For me, personally, it has been a joy to read this account, for it tells the story of my father and so many of his friends who were with him at Tsingtao, and who, like myself, have been part of the regimental family.

This story of one of the early battles of the 1914–18 war is full of interesting lessons. The politics of Empire; the important role of the navies; the problem of working closely with allies and not least, the early tactics of ground forces, leading to trench warfare, are all laid bare in this book.

More importantly, it tells once again of the indomitable spirit, endurance, courage and humour of the British soldiers of the Second Battalion the South Wales Borderers as they were in 1914 on the China Station, indeed as they were in 1944 in Normandy and as I am sure, they still are today.

I believe all who read this book will find it an interesting and thoroughly good read.

Preface

Tsingtao would hardly warrant a mention in most English language books written on the Great War. For the most part, it remains an almost unheard of town to the British, though many will have drunk the beer of the same name in Chinese restaurants throughout the country, and any link to the Great War would seem to be unlikely – after all, didn't we fight in Europe? It would perhaps come as a surprise to many that this was not the case in other countries of the world – Germany knows well enough what Tsingtao is or was to her, and of course, Japan also has reason to remember the adventure onto the European political and military stage in 1914. Therefore, it is not surprising to find that the bulk of information about the action in Tsingtao is written in German, and this in itself, may explain why the British have taken little interest. To the Germans, their protectorate was of vital importance to their imperial position and its loss was recorded in detail; to the Japanese, their part in the capture of Tsingtao was of huge importance to their future foreign policy, and so there is some reason to understand that they too have recorded the events carefully. To the British, the short campaign in Tsingtao and the small number of men involved in the action, is reason enough to avoid the issue – besides, the larger-scale events in Europe overshadowed the small Far Eastern event. That may explain why there is little in the way of British records of the events, but it does not really explain why the largest body of work on Tsingtao in English has been researched by American authors.

Nevertheless, the role of the British in the Far East at this time should not be underestimated. The involvement was such that their actions were to have repercussions which would affect the area for the next three decades. Taken simply, this results from the simple request that was made to the Japanese to assist in looking after British interests in the area during the opening phases of the war. This opportunity was too good to miss for the Japanese and thereafter, the Japanese became the senior partner in the area. The decision no doubt played an important part in the rise of the Japanese military that eventually led to the wholesale invasion of China in the 1930s and the Second World War. It would be too much to say that the latter conflict was a result of the Tsingtao campaign of 1914, but it was at the heart of the Japanese way of thinking at that time and no doubt, the origins of their great self-belief are found at this period.

It is, perhaps, for these reasons that I have attempted to write a work that gives some emphasis to all the relevant players of the period and why I have tried to place the campaign in context of the involvement of the British in China in the nineteenth century and the Japanese in the early twentieth century. It is still difficult for me to say that the Japanese would not have become allies in the war without the open invitation, but it is certain that events would have taken longer to occur had the offer not been made. For the Germans' part, they were so desperate to retain empire that loss of part of it at Tsingtao struck very deep – so deep that there was much soul-searching and condemnation of the British for the part they played in the event. To that extent, it has been difficult to strike a balance that would allow the story to be told and to allow the events to unfold in a logical manner to express the feelings of the time, as the grasp of empire slipped from one nation to another, whilst a third stood and watched and offered some assistance to the victor. It was as much an imperial affair as the conflict in the west, the empires of Great Britain and Japan fought against those of Germany and Austria, whilst Russia and France lent a hand to the allies to protect their interests and it all took place in the Empire of the Middle Kingdom – China. Now after almost 100 years, the world has changed and the rising star in the imperial firmament is the latter country. No-one at the siege of Tsingtao could have imagined such a thing!

Arriving at the end of the work has been an interesting journey which has taken many twists and turns and changes in direction. There is no doubt that I started off believing one thing, but by the end of the research, I found I needed to reassess my own opinions on the campaign. It is to be hoped that this work will allow others to experience those turns in events and to offer some reason to reassess the role of the west in its long-term involvement in the Far East. It is also to be hoped that it has done justice to the men, of all empires, who fought there.

Chinese names

Throughout the text, the spelling of Chinese names has tended to follow the usage most commonly used in the texts studied during the research – these may not all be the most immediately obvious in some cases. The city at the centre of the discussion is today called *Qingdao* in western texts, but for the Germans, it was always spelled *Tsingtau* and the British tended to use Tsingtao, although the German spelling does occur as do other variations. Throughout, I have used the spelling of Tsingtao, adopted by the Battle Nomenclature Committee when the Battle Honour of that name was awarded to the South Wales Borderers. The following gives a list of the usage in the text on the left and alternative spellings which can be found:

Tsingtao	Qingdao, Tsingtau
Kiaochou	Kiao-chau, Kiaochow
Tientsin	Tianjin
Nanking	Nanjing
Peking	Beijing
Shandong	Shantung
Jinan	Chinan, Tsinan Fu
Canton	Guangzhou
Tsimo	Chimo, Jimo
Yangtse	Yangzi
Hong Kong	Xianggang
Litsun	Licun, Li'tsun
Tsu Hsi	Ci Xi

Acknowledgements

The idea for this book was born out of a long association with the Royal Welsh Museum (South Wales Borderers) at Brecon and in the first instance, I am deeply indebted to Martin Everett, the curator, for suggesting the work to me. Of course, this was because the South Wales Borderers was the only regiment of the British Army to be awarded the Battle Honour 'Tsingtao', and as such, there was some vested interest in the suggestion. This would seem to be fair and it was not as if Martin was expecting something for nothing, as he put the museum's not inconsiderable resources at my disposal for the duration of the project, which included access to many items that would have been impossible to obtain otherwise. Martin also did most of the hard work in collecting the details of the South Wales Borderers who served in China at this time and which has been presented in the appendices. For that alone, I owe him a great debt of gratitude. The rest of the museum staff, particularly Celia Green, have always offered help and encouragement and put up with my frequent visits, getting under their feet when other museum business has needed their attention. I am grateful to all.

I have been a member of the Western Front Association for over twenty years and over that time, I have often given talks at the South Wales Branch meetings. I am grateful to the branch for allowing me to begin putting my ideas together by giving a talk about the campaign in China, though it is about as far away as one can get from the Western Front! I have, over the years, developed many strong friendships in the branch and there are those who will talk about the many facets of the war with little encouragement. I am grateful to them for sharing their wisdom and collective knowledge, and particular mention should be made of Peter Gorman, Viv John and Gareth Scourfield and, especially Terry Powell, our long-standing secretary, who went to a great deal of trouble to sort out the maps contained in this volume and helped to enhance some of the old photographs I have used to illustrate the text. Also, thanks to Jane Benjamin who has helped enormously in tracking down one or two of the more obscure titles in the reference list and I am extremely grateful for her assistance at some crucial times. The branch serves a further function to all its members by providing a good mix of talks and battlefield visits which help to broaden our outlook and assists in a greater understanding of the conflict that was the Great War. The varied programme is down to the work of Dr David Payne who scours the country and cajoles members to give the best cross-section of talks possible. This has all helped to stimulate the thoughts and ideas formulated in this work, although I am totally responsible for any mistakes or misconceptions that may occur.

I have been fortunate enough to have spent some of my professional life in China and that has assisted with my understanding of this massive country, although it would have to be admitted that I have not seen that much of it. Nevertheless, this work would not have been finished without the help of some of the people I met as a professional geologist in China. I would therefore like to especially thank my very dear friend, Dr Li Hongyu, who not only encouraged my interest in China but made a big effort to help organise my visit to Qingdao in 2006. Also, I must thank Miss Wu Yie (Kate) who acted as our interpreter and guide during the visit to Qingdao and our driver, Mr Gao, who got us to the main places of interest in the now much-expanded city. Every effort was made by all to ensure that the trip was a success and that I was able to research all I needed whilst there.

Thanks to Patricia Gilbert-Chappell for proof-reading the manuscript and for the critical eye she used during the process. I only hope that it was an interesting subject for her keen, enquiring mind.

Finally thanks should go to my wife, Francesca, who has, as ever, put up with the hours of abandonment whilst I researched the book and accompanied me to China to visit what little remains of the battlefield of Qingdao. Without her support, none of this would have been possible.

John Dixon
August, 2008

Chapter 1

The Struggle for China

Tsingtao, a modern city and sea port on the coast of Shandong province in north-east China, would today hardly seem to have been the place of a sharp action during the Great War. It is a popular seaside resort considered by the Chinese as one of their finest. Its modern hotels, wide boulevards, efficient multi-lane highways and good facilities attract tourists from all over the world who enjoy its fine beaches and good climate, particularly after the intense heat of the continental summer. It is hardly surprising that it was chosen for the sailing venues for the 2008 Olympics. It was not always so, and for a few brief months in 1914, was the scene of heavy fighting as the Great War swept across the globe affecting the far-off reaches of imperial influence. It can come as something of a surprise these days to discover that not only did the British Army fight in China during the Great War but also that the Japanese were their allies during this particular part of the bloody fighting that was to become known as the 'war to end all wars'. It is, therefore, a justifiable question to ask, 'Why was Great Britain involved in China?' The answer to this question is quite complex, the origins of which date back many years before the Great War. From the British point of view, it reflects, what is considered by some, a far from glorious period of British history. Compared to the fighting on the Western Front, the action at Tsingtao was a very small affair, but was, nevertheless, one that was to have a lasting impact on the influence of European nations in the Far East for years to come. Indeed, it could be argued that this action and the rise of Japanese militarism, not only produced the seeds for the next war in the Far East but also influenced the emergence of China into the nation and world power it has become. It is important to the story of this brief Great War campaign to have some understanding of the events that put Great Britain in a position that necessitated military action against the Germans in China and saw her adopt Japan as an ally. The following discussion deals with these issues, albeit briefly, to put the events of September, October and November 1914 into their historical and, to a lesser extent, political context.

It has been argued that by the end of the eighteenth century, China was in decay[1] and decline. It has been suggested that this was a direct result of the rule of the Qing dynasty which, it is said, had reached a peak at the beginning of the century and was by 1800 in a slow but steady decline. The dynasty itself was the source of some of China's problems in so far as it was Manchu and not Chinese. Following their conquest of China in the mid-seventeenth century, the early Manchu emperors had largely adopted Chinese ways and customs and they founded the Qing dynasty which ruled over China, in much the same manner as earlier Chinese Dynasties, for over 250 years. Nevertheless, the most important positions in the empire were all held by Manchu officials, often members of the imperial clan, clearly loyal to the emperor and his dynasty and this tended to set the ruling classes very clearly apart from the Chinese themselves. However, even under this non-Chinese dynasty, the country had remained essentially isolated from the rest of the world. It was an isolationism that was effectively sought by the Chinese. China was inward looking, content in its long established traditions and bound together, if loosely on some occasions, by a well-established order, based on the philosophy of Confucius, and a people who regarded all foreigners as barbarians. In itself, this attitude tended to encourage isolationism in which foreign contact was both unnecessary and undesirable. The Qing rulers saw no reason to change this stance and to that extent, they reinforced the strong Chinese xenophobic views.

During the first century or so of Qing rule in China, Great Britain and other western countries were expanding rapidly with influences reaching many parts of the world. India, the East Indies, Africa and the Americas had already been touched by the hands of western imperialism. China, the sleeping giant of the east, was an obvious target to the late eighteenth century entrepreneurs. She was looked upon as a source of trade and in the second half of the eighteenth century, the British had established trading links, mainly through the efforts of the East India Company. These links were tentative as the market was established and the cultural differences were understood, or ignored as the case may be. Initially, this trade was weighted in favour of the Chinese, since the west, Britain in particular, wanted as much of the Chinese produce as it could get its hands on. Of course, Britain wanted the fine Chinese teas together with silks and ceramics and, perhaps surprisingly, rhubarb. The Chinese believed that the western powers could not survive without these commodities, even going so far as to believe that rhubarb was essential for the health of the western digestive system. With this in mind, the Chinese thought they were bargaining from a position of great power. They had so little knowledge of the west that they believed that they could sell such items at will and that the British would pay anything they asked for the privilege. China, on the other hand, had little use for the goods produced in the west or the technological advances that were on offer. They saw most of what was available to them as unnecessary for the way their lives were ordered, and they saw little advantage in change simply to accommodate the western ideas. For instance, they had no use for fine woven cotton fabrics produced in Lancashire when the coarser fabrics were much more appropriate to their day-to-day way of life and besides, they could easily produce their own fine fabrics when necessary. However, it is believed that the early trading links established were beneficial to the Chinese on more general economic grounds. For instance, the value of tea exports to Great Britain was in excess of £3,000,000 in 1800, but the Chinese imported goods worth less than a third of this figure.[2]

For the traders, on the other hand, this deficit left a problem on how to balance the books for they were paying large sums into the Chinese economy and getting little by way of return trade. To the western business men, it was a situation that could not be allowed to continue and every effort was made to find something that the Chinese wanted to trade. It was not long before that commodity was found – opium. The drug was not new to the country since small amounts had been imported for medicinal purposes for some time and this trade had received the approval of the Chinese government. However, by the end of the eighteenth century, the trade in the drug was growing at a rapid pace as the East India Company brought Indian opium, from Bihar and Benares, into the country through Canton. From this point on, the cultures of China and Great Britain were to clash for over a century before the trade in this drug was finally abolished.[3]

The trade in opium has been seen in varying ways depending on the era, the nationality of the authority and the standpoint adopted. From a purely economic standpoint, it made perfect sense to a nineteenth century British businessman, whereas a more modern view is likely to see the trade as totally reprehensible. Indeed, it has been suggested by one American writer that the action of Great Britain in China in the first half of the nineteenth century was akin to the behaviour of Nazi Germany in the first half of the twentieth century.[4] Perhaps this comment is a bit harsh and the analogy unsustainable especially when a more balanced view of the trading relationship between the two countries is considered.[5]

Nonetheless, the effect of opium on the Chinese population should not be underestimated. Whilst China was happy to export, especially when trade was essentially in her favour, there was little problem and the Chinese were happy for the western powers to take all that they could pay for. The trade in opium grew out of a pure trading need to balance the books; the fact that the drug was harmful and its use frowned upon in both China and Great Britain seems to have made little difference to those purveying the drug and, to some extent, for London it was a case of 'out of sight out of mind'. Britain herself used significant quantities of the drug, medicinally as laudanum and recreationally in smoking dens throughout the country, although most notably perhaps, in London. In fact, the business was to become a triangular trade since Britain exported silk and tea from China whilst opium sourced in India was imported to China. In this way, as the years of the nineteenth century slipped by, profits flowed via the East India Company and others, to Great Britain. The trade in opium was not encouraged in Britain since the use of it was prohibited but nor was it actively discouraged – the revenue it provided was too great to ignore. By the early nineteenth century in China, opium use was essentially illegal so, effectively, the trade was little more than very lucrative smuggling through the port of Canton, which at that time was the only port through which Great Britain, and indeed other foreigners, was allowed to trade.[6]

In China, more and more opium saw more and more misery and greater profits for those drug dealers in the port of entry. Not only was the trade profitable to the western traders but the local Chinese officials were taking substantial bribes to allow the trade, and imposing such local taxes as were necessary to ensure that the trade continued. Accompanying the trade, a whole market of accessories to drug-taking such as bowls and pipes, grew up to such an extent that each area within the country had its favoured method of entering the opium world of temporary relief. By the end of the first quarter of the nineteenth century, vast numbers of Chinese were involved in some way with the trade and the number of addicts grew rapidly through all classes, from the lowest tiers of society to the very highest. It should be noted here that the drug was handled in China by Chinese dealers only. Once the drug had arrived in Chinese waters, the Europeans, and sometimes Americans, had nothing more to do with it, except to reap its profits, and in this way attempted to hold the moral high ground.

The Qing dynasty, as weak as it had apparently become, recognized the need to stamp out the trade and to break the cycle of addiction and misery for the users. Whether this was entirely altruistic in purpose may be questioned since the Chinese government saw a growing western influence that did not fit with their need for isolation and order, and the influence of the narcotic was clearly making things worse in this respect. By the 1830s, the situation had become so bad that the Dao Guang emperor appointed a special commissioner to handle the situation. This man was governor Lin Zexu. Lin was from an educated, but poor background, and was considered to be a brilliant administrator which enabled him to rise through the Chinese hierarchy of the early 1800s to reach a position of considerable respect and not a little power. Lin arrived in Canton in 1838 with a remit to clean up the city and free it from opium use once and for all and to a large extent, was given a free hand to carry out the work as he saw fit. His task was meant to be an internal affair in so far as he was meant simply to stop the Chinese dependence on the drug, but he could not deal sensibly with the situation without stopping the trade in opium and so it became inevitable that there would be some kind of international confrontation, particularly with the British. There can be few today who believe that Lin was wrong to have seized all the opium he could get his hands on and then destroy it. However, it was not seen quite like that in the summer of 1839. Moreover, Lin had actually assisted the traders since his action had effectively pushed the price of opium up in a depressed market and the dealers, although feigning outrage, were not entirely displeased by his seizure of their stock.[7] The situation was further complicated as Captain Elliot, who had become the

Superintendent of Trade in Canton after the death of Lord Napier, had persuaded the traders to hand over the supply of opium on the promise of compensation from the British Government and had thereby exceeded his authority.

The tight controls that were imposed on the traders at this time, which included a limited access to a huge market, and near confinement in Canton, was always going to be an issue that would inevitably lead to friction between the two nations. The foreign traders saw dealing with the Chinese through appointed officials, the Co-Hong, as a severe restraint on their ability to operate freely. This point had been raised some years earlier with the British government by Thomas Jardine who was one of the most influential traders in the area and the man who stood to gain most by any relaxations on the restraint of the trade. As early as 1834, he advocated military action against the Chinese to bring about the relaxation of these restraints – in fact, he believed that not only was military action necessary but it was inevitable if Great Britain was to continue to grow its trade in China and the surrounding area.

Tension grew between the British and Chinese and was brought to a head by the murder of a local peasant, Lin Wei-Hsi, by drunken British and American sailors in Tsim-sha Tsui.[9] The Cantonese authorities requested that the men be handed over, but the British refused, stating they would be dealt with under their own laws. The British argued that there was also the question of the identity of the murderer, since the man who delivered the fatal blow was unknown. It was unacceptable to hand over all the men since it was known that they would have all faced the death penalty under Chinese law. Perhaps, this was not a very strong standpoint as all those involved were as responsible as each other, but it was the one adopted by the British in Canton in 1839 and it did little to ease tensions between the two sides. Also, it was not a strong standpoint bearing in mind that the British, and other nationalities, were effectively little more than tolerated as guests in China. In fact, the British did hold a trial for one Thomas Tidder for the murder of Lin Wei-Hsi but it proved inconclusive. A number of other men were found guilty of lesser crimes, but even they escaped the punishment when they returned to England, since it was considered that Captain Charles Elliot, Superintendent of Trade with a responsibility, amongst other things, for the tea trade through Canton, had acted outside his powers. The Chinese did not attend the trial as they considered it to be invalid and, as can be imagined, they were deeply unhappy about the result. They responded by stopping the re-supply of ships in the harbour which further increased the tensions until an armed clash resulted, causing casualties on both sides. Initially, Elliot was in no position to dictate terms to Governor Lin who played a very patient game of diplomacy. However, it was not long before the Royal Navy arrived on the scene in the form of HMS *Volage* and HMS *Hyacinth* which gave Elliot the leverage he thought he needed to get the Chinese to give in to his demands and allow the re-supply of the ships in the port. On 4 September 1839, Elliot presented Lin with an ultimatum, to run until 2 p.m. that day, after which he would take action to ensure that all the British ships gathered by that time in Hong Kong, would be re-supplied. The Chinese ignored the deadline, believing that their large and impressively painted war junks would be a match for two rather small frigates, and allowed the deadline to pass. As a result, on the same afternoon, Captain Elliot ordered his ships to open fire on the Chinese junks:

> ... the junks then triced up their boarding netting, and came into action with us at half pistol shot; our guns were well served with Grape and round-shot; ... they opened up a tremendous and well directed fire upon us, from all their Guns (each junk had 10 Guns) ... the junks fire, thank God! was not well enough depressed, or otherwise, none would have lived to tell the Story (19 of their guns we received in the mainsail) ... We loaded with Grape the fourth time, and gave them Gun for Gun ... this is the first day I ever shed human blood, and I hope it will be the last.[10]

War that had been simmering since Lin had destroyed the opium now boiled over in this sharp naval engagement that was to become known as the Battle of Kowloon. It was the opening action of what was to become known as the First Opium War.[11] Although the Chinese had not been cowed by the assault, neither did they achieve the victory they may have anticipated with their large war junks although it was reported as such to the Emperor in Peking. In the fighting that was to follow, the technological gap between the two forces was to become increasingly obvious as indeed did the wide cultural gap between the two nations.

It should be pointed out here that whilst opium may be considered to be the root cause of the problems between Britain and China, it has also been argued that the main reasons for the war were not the drug itself but the restraint of trade that the Chinese placed upon the British as a result of the trade.[12] There was also the question of the protection of British citizens and how best to deal with the Chinese that had jeopardised the lives and livelihood of the traders in Canton.[13] However, the inter-relationship of the narcotic, for most of the imports to China at this time were in opium, in the situation that had developed should not be underestimated, although it may be true to say that the relationship between Britain and China was such that had it been any other commodity, the outcome would have been the same.[14] As such, it has been argued that opium was 'the immediate, but not the ultimate cause of war.'[15] The outcome, whichever line is adopted, was that British military might was directed at the Chinese.

In comparison to later conflicts, the First Opium War was a relatively small-scale affair that lasted for three years with limited engagements and, at least for the British, produced relatively minor casualties. However, the importance of the fighting to both sides should not be underestimated. For the British, it was essentially the muscle-flexing exercise of what was already a large industrialised empire. For the Chinese, the war was about holding onto the power of its Empire, deciding the course of action for its own people and dealing the 'barbarians' a bloody nose that would make them think twice in their dealings with China. With an almost medieval naïveté, China had no real idea of what to expect from the industrialised west, and even less of an idea of how to deal with a belligerent Britain – they were soon to understand what sort of military power was available outside their borders.

During the initial exchanges of the war, the British contented themselves with naval actions, blockading the approaches to Canton and seizing the port of Ningbo and this looked to be sufficient, as the Chinese offered a negotiated settlement. Governor Lin of Canton however reported to the Emperor that the Chinese forces had been able to pull off a number of victories that had brought the British to the negotiating table – carefully ignoring the facts almost completely since success was expected of him in far-off Peking.[16] Consequently, the negotiations were not a great success and stalled, and it became clear to the British that the Chinese were not really trying to bring about any sort of settlement which they would be likely to accept. This brought about renewed action and the British landed a force at the entrance to Canton that captured the Bogue forts guarding the waterway to the city. The forts were destroyed and although outgunned, did not willingly surrender their positions and there were a number of Chinese casualties. During this action, HMS *Nemesis* became the first iron-clad warship to enter Chinese waters. She was a 700 ton iron-clad paddle steamer with a very shallow draught which carried two 32-pounders and five 6-pounder guns as well as numerous smaller guns.[17] This ship was so powerful for the time that she alone gave the British absolute naval superiority – the Chinese had no answer for such military might and the ship was used to great effect throughout the campaign. It had also served to indicate that the British had no intention of dealing lightly with the Chinese.

The renewed action did much to shock the Chinese awake from centuries of a Sinocentric view of the world. Unfortunately for them, against such force, the Qing commanders were almost entirely powerless as the superiority of their enemy told on both land and sea. From that point onwards, the Chinese were fighting a largely defensive action whilst optimistic reports were still being sent to the Emperor that all was well – if a piece of British uniform was found in the sea, it was reported as severe damage or losses to the enemy. Such fabrications did little to end the war since the Emperor's belief in his forces was entirely dependant upon the reports he received. However, where the British fought the Chinese on land, a measure of respect developed as in the case of the death of Admiral Kuan, for instance:

> Many of the Chinese officers boldly met their death … Among the most distinguished and lamented was poor old Admiral Kuan, whose death excited much sympathy throughout the force; he fell by a bayonet wound in his breast, as he was meeting the enemy at the gate of Anunghoy … Kuan's body was recognized and claimed by his own family on the following day,

and was of course readily given up to them. A salute of minute-guns was fired to his honour from the *Blenheim*.[18]

Nevertheless, the British power was overwhelming the Chinese wherever they clashed and by early 1842, it was recognized that a final victory could be achieved against the Chinese by a campaign along the Yangtse River.[19] This would effectively cut China in two and the fall of Chenkiang would give Britain control of the Grand Canal, the result of which would be to disrupt supplies to Peking and effectively endanger the life of the Emperor. A force, under the command of Sir Henry Pottinger, began by taking the island of Chusan and then entered Shanghai. The biggest action of this short campaign in 1842, was the fighting around Chunkiang where the Chinese suffered heavy losses to the better equipped and better disciplined British force. The stiffest resistance was offered by the Tartar[20] soldiers who fought hard and often committed suicide rather than surrender to the British and suffer the subsequent dishonour. Unfortunately, they also prevented the dishonour of their women and children by putting them to death first.

> Frightful were the scenes witnessed by these men among the houses and enclosures of the city, as group after group of whole families lying stiffened in their blood, within their own homesteads, were discovered in the streets occupied by the Tartar troops and mandarins, so numerous and so painfully interesting in their revolting details, as to impress with deep and lasting horror all who witnessed this happily rare example of the miseries and ferocities of war.
>
> The bodies of most of the hapless little children who had fallen sacrifices to the enthusiasm of their parents were found lying within the houses, and usually in the chambers of the women, as if each father had assembled the whole of his family before consummating the dreadful massacre; but many corpses of boys were lying in the streets, amongst those of horses and soldiers, as if an alarm had spread, and they had been stabbed while they had been attempting to escape from their ruthless parents.[21]

The threat posed by Pottinger brought the Chinese to negotiations once again and the war was eventually ended by the signing of the Treaty of Nanking on 29 August 1842. The main provisions of the treaty as summarised by Lieutenant Ouchterlony were:

1. Lasting peace and friendship between the two nations.
2. China to pay twenty-one million dollars in the course of the present and succeeding years.
3. The ports of Canton, Amoy, Foochow, Ningpo and Shanghai, to be thrown open to British merchants. Consular officers to be appointed to reside at them and regular and just tariffs of imports and exports (as well as transit) to be established and published.
4. The island of Hong Kong to be ceded in perpetuity to her Britannic Majesty, her heirs and successors.

5. All subjects of her Britannic Majesty (whether natives of Europe or India) who may be in confinement in any part of the Chinese empire, to be unconditionally released.

6. An act of full and entire amnesty to be published by the Emperor, under his imperial sign-manual and seal, to all Chinese subjects, on account of having held service or intercourse with, or resided under the British government or its officers.

7. Correspondence to be conducted on terms of perfect equality amongst the officers of both governments.

8. On the Emperor's assent being received to this treaty, and payment of the first six millions, her Britannic Majesty's forces to retire from Nanking and the Grand Canal, and the military post of Chin-hae to be also withdrawn; but the islands of Ko-lang-soo and Chusan are to be held until the money payments and the arrangements for opening the ports be completed.[22]

The fact that China was to pay Great Britain such a large sum of money in compensation for the war and the loss of the opium, clearly indicates that there had been little compromise on behalf of the negotiators for the British government. To add to this, the opening of the ports and the cession of the island of Hong Kong indicates that the treaty was as successful for the British as had been military campaign.[23] However, it should be noted that the British government was not as enthusiastic about gaining Hong Kong, and Pottinger was rebuked by London for the deal he had struck – if anything was to be added to the empire then it should have been Chusan.

Perhaps for the British, the outcome of the war was never in doubt but to the Chinese, it was an immense blow to the national psyche. They were proven to be incapable of dealing with a relatively small force of invaders that they had seen as nothing more than barbarians. They had lost a war and, to some extent, had been humiliated by the terms of the rather one-sided treaty. It had not been a war for which the British could feel any pride since the Royal Navy had, by its intervention, supported the opium trade – a trade which was illegal in Great Britain. The war had been unpopular in Great Britain, so much so that no less a statesman than Gladstone, speaking in the House of Commons in April 1841, gave his opinion on the war, '… this I can say, that a war more unjust in its origin, a war more calculated in its progress to cover this country with disgrace, I do not know and have not read of.'[24]

However, not even this great politician could entirely relieve the Chinese of all responsibility for the war by their actions and posturing towards the western powers.[25] The justification for the war was difficult for the government of the day and it was argued that in taking the action, they were protecting the interests of British subjects in China. This was a belief held by many and was reported as such in contemporary accounts.[26] In fact, there was a feeling prevalent at the time, that the Chinese needed to be taught a lesson in their dealing with the western powers in general, and Great Britain in particular. The legitimacy of the opium trade cannot, and indeed should not, be defended on moral grounds, but many politicians, including

Gladstone later in his career, saw it as an acceptable trade item and a necessity if the books were to be balanced. John Quincy Adams, former President of the United States, actually saw the seizure of the opium by the Chinese in the same light as the Boston Tea Party, believing it was action to defend their sovereignty rather than to prevent legitimate trade, but this should be looked on as a peculiarly American attitude and would certainly not have been held by any of the major trading nations in China at that time.[27] There was, no doubt, an element of this but Lin's intentions were more direct and immediate. There can be little doubt that his commission to control the opium trade also carried with it the need for self preservation. He was required to do something so that his credibility could be maintained. His future treatment gives evidence of the Emperor's attitude towards failure in this matter. Whatever the reasoning behind the war or the justification for it, the outcome was the first of a number of so-called 'unequal treaties' – the Treaty of Nanking, in which Great Britain, and later other western powers, were able to exact some severe concessions from the Chinese. Perhaps the most significant thing to emerge from the Treaty of Nanking was the concept of 'extra-territoriality'. This allowed British citizens living in China to live outside Chinese law and made them subject to only the laws of Great Britain.[28] This has been seen by some as the greatest erosion of the rights of the Chinese at this time and extra-territoriality was to remain a contentious issue between Great Britain, the other western powers and China for the remaining years of the Qing dynasty.

For the Chinese, their difficulties were only beginning since the acceptance of certain foreign influence was not universally welcomed. The war and the unfavourable treaty had done much to weaken the hold of central government on this vast country and the Qing dynasty was to face years of unrest which, if not directly related to the Opium War, were a direct consequence of the humiliating defeat and the continuing foreign trade. In a number of violent uprisings, most notably the Taiping rebellion, which spread like wildfire throughout the country, millions of Chinese died (some estimates put it as high as thirty million)[29] and the conflict served to weaken the country even more and allow further influence from the 'barbarians' and in particular, from the western powers who were all eyeing up China and making plans to seize whatever they could get. The rebellions rumbled through the 1850s and to make matters worse, the problems with opium and its trade with the outsiders, and Great Britain in particular, were unresolved. The British government viewing the events from London, found the situation deplorable, but in reality, was practically powerless to prevent British 'merchants' selling more or less whatever they wanted. Besides, there may have been a lack of political will to do too much about the trade since it was providing a source of revenue which could not be ignored – at its peak as much as one fifth of India's total revenue came from the sale of opium in China.[30]

By 1856, relations with the British had deteriorated to such a level that a further military clash was inevitable. The conflict when it arrived was to become known as the Arrow Incident, or Second Opium War.[31] It arose when the crew of a merchant ship, the *Arrow*, was accused of piracy and all its Chinese crew members arrested on 8 October 1856. Although the ship, a ,[32] was not British owned, it had been registered in Hong Kong by its Chinese owner and was entitled to the protection afforded to all ships carrying the Union Flag. The master, Thomas Kennedy, a twenty-four-year-old Irishman, was later to swear on oath that the Chinese making the arrest had also removed the Union Flag and had thus committed a gross insult to Great Britain. It is believed that at least one of the Chinese crew of the *Arrow* had some contact with pirates and there could have been as many as three such men on board at the time, although perhaps it was difficult to prove this to everyone's satisfaction. Nevertheless, the evidence was sufficient for the Chinese to arrest the fourteen-man crew and ignore the protection offered by the Union Flag (albeit, in this case, a flag of convenience). The insult led the governor of Hong Kong, Sir John Bowring, ordering an attack by the Royal Navy upon the city of Canton. There has been discussion concerning the legality of the protection afforded by the British flag since the registration of the *Arrow* in Hong Kong had expired at the end of September. It has been argued that this situation had arisen since the ship had not docked in Hong Kong in the meantime, to allow the formality of reregistration to take place. Sir John Bowring chose to take this point of view when assessing the situation that was developing in China.[33]

Following the end of the Crimean War, Bowring had a large fleet at his disposal, under the command of Admiral Sir Michael Seymour, who was persuaded to send a number of ships, including HMS *Sybille*[34] and the steam frigate, HMS *Encounter*[35] to Canton to resolve the situation. The Chinese had nothing to match the fire power of these ships and by 29 October 1857, a breach had been made in the walls of Canton. Whilst the city could be readily shelled and perhaps captured, it needed troops to hold it which were not available. Only one British battalion, of the 59th Regiment (2nd Battalion East Lancashires), was awarded the battle honour 'Canton' for its part in the action, but the force as a whole was too small to subdue a city.[36] This meant that the capture of the city was a hollow victory and did nothing to resolve the long-standing issues between the two nations. At one stage during the early exchanges, the Chinese put a reward on any Englishman captured, dead or alive, with the huge sum of £1,000 being placed on the head of a British commander.

Bowring was replaced as Britain's plenipotentiary in China by the Earl of Elgin in the autumn of 1858. He had been charged with resolving the issues and arriving at a treaty that would both end the war and give Britain more access to the huge market in the Far East. To this end, he had also been charged with obtaining a treaty with the Japanese and thereby increasing the trading potential for Great Britain still further. In the latter, he was immediately successful, but the negotiations with the Chinese were fraught with

The main Treaty Ports in China.

difficulties since they had no wish to treat with the 'barbarians'. The Taku forts at the entrance to the Peiho river were forced to surrender in May 1858, after an artillery battle that lasted for ninety minutes. This forced the Chinese to the negotiating table, but procrastination and delay caused frustration to Elgin's mission over the coming months and no treaty could be arrived at. In 1859, it became clear that the Chinese standpoint had not changed and that Elgin would be required to undertake a further military campaign if his aims were to be met. A year had passed and there had been no progress. When it was ordered that the Taku forts should be captured again, the Royal Navy, under the command of Admiral Hope, attempted to carry out the order as expeditiously as the earlier action. However, the Chinese had strengthened the positions and increased the firepower of the forts. The result was a defeat for the attacking force and the loss of HMS *Plover*[37] Admiral Hope's flagship. A landing party had been set ashore but was badly mauled by the Chinese fire from the forts as it crossed the mud-flats of the river:

> We had a hard fight for it, but what could we do against such a fearful number of guns, and us poor little gunboats in such a small place, not much broader across than the length of the ship ... I had to fling my arms away coming back from the forts, and was nearly smothered once, only one of our bluejackets was kind enough to heave me out. You sank up to your knees at least every step, and just fancy the slaughter going 500 yards in the face of about 30 pieces of artillery right in front of you and on each flank. It was dreadful, horrible, work, but thank God I came out all right.[38]

It had been a costly action with a total list of killed or wounded in excess of 400.

This defeat, although relatively minor for the British, was a setback as far as the treaty negotiations were concerned, especially since it was now argued that there would be increased reparations for the losses sustained in this action. Of course, the Chinese saw things somewhat differently since, as victors of the latest encounter, they were very unlikely to give any ground in the discussions. It was August 1860 before another attempt was made to capture the Taku Forts when, with the assistance of a contingent of French troops, the British succeeded in taking possession of them for the second time:[39]

> All this time the fire of the enemy continued incessant. Cold shot, hand grenades, stinkpots and vases of lime were showered on the crowd of besiegers ... Ladders placed against the wall were pulled into the fort, or thrown over, and in vain did man after man attempt to swarm through the embrasures. If the defence was desperate, nothing could exceed the gallantry of the assailants. Between English and French there was nothing to choose. A Frenchman climbed to the top of the parapet, where for some time he stood alone. One rifle after another was handed up to him, which he fired against the enemy. But his courage was unavailing, and he fell, speared through the eye. Another, pickaxe in hand attempted to cut away the top of the wall. He

was shot and Lieutenant Burslem, of the 67th, caught hold of his pick and continued the work. Lieutenant Rogers attempted to force his way through the embrasure, but was driven back. He ran to another, but it was too high for him. Lieutenant Lenon, forced the point of his sword into the wall and placing one foot on the sword. Lieutenant Rogers leaped through the embrasure ...[40]

Such was the action involved in capturing the Northern Outer Fort. It should be noted here that seven Victoria Crosses were awarded for the gallantry shown.[41] Among these was the award to Hospital Apprentice, Andrew Fitzgibbon, who at fifteen years and three months became the youngest holder of the award. It was also the largest number of awards of the medal made for a single action until the defence of Rorke's Drift in 1879.

There then followed a rapid march on Peking with a view to increasing the pressure on the Chinese Emperor to re-enter negotiations. It was at this time that a number of events occurred that show perhaps the random fortunes of war. A party was sent ahead, under a flag of truce, to prepare the Chinese for the negotiations that everyone anticipated. The party included a number of army officers, as well as Thomas Bowlby of *The Times*, Harry Parkes, Consul to Canton, and a guard of Indian troops, a total of twenty-six men. This party was immediately taken captive and over half were to die of maltreatment or were executed by the Chinese. At the same time, Elgin carried on trying to make contact with the Chinese, being continually assured of the safety and good health of the party. Meanwhile, the French troops, lagging somewhat behind the British forces, ransacked the Emperor's Summer Palace taking away all that could be carried as loot and destroying what was too big to be removed. Shortly afterwards, Elgin heard of the mistreatment of his delegation and was furious that this should have occurred whilst everything was being done on his part to ensure the preparation of a peace treaty. He then ordered the complete destruction of the Summer Palace – an action which has been seen as, perhaps, one of the greatest acts of vandalism in warfare. It may have been that, but he rationalised it by the fact that the Palace had already been ransacked by the French – he had stopped short of the suggested destruction of the Forbidden City.

We went out, and, after pillaging it, burned the whole place, destroying in a Vandal-like manner most valuable property which could not be replaced for four millions. We got upwards of £48 apiece prize money before we went out here, and although I have not as much as many, I have done well. The people are civil but I think the grandees hate us, as they must after what we did to the Palace. You can scarcely imagine the beauty and magnificence of the places we burned. It made one's heart sore to burn them; in fact, these places were so large, and we were so pressed for time, that we could not plunder them carefully. Quantities of gold ornaments were burnt, considered as brass. It was wretchedly demoralizing work for an army. Everyone was wild for plunder.[42]

This action brought the Chinese to the negotiating table again. The Emperor had fled the city and left Prince Kuang to deal with the foreigners and to ratify the Treaty of Tientsin which had the result of releasing further Chinese ports to outsider trading and effectively increased the western influence that the Chinese seemed desperate to avoid. At each attempt to avoid further influence from outside, it appears that the Qing dynasty dug itself deeper into the mess that was eventually to bring about its own downfall. The treaty released further land in China, allowing western nations the opportunity for imperial expansion and, although it may have been recognized that the chances of turning China into a colony were remote, all the major western powers were aware that the country had much that could be taken by the strong. In this way, the influence of Great Britain was growing as she did everything to increase her markets for such commodities as cotton and opium.

The growing influence of Great Britain in China was the beginning of much greater western influence during the final decades of a century that had begun with China safe in its isolation. In a very similar manner, the influence of other western powers on China was growing. The French were particularly involved in Annam (Vietnam), traditionally a tributary state to China, and as their influence grew, they were keen to progress into south-western China. During the early 1880s, the French campaigned for control of Tongking which eventually led to the Franco-Chinese war, which also resulted in an unequal treaty, giving Vietnam to France and with it, all the economic possibilities of south-west China. A feature of the unequal treaties which the western powers squeezed out of the Chinese was the fact that any new concession gained by one power was also deemed to apply to the other imperial powers.

China was also involved in a war with Japan in 1894–5 which brought about a significant and humiliating defeat of the Chinese navy in September 1894 at the Battle of Yalu and subsequently, her army at Port Arthur.[43] Once again, China was forced to make huge land concessions and was separated from another of its tributary states, Korea. The expansionism of the Japanese in the area should not be underestimated for, although they were not in control of an empire that could rival Great Britain or France, they saw no reason not to build one as big as possible in the immediate environs of Japan and they were fast building the military know-how to accomplish this.

Not to be outdone, the Germans saw room for expansion and commercial gain in China and also a means of providing a base in the Pacific area of influence from which her growing navy could operate. At first, the imperialistic tendencies of Germany were muted in comparison to those of Britain and France, but Prussia had been party to an unequal treaty with the Qing dynasty in 1861. By the 1890s however, Germany was much more interested in China and saw her role there as a way to increase her influence throughout the Asian and Pacific spheres. To the Germans, Tsingtao, which had been identified by Admiral Alfred von Tirpitz in early 1896[44] as the perfect place for a port, would offer them both a foothold in China and a good safe harbour. Germany was to confront the Chinese following the murder of two German Catholic missionaries in 1897 which resulted in the first landing of German troops in Tsingtao. The Chinese had little option but to agree to a ninety-nine year lease of the area to Germany, together with permission to allow the Germans to build a railway line across Shandong province as far as Jinan. Along with this, they also conceded the right for the Germans to mine the mineral wealth from the area ten miles either side of the railway line. All in all, the Chinese had given up much to the foreigner.[45] Further details of the German concession in Tsingtao will be found in the relevant chapter.

To all this misery which appeared to descend upon the Chinese in the latter years of the nineteenth century must be added the encroachment of Russia onto its northern borders and into Manchuria. There were numerous skirmishes, particularly on the Amur River, between these two giant states and generally, the Chinese were bested. It must have been clear that the isolation and order that the Chinese had sought for themselves for centuries was soon to be lost for ever. There can be no doubt that the influence of the foreign powers was growing and at the same time, the Qing dynasty's grasp on China was weakening. The European powers vied for more and more of the Chinese cake whilst at the same time, China was becoming increasingly anti-foreigner. Although that was not an entirely new feeling in China by the end of the nineteenth century, it was almost actively encouraged in a kind of nationalism that was, at least in part, new to the Chinese themselves. It was difficult for them to accept that the traditional influences on their country and society were waning and that this was the root of the troubles that were to beset the country for at least half of the twentieth century. By the latter years of the nineteenth century, the old order was changing and before the century was over, the first expression of this change was felt in the so-called Boxer Rebellion.

The gradual emasculation of China, both actual and perceived, was seen by many millions of her citizens and her government, as something that needed to be stopped. The question was how could this be achieved so that China saved face and gained all she wanted in terms of the restoration of the old order and the removal of foreign influence. The nineteenth century had seen her embark on a number of wars with the western powers and Japan. All these wars and the internal rebellions had done little to achieve any of the aims that seemed to be so earnestly desired. Instead of limiting the influence of the foreigners, there had been a steady growth in their power within the country and the attitude of the Chinese was becoming increasingly xenophobic and they saw little need to change their view that all foreigners were barbarians. Of course, the Qing dynasty itself was not Chinese and to some extent, could be seen by the purists as part of the problem rather than being part of the solution. However, by the late 1890s, there was a new movement sweeping through parts of China which sought to bring together the xenophobic tendencies of the Chinese and strike at the very heart of the government, so that it questioned itself and its role in the destiny of China. Those involved in this movement were to become known as the Boxers.

The situation in China was not helped by the attitude of westerners who had done little to endear themselves to the Chinese throughout the nineteenth century. There was also no love lost between China and the Japanese whom they considered to be 'pygmy dwarves'.[46] In spite of the desire to be free of the grip of the foreigners, the Chinese had little in the way of military might with which to achieve this end. Soldiering was considered to be a lowly profession and consequently, the regular army, such as it was, was generally poorly led and ill-equipped. One commentator of the period suggested, 'The necessity of making an appeal to arms was to the Chinese in many ways distasteful. They did not wish to fight, but merely to be let alone.'[47] However, it should be noted that China had taken some steps towards a modern army and had purchased weapons and equipment from the Germans during the late 1890s.

Thus, by the end of the nineteenth century, the Chinese were in an invidious position. Their society, essentially feudal and ruled by an overbearing, often corrupt, bureaucracy, was failing under the influence of new ideas from the foreigners. Generally, these were viewed with a mixture of fear and loathing, particularly near the coastal fringes where western influence had been developing through the nineteenth century. It is, perhaps, surprising to think today that the trappings of the industrial age such as mining, railways and foreign trade were completely alien to, and unwanted by, the Chinese of 1900. They saw mining as tampering with the harmony of nature, and railways with their great iron rails and noisy steam engines, as upsetting the balance further. To a large extent, before the coming of western influence, foreign trade had been one way, as the states surrounding China paid tribute to the court. Hence, the encounter with western greed and expansionism could only have been seen as detrimental. Added to these material problems were more intellectual issues such as religion which saw hundreds of Christian missionaries fanning out all over China to bring the word of their god to the heathen Chinese. The China of 1900 had already experienced the Taiping rebellion which had been based on a peculiarly Chinese version of the Christian faith and this only supported the belief that, by and large, Christianity was something they did not want. Perhaps this was not unreasonable in a country where the main inter-mediary with their gods was the Emperor himself. Nevertheless, slowly and surely, a situation had arisen where some hundreds of thousands of Christian converts had been made by the industrious missionaries by the end of the nineteenth century. These converts were to become the focus of the hatred of the Boxers before the end of 1900.[48] Perhaps another factor that allowed China to be ready for revolt was the general attitude of the court which was in 1900, dominated by the Empress Dowager, Tsu Hsi who had been around long enough to remember the hard times during the Second China War and the Taiping rebellion, and hated the foreigners as heartily as anyone in the land. Thus, if there was to be a revolution against the foreigners, it was more likely to be supported by the court than prevented. The Empress Dowager was a powerful woman, described as the 'only man in China'[49] by one observer, and little of any importance happened but that she was aware of it or influenced it in some way.

It was with all these issues as a backdrop that the Boxer Rebellion took place. To the many Chinese whose lives were affected by it or were actively involved, it was not considered to be a rebellion with all that implies about conflict with the rulers of the country; but was rather an uprising of ordinary people against the foreigners who sought to dominate and destroy their country. The origin of the Boxers themselves is not entirely clear with some experts suggesting that they date back to the early part of the nineteenth century.[50] Other authorities trace their origins much closer to the events that gave them brief fame and notoriety, perhaps even to the German takeover of Tsingtao.[51] It has been suggested that they originated during the 1890s from two sects – the 'Boxers United in Righteousness' and the 'Spirit Boxers'.[52] As may be expected with names like this, the sects' activities revolved around the martial arts but there were also mystical beliefs. The followers believed that they could be made immune to bullets and that they could call up huge spirit armies in the defence of China. It may have been this alone that allowed the Boxers' following to spread like wildfire through the provinces of Shansi and Shandong[53] in north-eastern China in the latter years of the nineteenth century. To add a certain credence to their sect, they even coined the phrase 'Support the Qing, destroy the foreign (religion).'[54] On a somewhat darker side, the Boxers spread propaganda about the behaviour of the western peoples which can have done little to enhance the standing of the foreigners in the eyes of an already suspicious population. The Boxers insisted that the Christians stole Chinese girls and ripped out their hearts and other organs for medical purposes – a belief so widely held that it extended to the Empress Dowager – and that Christian priests were able to protect themselves by using menstrual blood smeared on their faces. This may all seem quite ridiculous today but it is a fine example of not letting the truth spoil a good story and sentiments such as these swayed hundreds of thousands of people in those provinces where the Boxers gained a real following – which were also the provinces where there were the greatest populations of foreigners.[55] The people in some of these areas needed very little persuasion to dislike the westerners and the Boxers simply provided them with the fuel.

Whilst the Boxers were seen by many Chinese and almost all western observers, as extreme and not necessarily dangerous, the last year of the nineteenth century saw a swift rise in the popularity of the cult and its gaining the tacit sponsorship of the Empress Dowager. In the early months of 1900, there were warnings from a number of quarters that the Boxers were getting out of control and that there could only be future confrontation. The majority of the ministers of the foreign legations saw nothing to worry about. The French minister, Monsieur Pichon, was not of a like opinion and warned about the growing strength of the Boxers.[56] Sir Claude MacDonald, the British minister, was totally unflappable about the situation but nevertheless made representations to the Chinese, through the official channel, the Tsungli Yamen,[57] with regard to the treatment meted out to a number of missionaries by the Boxers and the murder of one Sydney Brooks.[58] Sir Claude largely took the Chinese representatives' assurances at face value to such an extent that he saw no urgency to inform London of the situation that was developing rapidly in Peking. By the time the truth of at least some of Pichon's warning had been demonstrated, it was too late to inform the outside world of the situation. As the situation worsened, the ministers in the legations sent for troops for their defence, an action which was seen by some Chinese officials as inflammatory and the inevitable consequence of which was conflict. At all times prior to this, it had been necessary to seek the permission of the Chinese to have armed forces in the legations but under the circumstances and the inaction by the Tsungli Yamen, the legation ministers had decided not to wait for any response. Matters deteriorated rapidly in early June and it was clear that there would be some sort of confrontation. The Chinese government had issued, through the Tsungli Yamen, an ultimatum for the foreigners to leave their legations. This brought about much debate since there was a genuine fear that there would be a massacre as soon as the legations were abandoned.[59] On 18 June 1900, the German minister, Baron von Ketteler, was murdered by a Chinese soldier, an action which persuaded all concerned that it was better to stay in the legations and defend themselves.[60] This was, effectively, the beginning of the siege of the Peking legations, though until 21 June 1900, there was no open hostility between them and the Chinese.

There has been discussion about the timing of this 'rebellion'. What exactly had made the Chinese feel they could achieve in 1900 what they had failed to do against any foe throughout the nineteenth century. It has been argued that they knew of the very poor performance of the British in the first year of the South African War[61] and that this had given them courage. Also, as a result of the Italians withdrawing a request for a concession, the Chinese had gained greater self belief.[62] To some extent, the westerners had shown previously unnoticed signs of weakness and it appears that this may have been influenced by the rise of the Boxers and their quiet acceptance by the Empress Dowager. The latter also been considered that the Empress Dowager also saw the potential for using the Boxers to rid the country of the western influence once and for all, without the need for the court to take any of the blame should the rebellion fail. All the conditions would have seemed right for some kind of action – namely the siege of the legations in the first place, but also a number of other actions also occurred throughout this part of north-east China during the rebellion.

As the tensions mounted in Peking, there was still some contact by telegraph with the outside world and the foreign settlement at Tientsin was alerted to the deteriorating situation. The immediate action of Vice-Admiral Sir Edward Seymour,[63] senior British officer in the area, was to mount a rescue attempt. He was able to gain the support of the other nations represented and a mixed force was assembled as early as 31 May. At this time, the railway line between the two cities was operational and it was logical to Seymour to use this to speed his journey to Peking in order to rescue those besieged as soon as possible. This decision was, at least in part, the downfall of the mission. No sooner had he started out than there were problems as sections of the line needed to be repaired and each time there was a need to fight off the Boxers because, although better armed and trained, Seymour's force was heavily outnumbered.[64] Eventually, having reached to within thirty-five miles of Peking, Seymour had to admit that he could not continue with the rescue bid. Of course, this was not seen in a very good light by the besieged and he earned the nickname of 'Admiral see-no-more'. Although it is not difficult to understand the point of view of those inside the legations, Seymour's withdrawal made sound military sense. His problems were only just beginning, for as he withdrew, the net was drawing tighter about Tientsin, so much so that by the time his force had reached that city, its foreign quarter had also become besieged.

Thus, within a matter of days in June 1900, two crises had developed in China – one in Peking and one in Tientsin. Any relief force for Peking would, of necessity, need to follow the Peiho river and hence the relief of Tientsin would occur first, since this city was situated further down stream. The entrance to the Peiho was guarded by the Taku forts, two on each side of the river, and any relief along the river would first need to control these. The forts had commanding positions over the entry to the river and were, at least in theory, well-equipped after their rebuilding subsequent to the end of the Second China War. In 1860, it had been difficult to land forces to attack the forts and it was decided that some kind of flanking move would be needed for their capture this time. In the event, the forts fell relatively quickly on 17 June and the way was open to the Peiho and to Tientsin and Peking. Part of this action was the remarkable capture of four Chinese destroyers which were standing off the Taku forts. Commander Roger Keyes[65] brought his destroyer, HMS *Fame*, alongside the Chinese ships and boarded them without any loss of life – their crews seemed to have little will for fighting, and it was an early and important victory for the combined forces. A short time later, it was possible to land sufficient soldiers (including part of the 2nd Battalion the Royal Welsh Fusiliers) for them to break through the besieging forces and enter Tientsin.[66] However, getting troops to the foreign quarter of Tientsin was not the same as lifting the siege and it was to be over a month before there were sufficient troops in the area to allow for an advance on Peking.

Whilst this had been going on in Tientsin, sad news was received that all the occupants, both foreigners and Chinese Christians, trapped in the legations in Peking had been massacred. It was not true, but to those entrapped in Tientsin, it was a tremendous blow – they were in the same position and it must have seemed to them that unless something could be done quickly they would be next. Nevertheless, there was an increased resolve to break out of the siege. It was easier for the Tientsin garrison to be reinforced than it was for the garrison in Peking because of its position near the undefended coastal region and by early August, sufficient men and material had been gathered to allow for a break out. By this time, it was clear from messages smuggled out of the legations, that there were still survivors in Peking – and that fact made the break out all the more urgent and important. It was not long before the city of Tientsin was in the hands of the foreign forces and thereafter, they were able to make steady progress along the banks of the Peiho river towards Peking. There was fighting all the way, but to a large extent, it was much lighter than had been anticipated as the regular forces of the Emperor and the Boxer bands melted away not wanting to face the strong foreign force.

The siege of the legations in Peking was eventually lifted on 14 August 1900, the 2nd Battalion, Royal Welsh Fusiliers leading the British contingent into the city. The suffering and privations endured during the siege are difficult to imagine today but after fifty-five days, they could not have survived much longer. As can be imagined, the sight of the relieving force put everyone in the legation in a light-hearted, if not light-headed, mood but their generally poor condition was not wasted on the rescuers and many remarked on their thinness and paleness.[67] Even today, there is discussion as to why the legations had not been completely overrun at an early stage in the operation. They should have been, since they were so heavily out-numbered and the Chinese had modern weapons at their disposal.[68] Had such weapons been used, there could have been little to stop the Chinese gaining the victory they seemed to want so badly. It has been suggested by some authorities that there was someone senior in the Chinese camp who recognized that the action of the siege would do little for China and that the only likely outcome would be more foreign influence and a certain amount of retribution. The person most likely to have been responsible for not effectively pursuing the siege was Jung Lu, Commander-in-Chief of the forces arranged around the legations. It would appear that he recognized that over-running the legations and murdering the ministers and their families would create more problems for China than it would solve. In the days before her death in 1908, Tsu Hsi identified him as having 'saved the Manchus' at least in the short term.[69]

Following the lifting of the siege, the Germans and the French insisted upon punitive expeditions to seek out the ring leaders and exact revenge. At first, Britain also considered such measures but, probably under the influence of the more moderate United States of America, no action was taken. It is difficult to assess how effective the punitive expeditions were, but there is no doubt that the mass executions that followed did little to endear the Europeans to the Chinese or ease the fears that had hastened the rise of the Boxers. By the time these punitive expeditions were underway, the Chinese court had left Peking and it was not until it returned in 1901 that there were any discussions about reparations, the scale of which was so large that it took the Chinese until 1939 to pay off the money, some £67,500,000, extracted from them by a treaty signed on 7 September 1901.

The Boxer Rebellion marked the beginning of the final decline of the Qing dynasty. By 1908, both the Emperor and the Empress Dowager were dead and the new Emperor, a mere child, was only to rule for a period of three years before he was deposed and a republic declared. The effects of the rebellion were to reach far into the future as many of the Boxers were seen as heroes by the communist régime of later years. However, one of the immediate effects for the Chinese was perhaps small-scale, but visible in so far as it was common for the people of Peking to see foreign troops in their capital – the exact opposite of the Boxers' desired aims – a situation that came about because it was felt that it was unsafe to leave the legations unprotected. In 1912, the 2nd Battalion the South Wales Borderers sailed from their base in South Africa to take up the work of British Legation Guard in Peking.

> After a calm and uneventful voyage Chin-wang-tao was reached on the 3rd November 1912, having touched at Mauritius, Singapore and Hong Kong, at which latter place orders were received that we were to find the British Legation Guard of three companies at Peking and A, D and G Companies were detailed for this duty, the remainder of the Battalion being for Tientsin. At 8.30 am on the 4th November 1912, the Regiment left by special train for Peking and Tientsin, the latter place being reached at about 4.30 pm. Brigadier General Cooper CB, MVO, DSO, Commanding the Troops North China Command met the Battalion, also the band of the 15th Regiment the United States Infantry, the Band of the 2nd Battalion Somerset Light Infantry and the Drums of the 124th (DCO) Baluchistan Infantry besides a large gathering of various individuals representative of the different foreign contingents serving in China.[70]

This battalion was to remain in China for the next two years and, as a result, became the only British battalion to take part in the operations in front of Tsingtao in 1914.

For a little over one hundred years, there had been an ever-increasing foreign influence in China. From the tentative incursions by traders such as the East India Company, through the greed and duplicitous trading of the years of the Opium Wars, to the end of the Qing dynasty, there had been a steady flow of new ideas and new people into the vast country. It was something that the Chinese were powerless to stop and unsuccessful wars with Britain, France, Russia and Japan did nothing to stem the flow – in fact, the result of the wars and the onerous, unequal treaties extracted from them, had the opposite effect. The Chinese wanted to be left alone, rulers of their own domain, but there could be no possibility of that happening. By 1914, the influence, if not interference, of foreigners had assisted in changing China so fundamentally that there could be no return. The formation of a republic in 1911 discarded once and for all, the values that had been fought for through the nineteenth century. There can be no doubt that this had been, at least in part, down to western influence but whether it had been beneficial to the Chinese in the long term, perhaps only their position in the world of the twenty-first century will demonstrate. In 1914, the world was also changing for the western powers involved in China, as a result of a power struggle that had been building up through the nineteenth century. Foreseen by some of the soldiers and statesmen of the latter years of the century, this struggle was to destroy millions of lives and dismantle empires that had been built by trade, enterprise and conquest. China's involvement in this terrible conflict was small, but two of the major European powers were to clash in Tsingtao in the province of Shandong – ironically perhaps, the province that had been the birthplace of the Boxers – and between three of the nations: Great Britain, Germany and Japan, that had fought side by side to defeat them. The events in Tsingtao in 1914 should be seen against this backdrop of imperialism and the struggle for power in the Far East.

Notes

1. See, for instance, Cottrell (1990) & Collis (1946).
2. See Roberts (2003), 207.
3. A good discussion of the sources will be found in Inglis (1976).
4. Hooker, Richard, *The Opium Wars* (1996), published on the internet.
5. Gelber (2004), develops sound arguments for the trading relationship; similar arguments are not new e.g. Gorst (1899), 210 ff.
6. Collis (1946), Inglis (1976).
7. Inglis (1976).
8. See for instance Collis (1946), 98 ff.
9. Welsh (1997), 93–4. This is on the west side of the Kowloon Peninsula and was not in 1839 part of the area in which foreigners were allowed to trade.
10. From a first hand account published in Beeching (1975), 91.
11. Also known, more correctly, as the First China War.
12. See, for instance, Gelber (2004), 85–93.
13. Welsh (1997), 81.
14. Chang (1975).
15. Hsü (1983).
16. See, for instance, Walley (1958).
17. Beeching (1975), 117.
18. See Walley (1958), 139.
19. It should be noted that only four British Regiments were honoured with 'China Coast' as a result of the fighting. Baker (1986), 271.
20. Manchu warriors were known to the outside world as Tartars.
21. Ouchterlony (1844), 395.
22. Ouchterlony (1844), 451.
23. See Roberts (1996), 252.
24. See Cottrell (1995), 232.
25. See Gelber (2004), 94.
26. For instance, Ouchterlony (1844).

27. Roberts (2003), 252.
28. Ibid, 247.
29. Ibid, 277. Roberts also points out that this figure has been considered by some scholars to be too low.
30. Beeching (1975), 160. See also Keay (1991), 154.
31. Also, more correctly, known as the Second China War, see Baker (1986).
32. A   was a hybrid merchant vessel with a European-type hull but with mast and sail developed from the Chinese junks so that it could be readily manned by Chinese sailors. See Beeching (1975), 214.
33. Hurd (1967), 11 ff.
34. HMS *Sybille*, 1,633-ton wooden-hulled sailing ship with 36 guns – Commodore Charles Elliot.
35. HMS *Encounter*, 953-ton screw-powered wooden-hulled corvette, launched Pembroke Dockyard 1846 – Captain Dew.
36. Other infantry battalions were involved before the end of the fighting – a total of nine infantry and one cavalry regiments were awarded Battle Honours for the 2nd China War. Three Indian cavalry and eight infantry regiments were awarded similar honours. See Baker (1986), 275.
37. HMS *Plover*, 232-ton screw-powered wooden hull gunboat – Lieutenant Commander Rason.
38. From Hernon (2003), 373. This is an account of the action given by Midshipman John Fisher (in 1914, Admiral of the Fleet, Lord Fisher).
39. The French had become involved because of the murder of a French missionary for which they wanted justice. In the event some 6,000 French troops were involved in the Second China War.
40. Account of Thomas William Bowlby correspondent for *The Times*. He was
killed by the Chinese later in the campaign. See Hernon (2003), 380.
41. Awards of the Victoria Cross were made to Lieutenant Robert Montresor Rogers, Hospital Apprentice Andrew Fitzgibbon, Private John MacDougall, Lieutenant Edmund Henry Lenon, Lieutenant Nathaniel Burslem, Private Lane, Ensign John Chaplin.
42. A description furnished by Captain Charles George Gordon (later as a general, killed at Khartoum) of the Royal Engineers writing to his mother. See Hernon (2003), 389.
43. Paine (2003), 179.
44. Massie (1992), 171.
45. Roberts (2003), 304.
46. See Preston (1999), 12.
47. Preston (1999), 12.
48. See Tiedemann in Bickers and Tiedemann (2003), 17–41.
49. See Preston (1999), 16, and note 390.
50. For a brief discussion of these ideas, see Roberts (2003), 324–326.
51. See, for instance, Massie (1992), 276. It appears that this is not a univerally held belief, the reasons would appear to be more complicated.
52. See Preston (1999), 21.
53. See Preston (1999), chapter 1.
54. See Roberts (2003), 325.
55. Also, greatest influence of foreign religion, mainly Christianity. See Harrison (2007) in Bickers and Tiedemann, and Tiedemann (2007) in Bickers and Tiedemann.
56. Monsieur Stephen Pichon warned continually of the threat, and was considered by some to be a bit of a scare-monger but there was little he could do to prevent it whilst acting more or less on his own; see Preston (1999), for instance.
57. The Tsungli Yamen was the General Management Office for handling all
matters relating to the foreigners in China. It was not a ministry and was, under the control of the Chinese government who dictated the treatment of foreigners' requests. It was not a reliable means of dealing with the government since it depended on those serving on it at any one time and their attitude to the west as a whole.
58. Sydney Brooks became the first foreign victim of the Boxers when he was on his way back to his mission on the night of 31 December 1899. See Preston (1999), for details.
59. The concerns of the British were at least, in part, founded in the fact that such a massacre had occurred during the Indian Mutiny.
60. The Chinese soldier, En Hai, was captured six months later and executed at the behest of the Germans. He pleaded that he had followed orders on the promise of a reward and promotion – neither of which were received. Fleming (1956), 108.
61. See Bickers and Tiedemann (2007), introduction.

62. Preston (1999), 20 and 351. The claim to an Italian concession in Sanmen Bay, Fujian had been rejected. See also Bickers and Tiedemann (2007), introduction.
63. Sir Edward Seymour had plenty of experience in China. He had served under his uncle, Sir Michael Seymour, in the Second China War of 1860.
64. In one of these sharp actions, one of the casualties was Captain John Jellicoe and it was thought he would die. Of course, he did not and later became Admiral Sir John Jellicoe who commanded the British Grand Fleet at the Battle of Jutland in 1916. See Preston (1999), 92, 101 and 338.
65. In 1918, Admiral Sir Roger Keyes was to be the advocate and leader of the Zeebrugge Raid in an attempt to deny the Germans access to and from the captured Belgian port. Other officers serving in China at this time included Captain, later Admiral, David Beatty and Commander, later Rear Admiral, Christopher Craddock who went down with his ship, HMS *Good Hope*, at the Battle of Coronel in November 1914.
66. Cary and McCance (1923), 261. The Royal Welch Fusiliers (RWF) had 200 men engaged in this action during the course of which twenty-four were killed. The action was sharp and over 800 casualties were sustained by the mixed attacking force notably among the United States' 7th Infantry. The RWF were the only British regiment to be awarded the battle honour 'Pekin 1900'.
67. See, for instance, Cary and McCance (1923), 267.
68. The Chinese had a number of modern Krupp guns which they did not bring into use and it has been said that some were so new that they had not been unpacked. See Preston, 361ff.
69. Fleming (1956), 226.
70. Royal Welsh Museum (Brecon): note attached to embarkation orders for Tsingtao. The battalion had a strength of 863 men and seventeen officers on arrival in China. It should be noted that at this time the battalion was arranged on an eight company system, reorganisation to four company system took place on 1 December 1913.

Chapter 2

The German Protectorate at Kiaochou Bay

The Germans had looked on with some envy during the latter part of the nineteenth century, as their European neighbours and rivals had expanded their empires throughout the world, by both conquest and trade. Great Britain had been, more or less, in control of the oceans since the defeat of the French at Trafalgar in 1805 and had been able to extend her mercantile empire throughout the world, knowing that the trading routes were safe, under the tacit protection of the Royal Navy. France had managed similar expansion and, although the defeat of her army and navy in the early years of the century had no doubt slowed the progress, the French empire was large and vibrant, taking French culture, its values and the long arm of imperialism around the globe. The Germans had not been inactive during this period and by the end of the nineteenth century, had influence in scattered areas throughout the world, including Africa and the Pacific Islands. However, their two powerful neighbours, Great Britain and France, were controlling much of the trade and growing wealthy in the process and thus, Germany was finding the expansion of her influence very difficult as the country grew in military and economic strength. Even Germany's smaller European neighbours, Belgium and Holland, had aspirations for global influence with outposts of empire in central Africa and the Far East. Spain and Portugal also controlled a significant share of the world trade, controlling to a greater or lesser extent, most of South America. Nonetheless, it was to Great Britain and France that Germany looked with the greatest envy with a determination to put this matter straight, so that they could compete on equal terms and become a large, powerful economic and military empire.

Germany had, particularly as a result of Prussian militarism, built a strong, efficient army and a considerable navy by the end of the nineteenth century, but the scale and power of both seemed not to be reflected in the control of overseas territories. To extend German influence, and particularly to support the navy in some of the far-flung corners of the world, Germany needed more territory on which to provide coaling stations and supply depots that could serve the ships and feed the men who sailed them, thereby making German influence more widely felt. Amongst these concerns, was the need for a suitable base from which to operate and maintain their Far

East Squadron. There could be little prolonged influence in that region unless she could manage these issues. To many of the German military and naval leaders, it was clear that there was no better place to look for such a base than mainland China. Admiral Alfred von Tirpitz had made this clear after his reconnaissance of the Chinese coast in 1896 when his squadron had looked at the possibilities of a port and had favoured Tsingtao, although, at that stage, there were no immediate plans of how that was to be obtained from the Chinese.[1]

The Germans had not considered any diplomatic approaches to China and had simply recognized the potential importance to their long-term overseas strategy of this portion of the Shandong Peninsula. German influence in the region had been very limited during the nineteenth century, for they had not made the progress in trade with China that Great Britain and France, or even the United States of America, had been able to make. As a result of the unequal treaties signed after wars in Annam (by the French) and the Opium Wars (by Great Britain), the Germans expected similar treatment to other foreigners, should they also be able to wrest a treaty from the Chinese. However, by the 1890s, their presence in China was still mostly diplomatic and religious. Their missionaries were present and, alone with those of other nations, did their best to convert the heathen Chinese to Christianity and met with a similar, if limited, measure of success. It was, indirectly, as a result of this missionary work that the Germans were finally able to get the foothold in China they had been looking for. On 1 November 1897, two German, Roman Catholic missionaries, Franz Nies and Richard Henle, were murdered by the Chinese they were trying to bring into the flock. On 14 November, the Germans, full of righteous indignation, landed a force of 700 men in Kiaochou Bay, and raised the German Imperial flag. The murder of the unfortunate missionaries gave them the excuse they had been looking for to 'acquire' a naval base in China. The murders had allowed them to do so with perhaps a little more force than they had originally intended and, at the same time, gave them the moral high ground.

There was much indignation at the events but the Germans knew that by means of a treaty, they could get what they needed to maintain their Far East Squadron with terms that were most favourable to them. The treaty was signed in March 1898 and was published in Germany in April and again in July. It gave her a substantial concession around Kiaochou Bay and took the form of a ninety-nine-year lease on the territory on both sides of the entrance to the bay – this was clearly the thinking of the military mind to control the shipping in and out of the bay which would be essential in time of war and prevent any land-based attack on their shipping. The treaty also allowed for a fifty kilometre zone of influence around the bay and the construction of two railway lines, the longest of which would join Kiaochou Bay with the provincial capital at Jinan. Further, to add a bit more recompense for the murderous action of the Chinese, the Germans were granted mining rights for a distance of ten miles on either side of the railway lines for the entire length of the line[2] which allowed them considerable scope for mineral exploitation throughout the Shandong Province. For their part, the Germans very graciously allowed China to abstain from sovereignty within this area, but agreed to protect the Chinese citizens in their so-called 'zone of influence'.[3]

It has been suggested that the murder of the two missionaries was not a random act on behalf of the Chinese but rather, a desperate action to draw the attention of the outside world to the conditions prevailing in China during the 1890s. The divine rule of the Emperor could not be challenged, even the failing dynasty was too powerful within China for a direct assault on the throne. Many of the population, it would seem, recognized the decay of the central power which manifested itself as corruption in the provinces, together with a brutal subjugation of the peasantry. This was, in some provinces, including Shandong, surfacing as a lawlessness which the Imperial government seemed unable, or unwilling, to curtail.[4] Whether this was a cry for attention is perhaps open to discussion. However, the murders certainly attracted the attention of the Germans and gave them the excuse they needed to establish the port they had sought for their Far East Squadron.

The action of the Germans landing at Kiaochou Bay and the terms of the treaty that they forced from the Chinese has been seen by some[5] as the spark that started off the Boxer Rebellion and it has to be admitted that perhaps it is more than coincidence that the tinderbox of the rebellion was Shandong province in which Kiaochou Bay is situated. Similarly, it may be no coincidence that the murder of the German minister in Peking was the first act of aggression against the Peking legations. Whilst it may have been the spark, the rapidity of the spread of the rebellion owes much to the xenophobia of the Chinese and perhaps it is an oversimplification to suggest that all the blame for the Boxers' actions should be put upon the Germans. Nevertheless, they were undoubtedly as high-handed with the Chinese as any other of the European nations or, for that matter, the Americans or the Japanese.

The Germans set about converting Kiaochou Bay and the small town of Tsingtao into a small part of Germany, as far as they could. They also wasted no time in organizing themselves once the treaty was signed to their satisfaction. During 1898, they installed one marine battalion and one battery of field artillery to dissuade any immediate response from the Chinese as they set about planning their stay on mainland China. In 1899, they began their major construction projects on the railway, the barracks and the harbour. Germany did not have it all her own way in these early days, and between June and November, there was trouble with the Chinese and it was necessary to deploy troops to protect the workforce, particularly on the railway construction work. The railway was not popular with the local Chinese population and it appears that for a while, they did all they could to disrupt its construction, although it has to be said with no success. It did

The town of Tsingtao taken just before the outbreak of war in 1914.

Tsingtao, looking towards the railway station.

The contraversial Governor's House, later used as a Communist Party guest house and now more of a museum.

German warships in the harbour at Tsingtao.

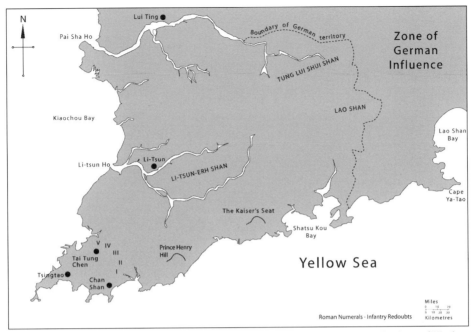

German Territory of Kiachou

not develop into serious unrest at that time or during the Boxer Rebellion, and although the Germans anticipated trouble in the area, Tsingtao was not troubled by events similar to those in Peking or elsewhere in northern China.[6] By 1902, the railway was carrying the coal from Shandong's first coal mines to the rapidly expanding port of Tsingtao and two years later, had reached as far as Jinan (then known as Chinan Fu or Tsinan Fu), the provincial capital. At this stage, the coal was used essentially to provide the power for the German navy, and in particular, the Far East Squadron, but by 1905, the first commercial coal wharf had been completed and by the following year, most of the harbour installations were complete. In the eight years after the treaty had been signed, the Germans had taken the small fishing town of Tsingtao and turned it into a military base and commercial port, serving a large area of the province. 'It will be seen thus far that Germany has, so far, not spared money or pains in the development of Kiaochou.'[7]

To the Germans, Kiaochou Bay was a prize and the development of the harbour was essential to the military goals of a growing military power and a militaristic society. The location of the harbour was ideal because it was central to the Yangtze, the Sea of Japan and the Gulf of Chihli which gave them the opportunity for trade and for the exertion of a certain amount of military control should that be necessary. In addition, the harbour was ice-free during the winter; to have had a base further north would have been to invite the possibility of ice-locked harbours for at least part of the time which would have been much less desirable to the Germans whose aim was to provide their Far East Squadron with ready access to and from the Pacific. Shandong province was ideal, in not only providing an excellent harbour, but but also large quantities of coal for both military and merchant vessels.[8] Thus, Tsingtao and its harbour was very important to the Germans who believed it could be fairly easily defended. The Germans were very pleased with their leased territory which was always known as Kiaochou, although the town of that name actually lay outside the area of the lease (which covered 152 square miles), but fell within the zone of influence covering a total of 3,000 square miles.

The topography of the concession was generally described as mountainous in the north, with land rising to as high as 3,700 feet in the range of hills known as the Laoshan Hills, with especially difficult terrain in the Tung-lui-shui Shan which had steep ravines and impassable slopes to summits of around 2,000 feet. To the south of these hills were a series of lower dissected ridges, such as the Litsun-erh Shan which rise to around 700 feet. The Kaiser's Seat (Wu Shan), on the south-east of the Tsingtao peninsula, rising as it does to 1,300 feet, marked the southern extension of the Laoshan Hills. The topography of this south-eastern part of the German protectorate was dominated by Prince Henry Hill (Foushan) which, at 1,250 feet, gave commanding views north to the Litsun Ho valley, Tung-lui-shui Shan and, to the south and south-west, the sea and Tsingtao and its bays. The importance of this hill and its usefulness for observation was not lost on the Germans nor, indeed, on the Japanese at a later date. Nearer the town, the topography had a tendency to remain hilly, with a girdle of three hills, Iltis, Bismarck[9] and Moltke running south-east to north-west across the peninsula south of the Hai-po Ho. These hills were not more than 500 feet high, but between this girdle and the sea were further hills, noticeably Government Hill and Diedrich's Hill which reached a little over 300 feet which in turn ran down to the sea in Tsingtao Bay and Augusta Victoria Bay. Overall, the Tsingtao peninsula should be considered as a series of tiered hills and ridges, often very steep-sided and dissected, rising steadily towards the north and east. Within this topography, flat land was at a premium, with most being used up for cultivation or habitation. From these tiered hills, a number of small rivers and streams ran towards the sea, although all were inclined to run dry during the long, dry summer months of north-east China.[10] In times of flood, the rivers could be expected to carry large quantities of silty sediment which was deposited in the bay, resulting in extensive mud flats.[11] The river channels were considered to be dangerous, even in the dry season, because of extensive areas of quicksand that developed from the large quantities of sediment that was transported and deposited in a short period of time. From the military point of view, the presence of quicksand was a problem that required careful consideration. In defence, the quicksand may have been a useful obstacle but in attack, or even in a withdrawal, it was a significant obstacle that would need to be overcome efficiently.

The northern portion of the German concession was considered to be good for agriculture, with gravelly soils in the lower areas and valleys that tended to be well-drained, though the hills were rocky and not generally suitable for agriculture. To the south of the Bay in the vicinity of Tsingtao, the land was considered to be poorer which was probably reflected in the fact that it was little more than a poor fishing village in the 1890s. However, by 1905, Tsingtao had become more like a European town than an oriental one. The Germans put a great deal of effort into the construction of public buildings, such as schools and a hospital, to accompany wide, metalled roads and stone-built residential areas. Sanitation had been a high priority as the town developed and efficient sewage systems were installed in the European quarter of the city. In the early twentieth century, the city had three more or less distinct areas – the northern Chinese quarter (Tapa-tao); an eastern, European quarter and, nearer the harbour, the western commercial quarter. To add to this Germanised town, there were a number of small towns and villages which came under the direct control of the Germans. These lay inside the zone of influence and the Germans sought to affect these towns to a greater or lesser degree, depending on their importance to the smooth running of the colony. Generally, in the years leading up to the Great War, the German influence on the area was seen, particularly by westerners, as being highly beneficial.

The climate in this part of north-east China was considered to be good and ideally suited to northern Europeans, since the summers were not too hot with temperatures in the range of 68° to 86°F (20 to 30°C), and although bitterly cold in the winter months when temperatures as low as 12°F (-11°C) were recorded, the sea does not freeze. It was a climate that, in its extremes, would not have troubled the Germans especially. The spring and autumn

The German railway station at Tsingtao, photographed in 2006.

Evidence of the German occupation of Tsingtao can be found in the architecture of many of the buildings which are typically European in style and occupy prominent positions in the older part of the city.

months, particularly October, were considered to be the best, and indeed are still considered so today, by the modern Chinese tourists who visit the resorts within the area of the old concession, and the large modern town of Tsingtao. Rainfall in the area was moderate, with an average of about twenty-four inches a year, most of which falls between April and September. It is easy to understand the German attraction to the area on the basis of the climate alone, and as early as 1906, it was 'considered without doubt to be the best summer resort in north China.'[12]

At the time of the 1904 British Military Survey of the area, the population of Tsingtao was given as 28,838, of which only 1,057 were Europeans,[13] mostly Germans. Such precise data for the years immediately prior to the Great War is not available, but it is known that the population grew rapidly over the next ten years, as the success of the protectorate continued, built upon the commerce that the Germans introduced. From this town, the Germans were overlords to more than 170,000 Chinese, in over 300 scattered villages throughout their zone of influence. They recognized the importance of Tsingtao at an early stage and, besides schools, hospitals and other public works, established a German bank to encourage the commerce they had instigated on their arrival in the area. This importance is further reflected in that the territory was different to other German colonies since it did not have a civil governor, and came under the control of the so-called 'Ministry of Marine', and a naval officer was in charge of both civil and military affairs throughout the protectorate. In 1914, the governor was *Kapitän* Alfred Meyer-Waldeck of whom more will be heard later. There was a council under the military governor that administered the local government. However, for all the organization and the energetic attempts to make the territory more attractive to the Europeans, it was apparently, well-known that, 'The Germans were cordially disliked by the Chinese.'[14] This, however, would not have been of particular concern to the Germans since the generally hostile attitude of the Chinese towards foreigners was well-known.

Although Tsingtao was developed as the main town of the German concession, its existing harbour was considered to be unsuitable because of its exposure to seasonal westerly winds that produced large swells and made for difficult berthing of large ocean-going vessels. It was for this reason that the Germans began work on the two harbours in Kiaochou Bay to the north and north-west of Tsingtao. The smaller of these, known as the Boat Harbour, was completed in 1901, and had one long pier which was equipped with a railway and cranes and was suitable for vessels drawing about sixteen feet. A second, shorter pier was provided for smaller, lighter vessels. The Boat Harbour had a narrow entrance and was considered difficult to enter in high winds. Additional berthing was eventually provided by the construction of a dock wall between the harbour and the main Shandong railway line. The larger Commercial Harbour, the more northerly of the two, was capable of handling ships of the deepest draught in all weathers. This harbour also had wharves and railways and a wide entrance which made it more easily navigated in high winds. The total area enclosed by the breakwaters of the Commercial Harbour was approximately 800 acres (roughly 1.25 square miles). Of course, a harbour of this size in an area where vast amounts of silt-laden waters discharge was prone to silting problems and the dredging carried out during construction needed to be revisited throughout its operational life to ensure that it remained serviceable. The opening of the coal wharf in 1904 signified the final stage of the exploitation of the mineral wealth of Shandong; coal could now be mined in the province and shipped out through its own port at Tsingtao. This also meant that Tsingtao was a suitable coaling station for the German warships of the Far East Squadron and was, by that time, only six years after occupation, fulfilling the purpose Germany had always intended for it.

It was some time later that the Commercial Harbour was finally completed and Germany's priority would appear to have been the provision of a facility for its navy in the first instance, with any other advantage coming as a useful trade-off against the costs involved in completing the venture. Warships were accommodated on the western side of the harbour entrance and a government naval workshop was set up close-by to provide the necessary repair and engineering facilities for these ships. The Germans had been very industrious in achieving their aims so quickly and everything was done with a sharp eye on the military advantage since it was noted that other landing places within the leased territory were very limited, although a number of smaller harbours were available to shipping of shallow draught. The Germans had captured, or rather landed at Tsingtao and it was not their intention to make it easy for anyone else to do the same and rob them of their prize.

German organization did not stop with the construction of the harbours for they also set about improving the infrastructure that would assist both in their control of the area and with the commerce of the area as a whole. The roads within Tsingtao were considered to be broad as they were two vehicles wide and were metalled and therefore good in all weathers. These roads extended outwards from Tsingtao to the larger villages, such as Tsíang kíou some ten miles to the north. Elsewhere within the concession, the unmetalled roads were improved to make them firm and allow all the villages to be connected and readily served. It is not too difficult to see the military thinking here – if the coast was defended fairly easily, then the improved infrastructure to important parts of the hinterland would also assist in the defence of the protectorate from a landward attack. At the same time as they were constructing and improving the roads, they were also constructing a railway line to connect Tsingtao to the provincial capital of Jinan, a project which included a grand terminus building in the latter town, although this was not completed before the start of hostilities in 1914. It was February 1904, just five years after construction commenced, that the first trains were able to travel along the completed track from Tsingtao to Jinan.

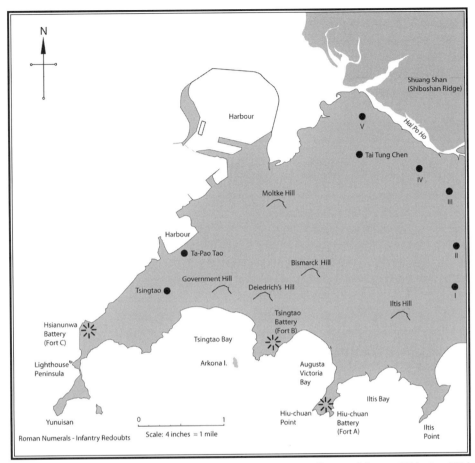

German defences at Tsingtao, 1914

The railway was constructed for much of its length on a low embankment some thirty feet wide which made it a marked feature that was not at all appreciated by the Chinese – even before the trains started running. Much of the area towards Jinan is flat loess plain and as such, the embankment would have seemed to be an eyesore but the Chinese also saw it as upsetting their old ways and, in the beginning, attempted to disrupt the construction. However, it was not long before the Germans were running a daily return service from Tsingtao to Jinan, a journey today of some six hours or so each way. As a result of the shipping and the railway links, Tsingtao became very prosperous, and from a commercial point of view, the Germans had been able to achieve great things.

To protect this most vital of colonies, the Germans had also been very industrious with regard to the provision of defences against the outside world. The Chinese, in the years immediately before the Germans arrived, had recognized the importance of the area and of the approaches to Kiaochou Bay as an entry into Shandong and therefore, the heart of northern China, and had begun to construct defences. The most noticeable of these,

The bay at Tsingtao before the outbreak of the Great War.

sometimes known as the Tsingtao Battery, was on the promontory between Tsingtao Bay and Augusta Victoria Bay. This battery was not complete when the Germans came into the territory and its completion became an early task for the military engineers. Known as 'Fort B' in the British military survey of the area, it was armed with four 150 mm guns.[15] In 1906, the British had also identified smaller guns, but it appears that these guns, of older pattern on overbreak carriages, were no longer part of the fort's defences in 1914.

The Hsiaunwa Battery ('Fort C' to the British) was situated south-west of Tai-tsi Chen on the west of Tsingtao Bay. Here, four large-calibre, 240 mm guns were situated in an open barbette[16] work some 250 yards long. The British had some considerable difficulty in deciding the calibre of these guns and it was estimated that guns as large as 305 mm had been placed in this position. However, by 1914 it had become clear that the earlier estimates were correct. On Light House Peninsula was the Yunuisan Battery ('Fort D') which comprised three 88-mm guns.[17] This fort had not been finished at the time of the 1906 British survey and by 1908, there seemed to have been doubts whether it would ever come into use. However, by 1914 it is clear that the three guns mentioned were positioned here.

The biggest achievement of the Germans in the seaward-facing defences was the completion of Huitschan (Hui-ch'uan) Huk Battery. This battery was described as having four 37 mm quick-firing guns and two 240-mm guns in an open barbette arrangement, with a further three 150-mm guns in a concrete-casemated battery. In the 1908 amendment to the British military survey, the size of the largest calibre guns was revised upwards to 305 mm and once again, this was proved to be incorrect at the time of the siege where the largest gun was 240 mm. The British had adopted a conservative approach in their assessment of the German defences but, in view of the covert manner in which the information appears to have been collected, that is not entirely surprising. The fire from these positions tended to overlap and hence provided protection from a little to the west of Iltis Point to beyond Light House Peninsula and into Kiaochou Bay. A small gap in this cover which occurred near the Tsingtao pier in the centre of Tsingtao Bay was obviously considered to be of little importance in the overall defence of the area and it is known that a number of guns of 88 mm calibre were available for further coastal defence if needed, though these do not appear to have been assigned to any particular battery.[18]

These batteries, which represented the coastal areas in which guns were placed to defend the town, were not the only seaward-facing defences. Between 1906 and 1914, the Germans completed a significant programme to strengthen their defences throughout the protectorate. During this period, a fort was built on Bismarck Hill[19] of thick concrete casemates and excavated to a considerable depth within the hillside to provide ammunition stores and living quarters for the garrison. This fort was armed with four 280-mm guns[20] and was capable of firing out to sea in support of the coastal batteries. Additional guns were placed on Iltis Huk (two 88-mm guns) and light guns on Hill 85 (two 50-mm guns) completed the seaward-facing defences. All these had been positioned to discourage an attack from the sea, for in the years following the Boxer Rebellion, few thought that the Chinese, or anyone else for that matter, would mount an attack over land towards Tsingtao, bearing in mind the difficult terrain that would need to be crossed at the northern end of the peninsula.

The Germans had never believed an over land attack was possible because they had little faith in the ability of the Chinese to mount such an attack and in the early years of the century, they saw no other threat either from within the region or from the European nations with which they had cordial relations. Nonetheless, they sought to protect their landward side by two more or less complete lines of fortifications. These defences were not present at the time of the British Military Survey of 1906 and do not appear to have been constructed when this was amended in 1908. However, by 1914, the Germans had constructed significant defences to face threat from an over land attack. The first of these concentric lines was sited on the hills near the town and focused upon Moltke and Iltis Hills where forts were established. The outer defensive line was constructed from a little south of the Hai-po Ho in the west, across the peninsula to finish a little in front of Hsai chan Shan to the north of Foushanso Bay. Agreement on the armament in these areas did not seem to be forthcoming.[21] However, it appears that Moltke on the west of the line carried relatively light armament with a total of eight 8.7-cm guns. Iltis fort seems to have been by far the most strongly defended position with at least six 120-mm guns and two 105-mm guns. Around the hill itself were further batteries with generally lighter armament, though it appears that the largest guns were two 150-mm guns which were

German observation post for howitzer battery on Bismarck Hill facing seawards, 1914. [Royal Welsh Museum, Brecon, BRCRM A1959.103]

Above: The author photographed at the same German observation post in 2006.

One of the entrances to Bismarck Fort, photographed in 2006.

situated on the northern flank about mid-way between Iltis Hill and Tai Tung Chen village.[22] The lighter batteries also appear to have been provided with searchlights.

Beyond these forts and assorted batteries were the defences of the Redoubt Line (*Infanteriewerks*). This line, running as it did across the peninsula from north-west to south-east, comprised five redoubts which were more or less strongly fortified and connected by trenches and earthworks and protected in front by a steep glacis and a high wall and ditch arrangement, with a considerable barbed wire entanglement. The armament of the redoubts was generally light but Redoubt N[o.] 1, north of Chan Shan, was supported from the rear by no less than six 120 mm guns and two 105-mm guns sited on the flanks of Iltis Hill. Similarly, Redoubt N[o.] 4, north-east of Tai Tung Chen was supported by four 120-mm guns and twelve smaller guns of a variety of calibres. Clearly, this area was considered to be of some significance to the defences, protecting as it did, the north central area and the potential crossing points of the Hai-po Ho. These redoubts were also furnished with machine-guns and searchlights to assist in the defence of their local area. It should be recognized that these were essentially infantry positions for the defence of the outer regions of Tsingtao.

The total number of guns present for the defence of Tsingtao appears to vary depending upon the authority (and the detail entered into by that authority) and ranges from as few as fifty-four guns of all calibres[23] to ninety-six guns of all calibres.[24] Although this may seem to be a significant number of artillery pieces, it should be remembered that in many cases, the guns were old, some reportedly dating back to the Franco-Prussian war and of 1870 vintage.[25] Some of the guns had certainly been acquired from the Chinese as part of the reparations from the Boxer Rebellion and were essentially out-of-date. Nevertheless, for the limited actions that the Germans envisaged, they provided support, but would be no match for the modern weapons of the day and the Germans were not foolish enough to believe that they would be. It was an example of making the best of what was available and what the budget would stretch to.

Beyond this organized defensive system were strong points and observation posts in the Laoshan Hills that were thinly manned and could be occupied in a time of need, and which allowed for a comprehensive defence system, extending several miles beyond the limits of the town. The arrangement of the defences afforded some protection to the rear of the city should it be necessary to make some stand from a land-based attack. However, in 1908, the British were of the opinion that:

> It would appear that the Germans do not intend to make Tsingtao an impregnable fortress. In its present state it is probable that it would speedily fall to the attack by a land force of suitable strength, supported by a squadron of first class armoured cruisers.[26]

This statement, although in some ways prophetic of the events of 1914, does not give any idea of what was considered to be a suitably strong land force and, as was to be shown, that force was considerably larger than the defenders who held onto the town and its surroundings for about eight weeks in 1914.

The forts were generally considered to be well-sited for the purpose of defending the coastal waters and the entrance to the harbours, although it was thought by the analysts responsible for the British report, that Fort B, north-west of Augusta Victoria Bay, could not bring sufficient fire to bear in the area to provide an adequate defence for the harbours. It was also considered possible that gun boats could probably come close in-shore under the guns of Fort C since there had been no provision for quick-firing guns to be sited lower down the coast and the guns at Fort C could not be depressed to the angles necessary to fire at targets located close inshore.

Whilst the Germans had thought their defences through carefully, it was recognized ten years before the Great War, that should Iltis Hill fall on the right and Moltke Hill on the left, then a general withdrawal would be necessary on Bismarck and Diedrich's Hill, and the command of these latter heights 'does not seem to offer great facilities for protracted defence.' This was at least partly the result of the attitude of the German hierarchy to the colony of Tsingtao. It was considered that whilst Tsingtao was an important addition to their overseas territory, great capital expenditure could not be justified in its defence, particularly on the landward side. It was unthinkable to the German military mind that there could be an attack from the landward side of their occupied territory. The Germans had witnessed the largely ill-disciplined Chinese army during the Boxer Rebellion and did not consider it to be a threat at all and, if an attempt was to be made, it could be dealt with easily by a small force near the new city. To defend the city on a more distant line through the hills at the neck of the peninsula would have required considerable effort and the deployment of at least a corps of trained troops. Germany did not feel she could afford 40,000 men to defend this rather small, though important, outpost from the unlikely event of an over-land attack by the Chinese. It was believed that the cruiser squadron, in 1914 under the command of Admiral Graf von Spee, would be the first line of defence.[27] To some extent, this echoed the belief of many of the British military thinkers who saw the Royal Navy as the most important arm in the defence of the British Isles and in a similar manner, the control of the seas for supply and lines of communication was also considered to be of great importance. The reliance on the navy, and the belief in a particular strategy, therefore negated the need for the Germans to maintain a large number of troops in Tsingtao. So it was with this in mind that Admiral Tirpitz vetoed the Outpost Line through the *Kaiserstuhl* (Kaiser's Seat) and the Litsun-erh Heights and then the possible line from Prinz Heinrich Hill (Prince Henry Hill) to Kuschan to eventually settle upon the line that was ultimately defended through Iltis, Bismarck and Moltke Hills. It was close to the city but, reasoned Tirpitz, the likes of the Boxers would not be able to break through and China could offer little more. As far as the possibility of

European enemies was concerned, it was reasoned that a large-scale land attack was unlikely, if only because of the logistics. Whilst the power of the Royal Navy was recognized and not underestimated, it was also believed that sea power would dominate throughout the region in the event of war and this negated the need for strong land defences.

The Germans envisaged a number of scenarios for war in the area, with a number of permutations of the likely enemy and alliances of European forces. All of these were more or less covered by the term *Kreutzerkrieg* or 'Cruiser War'. The Germans envisaged that their cruiser squadrons would move swiftly to destroy shipping and disrupt commerce, particularly of the British Empire.[28] This kind of warfare was eventually used in the Great War but was carried out most successfully by submarines. With these things in mind, Tsingtao had become the German cruiser squadron base and under Graf von Spee, the *Scharnhorst, Gneisenau,*[29] *Nürnberg, Emden, Leipzig,*[30] the destroyer *S90* and a variety of smaller gunboats were seen as the colony's first line of defence in the early months of 1914. It is interesting to note here that in the years before the Great War, the Royal Navy paid 'courtesy' visits to Tsingtao. Essentially, these were missions to keep an eye on how well the Germans were doing with the development of their port. The Germans always treated the visits as a great honour but were under no illusions as to their real purpose, although they always made every effort to entertain the crews of the visiting warships. For instance, the sailors of HMS *Monmouth* in 1913 and HMS *Minotaur* in 1914 were given a thoroughly warm welcome, and whilst peace lasted, the hospitality was unmatched but at the same time, both nations knew what was really going on.

To their land and sea defences, the Germans added air defence in the form of two Rumpler *Taube* monoplanes which arrived in the early months of 1914. These were not armed, of course, since they were initially intended for air reconnaissance to support the other defensive arms. However, there was one problem with the use of aircraft in Tsingtao – no-one had thought to prepare an airfield. It was difficult to find sufficient flat ground for use as an airfield and eventually, it was necessary to press the horse-racing track, known as Iltis Platz, into service. This open, relatively flat area made a short airfield that required considerable skill and not a little courage, to take off from and land on. By August 1914, one of these aeroplanes had been dashed to pieces on the rocks below the airfield after a failed take-off attempt, in which the pilot was seriously injured and was unable to take any part in the action of the defence of Tsingtao.[31]

The defences of Tsingtao required men to garrison the various forts and earthworks throughout the protectorate. These men were largely regulars who were rotated from home on a regular basis, serving for two or three years at a time, in a posting that was considered to be one of the best in the German colonies. Since the town was under the governorship of the German navy it was, perhaps, not surprising that the main body of regulars were provided by the 3rd *See Bataillon*. Many of the men who were to be involved

A Rumpler Military Aeroplane of 1914. This machine was usually referred to as a 'Taube' (dove) because of the swept-back wing shape.

in the siege of the town arrived in Tsingtao as replacements, a matter of a few months before hostilities in Europe broke out and were required to adapt quickly to their surroundings and prepare for war.[32] The breakdown of the forces in July 1914 may be summarised as:[33]

3rd *See Bataillon*	26 officers	1,161 other ranks
Pioneer company	3 officers	113 other ranks
A field battery	6 officers	130 other ranks
Sailors from Kiaochou in 5 companies	19 officers	907 other ranks
Other personnel (initially unattached)	65 officers	225 other ranks
Marine Detachment	14 officers	440 other ranks
Men from German warships	15 officers	700 other ranks
Volunteers at outbreak of war	30 officers	905 other ranks
Men from *Kaiserin Elisabeth*	5 officers	300 other ranks
Total	**183 officers**	**4,881 other ranks**

It was a small force to defend the town and its inhabitants but at the start of the war, there was little reason for concern, since things went well for the

Germans in Europe and a quick victory was anticipated. If that proved to be the case, there would be little need to defend their outpost in China, although they made preparations in a thorough manner as the clouds of war slowly descended. War in Europe seemed so far away to the men looking out over the Yellow Sea. It was difficult for the Germans in China to believe that there could be any outcome to that war, other than a quick victory – at least they did not differ in their thinking from the British and French who were seized by war fever in August 1914. To a great extent, this belief was essential to the continued management of the situation in the east – without it, morale would undoubtedly have suffered badly and the defence when it came, would have been more difficult. It was a situation that was encouraged by the commanders. However, within very few months, the Germans in Tsingtao had been proved wrong on all their assumptions in respect of the war and their long sought-after outpost in the Far East had ceased to exist.

Notes

1. Massie (1992), 171.
2. Jinan is approximately 200 miles from Tsingtao and hence the Germans gained control of a significant portion of China in one swoop.
3. The treaty will be found in the appendices.
4. Harrison (2007), 2.
5. See Fleming (1959, 2001 edn.), 29 and Massie (1991), 276.
6. Tiedemann (2007), 15ff.
7. Military Report (1906), 4.
8. In 1909, the railway brought 126,000 tons of coal to Tsingtao, see Hoyt (1975), 4.
9. This is the hill on which Qingdaoshan Park is situated and today has commanding views of the sprawl of the modern city.
10. The main rivers were the Pai-sha Ho; Chang-tsíun Ho; Li-tsíun Ho; Ch-wu Ho and the oddly-named Prince River. It should be noted that the Li-t'sun Ho and the Hai-po Ho are now totally dry for most of the year, their beds used for housing and cultivation.
11. The north-east of China is dominated by large quantities of loess deposits and this is easily eroded during the wet season. The Yellow River, famed for the vast quantities of silt it carries, runs through Jinan, the Shandong provincial capital, and perhaps the silty waters are not to be unexpected – certainly, they are not unique.
12. Military Report (1906). Today, its popularity is secure with mostly Chinese tourists.
13. The population in 2006 was in excess of 1.5 million.
14. Military Report (1906).
15. Burdick (1976), but Whittaker (1994) states that four 155 mm guns were present and the British Military Survey reports four 75 mm guns, two 120 mm guns and two 150 mm guns. There would seem to be no general consensus of opinion as to the armament but it is highly likely that the 1906 report, and its 1908 amendment, are inaccurate mainly because the forts mentioned had not all been visited in person and not all areas would have had ready access for foreign military personnel.
16. Barbette: *OED*, platform from which guns fire over the parapet without embrasures.
17. See also von Gottberg (1915), 57 and 58, for further estimates of the calibre of the guns.
18. See Burdick (1976).
19. The fort can still be visited and a number of rooms and levels are open for inspection.
20. Burdick (1976), though Whittaker (1994) gives only two 280 mm and four 155 mm guns for this fort.
21. See von Gottberg (1915), Burdick (1976) and Whittaker (1994) for the various ideas of the armament in the inner and outer areas of landward-facing defence.
22. See the map produced by Whittaker (1994) for the positions of the guns as understood by him.

23. Von Gottberg (1915).
24. Whittaker (1994).
25. Burdick (1976).
26. British Military Survey (1908).
27. See Hoyt (1975), 8.
28. Ibid, 9.
29. Armoured cruisers.
30. Light cruisers.
31. See Hoyt (1975), 65.
32. Burdick (1976), has a good description of how these men were acclimatised to Tsingtao in the weeks leading up to the outbreak of war.
33. These figures are those quoted in von Gottberg (1915), and do not appear to differ substantially from the totals quoted in other sources, although the breakdown is often not given.

Chapter 3

The Japanese Element

The Germans, in all the plans they had drawn up for war and the defence of Tsingtao, had ignored the growing power of Japan. This is somewhat surprising because they had acted as military advisers to the modernising Japanese army. They were aware of Japan's aspirations in the east as her influence grew to a point where she had a strong military presence in the area. Why the Germans failed to appreciate the growing strength of Japan is unclear, but it must be linked to the prevailing European attitude towards the peoples of the Far East at the turn of the twentieth century. Germany had an almost arrogant belief that an Asian country would not want to interfere in a European war – all her possible scenarios affecting Tsingtao had involved war with a similar imperial European power, such as France or Great Britain. Also, because Germany recognized that it had a certain amount of influence in Japan, it was thought that she could be kept out of any conflict by diplomacy alone. However, in the context of the war that befell Europe in 1914, it is important to look at the position of the Japanese as they struggled to assert their authority in the region that was of most interest to them – the area around their own home islands.

During the second half of the nineteenth century, Japan had moved quickly from an almost medieval warrior state to a modern imperial nation with a growing need to expand beyond her own borders and to influence both the policies and structures of the neighbouring states. They had modernised their army and navy, adopting European methods, so that the country became a potent force in the Far East. The army had been largely modelled on that of France and, to begin with, Japan had sought the assistance of French military advisers. However, their poor performance and near disastrous manoeuvres conducted under their direction, gave Japan the opportunity to seek advice elsewhere and they turned to Germany to complete the construction and training of their modern army.

The navy, on the other hand, was based solely on the British model, so much so that all orders issued from the bridges of Japanese warships were in English until well into the 1930s.[1] These features of Japanese military growth and modernisation indicate how closely interwoven the nation had become with the European powers and it is, perhaps, hardly surprising that when it was necessary to do so, they would take sides in any European-based conflict. The only question that really remained as war broke out in Europe was which side would the Japanese choose?

Japan's interests in China were not unknown. Japan had fought the Chinese in the bloody war of 1894–95 and, following her victory, had annexed Korea. In 1900, she had stood fast with the other 'foreigners' in Peking during the Boxer Rebellion. During that siege, her military commander, Colonel Shiba, had gained much respect for his quick action, and the endurance and tenacity of his command.[2] However, by 1904, Japan was fighting one of its Peking allies, as Russia felt the full force of this new power in the east. Japanese victories followed one after another as the Russians seemed to be continually on the back foot and favoured retreating to defensive lines. On land, from Yalu to Mukden, the Japanese forced the Russians back in a series of tiring battles and managed to lay siege to Port Arthur, while the navy defeated the Russian fleet at Tsushimo.[3] In some aspects, at least, this conflict was the herald of the total warfare that was to come. The Japanese ran out victors against the Russians but it had been a costly campaign, with heavy casualties, causing significant problems for the politicians back home. For instance, the Japanese, whilst defeating the Russians at Mukden, had not delivered the anticipated killer blow and it had cost them nearly 16,000 officers and men killed and just a little short of 60,000 wounded. It did not make much difference that the estimated casualties for the Russians were about 4,000 more – the battle had been a very costly victory.[4] The war also set the mood for future Japanese battles, where it was considered that a good fight was one in which victory was gained and heavy casualties were suffered. However, the outcome of the Russo-Japanese war was seen by the Japanese as a significant victory that was sufficient to allow them to move up a notch in the rankings of world powers; a position that they felt they had earned.

However, within Japan, there were conflicts between the civilian politicians and the armed forces, as well as between the army and the navy. Essentially in the early 1900s, Japan was governed by two clans[5] – the *Satsuma* who supplied recruits for and ran the army and the *Choshu*[6] who controlled the navy. As might be anticipated, the internal struggle for power led to rivalry between these clans, but ultimately their goals were the same. In a strongly militaristic society such as Japan, the civilian control of the armed forces was never better than tenuous, but whilst they were able to maintain the strong alliances with the western powers, particularly Great Britain, the politicians managed to hold the reins of power. To some extent, Great Britain had been favoured by Japan because she had not formed part of the international lobby which insisted that Japan gave up its gains on the Korean peninsula in 1896 as a result of the Sino-Japanese war. Russia, France and Germany had united in bringing diplomatic pressure to bear on Japan to give up what she had seized by force. It was particularly galling to the Japanese to see the Germans march into Shandong a couple of years later, on a much flimsier excuse – it looked as if the Europeans could do just as they wanted in China, including preventing any other Asian country from getting a foothold. The decision by the European nations to force out Japan at that time no doubt influenced her decision to support Great Britain in 1914 – that and the fact that the Japanese, particularly the naval leaders, could see no way that Great Britain could lose the conflict.

Of course, Japan held strong desires to be a big player in the affairs of the area and that would mean that she would need to dominate her giant neighbour – China. To do this, alliances were as important as wars to Japan and the choice of such alliances would play a large part in the Japanese foreign policy. Japan and Russia could not be considered as close allies following their war of 1904–05 and, although France and Germany had held a certain amount of influence at varying times in the recent history of Japan, they had gained little respect as a result of their attitude towards Japan following the Sino-Japanese war. To a large extent, these factors made Britain the obvious choice as an ally for the Japanese, and made the decisions that were to follow in August 1914 largely inevitable, particularly in light of their extremely pro-British Minister of Foreign Affairs, Baron Kato Takaaki.[7]

In the days immediately preceding the declaration of war against Germany, Britain had assumed that Japan would remain essentially neutral and would not become involved in the war that was setting Europe alight. But, this assumption had not allowed for the imperial ambitions of Japan herself. As war approached, it gradually became clear to some in the British government that it would be very difficult to keep Japan out of the conflict. As early as 2 July 1914, the British ambassador to Tokyo, Sir Conyngham Greene, was advising the Foreign Secretary, Sir Edward Grey, that 'Japan, as an extremely interested party, must in her diplomatic measures redouble her vigilance and take appropriate action …'[8] And, in Japan's eyes, appropriate action was to take part in the conflict to establish her influence in the area beyond any doubt. The British government had not, at that stage, declared war on Germany and, although they may have already reached a point of no return, it was believed by British diplomats that there would be no need for Japan to take part in a European conflict. To some extent, this may reflect a number of assumptions including a lack of understanding of the global nature of the war that was about to begin and a feeling that it would not be a long drawn-out affair – it was not only the soldiers who believed that the war would be 'over by Christmas'. On 1 August, Grey was informing the Japanese ambassador to London, Inue Katsunosukehim, that he did not believe there would be any need for Britain to ask Japan for any help under the terms of the alliance between the two countries.[9] Whilst the Japanese may have understood this, since war had not been declared at that time, they wanted to clarify their positions should Britain and her empire be plunged into war. Baron Kato did this by calling Greene to his ministry in Tokyo for a meeting on 3 August, during the course of which, Greene reported that Kato had commented:

... if British interests in Eastern Asia should be placed in jeopardy ... His Majesty's Government may count upon Japan at once coming to assistance of her ally with all her strength, if called upon to do so, leaving it entirely to His Majesty's Government to formulate the reason for, and nature of, the assistance required.[10]

This would seem to have been a reasonably clear statement of intent but Kato was not entirely convinced that Greene had understood Japan's wishes and followed up with a written statement, intended to clarify the situation further, in which he commented, '... the Imperial Government would wish to have the opportunity of considering (the action required) and consulting with His Majesty's Government before taking definite action.'[11] This tended to suggest that Japan was prepared to act, more or less independently, where she considered the alliance with Britain applied, whereas Greene's communiqué suggested that Britain would largely control the action of Japan under the terms of the mutual alliance. Thus, although allies, the two countries had different ideas on how the alliance would work in the event of a war commencing which involved Britain. A day later, Britain declared war on Germany and the differences in the standpoints taken were drawn into sharp focus as diplomats in both countries began negotiations that would draw Japan, albeit briefly, into the Great War.

In the days that followed, there was much diplomatic activity as both Britain and Germany sought to establish Japan's position in relation to events developing in the Far East. On 7 August, the British requested that the Japanese fleet be used to hunt and destroy the German armed merchant cruisers. This would, of necessity, constitute an act of war by the Japanese against the Germans and their interests in Asia. Japan did not dismiss this request, as Britain had assumed, since it was an opportunity for her entry into the war – Britain would also then secure the aid and assistance of their ally in the Far East. However, Japan saw greater opportunities for herself and as a response to the request, Baron Kato suggested that the best way of effecting the destruction of German shipping was to attack Tsingtao – the destruction of the base would make Germany's fleet ineffective and essentially put it out of action. Greene, whilst not approving the action, suggested that the Japanese government would be the best judges of the situation.[12] This cautious response may be understood if it is considered that whilst Britain wanted to secure Japan's assistance, the suggestion of a full-scale attack on Kiaochou Bay and the capture of Tsingtao, was not an entirely welcome proposal. It would appear that Great Britain did not want to give Japan carte blanche to enter China and probably recognized the expansionist desires of the Imperial government. On the other hand, Britain also recognized the difficulty of finding sufficient resources to have significant influence on any Japanese plans in the area. To clarify the Japanese standpoint, Baron Kato forwarded a note to Greene in which he stated:

Japan cannot restrict her action only to the destruction of hostile armed merchant cruisers, but it will become necessary for her to resort to all and every possible means for … the destruction of the power of Germany to inflict damage upon the interests of Japan and Great Britain in Eastern Asia.[13]

Britain had not really expected the firm proposal of action against the German protectorate and may have been somewhat embarrassed by Japan's resolve. For its part, the Japanese government was not standing still and awaiting events. At a cabinet meeting on 7 August, the Japanese Prime Minister, Count Shagenobu Okuma, had made it clear to his ministers that a declaration of war on Germany was not only an obligation under the alliance with the British, but also necessary to 'punish German militarism.'[14] Thus, the consensus in favour of war against Germany was developing. Subsequently, on 9 August, the German ambassador in Tokyo, Count von Rex, was called to a meeting with Baron Kato to be told that the situation between the two countries was becoming serious[15] and that war looked like being the outcome. This meeting was followed up the next day when Count Okuma called foreign journalists to a meeting to prepare the way for a declaration of war and suggested, with the full support of the armed forces ministers, that war with Germany was not far away. This was a political manoeuvre by which Japan sought to gauge foreign opinion, particularly that of the United States of America. There was concern in some quarters that the Americans would not tolerate Japan becoming involved in a European war, but as anticipated by Japan's government, there was no comment from the United States on the statement issued at the press conference. This has been seen as leaving the way open for Japan to declare war on Germany but whether there would have been any other outcome had the Americans objected, is difficult to assess. It should be remembered that the United States did all she could to stay out of the war and did not become fully involved in Europe until the end of 1917. Perhaps, their lack of response should be seen as an attempt to keep the war at a distance. Although this test of opinion had gone very well for Japan, it was still necessary for her to convince her main ally, Britain, that war was the only outcome and that an attack on Tsingtao was the consequence of such a declaration. Britain continued to try to limit Japan's involvement to the use of her navy, but Japan was not interested in anything except entry into the war as a full partner in any action in which she was likely to be involved. Sir Conyngham Greene, who was not totally against full Japanese involvement, commented:

> … I must say that Japan is willing to take steps for the protection of commerce at sea, but I am afraid that it is now impossible that operations should be confined to this. Japan wishes to do more and to do it with us, but if we refuse she will do it by herself … What we have to decide is whether it would be more advantageous to us to allow Japan to act alone, after having asked for her aid, or to give into her now, and by doing so, put her under an obligation which we can bring up when, after operations are ended, the process of cleaning up in China is begun.[16]

To a large extent, Britain had created her own problem as she wanted Japan as an ally in the area to help control German shipping and police the trade routes, and in asking for that help, had effectively allowed Japan to follow her own agenda in the Far East. This was recognized by Greene who realized that were Britain not to co-operate with Japan, the latter would take Kiaochou Bay anyway, and in doing so, would harm the alliance which was still important to British interests in the Far East. This point was not wasted on Sir John Jordan, British Minister in Peking, who wrote to Grey on 9 August stating:

> Should the Japanese move on Tsingtao without the British Navy participating (let alone the co-operation of land forces) a lasting blow will have been dealt to our prestige in the Far East.
> It appears very desirable that, pending the arrangement of a considered scheme of co-operation, the Japanese declaration of war should be put forward.[17]

British diplomatic efforts to control Japan had largely failed and the latter had moved from a position of no action, to limited maritime involvement, to a land campaign, to the capture Tsingtao. It might be argued that Britain had far more pressing issues in Europe with which to be concerned, but the steady shift in position, particularly since the declaration of war, had effectively played directly into Japan's hands, as they sought full involvement in what was, in August 1914, a very European affair. Caught between the needs of the European war and the need to maintain influence in the Far East, Britain had not been able to establish the diplomatic high-ground and there can be little doubt that Japan saw the achievement of her goals as a diplomatic victory which allowed her to significantly increase her own influence in the area at the expense of the 'senior' ally. By 11 August, Jordan had accepted the Japanese standpoint and he put this to Grey on the same day, stating that, 'The choice now being separate action by Japan and co-operation. I am entirely in favour of the latter.'[18] It then became only a matter of time before Japan declared war on Germany and began the proposed assault on Tsingtao.

Whilst there had been some reluctance on behalf of the British government to sanction the Japanese action in China, it was seen by diplomats in Peking and Tokyo as a more or less inevitable event. Even before Britain had shifted her position to that of accepting Japanese involvement on 11 August, Greene had recognized the need for co-operation and on 8 August had asked the British to consider the release of forces from Tientsin for the combined action against the Germans at Kiaochou Bay.[19] The request had rather pre-empted the decision in London and as such, was ignored to begin with, but on 9 August, Jordan had pressed the government in Peking by pointing out that, 'Our prestige and interests demand more than mere co-operation of our land forces at Tientsin, though that is itself most desirable and quite easy of achievement.'[20] This call also went unheeded since the government still had to decide its position and since that was shifting daily, it was impossible for it to act on such a request, although it probably took local knowledge into its deliberations in deciding the appropriate course of action. Of course, it was necessary for Britain to recognize the consequence of not co-operating fully with Japan and there would be tacit approval of any Japanese action and a reduction in her own power and influence in the area. However, Great Britain also needed to be mindful that whatever it decided, it was likely that it would place China open to Japanese expansionism and in that context, there was a recognition that some involvement by British armed forces would exert a measure of control over the Japanese. Greene was to write to Grey on 9 August to report Baron Kato's standpoint on this issue:[21]

> I said I thought it possible that public opinion at home might think it undignified for England to place all the risk involved in such an operation on the shoulders of her ally and to take none herself, and that I asked you if any of our troops from Tientsin should participate in the event of hostilities being resorted to. I suppose that his Excellency saw no objection? He replied in the negative.[22] To sum up, his Excellency said that what Japan wanted was a free hand and no 'limited liability'.

Whilst Japan was happy for Britain to assist in any operation, it was also made clear that if help was not forthcoming, then should the need arise, she would go ahead anyway. However, even before events had moved this far, it was clear that the British government did not want Japan acting alone, and the only way this could be avoided, was to co-operate if and when the need arose. By 13 August, the naval and military commanders on the China station were beginning to plan the co-operation that was considered necessary. Japan was still some days away from declaring war on Germany but Britain could not be left wanting when that apparent inevitability arose. Two days later, Baron Kato called Count von Rex to the Ministry of Foreign Affairs and presented him with an ultimatum:

> We consider it highly important and necessary in the present situation to take measures to remove the causes of all disturbance of peace in the Far East, and to safeguard general interests as contemplated in the Agreement of Alliance between Japan and Great Britain.
>
> In order to secure firm and enduring peace in Eastern Asia, the establishment of which is the aim of the said Agreement, the Imperial Japanese Government sincerely believes it to be its duty to give advice to the Imperial German Government to carry out the following two propositions:
>
> First, to withdraw the German warships at once from Japanese and Chinese waters also armed ships of any description and to dismantle those which cannot be withdrawn.
>
> Secondly, to surrender the whole Protectorate of Tsingtao forthwith – not later than the 13th of September – to the Imperial Japanese Authorities without conditions or claims of indemnity, with the prospect of eventually returning the same to China.

The Imperial Japanese Government announces at the same time that should it receive any but an unconditional acceptance from the Imperial German Government up to the 23rd of August 1914, to all the above mentioned conditions, it will consider itself obliged to take such measures as the situation necessitates.[23]

In all probability, the Japanese did not expect their demands to be met and were using them as a diplomatic excuse for war and an invasion of China. There was a tacit acceptance in the demands that this was the case, and that the Germans themselves had used a far flimsier excuse to get hold of a part of China and it was realized that they would not be giving it up easily. The ultimatum was careful not to point out what steps would be considered necessary if the demands were not met, but it was clear enough to all that this would mean some form of military action against the German colony at Tsingtao. The ultimatum also pointed out that the seizure of Kiaochou Bay would bring about its return to China, but no-one was fooled by this. Perhaps Britain pretended to be, since their diplomatic position in China had to bear in mind the situation that was developing in Europe as the her army was mobilized and sent to France to meet the threat from the Germans there. In reality, it was easier for the British to more or less ignore the situation that was developing in China and let the Japanese deal with it, particularly the military side of things since their army was large, was located close-by and was ready for action, if needs be. Count Okuma issued a statement to the effect that the alliance with Britain was the reason for war:

Japan's object is to eliminate from the continent of China the root of the German influence which forms a constant menace to the peace of the Far East, and thus secure the aim of the alliance with Great Britain. She harbours no design for territorial aggrandizement nor entertains any desire to promote any other selfish end. Japan's warlike operations will not, therefore, extend beyond the limits necessary for the attainment of that object and for the defence of her own legitimate interests. Accordingly, the Imperial government will take no such action as to give third Powers any cause for anxiety or uneasiness regarding the safety of their territories and possessions.[24]

This was designed to be reassuring but the delivery of the ultimatum had created problems for Sir Edward Grey who had tried to halt its despatch to the Germans by a telegram he had forwarded to Greene:

Unless the ultimatum has actually been despatched you should endeavour to get it deferred until I have discussed its terms with the Japanese Ambassador tomorrow. There are some important points of form to be considered. It would seem at first sight desirable that England and Japan should be associated in measures for the capture of Kiaochou, and that its surrender to both allies should be demanded, if at all, though we have no desire to establish any claims of our own on Kiaochou after the war.[25]

His efforts were to no avail, as Japan had already presented the ulti-matum to Germany without reference to Britain, an independent action that can hardly have been viewed favourably since it set a precedent for the nature of the alliance between the two countries – an alliance in which Britain assumed a more and more junior role. The pro-British Baron Kato tried to explain the actions of Japan more clearly with a statement that in part reads:

Early in August the British Government asked the Imperial Government for assistance under the terms of the Anglo-Japanese Alliance. German men-of-war and armed vessels were prowling around the seas of Eastern Asia, menacing our commerce and that of our ally, while Kiao-Chau was carrying out operations apparently for the purpose of constituting a base for warlike operations in Eastern Asia. Grave anxiety was thus felt for the maintenance of peace in the Far East.

As all are aware, the agreement and alliance between Japan and Great Britain has for its object the consolidation and maintenance of general peace in Eastern Asia and the maintenance of the independence and integrity of China as well as the principle of equal opportunities for commerce and industry for all nations in that country, and the maintenance and defence respectively of territorial rights and special interests of contracting parties in Eastern Asia.

Therefore, inasmuch as we were asked by our ally for assistance at a time when commerce in Eastern Asia, which Japan and Great Britain regard alike as one of their special interests, is subjected to a constant menace, Japan, who regards that alliance as a guiding principle of her foreign policy, could not but comply to the request to do her part.

Germany's possession of a base for powerful activities in one corner of the Far East was not only a serious obstacle to the maintenance of permanent peace but also threatened the immediate interests of the Japanese Empire.

The Japanese Government therefore resolved to comply with the British request and if necessary to open hostilities against Germany. After the Imperial sanction had been obtained I communicated this resolution to the British Government and a full and frank exchange of views between the two governments followed and it was finally agreed between them to take such measures as were necessary to protect the general interests contemplated in the agreement and the alliance.

Japan had no desire or inclination to become involved in the present conflict, only she believed she owed it to herself to be faithful to the alliance and to strengthen its foundation by insuring permanent peace in the East and protecting the special interests of the two allied Powers.

While regretting that Japan has been compelled to take up arms against Germany, I am happy to believe that the army and navy of our illustrious sovereign will not fail to show the same loyalty and valour which distinguished them in the past, so that all may be blessed by early restoration of peace.[26]

For Japan's part, they had begun preparing for a campaign against Kiaochou Bay in general, and Tsingtao in particular. This plan was not without diplomatic repercussions as Japan would have to bring a military force into neutral China to attack a German colony. Although China favoured the allies, and the bringing of foreign troops through her territory was effectively the same as the German action of breaching Belgian neutrality to invade France, the action had been the reason for Britain's entry into the war in Europe. It was necessary, therefore, to obtain China's goodwill for the enterprise before any operations against the German concession could commence. China was not in the least fooled by Japan's approaches, along the lines of the statement by Count Okuma quoted above. The Germans saw the opportunity of avoiding any fighting in the Far East and suggested that the colony should return to Chinese control immediately and thereby make any action by Japan unnecessary. China was open to this suggestion because it would prevent Japan having any legitimate reason to enter Chinese territory and thereafter carve up as much of the country she could get away with. However, it was not to be, for Berlin, like London, had more pressing issues to address as the war in Europe began to steamroller into France and Belgium. The small colony in north-eastern China was to be left to its own devices since there was little help, even diplomatic, that could be offered from Berlin. Although this proposal was not acted upon, it is difficult to understand how it could have helped the German situation in Kiaochou as she would still have lost control of her prized possession and her soldiers would, in all probability, have been interned in neutral China. The outcome of any battle for the protectorate would have been politically almost the same. It would appear that the Germans were not thinking too clearly, although perhaps they believed there was a chance that if the port was handed over then, by diplomatic means, they might gain a measure of control by manipulating the Chinese government to their wishes. In the end, no action was taken to return the colony to China, and Japan was able to organize its campaign against Tsingtao almost completely unhindered.

It was becoming increasingly obvious to the British in China that some sort of co-operation was inevitable and Colonel (later acting Brigadier-General) N. W. Barnardiston, commanding officer in north-east China, reported to the War Office on 10 August that his small force of little more than 2,000 men in Tientsin were ready to co-operate fully with the Japanese. He also pointed out that 20,000 men would probably be needed for effective co-operation. The War Office was not impressed by the figures and suggested that a small force would be all that would be provided and that such a force was unlikely to be more than a brigade, that is, not more than 5,000 men. On 16 August, still within the Japanese ultimatum, it was announced to Barnardiston that a force of three battalions from Tientsin in north China and an Indian battalion from Hong Kong would be brigaded for just such a purpose. Barnardiston asked to be allowed to contact his Japanese counterpart to discuss the joint operation, but the response from Grey was not encouraging though it is, to some extent, understandable:

Brigadier-General N. W. Barnardiston, MVO, GOC British Forces, Tsingtao.
[Royal Welsh Museum, Brecon, BRCRM A1959.103]

... until Japanese plan of operations against Kiaochou has been communicated to His Majesty's Government and agreed to, he [Barnardiston] should not arrange for any co-operation with Japanese military authorities that would involve violation of Chinese territory outside the 50 kilometre Zone around Kiaochou in which Germans have right of passage for their troops.[27]

Whilst Barnardiston may have been discouraged by such a response, he would also in all probability have been confused, for the War Office issued an order to him on the same day to make contact with the Japanese military authorities, via the British Minister in Peking, to arrange the joint plan of operations. It was not until 21 August that a joint operation was officially sanctioned by Grey. On this date too, the Japanese plan for joint action was handed to the British government which provided for a British force to land at Laoshan Bay. Once the action had been recognized, Barnardiston set about trying to assemble his force and draw up the chain of command that would be necessary for the operation to run efficiently. Gradually over the days since his first proposal, Barnardiston had seen his proposed force whittled away so that by the time that Japan actually declared war on Germany, he was to command no more than one battalion from Tientsin, the 2nd Battalion, South Wales Borderers, and half a battalion of Indians, the 36th Sikhs, from Hong Kong. Furthermore, he was not going to be allowed to act independently:

You will be under the control of Japanese commander and will co-operate with him as a complete formation. Let me know the plan decided on after consulting with the Japanese general.

Your force is purposely reduced to a minimum because British troops are only engaged to show that England is co-operating with Japan in this enterprise.[28]

It was further explained to Barnardiston that the 'exigencies at home and in India' required that the size of his force be limited. It is easy to understand this comment, but such a small force would have done little to impress the Japanese and much to encourage them with regard to their role in the campaign against the Germans and also, their position in the Far East as a whole. The Japanese had managed to get all, or possibly more than, they had hoped for by diplomatic negotiations when Britain placed her small force under their command.

For their part, the Japanese looked upon the Kiaochou campaign as an opportunity they were not going to let slip by inappropriate strategies and limited resources. They mobilized their army on 16 August, a week before their ultimatum with Germany expired. In 1914, Japan had a standing army of approximately 250,000 men but fully mobilized, she could field one and a half million soldiers. The 18th Division, with its base at Kurume on Kyushu, was earmarked for action in China and comprised the 23rd and 24th Brigades, a cavalry regiment, a field artillery regiment, a mountain artillery regiment, an engineer battalion and a transport battalion.[29] The strength of a division was approximately 19,500 men, that is somewhat larger than a British division of the same period. The division was to act on its own, since it was considered sufficient to deal with a force of approximately 5,000[30] Germans that were believed to be defending Tsingtao. It was considered to be unnecessary and inappropriate to designate the force an 'army' since that title was considered to be too grand for a small-scale campaign against a relatively weak enemy. Further, the division was considered to have been equipped with rather poor artillery which had short-range, and any large-calibre guns available tended to be those captured in Japan's wars around the turn of the century and as such, were old and considered to be of rather limited use. Further, it has been suggested that the Japanese infantryman was poorly armed and that the standard issue rifle, the Arisaka, was prone to jam in field conditions.[31] Nevertheless, the Japanese Army had plenty of men to put in the field and before the end of the operations, a further infantry brigade, field artillery, two engineering battalions and an ammunition column had been added to make the force up to a figure reported to be approximately 57,000 strong.[32] The division was commanded by Lieutenant-General Kamio Mitsuomi, an experienced soldier who had served in the war against China in 1895 and against Russia in 1904. He had developed a reputation for caution and steadiness and had commanded the division since 1912.

The Japanese navy, although intially cautious about entering the war for a number of internal political reasons,[33] was not to be left out and three squadrons of warships were used during the Tsingtao operations. The First Squadron protected the lines of communication, the Second Squadron blockaded Tsingtao, and the Third Squadron patrolled the waters to the south of Shanghai. For the most part, these were not the most modern ships available, being mostly of the pre-Dreadnought era, but they were adequate for the purposes of controlling the waters in the area of north-east China.[34] Early in the campaign, the Japanese did provide a show of naval strength when the *Kongo* was stationed off Tsingtao. This was one of the most modern ships in the world at the time and it so impressed the British that the Royal Navy immediately ordered two ships of a similar design. It was, however, far too important a vessel for blockading a small port such as Tsingtao and it departed the scene on 2 September, leaving the work of the blockade to the older ships of the Japanese Second Squadron. By this time, the Japanese navy had become more interested in the war and were determined to destroy the German bases in the Pacific, including those in the Marianas and the Carolines and which, by the end of the campaign, were unashamedly declared to be Japanese in perpetuity.[35]

The Japanese army was a modern army in so far as it had been rapidly reorganized from the medieval warrior caste during the latter decades of the nineteenth century, and although many of the traditional values and concepts had been transferred to the modern army, owed much of its military thinking to the European concepts of war. It was largely a conscript army in that military service was compulsory for all males between the ages of seventeen and thirty. Its strength lay in the loyalty of the men towards their superiors, a devotion to duty and a complete disregard for personal safety during combat. It was generally considered to be an intelligent and physically fit army and this, to a large extent, made up for the shortfalls it suffered in equipment. The officer corps was so devoted to its own cause, however, that it has been looked upon as a weakness by some authorities:

> The weaknesses were that the army officers tended to be narrow and poorly informed having lived during their training a claustrophobic existence excluding outside interests. In preparing for a military career, they had from a young age been cocooned and removed from ordinary society. Ingrown and narrow minded, they developed a dogmatic self-confidence in their own breed. They tended to be poor linguists and were not greatly influenced by forces outside Japan.[36]

Some of these features may not have been totally confined to the Japanese and certainly, similar criticism had been levelled at the British officer class over the period leading up to the Great War. However, this narrow-mindedness did not make the Japanese officers automatically suitable for the joint operations proposed for the attack on Tsingtao. On the other hand, the Japanese soldier at all levels was trained so that aggressiveness was almost second nature and there was an almost natural desire to attack the enemy and to get in close to use the bayonet. This attitude had already brought about high casualties in the war with Russia, but had not dampened the attacking spirit which was still clearly present in the army of 1914 and which was to be demonstrated in Tsingtao. Amongst the senior officers, there was a tendency towards a more cautious approach. Generals were trained to ensure the safety of the operation as a whole and therefore achieve the most favourable outcome to any action in which they were involved. This gave the impression that the Japanese generals were relatively calm and considered, and that they relied upon the aggressive junior ranks to bring about the ends required. This view is totally in keeping with the high casualties that the army was ready to accept. Perhaps these nuances of attitude set the Japanese army apart from its European equivalents and there can be no doubt that the relationship between the men, non-commissioned officers and officers was considerably more flexible than in the European continental armies. These differences in approach did not suggest that joint operations were going to be easy but, on the other hand, differences in language and approach made it clear that misunderstandings were going to be inevitable.

By 1 September, Japan was ready to move, but the issue of troops violating Chinese neutrality had not been resolved. Japan wanted to land at Lungkow on the north coast of the Shandong peninsula which would create a significant neutrality problem for China, since it was well outside the fifty kilometre zone established by the Germans. In an attempt to keep Japan out of her territory, China planned an official protest against this action. At this point, Britain stepped in and supported the Japanese request, rejecting the Chinese offer to declare war on Germany.[37] This weakened the Chinese position somewhat and they withheld their protest and on 3 September, issued the following statement:

> The Chinese Government will not accept responsibility for the passing of troops or war operations at Lungkow, Laichow, Kiaochou and their adjacent districts, but in the other districts of China the Government will strictly enforce neutrality as declared. The territory and diplomatic negotiations of China are recognized by the Powers and will likewise protect the property of the inhabitants in the region to be affected by the war operations.[38]

By this statement, China allowed a situation to develop whereby part of her country was to be used by three foreign powers to wage war while she attempted to maintain neutrality. It is another example of the government of China being manipulated by outside forces and having no position of strength from which to prevent the actions of more powerful nations. The course of the actions of the Japanese in China over the next thirty years demonstrates that she had been correct to object. The failure of diplomacy reflected badly on the nations involved since expedients based on their respective influence, prestige and war aims had taken little account of the wishes of China. China had attempted to issue a warning to Japan not to try anything outside the designated area but was effectively powerless to enforce it. It was not long before this statement was tested to the very limit of its intended meaning.

Thus, for Japan, the summer of 1914 had provided the opportunity she had been waiting for to expand her influence in the Far East. Like others before, Japan wasted no time in ensuring that the chance was not lost and in so doing, more or less forced her ally, Great Britain, to give her a free hand in China. It was something of a diplomatic coup for the Japanese and they were not about to lose the initiative as preparation for war proceeded at a pace which would allow Japanese forces to enter China during September. The pieces were beginning to fall into place for the assault on the German concession at Tsingtao.

Notes

1. See Denis (2000).
2. Preston (2002),175ff.
3. See Connaughton (2003), for a full account of these battles.
4. Connaughton (2003), 289.
5. Hoyt (1975), 50.
6. Denis (2000).
7. Kondo (1993), 3.
8. FO371/2014, quoted in Kondo (1993), 4.
9. NGB, quoted in Kondo (1993), 5.
10. FO371/2016, quoted in Kondo (1993), 5.
11. Ibid
12. Kondo (1991), 6.
13. NGB, 108 minute 9 August, see Kondo (1991), 6.
14. Dickinson (1999), 38.
15. Hoyt (1975), 57.
16. FO 371/2016, quoted in Kondo (1993), 7.
17. Ibid, 8.
18. Ibid.
19. Ibid, 10.
20. Ibid, 11.
21. Ibid, 12.
22. Hoyt (1975), 60.
23. Plüschow (2004 edn.), 31.
24. Hoyt (1975), 61.
25. Kondo (1993), 14.
26. Baron Kato's statement quoted on firstworldwar.com. *Source Records of the Great War* (1923), III.
27. FO371/2017, quoted in Kondo (1993), 17.
28. WO 106/663, quoted in Kondo (1993), 18.
29. See Kondo (1993), 21 and Denis (2000).
30. Based on the figures given by von Gottberg (1915).
31. The Arisaka was the Meiji 38th year pattern rifle and its name referred to the regnal year of the rifles first production.
32. Denis (2000).
33. Dickinson (1999), 75. It appears that not only were the Admirals cool on entering the war but had actively advocated neutrality in early August 1914.
34. See Denis (2000).
35. Dickinson (1999), 76.

36. Nish (1988) in Miller and Murray.
37. A full description of this is given in Xu (2005), 89.
38. Hoyt (1975), 81.

Chapter 4

The Battle for the Seas

It has already been discussed that the importance of Tsingtao to the Germans lay in the fact that they needed a base for their Far East Squadron, to allow them to extend their influence in the region as a whole. This fact had not gone unnoticed by the other powers who also wished to wield power in the area. Japan, who had attempted to use this area for its own purposes after her victory over China in the war of 1895, saw the German port as something that was worth fighting over, particularly as it had been the Germans who had been partly responsible for her losing the prize in the first place. Britain had no doubts about her own need for naval bases and, as the strongest imperial power in the area, sought to maintain ascendancy by exerting a strong influence all along the Chinese coast from Hong Kong to Wei-hai-wei. These foreign influences, whether British, German or Japanese depended upon naval power and, in a time of war, the importance of maintaining contacts with naval bases and providing replacements and supplies for the army in the field, was every bit as crucial as maintaining trade routes in times of peace.

The British had a particularly good relationship with the Germans in the Far East and had granted them the use of the dry dock in Hong Kong when they needed to carry out any repairs to the ships of their Far East Squadron. Although this was a workable arrangement, it was understandable, not least from the British standpoint, that the Germans would want their own facilities, in the long term. The British made regular goodwill visits to Tsingtao in the years preceding the outbreak of war – in the summer of 1913, HMS *Monmouth* paid such a visit to Tsingtao and a little over a year later, she was sunk, with all hands, by the German squadron she had visited, at the Battle of Coronel. In the middle of June 1914, with war barely six weeks away, on the occasion of the goodwill visit made by HMS *Minotaur* (the flagship of Admiral Jerram), the Germans held a grand ball in honour of their guests and sports of various kinds were laid on for all the crew, including a football match which the British sailors won by five goals to two.[1] Even though war was still some distance off (the visit was two weeks before the assassination of Archduke Franz Ferdinand), there was still a feeling amongst some of the German officers that the British visit was made simply to get a glimpse of the military arrangements in and around

Kiaochou Bay. This is, to some extent, borne out by the military survey carried out by the British of the protectorate in 1906 which must have been carried out in a clandestine manner mainly by naval personnel.[2] Perhaps, there was also a feeling amongst the British that the bay and its modern city with its useful harbour, should be in their hands, and apparently, in 1914, some officers aboard Jerram's flagship made no secret of this, one even going as far as to comment, 'Very nice place, indeed! Two years more and we have it.'[3]

To allow the Germans to hold a base from which to operate during a war between the great colonial powers was not something that could be countenanced by either Britain or France, since it was clear that this would eventually affect trade routes and therefore, impact upon the war effort in Europe. For their part, Japan wanted more influence on the Chinese mainland and, although they had been a long-time friend to Germany and had adopted many German military principles, they saw the outbreak of the Great War as an opportunity that was not to be missed to enlarge their empire. Their military successes during the two preceding decades had also given them much of the confidence needed to enter the power struggle in the Far East. Tsingtao was therefore seen as a prize by all the nations involved and the battle for the colony would pitch the navies of warring nations against one another. Although there was not to be a great sea battle, the control of Tsingtao was of great significance in the strategy of sea power in the area.

At the outbreak of war, the German fleet that used Tsingtao as its base was a significant threat to trade in the region and could readily disrupt the commerce between the various colonies and the war-torn lands of western Europe. It was fortuitous for the Allied Powers that when war was declared in Europe, most of Admiral Graf von Spee's fleet was elsewhere in the Pacific region. Indeed, von Spee's flagship, the *Scharnhorst*, was heading towards the south seas when news of the outbreak of war reached him in early August. The *Gneisenau* had met up with the *Scharnhorst* at Truk Atoll about two weeks before, and the *Nürnberg* had started her return journey from a peacetime good-will mission to Central America where she was to be replaced by the *Leipzig*. The *Nürnberg* had reached the Hawaiian Islands when the news of the outbreak of hostilities was received, and was initially ordered back to German waters, although these orders were immediately countermanded by Graf von Spee, and she joined his squadron in early August. Only the *Emden* was at her base and she too sailed soon after war was declared to join up with the rest of the squadron at Pagan Island, where von Spee called the captains together to decide on his course of action. The admiral decided that his squadron should remain together, but he allowed the *Emden* to detach, to begin the solo operations in the eastern oceans that were to make her infamous and hunted for the next three months.[4] The ships remaining at Tsingtao were a number of smaller gunboats and torpedo boats, together with an aged Austrian cruiser, *Kaiserin Elizabeth*, which were to a large extent, left to their own devices to defend Tsingtao from the British, the Japanese and, to a lesser extent, the French and the Russians. From a strategic standpoint, it would make no sense for the Germans to allow large, important, modern warships to be blockaded into their base when they could be of more use on the high seas. In actual fact, they could be of little use in the defence of Tsingtao if the colony was to be attacked from the land and their use in a defence against an attack from the sea would be dependent on there being sufficient room for the fleet to manoeuvre and there was little scope for that within Kaiochou Bay. Admiral von Spee recognized this completely, and knew that once Tsingtao had been abandoned by his squadron, there was no going back, an approach that tacitly accepted the ultimate loss of the German base. His duty, as he saw it, was to make himself and his ships, as useful as possible and this could not be done if his ships were confined to defending Tsingtao. The fine cruisers of his squadron could not be allowed to be blockaded in Kiaochou Bay, a decision that was clear to von Spee and one which he did not hesitate to make.

The presence of the *Kaiserin Elizabeth* in Kiaochou Bay initially presented something of a problem as the declaration of war by Great Britain on Germany had not included the Austria-Hungarian empire. Thus, even though the latter was an ally of Germany, she was not strictly at war with Britain. The Austrians were therefore left with something of a dilemma: if they were not at war, they were at risk of being trapped in Kiaochou Bay and could even have been interned by the Chinese. It was not thought to be feasible for the *Kaiserin Elizabeth* to make a run for it since, as an old ship, she was highly vulnerable. It was decided that she would be abandoned and her crew would make their way back to Austria, via Peking. There was, of course, a huge problem with this, for as soon as Austria became involved in

Artist's impression of the cruiser Kaiserin Elizabeth, *the* S90 *and the* Jaguar.

the war in Europe, she had to extricate over 300 sailors from a warring nation, through neutral China. The naval officers and ratings were advised to do this as civilians and in small groups and, in a short time, most had managed to make it to Peking, where they received the news that they must return the way they had come to assist their German allies in their defence of Tsingtao. Some of the sailors were apprehended by the Chinese but most made it back to Tsingtao where some were used to man their old ship in the harbour whilst others were converted to soldiers in readiness for the defence of Tsingtao.

The German Far East Squadron was a powerful one, dominated by two large ships, the *Scharnhorst* and the *Gneisenau*. These were sister ships, both built in 1907 and both displacing over 11,000 tons. Their armament, at eight 8·2-inch guns, was not considered heavy but they were relatively modern and both ships had a high reputation in Germany for their gunnery. Added to this, they were both fast, being capable of approximately twenty-two knots. To complete the Squadron were the three light cruisers, *Nürnberg*, *Leipzig* and *Emden* which were also modern, fast and each well-equipped with no fewer than ten 4·5-inch guns. It was a force that could not be left unattended in the Far East and the realization of this fact certainly influenced the thinking of some of the senior British naval officers in the early weeks of the war. To have given the Germans the luxury of being able to roam the Pacific at will would have meant risking supply lines for the main theatre of war in Europe. As the war developed, this not only meant war material but also manpower, as Britain called on troops from Australia, New Zealand and India. The threat was too great to ignore and everything pointed to the fact that not only would the squadron have to be dealt with but, in order to remove the threat completely, it would be necessary to take control of the squadron's home base. As it was, the British had lost the initiative almost before the war started, since the squadron was no longer in port and there was no precise intelligence as to its whereabouts.

Stationed in Tsingtao were also a mixture of smaller and older ships which, although forming part of the German naval presence in the area, were not considered either useful enough or modern enough to form part of von Spee's powerful squadron; some were so slow as to have hindered von Spee and the decision to leave them behind would not have been difficult since it was the most practical solution. At the outbreak of war, these older ships were also patrolling the waters in the area of the east China coast, but not all could be readily recalled to Tsingtao. However, at the same time, the *S90*, a torpedo-boat destroyer with four torpedo tubes, was at Chefu, further along the coast, and was able to return rapidly to its port where the old gunboats, *Tiger*, *Iltis* and *Cormoran*, and their crews, were awaiting developments. This small flotilla was soon joined by the *Jaguar* which had been patrolling on the lower Yangtze River. The other so-called river gunboats, the *Vaterland*, *Otter* and *Tsingtao* were not able to get to the port before hostilities commenced since they had been on duty further away from the

Tsingtao base. It appears that the *Tsingtao* was actually in the Pearl River, near Canton, when hostilities broke out, making its return to base impossible. To add to this defence force, the Germans had also converted a pleasure steamer, the *Lauting*, to serve as a mine-layer which was immediately pressed into service preparing a minefield on the approaches to Kiaochou Bay.

For the German navy in Tsingtao, there followed a period of anxious waiting. The British Pacific Squadron, under the command of Vice-Admiral Sir Martyn Jerram, was also for the most part, away from its main harbour at Wei-hai-wei, and thus, not in a position to challenge the Germans in Tsingtao immediately upon the outbreak of war. This delay gave the Germans the opportunity to do all that they could to secure the defences of Tsingtao against attack, both from the sea and from the land, although the latter was considered highly unlikely. The entrance to Kaiochou Bay was mined in a wide strip to prevent approach or entry to the bay by any warships. There were constant patrols by the smaller ships that had been left behind by the Far East Squadron so that early warning could be given of the approach of any enemy. The Germans were probably under no illusion as to the possible outcome of any action when the enemy could bring their ships to bear. Even though there were substantial defences on the seaward-side in the form of the forts that commanded the entrance to Kaiochou Bay, it was recognized that a bombardment from modern warships standing off beyond the range of the land-based guns would eventually have only one outcome and that was the fall of Tsingtao. The Germans were, nonetheless, anticipating the arrival of their enemy and there was a certain confidence that they could give a good account of themselves before the inevitable occurred.

The British Pacific Squadron comprised HMS *Minotaur*[5] (flagship of Admiral Jerram), HMS *Hampshire*[6], two cruisers, HMS *Yarmouth*[7] and HMS *Newcastle*[8]. To this was added the older battleship HMS *Triumph*. The *Triumph*, and her sister ship, HMS *Swiftsure*, were something of oddities in the British Navy. They had been designed by Sir Edward Reed to fulfil an order placed by the Chilean government to counter the threats posed to that country by the Argentinian armoured cruisers. Comments were made that Reed had 'forgotten the guns' in his design, for although *Triumph*, at 11,985 tons, had four 10-inch guns, she was considered to be relatively lightly-armed for a ship of her size. The Chilean government ran into financial difficulties well before the ships were completed and in 1904, both *Triumph* and *Swiftsure*[9] were bought by Britain at a little over £950,000 each, largely to prevent such ships falling into the wrong hands, particularly Russia. Thus by 1914, the ships were not especially old but were rather old-fashioned by the standards of the Royal Navy, added to which the armament, such as it was, was also non-standard. This tended to ensure that neither ship fitted well into the Royal Navy's doctrine of the time. Although it had been argued that they had been lightly armed to allow for greater speed (an approximate

The aged battleship, HMS Triumph.

top speed of twenty knots), they were slower than the powerful *Scharnhorst*, although somewhat more heavily armed. Whilst in the early 1900s, *Triumph* may have been considered quick, by 1914 this was no longer the case and issues that may have been important to Chile a decade earlier were of no particular interest to the commanders of the Royal Navy of 1914. With this in mind, the *Triumph* had been earmarked for decommissioning in early 1914 and, on the outbreak of war, was in dry dock in Hong Kong awaiting that fate. As early as 30 July, with war imminent, orders were received that the *Triumph* was to be re-commissioned, fully crewed and added to Jerram's command to assist in operations in the Pacific theatre and, in particular, the blockade of Tsingtao which seemed to all to be an inevitable consequence should hostilities begin. This re-commissioning was not achieved without some difficulty, since there were insufficient Royal Navy personnel in the area to man a warship of this size. To overcome this difficulty, General F. H. Kelly, GOC troops in South China, granted Admiral Jerram the unusual privilege of asking for volunteers from the garrison in Hong Kong. The war fever that was being experienced in Europe in the days immediately before and after the declaration of war on Germany may have not been as obvious in the Far East, but it came as no surprise that there were plenty of volunteers among the soldiers to take on the role of temporary sailors aboard the *Triumph*. From the volunteers, two officers, one hundred men and six signallers from the 2nd Battalion, Duke of Cornwall's Light Infantry were chosen which enabled the *Triumph* to sail from Hong Kong, under the command of Captain M. S. Fitzmaurice, by 6 August.[10]

It had been no mean feat to get the ship ready for action in such a short time and by all accounts, the soldiers performed their tasks as sailors well enough to earn the respect and thanks of Captain Fitzmaurice. The same day, the squadron was ordered to keep watch on Tsingtao and the *Triumph* was ordered to proceed towards north-east China to join with HMS *Yarmouth* and the French ship, *Dupleix*[11] and the five River Class destroyers[12] stationed in the area. The destroyers were essentially advanced torpedo boats, that sat higher in the water than the more up-to-date destroyers of the time, but were a step on from the old-style torpedo boats and in that respect, represented a transition point between the old and the new ships then coming into service. They were all relatively new vessels and were reasonably quick and up-to-date and a match for anything that the Germans had left to defend Tsingtao. The three larger ships of the squadron (*Minotaur*, *Hampshire* and *Newcastle*) sailed for Yap where, on 12 August, they destroyed a powerful German radio station, thereby significantly disrupting the communications for the German squadron which was by then scattered over the western Pacific.

One analysis of the relative strengths of the two belligerent navies in the area suggests that Jerram's squadron would be somewhat stretched to defeat the German squadron on the basis of fire power alone. The addition of *Triumph* to the squadron would certainly have given Jerram the edge in fire power, but her speed meant that this was an advantage that may have been difficult to use since he could not have brought the German squadron to battle. It was recognized that the German squadron was both powerful and fast and that any engagement with the British ships in the area would be a close-run thing. However, in the final analysis, it was believed that, 'He [von Spee] was a cut flower in a vase; fair to see, yet bound to die, and to die very soon if the water was not constantly renewed.'[13] This was an accurate assessment of the situation for von Spee as he was cut off from his Far Eastern base and to reach the relative safety of home, would be a very difficult undertaking when the might of the Royal Navy was looking for his squadron. Jerram had recognized the shortcomings of his own ships in respect of the German squadron but '*Minotaur* was such a good gunnery ship I should have been delighted to take them on.' This was typical of the Royal Navy's attitude at the time.

The Germans had not been idle while the Royal Navy mobilized its resources in the Far East, and had, to a large extent, disappeared from the eyes of the British and Australian navies in the Pacific. It was the intention of von Spee to sail his squadron back to the Atlantic Ocean, as he saw this as the main theatre of war and to that extent, he had decided to abandon Tsingtao to its fate. It is probable that this situation had been accepted and expected, since there was to be little chance of reinforcing its garrison sufficiently should Japan join the Allies, and no point in reinforcing Tsingtao if Japan did not enter the war on the side of the Allies. Whilst Britain had naval and ground forces in the area, mobilizing them towards an all-out assault on Tsingtao was not considered to be a high priority, bearing in mind the massive demands being made on Britain's armed forces much nearer to home. Nevertheless, when it became clear to the Germans that war had broken out in Europe, the last modern warship, the *Emden*, sailed from Tsingtao to begin its career as a surface raider in the Pacific and Indian Oceans, for which she and her crew became justifiably famous over a period of just three months. On 6 August, as the *Triumph* was completing her re-commissioning in Hong Kong, the *Emden* was capturing her first prize, the Russian Volunteer Fleet ship, the *Ryasan* which was taken to Tsingtao for refitting before returning to sea, having been renamed the *Cormoran*, taking the name and the armament of the old German light cruiser based in Tsingtao. The *Emden* continued her career raiding ships throughout the Indian and Pacific Oceans and narrowly missed an engagement with Jerram's squadron in early August when she sailed out of Tsingtao totally undetected, as the *Minotaur* and the *Newcastle* made for a rendezvous with the rest of the squadron at the Saddle Islands, off the coast of Shanghai.[14] It was to be 9 November before the Australian light cruiser, HMAS *Sydney*, was able to engage and destroy the *Emden* by which time Tsingtao, too, had fallen.[15]

The fact that the German squadron had been able to make an escape from Tsingtao is partly the result of an Admiralty decision thousands of miles away in London. Admiral Jerram had initially received orders that would have placed his squadron in position to cause problems for the Germans at Tsingtao. His command, based at Wei-hai-wei on the north side of the Shandong peninsula, was not too far from Tsingtao, when he received orders, on 30 July, to concentrate his force on Hong Kong:

> I must confess I was reluctant to do so, as it placed me almost 900 miles from what I conceived to be my correct strategic position. I assumed, however, that their Lordships had good reason for sending me there, and proceeded accordingly, at a speed of 10 knots, in order to economize coal.[16]

This he reported to the Admiralty and gave them the chance to change the orders but they did not and he was to comment later:

> I was so upset I nearly disobeyed the order entirely. I wish now that I had done so. Here was a definite plan of action formed in peacetime after mature consideration thrown to the winds by one peremptory telegram.[17]

It should be remembered that war was not declared until 4 August (5 August in the Far East). Jerram would have been able to do little to prevent the departure of the ships from Tsingtao before that date, but he would have been able to monitor the progress of the ships that did make the move. It appears that the Admiralty's decision was made by Churchill and Prince Louis of Battenberg, the First Sea Lord, the outcome of which was that at least part of von Spee's squadron was free and able to carry out considerable disruption to trade throughout the area. The *Emden* had not managed to get out of Tsingtao at that time and the *Prinz Eitel Friedrich*[18] and the re-manned and re-armed *Cormoran* (the captured *Ryasan*) were also able to make good their get-away. It also appeared that as a result of the Admiralty's decision, many of the ships that would supply von Spee's squadron were also able to leave Tsingtao and certainly one result of keeping them supplied was the loss to the Royal Navy of the *Good Hope* and *Monmouth* at Coronel, three months later. The decision not to follow the plan to concentrate off the south-east China coast was, ultimately, a costly one and one which was not corrected without the further expenditure of men and material at the Battle of the Falklands on 8 December when the German squadron was completely destroyed.

HMS *Triumph* and the destroyers headed north as ordered, to be in a position to maintain a watch over Tsingtao, although they were also detailed to provide an escort to the troop transports that were forming up in Wei-hai-wei to bring the British troops serving in north-east China into the war. Here, *Triumph* would replace her crew of soldiers with sailors and the men of the 2nd Duke of Cornwall's Light Infantry, who had carried out their seafaring tasks so well, and would replace the 2nd South Wales Borderers who had been warned that they were to form part of the expeditionary force to move on Tsingtao. The order to keep a watch on Tsingtao was already of little purpose, since the modern ships were on the open sea, leaving only smaller and older ships to assist in the defence of the colony. There were only three warships of significance left in Kiaochau Bay: the *Kaiserin Elizabeth* with two 7·5-inch guns and eight 6-inch guns; the *S90*, an old-type torpedo boat destroyer and the *Jaguar*, a small gunboat. These ships should not have been any threat to the larger more powerfully-armed vessels then making their way towards the Shantung peninsula, but that did not mean that they had no further part to play in the defence of Tsingtao, as later events were to demonstrate.

By 20 August, the Germans had more or less completed their defensive preparations on both land and sea, in and around Kiaochau Bay. They had completed a minefield to the mouth of the bay by improvising mines from a variety of munitions available within the German territory and placed there, using the converted pleasure cruiser *Lauting* as a minelayer. It was, therefore, unlikely that the *Triumph* or any of her accompanying ships, could enter into the bay, at least until some thorough minesweeping had been accomplished, a situation that was underlined by the presence of the coastal forts covering the entries to the bay. On 23 August, the Japanese ultimatum to the Germans to evacuate Tsingtao expired – no-one, least of all the Japanese, had expected the Germans to comply – and a state of war existed between the two countries. The day before, HMS *Kennet*, one of the destroyers attached to *Triumph*, almost caught the *S90* unawares as she was patrolling outside the minefield. The *S90* should have been no match for the newer and faster *Kennet*, but her commander, *Kapitanleutnant* Brunner, was able to avoid destruction by a mixture of good fortune, good seamanship and good gunnery. He took his ship in towards the minefield and under the coastal batteries, and dared *Kennet* to follow. Hot in pursuit, the *Kennet*, firing all the while, tried to cut the *S90* off from the safety of the minefield, but suffered a direct hit on one of her guns and was forced to withdraw, with three men killed and six more wounded, two so severely that they were to die in the ship's sick bay a little later.[19] With darkness falling, and with one gun out of action, the *Kennet* had little option but to break off the engagement and the *S90* threaded her way back through the minefield and into the relative safety of Kiaochau Bay. It had not been a good start to the British naval blockade and had helped German morale just a little:

> On the way back to the battery we heard firing, the alarm was at once sounded along the sea front. The Torpedo Boat *S90* had gone out and is now outside the protection of our coastal batteries. Some islands lie just outside the range of the guns and beyond them two small islands are looking like haystacks as they run up straight to a point. An English destroyer had hidden herself behind the latter and as *S90* steamed past at a range of about 6,000 metres the former opened fire, she fired about 80 rounds but none took effect.[20] *S90* replied with her two 8.8 cm guns and scored a direct hit before she fired two shots. The shooting of the English ship must have been very bad as from our position shots were seen to strike 1,000 metres short – the Englishmen then went away.[21] We thought she was probably a scout of the English and would probably return shortly with her squadron, unfortunately no such luck, nothing happened.[22]

This was to be the only action in which the Royal Navy acted alone during the blockade of Tsingtao. The following day, Japan entered the war and in three days, provided ships to assist in the blockade. Captain F. A. Powlett had also arrived in the area with HMS *Newcastle* to strengthen the British presence. The *Triumph* and the *Usk* were then temporarily detached from the flotilla and departed for Wei-hai-wei, in order to escort the 2nd South Wales Borderers troop ships south to Laoshan Bay, where the soldiers would disembark in preparation for the assault on the German colony. The Japanese warships, the *Ibuki* (an armoured cruiser) and the *Chikuma* (a light cruiser)[23] were placed at the disposal of Admiral Jerram to provide fire-power to the blockade. The sea power amassed around Kiaochau Bay meant that for the Germans there was no longer much hope of support or rescue. The modern warships of Admiral von Spee had left and could not return, their futures would lie elsewhere. For the Germans in Tsingtao, the die was cast; all they could do was wait for the assault that they all knew must come. They were an isolated garrison in a sea of enemies. Germans who had travelled to Tsingtao from all over that part of China had swelled the garrison to about 5,000 men by the time Japan entered the war. After 23 August, there was little chance of any further reinforcements. Whilst the garrison may have been sufficient if the Germans had only the British to fight (they also had limited resources in the area), it was clearly insufficient once it was known that the Japanese had thrown their lot in with the Allies. The Germans knew that they had a reasonably good defensive position, but in the absence of relief or replacements, they realized that all they could do was to fight to the bitter end – an end that would be dictated as much by the finite supplies and ammunition available as it was by the number of willing defenders.

The Allied naval build-up in the area continued as the Japanese committed more of its resources to the blockade of Tsingtao. No fewer than five battleships would use their 10-inch and 12-inch guns during the bombardment of the port. They were supported by seven armoured cruisers, five light cruisers and fourteen destroyers to complete the Japanese blockading force, supported by the *Triumph, Kennet* and *Usk*. To add to this, there was a seaplane mother-ship, with four seaplanes, general mine-sweepers and various support vessels which ensured that the fleet could be supplied and maintained. The small German naval force in Tsingtao may have been outnumbered and outgunned, but later events demonstrated that they remained undaunted.

Following the entry of Japan into the war, the action around Tsingtao became increasingly land-based as troops were brought to the area to carry out the overland attack that the Germans had thought unlikely. Control of the sea had been more or less handed to the Allies as the German Navy recognized its priorities were elsewhere. Although the decision to effectively abandon Tsingtao was not made lightly, and had been based to a large extent on the hope that Japan remained neutral, the ensuing events proved that the decision had been correct. While the Germans recognized that they could not be supplied or reinforced, they were aware that the British and the Japanese, could do both at will. All that remained for Tsingtao and its defenders was to await the outcome of the land-based campaign that was about to begin.

Notes

1. Massie (2003), 182. The German flyer Gunter Plüschow seems to have been confused by the details of this event since he identifies the visiting ship as HMS *Good Hope*. There is no record of that ship visiting Tsingtao in 1914. See Plüschow (2004), 24.
2. Military Report (1906) and amendment (1908).
3. Massie (2004), 186. Of course, the officer was mistaken as, although the British were involved when the town fell, it never came under British control.
4. See Massie (2003), 185.
5. HMS *Minotaur*, armoured cruiser of 14,600 tons built in 1908 with a main armament of four 9·2-inch guns and ten 7.5 guns.
6. HMS *Hampshire*, armoured cruiser of 10,800 tons built in 1905 with a main armament of four 7·5-inch guns and six 6-inch guns.
7. HMS *Yarmouth*, light cruisr of 4,800 tons built in 1912 with a main armament of eight 6 inch guns.
8. HMS *Newcastle*, light cruiser of 4,800 tons built in 1910 with a main armament of two 6-inch guns and ten 4-inch guns.
9. HMS *Triumph* was built by Vickers Limited while HMS *Swiftsure* was built by Armstrong Whitworth.
10. *Official History of the War. Naval Operations* (1920), I, 142.
11. The *Dupleix* had been built in 1903, displaced 7,432 tons and was armed with eight 6·4-inch guns. See *Official History*, 140.

12. HMS *Usk, Kennet, Welland, Ribble* and *Colne.*
13. Churchill (1938), 251.
14. See the *Official History*, 143.
15. A 4.5 inch gun from *Emden* acts as a permanent memorial in Hyde Park, Sydney, Australia, to this action. HMAS *Sydney* was a modern light cruiser of 5,000 tons and armed similarly to the other British-built light cruisers of the day. Its defeat of the *Emden* at the Battle of Caicos also recorded the Royal Australian Navy's first ship to ship battle.
16. See Halpern (1994), 73 and Nish (1970).
17. Ibid.
18. *Prinz Eitel Friedrich* was a 9,000 ton passenger ship which was converted to a light cruiser while at Tsingtao and served as a surface raider into 1915 before being interned in Newport News, Virginia, in March of that year.
19. Hoyt (1975), 75 and *Official History*, 149. There are records for four of the sailors killed but a search has not come up with the name of the fifth (see Appendix II). These are amongst the first British fatalities of the war – the British army did not fight its first action until 23 August at Mons.
20. A later entry concedes that one shell had passed through the flag of the *S90!*
21. The poor British gunnery at this stage of the war has been remarked upon by others, e.g. Halpern (1994).
22. From an unknown German's diary picked up in the observation station of Bismarck Fort by Major Margesson of the SWB following the fall of Tsingtao in November 1914.
23. The *Ibuki* at 14,600 tons was built in 1910 and had four 12-inch guns as its main armament. The *Chikuma* at 4,900 tons had been built in 1912 with a main armament of eight 6-inch guns; see *Official History*, 150. Both these ships were later involved in hunting the *Emden* in the Indian ocean, particularly around Ceylon.

Chapter 5

The Opening Acts

In the early years of the twentieth century, Tsingtao was seen as a good posting for the German military. The climate was reasonably good, the environment pleasant and generally, the work was not too taxing, although the town's role as a port for the Far East Squadron meant there was usually enough to keep everyone busy. *Oberleutnant sur See* Gunther Plüschow, a naval pilot, arrived for his second visit to Tsingtao in early June 1914. The first time he had visited, he had been a naval cadet and had travelled there on the Imperial Mail Ship, *Prinzregent Luitpold*, to join his ship, the armoured cruiser, *Fürst Bismarck*[1], then berthed in the newly-completed harbour.[2] On his second visit, he had travelled overland by train through the Russian steppes to Mukden which had been the scene of ferocious fighting some ten years earlier during the Russo-Japanese War.[3] From there, he had continued via Peking and Jinan, the provincial capital, before reaching Tsingtao, making use of the recently finished railway. After over 6,000 miles and endless days of being confined to the train, he was understandably very happy to be back on 'German soil'. He was a young man who was particular about his appearance, and throughout the long journey, had managed to keep one of his uniforms in good order so that, after shaving and changing on board, he was able to step from the train as fresh as when he had left Germany. This particular attention to detail was something that tended to set him apart, even from his fellow officers, and was something that enabled him to survive the difficulties of the coming months in Tsingtao when he proved to be of the greatest assistance to the rest of the German colony. Although he was pleased to be in China again, for him at least, there were a number of complaints about the way of life in the colony during the first few weeks of his new posting:

> Life in the East was very monotonous for Europeans. Very little socially, no music, no theatre – things one misses. One's only consolation is that one lives better than at home, and sport makes up for a great deal. I took up polo with enthusiasm, and soon as I had accustomed myself to the unusual pitching and tossing to which my horse subjected me I was very successful.[4]

Perhaps the lack of adventure was understandable for Plüschow; not long before his departure for China he had, with another pilot named Guido

Kapitän *Meyer-Waldeck, Governor of Tsingtao.*

Linnekogel, set the altitude record at 5,500 metres – a significant achievement in those early days of powered flight and not without considerable risk.[5] Peacetime life in Tsingtao was good for the Germans and the many other nationalities that lived, worked and visited the prosperous well-organized colony. For all that, it is as well to remember that Tsingtao was essentially a military base, governed by the German Navy; in 1914, its governor was a naval officer, *Kapitän* Alfred Meyer-Waldeck who had held the position since 1911. The Governor's residence, set a little apart from the main German area of Tsingtao, had gained a certain amount of celebrity in Germany having been built by a predecessor who had spared no expense nor omitted any luxury, utilizing only the finest materials, such as polished marbles and high-quality timbers, and the cost had eventually led to the governor's dismissal.[6] However, it did mean that Meyer-Waldeck lived in a certain degree of comfort and, of course, the residence, perhaps somewhat grotesque to the modern eye, was also used for the purpose of entertaining and impressing foreign visitors.[7]

To the Governor fell the routine tasks of running the colony with its city, docks, harbours and railway, to ensure that the German Far East Squadron was well-maintained and suitably supplied. The task of entertaining the foreign dignitaries who came to the area from time to time also fell to him. One such visit was that of HMS *Minotaur*, the flagship of Admiral Jerram, which called in an official capacity in June 1914. For the most part, these were not onerous duties, and there were also defences to build and maintain, and the garrison of Marines and Marine Artillery to discipline and keep in order. In 1914, Tsingtao was well-run and as Plüschow mentions, the Germans, civilians and armed forces alike, lived better than they did at home. As the heat of the north-east Chinese summer developed in 1914, these pleasant and happy times were running out for the German colony as developments in a small Balkan city, Sarajevo, took centre stage. When the news of the assassination of Archduke Franz Ferdinand reached Tsingtao in the early weeks of July, it all seemed so far away:

July had come, and brought with it the loveliest weather, most radiant sunshine, and the bluest skies. It was Tsingtao's best month. The bathing

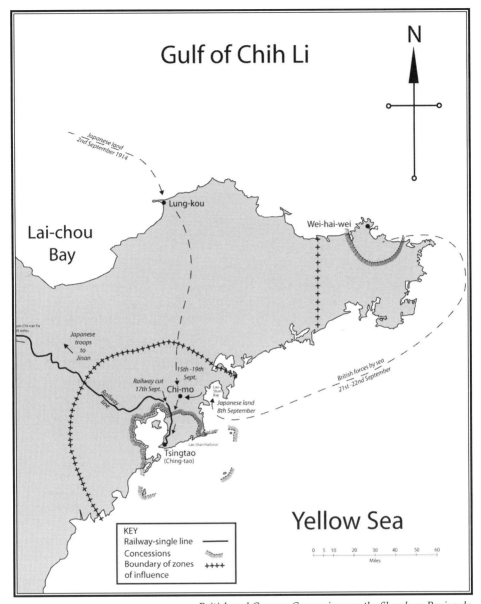

British and German Concessions on the Shandong Peninsula.

season was at its height. There were many charming ladies, most from European and American settlements in China and Japan, visiting the 'Ostend of the Far East' and enjoying the beauty of Tsingtao.[8]

It was to be the last month in which the Germans in Tsingtao, or for that matter anywhere else, could enjoy the summer weather in peace. The days took on a feeling of unreality as no-one could believe that the events in Sarajevo were having such far-reaching consequences. As the months wore on, and one rumour-filled day followed another, it was clear that tensions were growing in Europe. Nevertheless, on 30 July when the order 'Danger of War' was issued by Meyer-Waldeck, it still came as a real shock to most of the inhabitants of Tsingtao, whether German resident or foreign visitor. From the moment the order was issued, Tsingtao was put on a war footing to await developments in Europe.

> On the 31st July the Marine Artillery manned their works. Shortly afterwards the 3rd Marine Battalion manned the infantry works. Naturally we were, at first, very pleased that it was going to be war.[9]

As the days slipped away, Plüschow's polo team had to cancel a match with the British team in Shanghai which seemed to the young aviator to be a good indication of the severity of the situation. All the talk was of war and the consequences of it, no angle was left unexplored by the barrack-room politicians and strategists, as every piece of news and rumour was examined in minute detail. British ladies in Tsingtao, visiting the colony perhaps for the first time, were shocked at the very thought of war and considered it to be very unlikely that Germany and Britain could go to war with each other. Perhaps some of the officers amongst the German Marine Battalion thought so as well, after all King George V and Kaiser Wilhelm were first cousins. Far more probably thought that was inevitable and perhaps even a consequence of that relationship. There were also those professional soldiers, both officers and rank and file, who actively welcomed war and could not wait for it to start, only bemoaning the fact that they were so far away from Europe which they thought would be the cockpit of the action. It was hard for anyone in the German settlement to believe that there was any real danger to Tsingtao from any of the European adversaries that had a presence in the Far East. Britain and France posed no danger to their security since they had only small numbers of troops close at hand. In the early days of August, no-one gave a second thought to the nearest external imperial power – Japan. There was a sense of unreality in the colony which was at least partly the result of its extreme distance from Europe and, as a consequence, a feeling of being out of the action; but even that could not last as the days passed and events in Europe began to have far-reaching effects.

On 1 August, following an ultimatum issued at midnight on 31 July, Germany declared war on Russia and invaded her territory on the pretext that the Russians had entered Germany first. This seems to have been a well-organized plan since the German declaration which was timed at 5 p.m. implied that Russia had pre-empted the declaration by an invasion earlier in the day. Germany had decided on war with Russia on the last day of July and nothing the Russians did after the ultimatum was delivered would have made any difference. Germany sought to place the blame for war on Russia and, in so doing, appeared to be the injured party.[10] Whether or not the Russians invaded first mattered not to the Germans in Tsingtao – everyone was mobilized for war in the colony, the waiting was over and when the news of the declaration reached the colony, there could only be one course of action. Germany was officially at war with a major European power and, even if Tsingtao was under no immediate threat, there was at least an identifiable enemy, and they planned to be as ready as possible. In the unlikely event of Russian troops turning up in Kaiochou Bay, they would meet with the stiffest resistance that Meyer-Waldeck and his limited garrison could muster. Whilst there was great enthusiasm for the war amongst Meyer-Waldeck's command, the conditions at some of the war stations in China were not all pleasant, particularly for some of those serving in the Marine Artillery:

> The garrison of a Battery is about 180 men, the rooms are at present very wet. Water is running down the walls and comes from the ceiling, in fact everything was wet, this is due to it having rained for at least fourteen days.[11]

According to this soldier who was stationed in Bismarck Fort, the weather had not been as good as *Oberleutnant* Plüschow had described during July. It is just as clear that the Germans had not managed to waterproof or ventilate their concrete structures successfully, though it was, perhaps, considered to be too much of a luxury in such an utilitarian structure. However, the bad conditions were to have an effect on the health of the men and on their equipment:

> This morning we had a parade for one hour cleaning arms – owing to the wet state of the Batteries the small arms rust very quickly. A certain amount of emery paper comes in very useful for cleaning purposes. The side arms were cleaned today.[12]

Conditions were certainly uncomfortable in the damp forts, and were probably made worse by the tense waiting for something to happen, but there was a determination that it would make no difference to the preparations and generally, spirits were high amongst the men of the Marine Artillery, and morale and discipline did not falter. Tsingtao may have been a relatively 'comfortable billet' but it was by this time, recognized as being an active service, and the artillerymen wanted to use their big guns as soon as possible and therefore their care and maintenance was of great importance if they were to be serviceable for the defence of the town. The duty of the men in Tsingtao was clear and they were determined not to be found wanting.

> Of course, our minds were filled with this contingency. The tension was even worse than during the first days of mobilization. And when, on the 4th August, we got the news that war had been declared against England it became a deliverance – the die was cast in Europe.[13]

Britain did not have a large force in China, a total of eight battalions between Hong Kong in the south and Peking in the north, numbering fewer than 10,000 men, far too small a force to put in the field against a reasonably

HMT Soudan *which took the 2nd Battalion South Wales Borderers from England to South Africa in December 1910 and from Durban to Teintsin, China in October 1912. [Royal Welsh Museum, Brecon,BRCRM 1949.48]*

well-fortified town like Tsingtao, even though the defenders numbered only half that figure. The Germans therefore felt a certain security and in the early days of August, the colony lived on a diet of fact, mixed with a liberal helping of propaganda fed by the telegrams coming out of Europe, in which the German Army always seemed to be doing very well indeed. The news of further successes as the German Army marched across Belgium and into France, brought immense pleasure to the messes in Tsingtao, but this was tinged with sadness since most serving men wanted to be where the real action was, with their home armies in Europe. They felt unable to prove themselves, believing the minor British presence in China would be very unlikely to allow them that honour.

Further north in Tientsin, during the final days of July, the British garrison had not noticed anything especially odd – there was an element of tension between the various Europeans, but this was no different to anywhere else in China. Like the Germans at Tsingtao, the garrison of Tientsin, the 2nd Battalion the South Wales Borderers, also felt isolated and rather left out of things. Theyprovided the Legation Guard in Peking, and a company for duty in Fengtai, a southern suburb of the capital city. During the course of their duties, the Legation Guard came into contact with soldiers from many nations in the confined Legation district of the city, which was situated within easy walking distance of the Forbidden City. This gave them the opportunity to make many international friendships as the nations that had been involved in the siege during the Boxer troubles had all insisted on the right to have an armed guard within the confines of the city as part of the subsequent treaty with the Chinese. The Borderers would therefore have come into contact with Russian, Italian, French and Japanese soldiers to name but a few; in fact, a series of photographs was issued to enable the Legation Guard to recognize the uniforms of the other nations present in the District, so that there would be as little confusion as possible. The Borderers provided a company for this purpose which was rotated with those based in the barracks at Tientsin (and the one based in Fengtai) so that during their China posting, all the officers and men would have been on duty at all the locations on several occasions.

The Borderers had been away from their home station for some time and had arrived in Tientsin from South Africa in 1912. Many were old hands, with years of experience of soldiering and foreign postings. Some were veterans of the second Anglo-Boer War. The battalion departed from Durban aboard the HT *Soudan* in October 1912, and after an uneventful posting, there can have been no-one who thought that the tour of duty in China would be any different. The battalion reached Chin-wang-tao on 3 November and arrived in Tientsin the following afternoon, where they were met by an honour guard commanded by Brigadier-General Cooper, officer commanding troops of North China Command.[14] Five companies of the Borderers remained at Tientsin, billeted in a 'go-down' or warehouse, while the three companies earmarked for duty in Peking carried on their journey to commence the work immediately.[15]

By 1914, the Borderers in the barracks in Tientsin were perhaps best placed to notice any changes in the composition or attitude of the German garrison, since the barracks of the East Asia Marine Detachment were immediately next to them. At this time, with war just weeks away, relations between the British and Germans were nothing but cordial and, both officers

2/SWB Legation Guard leaving Tientsin for Peking. [Royal Welsh Museum, Brecon, Box 91]

and men of each nationality, had friends amongst their counterparts:

> Tientsin, like Peking, was divided into concessions (in Peking called
> Legations) or areas limited solely under the control of the British, French,
> German, and other nations, commanders whose troops were held responsible
> for law and order in their own respective areas.
>
> The German concession was nearest to us and was under the command of
> Colonel Kuhlo, a giant of a man, who, together with his officers, were
> particular friends of ours.
>
> In June or July, 1914, Colonel Kuhlo invited, and we accepted, Colonel
> Casson and the officers of the Regiment to a dinner in their officers mess, I
> recollect that though we attended in Mess Kit the German officers did not
> have Mess Kit and wore their ordinary daily uniform.
>
> At dinner Colonel Kuhlo and Colonel Casson each spoke of the great
> friendship existing between us and hoped that it would never be interfered
> with. We all drank the toast to our respective sovereigns, King George V and
> the Kaiser, and the band played the national anthems, which, incidentally,
> was the same tune for both of us![16]

Of course, the events in Europe rapidly overtook the friendships of
peacetime. The declaration of war brought first Russia and then France into
open conflict with Germany. Since both were, at least in theory, allied to
Great Britain, it was inevitable that she should, in turn, declare war on
Germany. This action was precipitated by the German invasion of Belgium.
Britain, France and Germany had signed a treaty in 1840 which guaranteed
the safety of Belgium, should it come under external threat. The Germans
broke this treaty and compromised Belgium's neutrality, seeing that country
as a back door into France, whose border with Belgium was largely
undefended as a result of the treaty. Germany saw Belgium as a weak
country and so had nothing to fear from disrespecting the seventy-four-
year-old treaty and had detailed plans in place since 1905 for the manoeuvre
they were then carrying out.[17] Whilst this is all true, the declaration of war
by Britain and France was as much about supremacy in Europe as anything

*Facing: The King's Birthday reception at British Legation Peking, 2 June 1914 shows the international
nature of the troops in the city. Back row: Sgt C. Dipper (2/Glosters); Cpl F. Roberts (16/Colonial
Infantry, France); Sgt J. Galbraith (2/Glosters); Sgt Drew (US Marine Corps); CQMS W. J. Gwinnell
(2/Glosters); Sgt Saliou (16/Colonial Infantry, France); Sgt A. Layton (ASC); Sgt J. Eagles (RAMC).
Second row: Sgt Coopery (2/Glosters); P/O H. Billi (Royal Italian Navy); Sgt Tusuda (Japanese
Infantry); P/O Tobros (Austrian Navy); CSM W. J. Watson (RGA); Sgt J. Roevens (Belgian Guard);
Sgt Thorne (RGA); Sgt Maj Azuma (Japanese Infantry); Sgt G. Baines (RGA); Sgt Lengmuller
(German Infantry); P/O B. Pons (Royal Italian Navy). Third row: CSM C. Basdell (2/Glosters); Sgt
Popoff (Russian Cossacks); Sgt J. Seabright (2/Glosters); C/Eng Cronan (US Marine Corps); Sgt R. B.
Hicks (ASC); Sgt J. G. Bronius (Dutch Marine Infantry); Sgt R. Jamieson (2/SWB); Sgt De Zetter
(Belgian Guard); Sgt C. Fairbrass (2/SWB); QMS H. T. Cox (RE); Sgt May Creamer (US Marine
Corps). Seated: Sgt W. Oxenham (2/Glosters); Sgt Maj Samp (German Artillery); Sgt W. J. Keywood
(2/Glosters); Sgt Shenikoff (Russian Cossacks); Sgt F. Toop (2/Glosters); Sgt G. H. Battereld (Dutch
Marine Infantry); Sgt S. D. Bean (2/SWB); P/O Tribran (Austrian Navy). Front row: Sgt F. Chaston
(2/SWB); Sgt C. Iggledon (2/SWB); Master W. G. Keywood; Hospital Steward Rogers (US Marine
Corps); Master H. M. Cox; S/Sgt W. G. Penn (ASC).   [Royal Welsh Museum, Brecon, Box P9]*

SERGEANTS MESS 2ND BATTALION SOUTH WALES BORDERERS
DECEMBER 1914

else and if the Germans had not invaded Belgium, then another reason for the war would almost inevitably have been found – the invasion of France would have had the same effect if Britain stood by its newly-developed friendship with her. Thus, by 1914, war was almost a certainty and little could have been done to prevent it. Seven thousand miles away in Tientsin, with the nations' representatives living in their respective concessions, there had been no signal to let them know how they should behave in the event of war or how they should prepare for that eventuality or indeed, if they were to take any action at all.

I recollect that my friend Leutnant Wendt[18] of Colonel Kuhlo's garrison, met me in the street about August 11th, 1914, and asked 'What are your people going to do here?' and then he mentioned that the Germans had captured many prisoners on both the French and Russian Fronts.

I replied, 'I don't know what we're going to do but we don't want to fight you chaps because you are friends of ours.' We never met again.

About this time I heard that Colonel Kuhlo and his whole garrison had entrained at a small station some 6 miles from Tientsin and had all gone to Tsingtao. We heard that every German officer and other ranks had quietly left their posts all over China, including the German Legation Guard in Peking, and had headed for Tsingtao.[19]

Whilst other nations were deliberating their action in China, the Germans had made the decision that they would defend their important colony on the Shandong peninsula and, as Lieutenant Walker had pointed out, Germans from all over China made their way to Tsingtao to swell the ranks of the

Facing: Sergeants of the 2/SWB in Hong Kong, after the successful action against the German held post of Tsingtao in November 1914. [Royal Welsh Museum, Brecon, Box 91]

Right: 2/SWB Sergeants in winter dress at Tientsin. [Royal Welsh Museum, Box 91]

Tientsin Garrison– 2nd Battalion on Guard Duty in Winter of 1913.
[Royal Welsh Museum, Brecon, Box 91]

would-be defenders. Although there were precious few of them, they felt strong in their fastness knowing full well that it would take a large force to dislodge them – a force larger than their enemies had in China in the early days of the war. Of course, they had chosen to forget Japan believing, or perhaps hoping, that she would remain neutral. On 1 August, Colonel Kuhlo, wrote the following to the British General Officer Commanding, Brigadier-General N. W. Barnardiston:

> I have the honour to inform you that I have received telegraphic orders to move my detachment as soon as possible to Tsingtao.
> On account of the haste with which I have had to carry out this order, it had been impossible for me to say 'Goodbye' to you personally.
> I therefore beg you to forgive the omission which was due to the unsettled state of the Political outlook.
> I should also be especially grateful if you would say 'Goodbye' for me to the Officers and Troops of your command, and to convey to them my very best thanks for the friendship and comradeship which they have extended to us, both in Tientsin and Peking.
> The friendly relations which have always existed between us remains a very pleasant memory.[20]

This very formal letter which, nevertheless, voices some of the regret of the coming of war was replied to in a similarly formal manner by Barnardiston on 4 August, during the course of which he commented:

On my own behalf, and that of the Officers, NCOs and men of the British Troops under my command, I can only say that we sincerely regret the severance of those friendly relations – a severance which we earnestly hope may only be a temporary one.[21]

For the 2nd Battalion, the South Wales Borderers, early August 1914 was a time of waiting as they held themselves in readiness for action. It was anticipated that they would be sent to France – to the main theatre of the war – there was no real expectation amongst any of the men of fighting in China. Like the Germans, the officers and men of the Borderers felt that their place was with their home armies in Europe, but all they could do thousands of miles away from the action was to await orders to move. They had not however, been forgotten by the military hierarchy in London and their time was not far off. It is probably fair to say that, for the most part, the Borderers would have been entirely ignorant of the political moves going on behind the scenes but events in London were to affect them in an unexpected manner.

As discussed earlier, the British government had asked the Japanese for assistance in the Far East and, for their part, the Japanese could not wait to get involved – it was their chance to get the foothold in China which they had sought, for at least twenty years. It was also their opportunity to be recognized as a world power by the great nations of the world and it was simply too good an opportunity to miss. Britain had wanted rather limited assistance from the Japanese which was, perhaps, a little naïve as the latter were only interested in full involvement and would not be content to use their navy simply to patrol the area, to ensure that German ships were kept away from China and the ports, particularly Tsingtao. To the Japanese, this option meant them taking a considerable risk without any potential benefits. It soon became clear to the British government that Japan was going to use her not inconsiderable military power to full effect against the Germans in Tsingtao and, after asking for assistance, Britain was put in a rather awkward diplomatic position and could do nothing to prevent her ally declaring war on Germany on 24 August. Nevertheless, Britain could use locally-based forces to assist the Japanese in any action they chose to take in the area and it was clear that this would mean establishing a force to take the field in north-east China. Initially, the view from London was that such a British force in the field with the Japanese would not be acting simply as support, but would also be acting as observers and, as such, might be able to control events to some degree. Again, this was probably somewhat naïve as, with the intended action close to the Japanese home bases, they could call upon a large force more or less at will. As such, any British force (bearing in mind there was a maximum of only eight battalions in the whole region), would be in such a minority that there could not really be any serious consideration of controlling the Japanese and that at best, the British could take no more than a minor part in any operations. With all these things going on in the background, the 2nd Battalion the South Wales Borderers were, on 17

September,[22] placed on readiness for a move at short notice and orders were received the following day.

The Borderers were to come under the command of Brigadier-General Nathaniel Barnardiston, a career soldier who had seen service in a number of overseas postings before reaching North China. He had commanded the 2nd Battalion the Middlesex Regiment during the latter stages of the Anglo-Boer War, but it was considered that he lacked the robust physique required for field command. He was, however, considered to be a charming man with considerable diplomatic and social skills which made him eminently suited for a command such as North China. As the senior officer in the region, he was placed in command of the joint operations with the Japanese, in which the British were to play a strictly limited role. Nevertheless, he had asked for a substantially larger force, hoping that it would include a full brigade of four battalions, as well as artillery. In spite of all his lobbying and protestations, he was only given the 2nd South Wales Borderers and half a battalion of the 36th Sikhs, and no artillery whatsoever, with which he was to take the field and play an important and integrated part in the overall campaign. It was a great deal to ask of any commander, but for the soldiers who were to be involved, it was simply another job to do and since many of the Borderers had experience of soldiering throughout the Empire, it probably seemed little different to anything else they had done during the last few years, albeit this time, they were going to war. In due course, an agreement for joint military operations was drawn up and signed by Japan (Lieutenant-General Kamio) and Great Britain (Brigadier-General Barnardiston), with the latter being given only a very minor role.[23]

Whilst these discussions were going on, the Germans in Tsingtao took the opportunity to improve their preparations for the assault that, by the end of August, they knew must eventually come. Two Rumpler Military Mono-planes of the *Taube* design, that were to form the basis of an air force in Tsingtao, had arrived in crates aboard the steamer, *Patricia*, in July and *Ober-leutnant* Plüschow and his crews spent two days assembling the machines. The assembly was the easiest part of the task, Plüschow's biggest problem was the choice of Iltis Platz as his aerodrome.[24]

> The aerodrome was extraordinarily small, only 600 metres long and 200 metres wide, full of obstacles, surrounded by hills and rocks. I was only to learn later how very difficult starting and landing were made hereby.[25]

Not only was the aerodrome small, but it was also surrounded by hills on three sides and on the fourth, the seaward side, which was effectively the end of Plüschow's runway, was a further hill which dropped steeply to the rocks and sea below. It was not a good airfield, but there was no alternative and the pilots needed to make the best they could of it. This was a little worrying for Plüschow and his hopes for the future of the air force in the area. As if to confirm the difficulties with the siting of the airfield, Plüschow, an experienced pilot, discovered that the cross-winds and down-draughts over the edge of the airfield caused problems as the *Taube* was light and very susceptible to the small changes in wind speed and direction. He completed three flights, cautiously investigating both the suitability of the airfield and the capabilities of his aircraft. On the fourth flight, all went well until almost at touch-down, a sudden gust of wind brought the nose of the aeroplane down sharply, causing it to crash. Fortunately for Plüschow, the damage to himself and the machine was relatively light which proved to be a great bonus to the defenders of the town in the coming weeks, as his reconnaissance flights took on great importance. However, the propeller of the small aeroplane had been damaged beyond repair which at first, did not cause Plüschow undue concern because along with the crated aeroplanes, there were also crates of parts to keep them airborne. As is often the case, things were not as simple as anticipated. In those days, propellers were crafted from wood and when the crates of spares were opened, the spare propellers were found to have been damaged as a result of the crate having leaked during the voyage, causing the wood to warp and rot beyond repair. With some ingenuity, and the skill of Chief Engineer Stüben and his Chinese workforce, a new propeller was fashioned to the specification of that damaged in the crash. The Chief Engineer did not have all the benefits of a modern aircraft workshop and, although he had made an excellent job of the replacement, it was to require regular maintenance thereafter, as the glued laminations of the propeller started to separate during each flight. After every couple of hours flying, the propeller had to be removed and repaired which was all very time-consuming but the diligence of Stüben, and Plüschow's determination, experience and skill as a pilot, kept the *Taube* in the sky throughout the entire siege and there were no more accidents in

taking-off or landing. The problem with the airfield had to be managed by the pilots but, as *Leutnant* Müllerskowski, was to find out, that was easier said than done. His first flight ended in disaster when his aeroplane failed to gain height and crashed over the edge of the cliff onto the rocks below the airfield. The machine was completely wreck-

Oberleutnant *Günther Plüschow seated in the cockpit of his Rumpler aeroplane.*

ed and Müllerskowski seriously injured and he took no further part in the defence. As a result of these accidents, instead of having two aeroplanes and two pilots, the nascent air-force of Tsingtao was reduced to one pilot and one barely serviceable machine.

Also aboard the *Patricia* were two observation balloons which were also in Plüschow's charge. These balloons, each of 2,000 cubic metres, were to be used to observe troop movements and Meyer-Waldeck had placed considerable store on their usefulness in the event of a siege of the town. However, the realisation of this ideal was far from the truth when Plüschow eventually got to try them out.

> Our Governor expected great things of the observation balloon. It was hoped that it would be of great service in reconnoitring the approach of the enemy and the disposition of his artillery. These hopes were doomed to disappointment and my fears that the erection of the balloons would serve no useful purpose were soon justified.
> Though I was able to send up the kite balloon to 1200 metres from the ground, we did not succeed in visualizing the range of hills which lay behind our fortified positions, thus observing the enemy's movements, above all, his heavy siege artillery [was impossible]. And this would have been of capital importance to the defenders of Tsingtao.[26]

Life for the troops manning the forts was no less busy as there was plenty to be done in preparation for war. At first, this kept the men fully occupied but as the days passed without any significant incident, the men became bored, looking and waiting for work to do and, in particular, wanting to have a go at the enemy. The artillerymen in the forts longed to man their guns, but there was little cause for excitement aside from the short engagement that saw HMS *Kennet* damaged by the *S90*, which gladdened the hearts of the witnessing Germans. Then almost unexpectedly, on 27 August, a fleet became visible to the German gunners. The ships were at some considerable distance from the bay, but it was clear to all that they were Japanese with all the implications that this realization involved.

> At daylight tomorrow the attack from the sea will surely begin, we are very pleased at the idea of it. I expect at home they have already given us up as lost, we are in very good spirits here. It all depends on whether we can beat off the contemplated attack. Yesterday the following telegram was received from His Majesty 'God be with you in the impending difficult fight, my thoughts are with you. Wilhelm.'[27]

No doubt this message from the Kaiser lifted the spirits of the German force as the Germans, like the British, were fiercely loyal to their monarch, and any recognition of their efforts from Germany would have helped to sustain their morale. There was however, to be no immediate attack from the sea. As part of their preparations, the Japanese attempted a landing at Cape

Jaschke, across the bay, south of Tsingtao, with the view to preparing positions for heavy guns. The landing party was shelled with shrapnel from Fort A on Hui-ch'uan Point and, when a small party of Germans was landed from the *S90* to investigate the situation, it reported that the Japanese had departed the peninsula, leaving behind several dead soldiers. The Japanese had lost the first round of the action of Tsingtao and had suffered their first casualties. Many more would follow before Tsingtao was to fall into their grasp.

Notes

1. SMS *Fürst Bismarck* was an armoured cruiser of 10,690 tons built in 1896 and like its more famous namesake of the Second World War named after Otto von Bismarck.
2. See Whittaker (1994),11.
3. Many of the battlefields had been left untouched since the end of the Russo-Japanese War. During 1913, a group of officers of the 2nd SWB visited the battlefields and Major Margesson made a record of the occasion in his diary preserved in the Royal Welsh Museum at Brecon.
4. Plüschow (2004), 26.
5. Plüschow (2004), 17.
6. Oskar Truppel was Governor from 1901 until Meyer-Waldeck replaced him.
7. The Governor's House is still standing in Tsingtao and for a small admission fee, it is possible to visit the rooms that were used by Meyer-Waldeck during the siege. The building was used by the Communist Party as an official guest house and the bedroom used by Chairman Mao is important to Chinese visitors.
8. Plüschow (2004), 28.
9. German diary found in Bismarck Fort.
10. Gleichen (1988), 10.
11. German diary found at Bismarck Fort entry for the period 31 July to 3 August. The author of the diary has been tentatively identified as Heinrich Pauer of the Marine Artillery.
12. Ibid
13. Plüschow (2004), 30. Note Plüschow states 4 August. North-east China is eight hours in front of GMT and hence it was 5 August in the colony before war was declared.
14. Anonymous account from a document held in the Royal Welsh Museum, Brecon.
15. The 2nd Somerset Light Infantry were in the British Barracks in Tientsin at this time and remained there until posted out of China. Also note it was 1 December 1913 before the 2nd South Wales Borderers was organized on a four company system.
16. Lieutenant Walker's notes on the Tsingtao campaign held at Royal Welsh Museum, Brecon.
17. The 'Schlieffen Plan'.
18. *Oberleutnant* Paul Wendt. He was later captured by the Japanese and was held as a prisoner of war at Oita Camp in Japan from where he was released in December 1919.
19. Walker, Royal Welsh Museum, Brecon.
20. Routine Orders 5 August 1914 – Royal Welsh Museum, Brecon. Note that at the time the note was sent, the two countries were not at war.
21. Ibid.
22. Embarkation orders can be found in Appendix X.
23. See appropriate Appendix for the agreement.
24. Today the area of Iltis Platz is given over to parks and football pitches remaining largely undeveloped – the confines of Plüschow's airfield can be identified.
25. Plüschow (2004), 27.
26. Plüschow (2004), 36. Plüschow does not indicate that these balloons were trialled or whether a variety of options were tested. They were certainly visible to the British forces when they arrived in the siege positions.
27. German diary found at Bismarck Fort. Royal Welsh Museum, Brecon.

Chapter 6

The Landings

The declaration of war by Japan left no-one in Tsingtao in any doubt as to the events that were likely to unfold in the coming months. The appearance of Japanese warships off the coast confirmed their intentions, but there was still the question of how they were to get troops to Tsingtao. The Japanese had assessed their options for making war on Germany thoroughly, and it was clear to them that a frontal assault on Tsingtao from the sea was both impracticable, as far as finding a suitable place to establish a beachhead was concerned, and likely to be very costly in terms of the casualties they would probably sustain during such an assault. The German forts could bring heavy fire to bear on any attack from the sea and, whilst they might ultimately be overcome by superior Japanese numbers, they could inflict serious casualties whilst they were in action. They had also mined the approaches to the harbour as soon as war became inevitable, converting the pleasure steamer, *Lauting*, for this purpose. Much of the immediate coastline of Kiaochou Bay was rocky and totally unsuited to a sea-borne invasion and where there were no rocks, the Germans had the beaches covered by one or more of their forts. Consideration of other beaches in the general area of the German concession, and the German zone of influence, produced similar issues which caused the Japanese to reassess their overall strategy for an attack on Tsingtao. Any landing they made needed to be secure, or very quickly secured, if they were to get sufficient troops ashore; it was certainly desirable that they should not meet any stern resistance that could inflict heavy casualties before being able to establish a suitable beachhead. Any landing site chosen would need to have a reason-able beach and preferably a bay which would serve to protect the transport and supply ships. This suggested to the Japanese that probably the best thing to do was to look beyond the German zone of influence, which would ensure that the waters would not be mined and that any chosen beach would be free of German defenders. However, if this was considered to be the most favourable option, it would be necessary to violate Chinese neutrality, for if they were not attacking Kiaochou Bay (effectively German territory) directly, then they would have to do so indirectly, through China. There were, clearly, problems with this approach that were fully acknowl-edged by the Japanese. The international community, particularly Britain, was not happy with this approach but recognized that they were powerless to intervene; if the Japanese set their mind to the task, no amount of diplomatic pressure could persuade them to do otherwise. The Chinese government had offered Britain an alternative, by way of her ambassador in Beijing, John Jordan, suggesting that China should also declare war on Germany and put a force into the field immediately. This would seem to have been a sensible way to solve the problem and would have brought the Chinese into the war from the outset. Jordan however, appears to have taken a rather high-handed attitude and dismissed the Chinese offer which would have resolved the neutrality issues, and hence the difficulties associated with the Japanese search for a suitable landing place. This was seen as a stinging rebuke to the Chinese and a considerable loss of face for their government. Of course, the Chinese had their own reasons for making the offer. By declaring war, they could, in theory at least, have a say in the outcome of the campaign in Kiaochou with the ultimate aim of seeing Tsingtao returned to their control. Secondary to this was the rather longer-term goal of being able to attend any peace conference on an equal footing with the Japanese and hence, ensure that Japan would not gain their long sought after foothold in mainland China.[1] Therefore, at this early stage of the campaign, the political manoeuvres associated with the whole of the Kiaochou situation were becoming complex and very sharply focused.

By the time Japan had declared war, it was clear that any action they might intend undertaking would be without the permission, implied or otherwise, of any European power or China. Britain recognized very early on in the discussions that it was not really within her power to direct the military operation, or dictate the foreign policy of a sovereign, independent nation even though she may have inadvertently provided the means to allow Japan to enter the war. For Britain to withdraw her tacit support for Japan would not achieve anything either, since Japan had decided to enter the war to establish herself as a power in the Far East and would have continued her course of action without recourse to anyone. Japan saw the removal of Germany, and German influence, from Kiaochou Bay as an integral part of her foreign policy and once she had been offered the chance to enter the war, she would not be easily stopped. After due consideration of the options, the Japanese came to a decision to make theira landing in China. Lungkow, on the north coast of the Shandong peninsula was considered ideal for the purpose and everything was put in readiness for an assault on Tsingtao by means of a passage through China. It should be recognized here that this decision was not dissimilar to that made by the Germans when they breached Belgian neutrality in order to fight the French. In view of the stance Britain took over this latter event, the Japanese actions clearly placed the British government in an uncomfortable, but largely unavoidable, position.

During this period of deliberation, the Japanese navy maintained a steady watch on the entrance to Kiaochou Bay – nothing went in or out without their knowledge, but as far as the warships were concerned, the big

German cruisers had gone and the smaller warships were of little real consequence. Tsingtao's fate was not going to be decided in a sea battle. However, it was not as straightforward as the Japanese might have hoped. On 31 August, the Japanese destroyer *Schiratai* ran aground on Lientau Islet, one of the small islands in the bay, during a heavy storm. Although attempts were made by three other Japanese destroyers to re-float the stricken vessel, it soon became clear that this would not be possible. As the storm cleared, the Japanese, realizing that the vessel would be a ready target for the Germans in Tsingtao, evacuated the crew and all important documents to the attending destroyers. As if to emphasise this vulnerability, one of the forts let off a salvo and the Japanese destroyers made off quickly leaving the *Schiratai* to her fate:

> This morning a Japanese destroyer ran ashore on a small island opposite H. Battery (Fort A) and remained fast. Unfortunately, our batteries are unable to reach the island.[2] The Gunboat *Jaguar* steamed out and opened fire on the destroyer, she got in some good hits and we were easily able to watch the effects of the shots. A Japanese Cruiser lay away on the horizon and allowed the destroyer to be bombarded without coming to her assistance. The Gunboats cannot take on a cruiser, they are, however, suitable for an opportunity when there is no heavy gun firing, they can steam out for a short distance and afterwards make a bolt for the harbour. Four destroyers came to the assistance of the bombarded destroyer but it was now too late, the work was completed, she lay over on one side and the SMS *Jaguar* returned into the harbour.[3]

The *Schiratai* was completely destroyed by the action of the *Jaguar* and, although all the crew escaped, the incident provided a lift to the Germans in Tsingtao, their only disappointment being that the ship was too far away to allow the big guns in the forts to get in on the action. It was a small victory before the main event which was all but ready to begin.

The Japanese began their landings at Lungkow, about 100 miles north of Tsingtao, on 2 September. The force to be used in the campaign was the 18th Independent Division which had mobilized at its base at Kurume in the south of Kyushu by 24 August, and had been awaiting confirmation of the assault. It had been styled an 'Independent' division to reflect the fact that it was not part of an army corps or larger formation. The Japanese had not considered the campaign against Tsingtao of sufficient size and importance to warrant the formation of an Army though, ultimately many more troops than would have been considered normal for a division, were to become involved in the siege.

The final decision to land at Lungkow was taken on 30 August and the 18th Independent Division wasted no time making its landings only three days later. The principle behind the landings in Lungkow was to split the force into two main assault groups. The first troops to land were to be the main body of the fighting troops (mainly infantry and associated field artillery) and their supply columns which were closely followed by the siege troops and the remainder of the supply columns. The second group would include the large siege pieces that would be needed to complete the campaign. The first troops to land in China in September were referred to as the Yamada Detachment (*Yamada Shitai*), after the general-officer commanding, a complete brigade which was to establish the beachhead and then push rapidly south towards Tsingtao.

> The Japanese landed on the 5th (sic) of this month at Tongku,[4] north of Tsingtao, altogether a force of about 10,000 Infantry, Cavalry and Artillery. 4,000 men were landed on the 5th and started to march towards Tsingtao – in 2 days they may possibly be here – everyone is breathing with relief, at last they are coming. The Japanese Squadron of about 20 ships again came in sight this morning, against these we have out 4 sea batteries, 17 guns. How it will end here is in God's hands.[5]

Although there are significant mistakes in the artilleryman's account, it is clear that there was an expectation of battle in the not too distant future and an eagerness to get on with it, tinged with the realisation that the Germans were under-equipped for the forces ranged against them. However, the Japanese had chosen a bad time to commence an invasion since on the day of the landing, a storm broke that was to lash the Shandong peninsula until 10 September. The storm, described as the worst for a generation, caused significant delays to the operation but the Japanese continued the landings. The veritable deluge that fell in a short time meant that tracks and unmade roads which would have allowed an army to pass in dry weather, albeit with some difficulty, became more or less impassable. Roads became rivers of mud, streams became raging torrents and the Japanese army, slowed to

Japanese troops landing at Laoshan Bay.

almost a crawling pace, edged its way towards Tsingtao under very difficult conditions. Any expectation which the defenders in the town may have had of an early engagement were gone – little could be done in the face of the weather which was for a few days the biggest enemy of the Japanese. For all that, what little progress the Japanese did manage was completely unhindered.

The Chinese, although neutral, tended to support Britain and her allies, but naturally, they were not happy with the high-handed approach adopted by the Japanese and their landings in strength at Lungkow. The Chinese could not stop them without creating a diplomatic incident in which they recognized that they would probably come off worse. China managed to resolve this dilemma by creating a so-called 'war zone' which allowed the passage of Japanese troops through a portion of Shandong Province, whilst insisting that the invading force remained within the zone. In fact, the Chinese had more or less washed their hands of the whole situation, in part as a result of Ambassador Jordan's reaction, and were awaiting the outcome almost as much as the Germans. The Chinese, in creating a war zone, had recognized their inability to prevent the Japanese taking any action they chose; this was further emphasised when China was unable to prevent the Japanese moving outside the zone to take control of Jinan. There was nothing the Chinese could do but await developments and hope they would not become embroiled in the conflict unnecessarily.

For their part, the Germans were unable to operate outside their concession since that would have broken the terms of their lease and violated Chinese neutrality. Although that may not have worried them too much, they had far too few men available to enable them to take any sort of action beyond the area of the concession – but they were not without intelligence about the manoeuvres:

> I was soon to receive my baptism of fire. It was during the first days of September, on a Sunday, at an altitude of 1,500 metres, far out over the territory, basking in sunshine. I suddenly caught sight below of a fairly important detachment of Japanese, which greeted me with volleys of infantry and machine gun fire. I returned home, exhibiting ten holes in my planes. But in future I did not descend below 2,000 metres, thus avoiding unnecessary risks to my engine and my propeller.[6]

Oberleutnant Plüschow was able to report the incident shortly afterwards, and it would appear that he had encountered the Japanese force that had entered Tsimo, inside the German zone of influence, on 12 September. The Japanese had planned to be in Tsimo in force by not later than 15 September, but the advance guard from the one cavalry regiment in the force had entered the town of some 30,000 inhabitants a few days ahead of schedule. The Germans had no more than twelve men stationed there who were forced to withdraw, despite the fact that the Japanese had not arrived in great numbers. There were no casualties and the remainder of the cavalry regiment, which had pushed on in front of the Yamada Detachment, reached Tsimo on 14 September, at which time the main force was still struggling through the difficult conditions created by the storm. These delays were not as bad as they might have been, had the Japanese been less persistent in their approach. The infantry of the Yamada Detachment slowly moved forward but greater difficulty was experienced by the artillery which struggled to move siege guns along the flooded, muddy and rutted roads, at anything like the pace required to keep in contact with the main body. The idea of attacking Tsingtao from the north had not paid off as well as had been hoped and Lieutenant-General Kamio, in overall command of the operation, decided there was sufficient scope for him to consider opening another flank, and thereby enable him to speed up operations and invest Tsingtao at the earliest possible date. He revisited his original plans and decided to support the Lungkow landings by launching a new assault from a landing in Laoshan Bay. A landing here, to the north-east of Tsingtao and within the German zone of influence, had originally been rejected because of worries over the disposition of the enemy forces in the area and the possibility of mines in the bay. Kamio needed to seize the initiative and decided to prepare Laoshan Bay by minesweeping, detaching the rearguard from the Lungkow force to act as support for the new landings which he ordered to be made as soon as possible. Although Kamio was still short of the intelligence he had thought necessary during the early stages of planning, he was under pressure to invest Tsingtao as soon as possible, and this outweighed any other considerations.

The landings at Laoshan Bay commenced on 18 September with a preliminary naval bombardment of the area, covering the areas thought to be most defensible, followed by the landing of the Horiuchi Detachment (*Horiuchi Shitai*). Surprisingly, the Japanese met no resistance as they moved away from the beachhead, as the Germans had decided not to defend the area and the Japanese warships had bombarded no more than rocks and sand. Although the reason for the absence of any defenders or

Mules on lighter at Wei-Hai-Wei 21 September 1914. [Royal Welsh Museum, Brecon, BRCRM A1959.103]

defensive positions is not immediately obvious, it is likely that the Germans considered it imperative to conserve their force for the ultimate defence of Tsingtao. With limited resources, their commanders always had difficult choices to make and the decision not to oppose the landings was simply one of these. Not only were there too few troops available to Meyer-Waldeck, there were also a lack of suitable artillery pieces, especially field guns, with which to prepare defensive positions. It is possible that the German governor considered it pointless to offer a token defence of the beach at Laoshan Bay, when all that could be achieved was a reduction of his already limited resources.

To support this second landing, the main Japanese force from Lungkow had succeeded in cutting the railway link between Tsimo and Tsingtao on 17 September and effectively further isolated the defenders of Tsingtao. The following day, a patrol of Yamada's cavalry had a skirmish with a German patrol to the south of Luiting, during the course of which the smaller German patrol was forced to withdraw but kept up a busy fire as it did so. The officer-in-charge of the Japanese patrol, Captain Suida Sakuma, was hit in the chest by a rifle bullet and died almost immediately. His counterpart in the German patrol, Baron von Riedesel,[7] was severely wounded in both legs and ordered his men to continue to withdraw while he covered them as best he could. It was later discovered that he bled to death. These were the first casualties recorded in the land fighting around Tsingtao. The main body of Yamada's Detachment reached Tsimo on 19 September, four days behind the original schedule, but the bulk of the 18th Independent Division did not arrive in Tsimo for another three days. The effects of the storm had been to delay the siege of Tsingtao by about a week. When one considers the appalling conditions caused by the storm, this was a significant achievement and shows the total commitment of the Japanese to the campaign.

On 18 September, the same day that the Japanese had commenced their landing at Laoshan Bay, the 2nd Battalion the South Wales Borderers, in Teintsin, received their orders to move the following day.[8] The period of waiting had been difficult to bear, especially since news of the actions in France and Flanders was now reaching China. The Borderers felt that it was time for them to be taking part in the war and, like their comrades in Europe, none of them wanted to be left out and none of them wanted the war to be over before they had the chance to get involved.

> The British Force embarked at Tientsin on September 19th in three hired transports, *Kwang Ping, Shao Shing* and *Shuntien* and were escorted from Taku Bar by HMS *Triumph* … the torpedo boat destroyer HMS *Usk* and a Russian warship, *Askold*[9], with five funnels. The *Askold* early got the nickname of 'packet of Woodbines' by our troops … The naval escort met our convoy at 2.15 pm on September 20th at Wei-Hai-Wei. A number of mules, necessary to complete our transport requirements, had been purchased by Captain Knaggs, Indian Army, and were put on board. The steamship *Shanking*, chartered by the naval authorities as a hospital carrier for the conveyance of

wounded to Wei-Hai-Wei joined us and we sailed at 4 pm September 21st for Laoshan Bay.[10]

The three ships that had been chartered as troop transports for the journey to Laoshan Bay were colliers and since the move had been made very quickly when the orders arrived, there had been no time whatsoever to clean the ships and holds of coal dust. To lessen the effects of the dust, the decks of each ship were covered with straw matting and to compound the problems, there were no sanitary arrangements on board.[11] Although far from satisfactory, conditions on board the troopships were the best that could be arranged at short notice. Fortunately for everyone, it was to be a relatively short journey and, after waiting for a month to become involved, it was not considered to be much of a hardship. All arrangements for the move were inspected by Brigadier-General Barnardiston before the convoy was allowed to set sail. When he wrote his campaign despatch, he was to make special reference to the good work done by Captain A. E. House, RN[12] and Fleet-Surgeon Clarke who had worked quickly and methodically to provide facilities for any sick and wounded. Barnardiston and his staff were satisfied that everything was ready for the convoy to move off to war. Major Margesson, travelling on SS *Kwang Ping*, commented on their departure on 21 September:

> Cold morning. Orders to leave at 4.00 pm. Rumours of typhoon coming up from Hong Kong. This will be very unpleasant as all men sleeping on deck – over 200 – will have to go below with hatches battered down if it is really rough … We left line ahead, smooth water all the way. Light partially screened at night, i.e. saloon and cabin lights. *Triumph* led way and *Usk* whipped in – calm.[13]

Japanese troops bringing their artillery ashore at Laoshan Bay.

SS Shuntien *leaving Tientsin with 2nd Battalion South Wales Borderers on board for Tsingtao. Total accommodation: 20 officers, 336 men, 50 Chinese, 64 mules and 40 carts*
[Royal Welsh Museum, Brecon]

Thankfully for all concerned, the typhoon had been no more than a rumour and the sea remained calm throughout their short voyage and, on the morning of 22 September, the Borderers caught their first sight of Laoshan Bay, crowded with Japanese warships and transports. It was necessary for a Japanese destroyer to escort the Borderers' transport ships to their allotted positions to be ready for disembarkation to commence. At about 8.30 a.m., Captain Fitzmaurice of the *Triumph* signalled that stations had been well-kept during the night, a gesture from the Senior Service that the collier masters appreciated.

The Japanese had commenced their landings and were well advanced by the time the Borderers arrived on the scene and there were piers in place ready to disembark those troops, including the Borderers, arriving later to swell their ranks.

> One could not help being struck by the excellence of the Japanese arrangements at Lao Shan Bay. All kinds of military stores from 11" guns down to ration biscuits were being landed simultaneously, mules, horses and transport carts, also a light railway in sections. These piers were being built on piles, in fact the Bay was like a beehive, yet everything were plainly cut and dried. Large numbers of Chinese coolies, controlled by a few Japanese soldiers armed with sticks, were kept continually on the move in a long string, moving supplies from the beach up to large depots which had been formed a mile inland. Howitzers, field guns and weapons were pushed on towards the front as they arrived on the beach. At the same time the railway as it landed was put on trucks, shoved up to the railhead and laid on the roughly prepared track. The Japs. stated that they could lay about eight miles per day.[14]

It was 1.45 p.m. before the Borderers' transports were allowed to drop anchor in readiness for disembarkation. The sight of all the war materials being unloaded by the Japanese must have been very sobering to Brigadier-General Barnardiston – he had not been allowed to bring anything other than the infantry in the transports – his request for additional men and material having been rejected without discussion. If he had not already realized that he was to be totally dependent upon the Japanese for these things, the situation would have become painfully obvious to him as the transports awaited to unload on that late September afternoon – his force was to play a very minor role.

The lack of equipment and supplies, must to some extent, reflect the seriousness with which the British government viewed the entire endeavour. Once again, it was rather a case of 'out of sight, out of mind' and, whilst there were obvious pressing needs elsewhere for British troops, the paucity of supplies and the lack of preparation for Barnardiston's command was close to negligent and is something that did not go unnoticed by the officers of the South Wales Borderers. The effect of this weak approach to the campaign on the lasting credibility of the British in the Far East was, to say the least, negative. Even in the short term, it did little to impress the Japanese or convince them of the British commitment to the operation.

The agreement[15] by which the two nations were to act had placed Barnardiston under the Japanese commander, Lieutenant-General Kamio. However, for his line of communication, Barnardiston preferred to use the Admiralty directly, since any communication passing through the Japanese lines of communication would, of necessity, need to be translated. This arrangement was found to be a practical solution as the alternative would have placed an excessive burden on the few Japanese interpreters attached to his force. General Kamio was under orders from his government to act in

HMS Triumph *and HMS* Usk, *23 September 1914.*
[Royal Welsh Museum, Brecon, BRCRM 1984.64]

Commander and staff aboard SS Shuntien. *Brig-Gen N. W. Barnardiston,*
Capt C. D. Hamilton-Moore (Brigade Major), Maj Hiwatashi (Japanese
Liaison Officer) 19 September 1914.
[Royal Welsh Museum, Brecon, BRCRM 1984.64]

a spirit of co-operation with the British force and had been sent strict
guidelines on 11 September to ensure that the joint operations were
conducted in a suitable manner:

1. To show sympathy and friendship with the allied force by providing
   the British force with every convenience, as far as it does not impede
   our operations. This contributes to the smoother relations between
   two countries.

2. The British force is small in number. Therefore, to give full
   consideration to the difficulty of filling up its loss while it is
   important to offer opportunities to enhance the glory in action.

3. To be especially careful in contacting with and deploying the allied
   force in order to avoid mistakes caused by the difference of race or
   language, such as firing on each other.

4. Leaks of military intelligence tend to happen by unexpected routes.
   Therefore it is necessary to keep secrets even from the allied force.
   However, be careful not to offend by that.[16]

The Japanese had realized that there were likely to be problems when the
field operations began and took on an almost conciliatory role towards the
British, although in terms of numbers, they were by far the senior partner.
They accepted that the British were to be included and had, at least on the
face of it, extended their goodwill unreservedly. However, at a later date,
there was to be discussion at the highest levels as to just how useful the

British force actually was. It was likely that many of the British soldiers were thinking the same thing when they saw the great effort that their ally was expending on the operation. Some of the issues arising from this co-operation are examined in a later chapter.

The British transports had arrived a little sooner than the Japanese had wanted. Originally, the arrival of the Borderers had been planned for days two and three (19 and 20 September) after the Japanese had first set foot on Laoshan Bay, but the problems that had been experienced at Lungkow, and the thought that there might be German defenders, had suggested that an early British presence was not advisable and they had argued that they should be allowed to complete their landings before the allied force arrived. The arrival of the Borderers on day five of the landings (22 September) was essentially a compromise, but perhaps it was fortunate that there were no Germans present because there is little doubt that since neither force had operated together before, there would have been confusion. The language would also have been a significant issue with few Japanese speakers available at any rank in the British force and a very limited number of English speakers in the Japanese divisions.

The British soldiers were not only struck by the industry of the Japanese in Laoshan Bay but also by the countryside. Major Margesson was to note that the hills of the Laoshan Ridge, rising to over 3,000 feet were steep and rugged and came right down to the sea at Laoshan. The landing area near the village of Wang-ko Chuang in the north of Laoshan Bay had been described by Major Kihara of the Japanese army as a broad shelving beach with a suitable tidal range, with flat ground not too far inland that would allow for the storage of supplies. It was also important that there was suitable ground to allow a light railway to be constructed, although perhaps

Some of the Japanese motor transport.

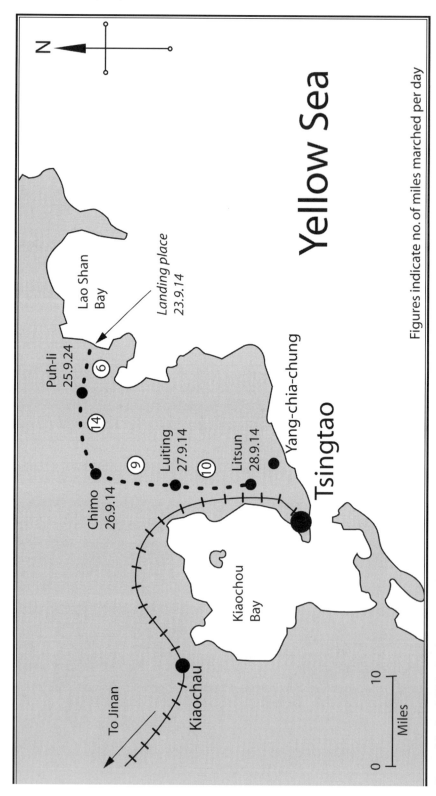

N

Lao Shan
Bay

Landing place
23.9.14

Puh-li
25.9.24

⑥

⑭

Chimo
26.9.14

⑨

Luiting
27.9.14

⑩

Litsun
28.9.14

Yang-chia-chung

Tsingtao

Kiaochou
Bay

To Jinan

Kiaochau

10

0   Miles

Yellow Sea

Figures indicate no. of miles marched per day

Route of the South Wales Borderers approach to Tsingtao.

Pile driving in preparation for the construction of a pier for the Japanese force to land supplies and equipment at Laoshan Bay, September 1914. [Royal Welsh Museum, Brecon, BRCRM 2005.70]

a major feature was the size of the bay which would allow for large numbers of ships bringing men and material to the area to be accommodated at any one time. This latter factor was significant since there were large quantities of both to be off-loaded before the end of the campaign.[17] However, the hills formed a barrier which tended to cut off the eastern end of the peninsula from Kiaochou Bay and Tsingtao. For the Germans to have a truly secure port at Tsingtao, it was these hills and their approaches that would have to be defended. It must have been very clear to British and Japanese officers alike why the Germans had chosen not to expend man power on such an exercise and trust to their analyses that any assault on Tsingtao would come from the sea rather than overland. It must have come as quite a blow to Meyer-Waldeck and his staff to discover that the Japanese were not only getting involved but were attacking Tsingtao overland. This was not the scenario that the Germans had planned for, and in that context at least they must be deemed guilty of a major oversight in their preparations for the defence of their colony.

Although the Japanese progress from Lungkow had been slowed by the storm, by the time the South Wales Borderers were preparing to land, there were reports that the Japanese were well inside the German concession as the Mecklenberg Hotel, in the hills to the north-east of Tsingtao, had fallen after a short fight. The Germans had reportedly withdrawn without losses but had set fire to the resort hotel as they departed, making much of the fact that they had caused casualties amongst the assaulting Japanese force. The Japanese however, were moving inexorably forward, making use of the

Landing at Laoshan Bay. Captain J Gray 36 Sikhs (DAA & QMG) in left foreground, 23 September 1914. [Royal Welsh Museum, Brecon, BRCRM 1984.64]

Disembarking the ponies at Laoshan Bay, 23 September 1914. [Royal Welsh Museum, Brecon, BRCRM 1984.64]

tracks and passes through the Laoshan Hills, and no amount of propaganda could disguise that fact. They were prepared to suffer a few casualties since they had men and supplies close at hand but the German defenders were a small and finite resource that they knew from the outset was inadequate to forestall any sizeable action against them.

The right flank of the Japanese army, moving south from Lungkow, began to fan out east and west of the intended route – thereby flagrantly ignoring any pretence of acknowledging Chinese neutrality – tightening its grip on the railway links to Kiaochou Bay and the colony. One of the main Japanese interests in this part of China was the rich coal deposits which they coveted to enable their industrial growth to continue, since Japan was, and still is, relatively fuel poor. The power that came with the increased energy source would allow Japan to gain respect amongst the western empires that they so admired. The coal mines of Shandong, operated by the Germans since their treaty with China, would be an ideal source if the Japanese could get control of them and the action against Tsingtao proved a ready excuse to achieve just that. The Germans had made some efforts to thwart the Japanese in this enterprise by offering the concession and the coal mines back to China, seeing this as a means to possibly protect their interests and prevent aggression against a neutral country. However, the Chinese did not want to be part of these machinations and whichever way the action was viewed, China was not in control of a large part of her own territory – and that was an unsatisfactory situation. There were also rumours that, in an effort to keep the Japanese away from the mines, some were being turned over to the control of American entrepreneurs in order to get the Stars and Stripes flying over them since 'the Japanese will be very careful not to pick a fight with the Americans.'[18] Whether or not this rumour had any truth in it does not matter since what is really important is that the defenders of Tsingtao believed it and it can have done little harm to the morale in the damp forts around the city. The truth of the situation was that before long the Japanese were in complete control of the Jinan–Tsingtao railway and entered Jinan in force, finally cutting Tsingtao off from the rest of the world.

About this time, there was also a report of the capture and execution of a Japanese spy. Perhaps this is not too remarkable during a time of war, but this particular spy, a Japanese staff officer, had been making every effort to poison the water supply to Tsingtao by adding the typhus bacillus to it in numerous parts of the colony.[19] In 1914, the poisoning of water supplies was strictly forbidden by the Hague Convention of 1907 which, rather like the modern Geneva Convention, set out the rules of civilised warfare. If it were attempted, it does not seem to have been very successful since the colony only surrendered when the ammunition supply dwindled and they had nothing with which to continue the fight – disease does not seem to have been a significant feature during the siege, although inevitably some of the soldiers were taken sick at that time. If there was any truth to this story, then it would be a very early example of biological warfare which would have been frowned upon by the European allies had they been aware of it. It is also a frightening precursor to the experiments perpetrated by the Japanese in Manchuria during the late 1930s.

The South Wales Borderers began to disembark on 23 September:

> Cool cloudy day. Disembarked at 8 am. Jap. Men of War boats took men off our ship and lighters took off mules and stores. Camping ground close to the beach. Water much contaminated low down on the hillside by Japs. They are very insanitary in their habits. Piers are being pile driven on which to land heavy guns. We landed on floating pier, made of rafts joined horizontally by wire cables, with barrels at sea end. General says that the Japs are now at Mecklenberg Hotel, close to Tsingtao. We move on day after tomorrow about 5 miles. SS *Kwang Ping* and *Shuntien* empty by noon.[20]

Major Margesson, commenting on the battalion's first association with its allies, raised an issue that was to recur throughout the next two months and that was the insanitary attitude of the Japanese. This was to cause some friction, and frequent comment, but there was nothing that could be done, except for the officers of the Borderers to ensure that their men did not follow their Japanese comrades-in-arms in their approach to the sanitary arrangements.

> The men worked hard and cheerfully at landing and stacking stores etc. and the entire disembarkation was completed by 6.00 am September 24th with the exception of the base stores not yet required and left on board the steamship *Kwang Ping* in anticipation of a change of base to Shatzukou Bay, 10 miles from Tsingtao.[21]

The crossed Japanese flag and the Royal Navy's White Ensign on the beach

It was a busy twenty-four hours for both the Borderers and the Japanese, an army was slowly being landed in readiness to link up with the Yamada Detachment and then move on towards Tsingtao. All this needed to be accomplished in a matter of days, so industry and urgency was considered necessary.

> Landed in Japanese lighters at 9.30 am (23rd September) at Japanese 10th Landing Base on pontoon pier and Jap. flag and Union Jack[22] crossed at head of pier in front of Jap. headquarters. Unloading stores all day. Continued unloading stores all day (on 24th September). Japs swimming horses ashore all very young and apparently unbroken. Jap. Engineers busy building pier for landing heavy guns. Railway Regiment commence laying light railway.[23]

The unloading of the mules was a very lengthy business as each individual animal was slung over the side of the transport ship and lowered into a lighter which then took them into the shallower water from where they were cajoled into the water with some difficulty by increasingly frustrated handlers.[24] This was time-consuming and the men worked hard. Even the carts presented unexpected problems for they had been loaded at a quay in Teintsin but now, in Laoshan Bay, with ships standing off the landing beach, each cart had to be, more or less, completely dismantled before being man-handled ashore and reassembled. The work did not go unnoticed and Brigadier-General Barnardiston made special reference to the way in which the Borderers threw themselves into their duties. The battalion was now well and truly at war with the Germans.

Notes

1. See Xu (2005), 89.
2. This comment and the Japanese reaction to the situation tends to suggest that perhaps, even at this stage, there was little accurate intelligence about the full capabilities of the guns in the forts.
3. German Diary, Royal Welsh Museum, Brecon.
4. The diarist is mistaken here since Tongku is much further north along the coast than the actual landing point in Lungkow.
5. German Diary, Royal Welsh Museum, Brecon.
6. Plüschow (2004), 39. This flight would appear to have been on 13 September.
7. *Riedesel Freiherr zu Eisenbach*, Gottfried; *Leutnant der Reserve in der 5. Kompanie des III. SB.*; kia 18.09.1914 Tsingtau.
8. See Appendix 10 for the Embarkation Orders and the disposition of the officers and men amongst the three transports.
9. *Askold* was a protected cruiser that had been commissioned in 1902 and was one of the fastest ships of the time with a design speed of 23.6 knots. She displaced 5,905 tons. The ship was captured by the British from the Bolsheviks in 1918 and was finally scrapped in 1922.
10. Lieutenant Beaumont-Walker, 2/SWB, Diary, Royal Welsh Museum, Brecon.
11. See Sgt. Bean's Diary. Royal Welsh Museum, Brecon.
12. The King's Harbour Master and Naval Executive Officer in Wei-Hai-Wei.
13. Margesson Diary, Royal Welsh Museum, Brecon.
14. Bradstock Diary, Royal Welsh Museum, Brecon.
15. See Appendix.

16. Japanese original (NDS) translated in Kondo (1991).
17. Whittaker (1994), 83.
18. German Diary, Royal Welsh Museum, Brecon.
19. German Diary, Royal Welsh Museum, Brecon.
20. Margesson Diary, Royal Welsh Museum, Brecon.
21. Beaumont-Walker account of operations, Royal Welsh Museum, Brecon.
22. Not actually the Union Jack, but a large White Ensign.
23. Bean Diary, Royal Welsh Museum, Brecon.
24. Going account of operations. Royal Welsh Museum, Brecon.

Chapter 7

Towards the Siege

The unloading of the stores at Laoshan Bay continued until 24 September when the last transport, SS *Shaoshing*, was emptied of the paraphernalia of war. There was time for some organization and a night in camp, before the 2nd South Wales Borderers were ordered to march towards the front line and to where the Japanese were moving towards the complete investment of Tsingtao. The Japanese intention, and it should be stressed here that the Borderers had clear instructions to fit in with their ally's plan, was to bring the troops together from the landings in a line across the small peninsula at the end of which Tsingtao was situated. This would, in effect, place them immediately in front of the German Redoubt Line and north of the Hai-Po River. From that point on, the campaign was to be an exercise in siege warfare as successive assault positions were prepared and occupied by the besieging force and thereby, increase the pressure being brought to bear upon the defenders. The Japanese had relatively recent experience of this approach to warfare, as during the Russo-Japanese War of 1904–05, they had employed such methods successfully, to capture the town of Port Arthur (Lu-shun) in Manchuria.[1] The task ahead of them in 1914 was much smaller, although perhaps the German force in Tsingtao was a more determined foe than the Russians had ever been, but it was still an assault on prepared positions and that meant that there was no room for complacency or lack of determination. Planning and organization were essential and every unit was required to perform its task fully and to a timetable which, although it allowed some room for flexibility, was reasonably tight to allow the siege to progress satisfactorily. Before the siege lines could be drawn, it was necessary to clear the country of the enemy in front of the main Tsingtao defences and, during the second half of September, this was done in a series of small, but nonetheless, sharp actions that forced the Germans back on their defensive lines north of Tsingtao. It was into this position, to bring continued pressure to bear on the withdrawing Germans, that the Borderers were being marched:

Marched out 10 am. General Barnardiston made a speech; said he was very pleased with good work done by Battn. Disembarking. Read out Kitchener's speech to soldiers of Expeditionary Force. Camped at 7.30 pm at Pu-li. Road fairly good, but blocked by Jap. Guns and transport. Great difficulty getting along past teams etc. On narrow road. They drive badly and always put on brake coming down hill. Orders to go to Tsimo. All kit cut down. We are short of transport, as usual. Have a bathe in the river with Going, Johnson, Jones and Bradstock.[2] Washed my socks. Warm sunny day. Japs expect to complete investment in about three days. Gipps and [Hasle] from HMS *Triumph* rode out to see us.[3]

Once again, there was some irritation amongst the British officers directed at the Japanese, as well as considerable frustration at their ally's march discipline which was slowing the progress of the South Wales Borderers. Similarly, there was during this first day's march, further comment about the sanitary arrangements made by the Japanese:

> Japanese sanitation was in every way inferior to ours. They left the ground in a filthy condition when they moved. They also admit that our rations are more readily prepared for eating than theirs and that the fact that we can get along on tinned meat and biscuits gives us many advantages.[4]

The Japanese approach to their field operations was very different to that of the British. The ordinary Japanese soldier may have been fairly fastidious about his personal hygiene – body odour seems to have been frowned upon and bathing was encouraged – but he cared much less about latrines and, according to some sources, happily left faeces anywhere.[5] This behaviour appalled the British, soldiers and officers alike, since faeces should never be left unburied. On the other hand, however, the British soldier was less worried about his own personal hygiene; he was happy to bathe but would put up with the dirt of campaign with much less discomfort than his Japanese equivalent. There was a certain amount of racial stereotyping here, since the British soldiers seem to have thought of the Japanese as 'coolie soldiers' whilst the Japanese looked upon the British as 'smelly barbarians'.[6] However, it was recognized that, for the benefit of good relations between the two countries and the overall success of the operations, there was a need to forget such differences and realize that, in the long run, they were of little significance. The two forces simply had to operate as closely together as possible, all under the command of Lieutenant-General Kamio.

The orders received by the Borderers from the Japanese General Staff for the move took the British around the Laoshan Hills in a generally westerly direction, that is, not directly towards Tsingtao. This was against the better judgement of the British commanding officer, and Barnardiston had met with General Kamio to argue his case for the force to be placed on the left of the main assault on Tsingtao, which would place it close to Laoshan Bay and ensure the shortest supply lines possible. This request for what was essentially an easier approach march may seem unfair on the Japanese who had landed at the same place, at more or less the same time. Since Barnardiston's force was less well-equipped with transport, it is assumed that he had made his request to compensate for the lack of carts and wagons. However, whilst

2/SWB transport mules. [Royal Welsh Museum, Brecon, BRCRM 1984.64]

the meeting between the two officers was entirely amicable (it could not have been otherwise since both soldiers were consummate diplomats and gentlemen), it has been reported that Kamio remained somewhat aloof, but respectful, and flatly refused Barnardiston's request. Kamio wanted the small British force close to the right flank of the advance, though no reason for this decision appears to have been offered. It is possible, however, that Kamio saw the British force as being so small that it could not be left without substantial Japanese support, and therefore could not be left to its own devices on the left flank of the advance, even if it were nearer to its own somewhat meagre supplies. Kamio's insistence saw the British force more or less totally assimilated into the Japanese effort. Barnardiston could do nothing but accept the general's decision with good grace and pass the order down to his command. When this was heard in the ranks of the Borderers, there was even a rumour, no doubt started by some 'old sweat' with a sense of humour, that Kamio had requested the Borderers as his personal bodyguard and it was a relief to many of the men that this proved to be false and that they were going to be involved in the proper soldiering of the campaign.

The first day of the march took the Borderers to Pu-li, a distance of eight miles from their camp at Laoshan Bay. Although under normal circumstances, it was no great distance, as Major Margesson was to point out it was a very trying march for a number of reasons. The preparation of the Borderers, or more likely the staff, for the campaign should be questioned since the troops were not equipped for the conditions in which they found themselves. The soldiers had arrived in Laoshan Bay in their summer kit of light cotton shirts and shorts with one blanket and a waterproof cape per man, hardly the kit that was required for a campaign in north-east China as autumn approached. Their winter clothes did not catch up with them for some time, though by the time they did, they were most welcome as the weather was to deteriorate rapidly. That night, 25 September, the battalion bivouacked in a field and began to feel the effects of the weather for the first time since their arrival:

> Very cold last night. Wakened at 3 am by convoy coming in from Laoshan Bay. Heavy dew. Reveille 4.45 am. Carts packed [full]. March at 6.30 am. Road as usual blocked by Jap howitzer and limbers. Good road but marching made very irksome by these constant unnecessary halts.[7]

Major John Going was also to point out that Chinese roads did little to help the battalion on their first march since at best they were poor, but the bad weather experienced in the area in early September had turned them to rivers of mud with boulders and, even then, they were blocked with Japanese guns and equipment.[8] The Borderers were forced to halt often and were even forced off the road to march along in the fields as Japanese guns and transports broke the line of march. The tendrils of the sweet potato in many of the fields into which they marched soon wound themselves around their legs and slowed down progress still further. The march of 26 September took all morning for the battalion to accomplish thirteen miles, at the end of which they were in Tsimo, a small provincial town:

> Bivouacked in a yam (sweet potato) field. Convoy not arrived, one biscuit per man issued. Heavy firing to be heard all day some considerable distance off.[9]

The issue of a single biscuit per man added to the woes of the Borderers on this march and clearly highlighted the problems of supplying an army in the field, for which there had been limited and hasty preparation and which was moving away from its source of supply. That the British Government was not fully committed to the Tsingtao campaign, is clear from its refusal to Barnardiston's request for additional troops and guns. Unfortunately, that lack of commitment was also reflected in the poor supply system, as inadequate rations and support was lacking for the force that was put in the field. Barnardiston's request to be closer to his supply, such as it was, would probably have helped the situation, but would not have solved the problem. As a result, the supply of the battalion was left, to a large extent, to the officers who took things into their own hands, initially, at their own expense:

> Arrived Tsimo 12 noon. 13 miles. Got hold of a butcher who said he would bring beef and pork. No arrangements made by the staff to give us a full ration; this has to be done by the Regt. Bought 240 eggs, 18 fowls, grapes for $10. Supplies should be no difficulty now Tsingtao is practically invested. The supply officer is useless and remains at Laoshan and has no advance depot. Japanese have given us some chickens and vegetables and promised pork and beef; so they mean now to help us with supplies.[10]

The firing that Sergeant Bean had referred to on 26 September was the result of the first movement of the Japanese forces against the outer defences of Tsingtao. The Germans had arranged a number of widely-spaced, lightly-defended defensive positions, with perhaps no more than fifty men, each supported by a machine gun. These positions between the Pai Sha Ho and Li-tsun Ho rivers, were never intended to form a strong line of defence and as such, their loss to a determined enemy assault was expected. They did, however, provide a means of giving to those Germans behind the Redoubt Line and essentially south of the Hai Po River, an early warning of the enemy's approach and, therefore, time to prepare a more determined defence of the town. The following Japanese account uses the Japanese names for the hills and, whilst there is some jingoism involved, it gives a reasonable impression of the kind of skirmishing that was going on as the South Wales Borderers moved up to take part in the effort to push the Germans back on the town – or as the Japanese called this steady forced withdrawal, 'marching backwards.'

> On the 26th September, the whole army commenced their attack against the first lines of defence, and the forts Nyoko, Kotofu[11] and Ryuten. Some of the forts near the mouth of the Hakusa[12] were easily captured by Japanese charges; but the forts near Kokken[13] resisted very strongly being held and fortified with mines and wire entanglements. Lieutenants Tamazaki and Ikeba were killed in scouting about this region.
> The invading army then smartly made a diversion, and when the left wing attacked Kokken and its sister fortresses heavily, a detachment went around Sikoman-zan,[14] the steepest hill in the region and came out just behind Kokken. No enemy could have sustained this sudden attack from the part which was defenceless. Thus even the strong forts were taken by a single charge of Japanese troops.[15]

This account suggests that this was a major feat of arms and whilst it was an important step in the campaign, it should be remembered that these 'forts' were not of the same order as those immediately around Tsingtao or even those of the Redoubt Line south of the Hai-po Ho river. The Japanese had successfully broken the German Outpost Line (it was no more than that) of lightly-defended vantage points. The Germans were far too short of troops and material to defend such positions for any length of time, and although their capture on 26 September would not have come as a particular surprise to Mayer-Waldeck and his staff, it was the first indication of the determination of the Japanese and the speed of their approach. It would have been of little consequence to the Germans as they withdrew to their second line of defence which was better prepared and which, being much closer to their city, they were more determined to defend. The capture of the outer defences was, however, of greater significance to the Japanese as they swept the countryside clean of Germans in their progress south, although in doing so, it would appear that they had suffered rather more casualties than the Germans.

It should be noted here that, for the Japanese to simply engage their enemy, was no small feat of arms. The hills separating the landing areas of Lungkow and Laoshan Bay from Tsingtao were steep and rugged and, at over 3,000 feet high, presented a considerable obstacle to the approach to the port. The Laoshan and Tung-Lui-Shui hills were dissected by a number of steep-sided valleys and passes. It was necessary for the Japanese – and later the small British force – to negotiate first the Ho Hung Pass and then the Laoshan, the Marsch and the Kletter Passes which were little more than single-file tracks over rough terrain and not well-suited to the movement of a large body of men and equipment. Any defence that the Germans made in these areas, no matter how small, was designed to cause as much discomfort and delay as possible and at little loss to themselves. It was also along these narrow mountainous tracks that the Japanese needed to bring their siege pieces, though by the time these arrived on site, the routes had been secured by the infantry. To achieve any sort of engagement demonstrates the Japanese determination and commitment to the operation against Tsingtao. It is, perhaps, a pity that the British government had not showed the same level of determination and commitment, but their attention was focused on events in France and Flanders.

Whilst the Japanese army was attacking the outer German defences, they were also mounting an attack on the German and Austrian ships in Kiaochou Bay. The *S90* and the *Jaguar* were in position off Tsang-kou and were themselves supported by the larger *Kaiserin Elizabeth*. It was clear to the Japanese that it would be necessary for them to discourage the naval bombardment that these ships could bring to bear on their troops advancing on the right flank, close to the coast. At this time, the Japanese were still largely without their own artillery support and thus, had little opportunity to return the fire. Therefore, it was decided that they should mount an aerial

The rain turned the roads in the region to mud that was almost impossible for the transport to negotiate.

attack. Three aeroplanes, one Nieuport and two Farmans, were used in a mission which it was hoped would cause some damage to the ships. However, this early example of a bombing mission, considered by some to be the first such attempt,[16] met with no success except for perhaps causing some panic amongst the crews as the ships were manoeuvred within the confines of the bay in an effort to avoid the machines and their bombs. However, one of the Farman aircraft that followed up on its bombing mission with a reconnaissance of the ground to the north of the town, confirmed that the Germans were, in fact, withdrawing from their outer defences and their redoubt line.

For the Borderers in Tsimo, these actions were some way off to the south, but the sound of the firing was clear, and when the order arrived for them to move to Luiting, on the Pai Sha Ho river, a distance of some nine miles, they realized that they would be moving towards the sound of the firing and the battle-front. As it marched south, the battalion was aware of shelling to its right and once again, the Japanese right flank came under fire from the German warships in Kiaochou Bay. The enemy had not been discouraged by the Japanese bombing attack.

> Left 7.30 am: good road, but very cut up close to Tsimo. March impeded as usual by Jap howitzers. Got to Lui-Ting at 11.30 am. Gen off to Jap headquarters at Li-tsin. Pte. Bent of my company interpreted in Japanese for the general. We camped the other side of the river Pai-sha-ho, a broad sandy river; good water. We heard guns firing all day and saw either a shell or mine burst. There were two vessels in the harbour; one a destroyer and one a cruiser, we could see their masts; they were apparently firing on the Japanese right column. Japanese had only about 16 casualties yesterday. Two aeroplanes out from Tsimo, one a biplane and one a monoplane. We ought to get busy tomorrow as the Japs have advanced $1^1/_2$ miles South of Li-tsin.[17]

The bombardment from the German ships patrolling the bay caused some casualties and proved a great nuisance to the advancing Japanese who were trying to force the pace and to keep up the momentum of their assault against the withdrawing German force. The British column reached Luiting by about midday on 27 September and Barnardiston went to confirm their arrival immediately to General Kamio and to discuss the next moves expected of his command. On this occasion, he was accompanied by Private Percy Temple Bent of D Company, the South Wales Borderers, as a Japanese interpreter. Bent had grown up in Japan where his father was a businessman and he spoke the language sufficiently well to be very useful to both the battalion and Barnardiston. At only nineteen-years-of-age, it must have been a very nerve-racking experience for him to have been summoned to act with his own GOC, in the presence of the overall commander of the field operations. However, Lieutenant-Colonel Casson was later to record Bent's usefulness during the campaign and recommended that he be commissioned. Bent was duly commissioned into the 1st King's Own Scottish

The harsh nature of the terrain is clearly evident in this photograph of Chinese labourers bringing up supplies for the Japanese. The railway is under construction on the right of the photograph.

Borderers and was killed in action on the first day of the Battle of the Somme in 1916, fighting alongside the 2nd Battalion the South Wales Borderers in the bloody action at Beaumont Hamel. Barnardiston received orders for his next move which was to be to Li-tsun, but everything was a little imprecise at this stage, as there had been no reconnaissance of the position which he was meant to occupy within twenty-four hours. He was assured that it would be pointed out to him by a Japanese staff officer on their arrival in Li-tsun.[18] At this stage of the advance, the Japanese insisted that the brigade transport and ammunition column were to be left behind under the control of the Japanese troops in Luiting, and Captain Dow (Indian Army) and Captain Colyer (Australian Intelligence Corps) were detailed to remain behind and take responsibility for it when the move began on 28 September. A further outcome of Barnardiston's meeting with General Kamio was the issuing of an order to the Borderers for their first action in China, which was to follow immediately upon their deployment in the area of Li-Tsun:

> GOC ordered us to make a night attack on the German line if they didn't retire. Their position was unreconnoitred and it was not known whether they actually were there or not. A very sketchy scheme; a good thing that the Germans retired. The scheme does not inspire one with great confidence in our staff.[19]

Fortunately Margesson's fears, and those of his fellow officers, were unfounded since the Germans simply melted away from their position under pressure from the advancing Japanese, and the Borderers were not called upon to make an unnecessary, ill-prepared night attack. The rapid Japanese advance between the Pai Sha Ho river and the Li-tsun Ho river had dissuaded the Germans from attempting a strong defence of the area immediately south of Li-tsun. They continued to withdraw, having clearly decided to consolidate their defence in the immediate vicinity of Tsingtao.

The move to Li-tsun had not been as uneventful as the previous day's march and it was soon clear before much of the ten miles had been completed that the Germans were actually shelling the village as the Japanese approached. The Borderers were ordered to move to the east of Li-tsun and occupy an area around Tung-li-tschuang, where they were soon aware of action to the south and south-east of them and saw German shrapnel bursting over the advancing Japanese infantry. The Japanese had begun their assault on the second line of defences, or more specifically, Prince Heinrich's Hill which, with a peak at over 1,200 feet, dominated much of the battlefield to the north and north-east and thus, the approaches to Tsingtao. The hill was of great importance to the Germans for artillery observation and therefore enabled the forts of the last line of defences to support the redoubts and earthworks of the outer defences. The importance of the hill had clearly been recognized by the Japanese who, realising that it must fall before any further progress could be made against Tsingtao, began their assault on it on the morning of 28 September. They used approximately 300 men, known as the *Kesshitai* (men resolved to die)[20] under the command of Captain Sato, and anticipated heavy casualties. The German defenders of the position numbered no more than fifty-four men who held out for four hours against a strong and determined attack by Sato's men. During the fighting, both Sato and his second-in-command were killed, along with twenty-two of the assaulting infantry and a further hundred were wounded.

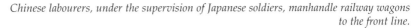

Chinese labourers, under the supervision of Japanese soldiers, manhandle railway wagons to the front line.

German gun, guarded by the Japanese after capture in the Coastal Redoubt, indicates that many of their field pieces were out of date.

Nevertheless, by midday Prince Heinrich's Hill was firmly in Japanese hands and all but twelve of the garrison had been killed or taken prisoner. The twelve surviving Germans, led by a sergeant, managed to fight their way back to Tsingtao where they could be usefully employed to fill the ranks immediate to the defence of the town.

At about 2 p.m., to the west of Prince Heinrich's Hill, the Japanese were engaged in another skirmish. During the advance of the left flank, they had occupied a ridge of low, prominent hills (not more than 200 feet high) which was known to them as the Shiboshan Ridge.[21] Located to the north of the Hai-po Ho river, this ridge was important as it offered the Japanese their first view of the Redoubt Line and its defensive ditch which stretched across the whole of the peninsula from this point. The hills, though partially wooded, were considered important enough for the Japanese advance guard to hold until the main body of the infantry could be brought forward. It was also clear that they would not only form a suitable position from which to protect the crossing of the small river in front of the Redoubt Line but would also serve as a position which could be used to protect the artillery when it eventually came forward. It was not long before the Germans mounted a counter-attack, using less than 100 infantrymen, which was readily beaten off by the Japanese who were in control of the stronger position. The Germans, unwilling to let the matter rest there, mounted a second stronger counter attack later in the afternoon, led by Colonel Kuhlo, who had been well-known to the Borderers when they were stationed in Tientsin. Although this was pressed home with considerable determination, the small force of Japanese on the ridge had been reinforced with a machine gun section and the attack was beaten off with numerous casualties – having achieved nothing. The Germans withdrew leaving their dead on the battlefield but appeared to have removed their wounded in wagons brought up for that purpose before the attack had commenced. The Japanese then consolidated the position and awaited the arrival of the main body of their force on the right flank.

Whilst all this was going on around the outer defences, the Japanese were also paying some attention to the forts of the inner defences and those facing seaward near the entry to Kiaochou Bay. Their navy shelled the forts of the inner defences and, although initially, this met with little success, the vulnerability of the carefully chosen German positions was becoming clear to everyone. This was particularly significant since at this stage, the Japanese had not completed the movement of their large siege pieces onto the battlefield ready for the bombardment of the town to begin in earnest. As the encircling attackers drew ever closer, it was becoming clearer to the defenders that their defence, no matter how determined, could not match the power the Japanese were ranging before them. However, morale appears to have remained good amongst the Germans, and at this stage, there was plenty of ammunition to carry on the fight and no shortage of food or water. Thus, whilst the situation inside Tsingtao was becoming critical, there was no-one in the town who felt there was any need to panic. They were still capable of putting up a fight and were determined to do just that for as long as they possibly could.

Above the battlefield, *Oberleutnant* Plüschow was flying his *Taube* on one of his, by now, routine observation missions to record the progress of the Japanese force. He was confronted by one of the Japanese Farman aircraft that tried to force him down and prevent his important work. After a similar event a day or two before, when he had almost lost control of his machine, Plüschow had taken off well-prepared on the morning of 28 September:

> Next time I was more careful. And on sighting one of my enemy colleagues I followed him and shot him down with my Parabellum pistol after firing thirty times.[22]

After watching the Japanese aircraft go down into Shiatsu Bay on the east of the peninsula, Plüschow made a safe landing at his airfield in Tsingtao. This was one of the very earliest aerial combats recorded, and it was not until news of it reached the Western Front that the French announced that they too had brought down an aircraft by rifle fire in aerial combat over France. There is, still some doubt about the authenticity of the French account, but there is no doubt that Plüschow's victory was the first such action in Asia.[23] It has been argued[24] that the Japanese were determined to prevent Plüschow's missions and to do this, Japanese pilots needed to try and force him down. As the siege developed, each time Plüschow took off, he was met by an equally determined adversary which had resulted in this early aerial combat, although none of the aeroplanes at that time were armed and relied totally on the side arms carried by the pilots. There can be no doubt that Plüschow's flights became shorter and shorter but, since the Japanese were getting closer and closer to the town, he did not need to fly so far or be in the air for as long to gain the information required. There is no question that the Japanese pilots had an effect on Plüschow's work, as he mentions it on a number of occasions in his own account of the events. However, he continued to fly missions each day until almost the end of the siege and his flying was never bettered by the Japanese. The limitations on Plüschow's flight would seem to have been caused by the limitations of his damaged propeller, rather than by any specific actions of the Japanese. Of course, the latter had more aircraft and more pilots and it is certain that no matter how tired Plüschow was becoming as a result of his missions, he was met each day by a fresh Japanese pilot and machine. Viewed in that context, the Japanese were slowly gaining air superiority, although by the time Plüschow had ceased his flying missions, it no longer really mattered.

The Borderers having continued their march towards Li-tsun, had marched passed General Kamio who remarked positively upon their general soldierly appearance and bearing. Apparently, the general thought that the summer-weight shorts were a very practical idea but wondered how the troops managed to keep their knees warm in winter! The march of 28 September eventually ended up in the village of Yang-chia Chin, to the south of the Li-tsun Ho, where the Borderers were bivouacked close to the Japanese 55th Regiment. The cruiser, *Kaiserin Elizabeth*, clearly visible from the camp, steamed up and down Kiaochou Bay, but fortunately, had stopped shelling the area by the time the Borderers arrived. It is worth noting however, according to Sergeant Bean, that just after passing through Li-tsun, the battalion came under artillery fire for the first time and were forced to deploy rapidly in artillery formation as several large shells fell in the area. The shells did no damage and caused no casualties but served as a reminder of the nearby actions that they had been aware of all day during their march.

Conditions in this village were far from ideal. There was no running water at their bivouac, even though it appears that the battalion was camped in a dried river bed.[25] Major Margesson went in search of water and encountered a Japanese sentry from the 55th Regiment who immediately mistook him for a German until Margesson was able to show him the rest of the bivouacked battalion just beyond the sentry's post. The problem of mistaken identity was to become something of an increasing issue since all the European troops and their uniforms were very similar, at least to the Japanese, and it led to a number of incidents before the campaign was ended. As daylight faded, the Germans continued to shell the advancing Japanese.

> After dark heavy shell fire from Tsingtao all night on the Jap Outpost Line; they did a certain amount of damage. No reply from Jap artillery. About 700 rounds fired, mostly from big guns. Spent a bitterly cold night; only a great

coat on; carts did not get up until 8 pm and then could not get closer than a mile.[26]

The continued shelling and the amount of ammunition used suggests that the Germans had begun to stiffen their resistance. With the Japanese quickly approaching the Redoubt Line, they could scarcely wait much longer. The 28 September had been a difficult day for all and, in spite of all the difficulties of the march, with poor equipment and inadequate supplies and rations, the Borderers were still in good spirits. Fortunately, the Japanese attitude was one of co-operation and the battalion was able to obtain some food from them to ease the ration shortage. Nevertheless, for much of the march from Laoshan Bay until some time into the siege works, the Borderers were on half rations. Although generally there was a spirit of co-operation, there was some concern on the British part about the Japanese approach to bivouacking, always camping near a village, then stripping it bare of anything useful and ignoring any unfortunate villagers who had the temerity to complain. They made shelters from whatever was available before moving on, dismantling their camp and starting again elsewhere. It can only be imagined that as successive units passed through the villages, they were stripped of every available material as the army looked for shelter. This, however, was not the British approach; they generally bivouacked away from the villages and the soldiers were strictly forbidden to cause damage or loot the villages through which they passed. The marching column even required permission, when rations were short, for the men to help themselves to the fruit in an orchard through which they passed during 28 September and, even though permission was given, it was on the understanding that no-one fell out. On the basis of the British eyewitness accounts, the Japanese had no such qualms and paid no heed to the discomfort their passing through caused to the Chinese villagers. This really begs the question as to how the population of the area coped as their meagre possessions were taken from them, as winter approached. It appears the Japanese believed that, as an invading army, they could do as they wanted, particularly since most of the villagers they were encountering at this stage of the campaign were in the German zone of influence and presumably, were looked upon as legitimate targets. According to contemporary accounts, it was not unusual to see the Japanese moving between the old and new camp-sites ferrying the chattels they had acquired at the old site to the new and it was equally common for Chinese civilians, the so-called 'coolies',[27] to do much of the carrying for them.[28] The fact that they had invaded a neutral country did not seem to play any part in the manner in which they treated the Chinese throughout the campaign. The British did not see things in quite the same light, although this would not always have been the case, if one considers the events of the two opium wars, and the Japanese behaviour was remarked upon by the observers of the events during the march to the front in September 1914. However, the Borderers do not seem to have taken undue advantage of the local Chinese population to improve their lot during their march, 'Too cold to sleep all night. Everyone up at dawn looking for breakfast but all we get is a small drop of hot tea without milk and sugar.'[29]

Thus began 29 September for the Borderers. The weather was changing rapidly and the battalion, lacking their winter kit, was not prepared. Whilst the men remained in good spirits, the officers were becoming concerned about the effects that the lack of rations and warm clothing were having on their condition and the impact that would have on the battalion's effectiveness as a fighting force.[30] It was not long after reveille that things were made even more unpleasant as the *Kaiserin Elizabeth* began to shell the general area with supporting fire from the forts. It became necessary for the Borderers to abandon camp and set up another within the shelter of a nearby hill. There was no reply to the enemy shellfire which caused a measure of complaint and irritation amongst both the Borderers and the Japanese, since they were all awaiting the arrival of the Japanese big guns before there could be any redress in the balance of the artillery. On the basis of the progress that had been made to that date, it looked as if it would be some time before the guns would arrive. The impact of the bad weather during the first two weeks of September was continuing to have an effect on the movement of the heavy artillery. So, for the time being, the allies had to suffer the intermittent German shelling with patience as their infantry attempted to push the enemy back as far as possible, exposed to the enemy's guns of all calibres.

By this time, the Borderers were more or less in the front line and it was necessary for them to dig themselves in for the first time since landing. It was not long before they found another problem. The light entrenching tools that the soldiers of the battalion carried as part of their normal kit were

Hill 89 near Yang-Chia-Chun – C Company's cookhouse dugout with bomb, made of a large coffee tin and dropped by Plüschow from his Taube, on its roof. Tsingtao. Thought to be the first incident of a bomb being dropped by a hostile aircraft, 10 October 1914.
[Royal Welsh Museum, Brecon, BRCRM A1959.103]

Hill 89 near Yang-Chia-Chun – C Company 2/SWB store dugout. Left to Right: Private P. Powley, Sergeant A. G. Larley, Company Sergeant Majoror C. H. Heal, Company Quarter Master Sergeant R. Smith. [Royal Welsh Museum, Brecon, BRCRM A1959.103]

totally unsuited to the heavy ground conditions, making progress very slow. There were very few picks and shovels to go round, to cope with the often rocky subsoil encountered within a foot or so of the surface. One of the officers remarked that it seemed 'criminal not to bring plenty of entrenching tools'.[31] Lieutenant-Colonel Casson had asked for more tools so that his men could provide themselves with cover, but there were none to be had at this stage of the campaign – it was not the first time the British soldier had entered the field under-equipped and it was most certainly not the last. As they prepared for the night of 29 September, the Borderers had noticed that the German kite balloon, under the command of *Oberleutnant* Plüschow, had been raised to observe the positions, now that the allies were closing in on Tsingtao. The Japanese guns opened fire but failed to shoot it down. It was probably the result of this observation balloon, and the fire it drew, that the second bivouac and that of the 55th Japanese Regiment, was shelled. The Borderers abandoned their position and moved once more from Yang-chia Chin to a yet more protected area on the reverse slope of a nearby hill which thwarted the German efforts to search them out. The regular and reasonably accurate shellfire, particularly against the Japanese hospital, from the German heavy guns in Tsingtao also encouraged General Kamio to move his headquarters out of Li-tsun to a safer area some distance away, which was less obvious to any airborne observers. At this stage of operations, there was a feeling amongst the Borderers that they were being specifically targeted by the Germans, but there is little evidence to support this belief. No doubt, they thought this was possible because two of their bivouacs had become untenable in a very short time.

For the next ten days, the Borderers maintained their position close to

Yang-chai Chin, anticipating orders for action but receiving none as the Japanese prepared themselves for the next phase of the siege. The Germans continued their intermittent harassing fire, but could do little to prevent the steady build-up of men and equipment in front of Tsingtao.

Notes

1. Connaughton (2003), 227 ff.
2. Major John Going, Captain Dudley Johnson, Major Ernest Jones and Captain John Bradstock.
3. Margesson Diary, 25 September 1914. Royal Welsh Museum.
4. Lieutenant Simson's report.
5. See, for instance, the discussion in Burdick (1976).
6. Whittaker (1994), 88.
7. Margesson Diary.
8. Major Going's account, Royal Welsh Museum.
9. Sergeant Bean's Diary, Royal Welsh Museum.
10. Margesson Diary – the supplies purchased would appear to be barely enough for one company – in this case D company since Margesson was its OC.
11. Kou-ta pu just to the south of the river Pai Sha Ho.
12. Pai Sha Ho river.
13. North of Li-tsun.
14. Possibly the hills know as Shih-men to the Chinese.
15. Yamada (1915), *USM*, 271.
16. See Whittaker (1994), 171.
17. Margesson Diary, Royal Welsh Museum; note Margesson was only aware of two ships in the bay at this time.
18. Brigade War Diary.
19. Margesson Diary, Royal Welsh Museum.
20. Compare this with the 'forlorn hope' of the days of the Napoleonic wars.
21. Shown on contemporary British maps of the area as Shuang Shan by which name it is still known to the Chinese.
22. Plüschow (2004), 49. Lieutenant Shigematsu became the only Japanese pilot reported as killed in action during the Great War.
23. Whittaker (1994), 103.
24. See for instance the discussion in Burdick (1976).
25. It is interesting to note the river bed was dry approximately two weeks after the biggest storm for years. This indicated the very sandy, permeable soil in the bed and probably that the local water table was very low and incapable of maintaining a bed load. This probably means that the soils were also very loose in the area.
26. Margesson Diary, Royal Welsh Museum.
27. It should be noted that the term 'coolie' was extensively used in the east, especially India and China, for any hired labourer – it was not a derogatory term.
28. See, for instance, Simson's report, Royal Welsh Museum.
29. Sergeant Bean's Diary, Royal Welsh Museum.
30. See, for instance, Margesson's diary and the account written after the campaign by Lieutenant Colonel Casson.
31. Margesson Diary.

Chapter 8

Divisional Reserve

On the last day of September, there was significant shelling of the Japanese positions throughout the day, which had come disturbingly close to the Borderers' positions. It was believed by those at the receiving end of the bombardment that the German observation balloon had called down the fire on a nearby Japanese battery which was getting ready for action. As a result, both the German Battery BXII on Bismarck Hill and the *Kaiserin Elizabeth* had done their best to destroy the Japanese battery. However, there is a suggestion in Plüschow's account that he did not keep the balloon manned, as he did not believe it was of much use for accurate observation of the approaching enemy.[1] Whether or not this was the case, the effects were still significant:

> The general says that the big German gun is a naval one and must be 15,000 yards away from Li-tsun village, which she has been accurately shelling; so much so that General Kamio has moved his Head Qrs elsewhere. The Japs will have an awkward time from the cruiser in the bay bringing up their big guns as the road is in full view of the harbour and under fire from the big naval gun. A large shell landed 50 yards in front of our convoy the other night on the road. The German fire is very accurate and is directed on the road at night.[2]

To some extent, the destruction of the Japanese positions was of less importance than the harassment that shelling of the approach roads caused which made all movement in that part of the Japanese front difficult. The shelling was good for German morale after weeks of waiting, as there was a very definite need for the men to have something to do, to feel that they were taking some action against the threat posed by the Japanese.

> In general orders it was announced that up to the 28th September the Japanese losses had been 1,784 killed and 8,000 wounded – our total losses are 110 killed and wounded. Four of the English Staff and three of the Japanese, are quartered in the Market Place at Lit'sun. So far no English or Russian troops have taken part in the fight. The shooting of the Japanese troops is very bad while that of our Marines is very good. During the last year the 3rd Battalion of the S. M. have regularly received decorations for shooting. The Chinese report that the Japanese are in a blue funk when they think they are

up against the Marines. Out Infantry appeared to be very done up when they fell back, their toes were sticking out of their boots, their helmets were shot through etc. Here we sit and are allowed to do nothing! No firing since 6 pm.[3]

It was not only the business of fighting that was good for morale as the diary entry above indicates. It had been reported that the Japanese losses were extremely high and there was no doubt that in attacking, the Japanese had lost far more men than the Germans, but those quoted in the latter's 'general orders' were probably greater than the actual figures. It is also quite typical for an army to believe that the capabilities of its men with a rifle or artillery, are second to none[4]; a means of boosting morale, for while the beleaguered force believed it was out shooting the enemy, it had no reason to despair, and even had some hope that perhaps there might be a favourable outcome to the events.

Gradually, the 2nd Battalion the South Wales Borderers, became aware of the plan of attack and that they were acting as the reserve for the Japanese 18th Independent Division. They were busily involved in making their positions suitable for their stay and, during the first ten days of October, expended much effort digging trenches and building shelters. They were well aware of both the need for the Japanese to bring up their heavy guns before the situation could be moved on to a full siege; and also the diffi-culties caused by the *Kaiserin Elizabeth*. At this stage, they were doing little more than marking time, while all the elements of the siege were assembled. Once again, Margesson remarked on the accuracy of the German shelling every day during the early weeks of October, and continued to attribute it to the work of the fire observer in the German kite balloon. On the other side of the front, to assist with the work of the observation balloon, Plüschow took his *Taube* into the skies every day and usually attracted fire from the Japanese infantrymen, although as the sole German pilot and by now, well-accustomed to his work, he seldom flew below 2,000 metres, and con-sequently, his aeroplane suffered very little damage. Plüschow provided a very useful service and earned the appreciation, respect and admiration of his superiors:

> Our aviator, *Oberleutnant* Zur-See Plüschow made an ascent yesterday in his monoplane – two Japanese biplanes chased him but could do nothing as a monoplane can fly much higher – we have a great respect for *Oberleutnant* Plüschow, he is always cheery and ready to joke and runs great risks, at the same time he is a small man.[5]

Although the Japanese were making great strides with the investment of Tsingtao, there was a significant set-back at the end of September. Their navy had been intent on clearing the mines laid in Kiaochou Bay, in order to allow them the opportunity to attack from the sea as well as from the land, and in so doing, rapidly compromise the defence of Tsingtao. During these minesweeping operations, the Japanese lost two of its ships on 30 September, when they struck the mines they were attempting to clear. Both ships sank and their crews were lost and all minesweeping operations were suspended for a time, forcing the army to act alone. To counter this downturn of fortunes, it has to be said that the land operations were proceeding well and to a large extent, the loss of the mine-sweepers was to have very little long-term effect on the outcome of the operations against Tsingtao.

Despite these losses, the Japanese remained irrepressible and, in an effort to strengthen allied relationships, the Borderers were honoured by a visit from the Japanese Emperor's aide-de-camp:

> Jap[anese] Emperor's ADC came, received by guard of 1 subaltern and 25 men. We were all (officers) drawn up. He made a speech that the Emperor was gratified at the co-operation of our two armies (our army being 1 Battn). The Emperor and Empress were sending a gift of saki for the officers and cigarettes – 5,000 – with Imperial crest for the men. The ADC staff consisted of a Japanese clad in a black frock coat, putties, elastic sided boots and a bowler. A quaint dress for campaigning in.[6]

This was a polite gesture in the midst of the preparations for the main siege and it was one that was not wasted on the officers and men for, although the ADC may have looked quaint, his rank demanded respect which was duly afforded to him and the issue of five cigarettes per man was most welcomed.[7]

During early October, the Borderers established themselves in positions on Hill 89, near the village of Yang-Chia-Chun, and got to grips with everything that was required of them, both as soldiers and, to a lesser

The visit of the ADC to Mikado on 2 October 1914. Left to Right: Majoror H. G. Pringle, Lieutenant-Colonel H. G. Casson (hidden), Major E. F. Cathrop, Captain C. D. Hamiton-Moore, Brigadier-General Barnardiston, Japanese ADC. [Royal Welsh Museum, Brecon, BRCRM A1959.103]

degree, as representatives of their country. They were fully occupied digging themselves into their portion on the Shiboshan Ridge and found the work very tough as they were still without the proper tools for the job – they had no more than twenty picks and shovels per company. There was much discussion regarding the construction of trenches and shelters. In the case of the former, the Japanese, with their relatively recent experience of the Russo-Japanese war, had a set method of preparation which the Borderers found difficult to adopt in some of the rocky areas of their position, without the help of more efficient tools, but they did what they could. As for the construction of shelters, there was even more discussion about the best way to proceed; Lieutenant Simson tended to believe that the Japanese approach was the best, an opinion that was reflected in his post-campaign report:

> The shelter is made in two ways. The best and quickest way is to lay the material for the roof on the ground and start digging the trench throwing earth for the parapet over the material. When sufficient depth has been reached, cut a groove in the face of the trench so that the centre upright can be fixed in to take the weight of the roof. Then dig the earth out under the roof. This prevents anything slipping and gives a broad surface on which to make the edges of the roof board rest. If sound timber is used as a bearer it should be squared at least where it rests on the top of the upright. A sandbag or stone should be placed under the upright to prevent sinking and the outer edge of the roofing materials on logs, planks and sandbags to prevent the earth crumbling and falling in. A shelter for five or six men could be rigged up with … a log for upright and a plank for bearer and a few sandbags. Later on cut timbers were issued by the engineers and made use of for making shelters.
>
> The other way, which wastes time, is to put in the shelter after the trench has been made. This means demolishing the parapet and throwing the earth well forward to make room for the roofing materials. Then, when they are laid, start digging out the earth underneath and remake the parapet over the top. This method seemed the more easy one for the men to understand and was always used by the British and Sikhs.[8]

The Japanese approach required an element of planning in order to predetermine the position of the shelters before the excavation of the trenches was commenced. In rocky ground, this caused some problems and the British, whilst perhaps requiring more labour, allowed for a measure of flexibility in the positioning of shelters as they could be sited at the most appropriate parts of a newly-completed trench. However, the relative advantage of one method of preparing a shelter over the other was rather academic at this time, as it was more a matter of keeping the battalion busy and ensuring that while they were in divisional reserve, they were not losing men by taking unnecessary risks, as a result of being exposed to shell-fire. The shelters they built served their purpose for the time they were in this part of the line and there were no casualtes.

On 4 October, Brigadier-General Barnardiston visited the Japanese headquarters at Chang-Tsun, to return the compliment paid by Colonel

Tanak, the Emperor's aide-de-camp, and in so doing, maintained the good relations between the two forces:

> At the same time he obtained an interview with General Kamio, the Japanese Commander, who informed the GOC that the British Force would be given a definite task in the investment and assault and that in the first instance we should be given a German Redoubt to capture. General Kamio then showed the GOC a copy of a letter he proposed to sent to the Governor of Tsingtao calling upon him to send away any non combatants before the bombardment began. This letter was signed by General Kamio and the Japanese Admiral. The GOC suggested that his name should be associated with the document as we were allies acting in conjunction. The Japanese seemed rather taken back at this proposal and said they would have to refer the matter to their Government. The GOC also wired the War Office for instructions.[9]

The suggestion made by Barnardiston would appear to have been well-meaning, and although he fully recognized that Britain was a very junior partner in terms of her military effort, he also recognized that his force was representing one of the most powerful nations of the day. It would not appear to have been an unreasonable suggestion to be acknowledged as an ally. Barnardiston's answer from the War Office was that he would only be a signatory to any declaration should it be the wish of General Kamio and clearly, the latter had no such wish in this instance. When the letter was sent to Meyer-Waldeck on 10 October, it did not carry Barnardiston's signature, in fact, as if to emphasise the situation, it has been suggested that Kamio signed the document as Commander-in-Chief of the Army Besieging Tsingtao, further emphasising his complete control of the situation.[10] This did nothing to improve the relationship between the two allies. Looked at from the Japanese point of view, perhaps Barnardiston's request was unreasonable since they were the country putting in the greatest effort and stood to lose the most men, and were therefore taking the biggest risk, both politically and economically. After all, what would become of them if the Germans were victorious in Europe? The Japanese were not prepared to be compromised, they had been asked for assistance by the British and had given it wholeheartedly – perhaps too wholeheartedly for some – by declaring war on Germany. The motives for this declaration may not have squared with British thinking on the Far East, but there could be no denying their energy and effort in responding to the request. Barnardiston was, therefore, not included in the gesture of humanity to the beleaguered enemy:

> The undersigned have the honour to convey to your Excellency the most gracious wishes of the Emperor of Japan, who desires to save non-combatants of the belligerent country as well as the subjects of neutral countries at Tsingtao who desire to escape from the loss that may arise from the attack on the fortified port. If your Excellency desires to accept the proposal of the Emperor of Japan you are requested to furnish us with a detailed communiqué about it.
> Lieutenant-General Kamio, Vice-Admiral Kato.[11]

Captain J. Bradstock, SWB.
[Royal Welsh Museum, Brecon,
BRCRM A1959.103]

Governor Meyer-Waldeck circulated the letter within the colony with a special note to the foreign nationals, that is non-German, who might wish to leave. On 12 October, a dozen residents of the town, missionaries and diplomats, assembled and were escorted towards the Japanese lines where it was reported that they were well treated before being allowed to travel to Shanghai or to Peking where they were, effectively, under the protection of the neutral government of China. It was to be the last such opportunity that was offered.

While this was going on, and perhaps the British command was feeling slighted by the apparent lack of respect from the Japanese for Barnardiston's request, there was another incident which did little to encourage the harmony of the operation. On 9 October, General Kamio received notification by telegram of an article in a Peking newspaper which was supposed to have arisen as a result of an interview with Major D. S. Robertson,[12] the British Military Attaché to Peking. In the course of the interview, it was stated that the British force at Tsingtao had been deliberately kept out of the fighting on 28 September and 'that from a political and military point of view it was a great mistake for us to be fighting alongside the Japanese and that the whole of Europe would look down on us for doing it.'[13] This was not the least bit helpful to the forces in the field and Barnardiston, as soon as he was made aware of it, wrote to Kamio disassociating himself from the views expressed by Robertson. Whether or not Robertson actually made the comments, in either an official or unofficial capacity, was irrelevant since they had been published in the press and it had been brought to the attention of General Kamio. There were already minor irritations between the two groups in the field, originating from the problems of bivouacs and the lack of discipline on the line of march. It had not helped, and Barnardiston was left to handle the situation that was becoming more of a diplomatic problem and less and less a military one. It would seem a strange comment for Robertson to have made since he had spent a long time in the Far East – he had even been decorated by the Japanese when he had been attached to the Japanese Army in Manchuria – and he would have been well aware of the situation that was likely to arise as a result of any unguarded comment. This fact alone tends to suggest that perhaps Robertson would not have been this careless in his remarks and that they were no more than a journalist's fancy and should never have been printed. Whether or not Kamio felt the least bit bothered by the insult from his ally is not known, but it can be imagined that he was not pleased and, perhaps, he privately viewed the British involvement differently afterwards. Nevertheless, he did issue operational orders on 8 October which were to be those that would take the Borderers into the next phase of the operations before Tsingtao.

Throughout this period of intensive Japanese preparations, the Germans had not been idle and the Borderers did not escape the attentions of *Oberleutnant* Plüschow who had manufactured some primitive bombs from old, large coffee tins packed with dynamite and bits of iron of all kinds[14] which he threw over the side of the *Taube* in the general direction of the enemy. One bounced off the cook-house tent and its contents scattered over the bivouac but failed to explode. It was left to Captain Johnson to tidy up the camp which he did by detonating the sticks of explosive using a rifle! It was pointed out by Lieutenant Walker that this was probably the first time British troops had suffered aerial bombardment anywhere in the world[15] and it was, without doubt, the first time British troops had been bombed in Asia. Fortunately, there were no casualties.

There was also time while they were in divisional reserve for the Borderers to reconnoitre the ground and get a feel for the general topography around the positions on the Shiboshan Ridge that they would be expected to take over in a few days' time when the guns were all in place and ready for the bombardment to begin and the full siege operations could start.

Ellis, Somerville, Sgt Bean and Sgt Pearce, LC Cooke and Pte. Terrill[16] reconnoitring a road from Yang-chia-chun towards Japanese outposts. Walked up to top of Hill 58, saw *Kaiserin Elizabeth* steaming slowly down the harbour, shelling the hills on which are Jap outposts. This she can do with perfect impunity, till the Jap big guns come up. Saw three ships and one destroyer (Jap) in Shan-tung-tao Bay N of Prince Henry's Hill. German big naval gun has not fired so much today as at first. The shell seems to wobble in the air. The Li-tsun non-stop express, we call it. A drop or two of rain last night but not enough to make one get up.

Bradstock, Petre and Habershon[17] were very nearly hit by 9' shells when reconnoitring the road on Jap right by Pau [erl] village. A shell burst 100 yards away right inside a trench Jap Inf were digging. A main road runs here and night and day is shelled by German howitzers. Two Jap 4.7' guns were firing on German gunboat. They claim 4 hits but this is doubtful and observers say Jap gunnery was poor. In afternoon Going and I walked to Shan-tung-tao Bay to hill overlooking it and saw HMS *Triumph*, 3 Jap cruisers and a hospital ship[18] and several destroyers. Heavy firing went on all night, principally at the 'nek' where Japs are constructing a gun emplacement, near Pau [erl] village. Pringle[19] thinks that 5,000 shells have been fired; this would average 100 shells a gun.[20] At 10 pm a fire broke out in Lau-chi-ham-ko village where the Jap 55 Regt is in reserve. Fortunately it was not observable by the Germans.[21]

Routine duties for the Borderers in their trench.

There was a need for the battalion to get to know the ground, it would be very different when they came to man a section of the Japanese Outpost Line. The first line that would be occupied was to be known as the Artillery Covering Position and there was a measure of protection for this line because of its position just below the crest of the Shiboshan Ridge. Once this position was manned, there was an immediate need for the Borderers to push forward towards the German redoubt line, or outer defence line, in siege style, to prepare another line, the First Attack Position, constructing communication trenches as they proceeded. There would be little cover for this work since the southern slopes of the Shiboshan Ridge were treeless[22] and in direct view of the enemy's forward positions in the redoubts some distance below. This would mean that most, if not all of the work would need to be carried out in the dark and therefore, everything that the Borderers' officers could do to get an idea of the overall topography of their allotted section of the line, and that immediately adjacent to them, would be of great help in the days to come.

To the relief of just about everybody in the battalion, 5 October saw the arrival of the transport convoy and with it, additional kit and, as Margesson put it, 'luxury again' as items like waterproof sheets, Burberrys and basins were delivered. On the same day, Lieutenant Simson reported that he had visited the Japanese field hospital to discover the rather depressing news that the Japanese had suffered 300 casualties in only eight days, all but thirteen the result of enemy shell-fire from the bay and the forts. This was considered at the time to have been a particularly heavy casualty list, as the Japanese had not been involved in any heavy fighting with the enemy in this area. Since the Japanese had done no more than consolidate their positions and move guns forward, they had not been returning fire to any great extent that was likely to cause the Germans any real problem. It was a patient build-up of their power but it was proving to be quite costly in terms of manpower.

During their period in the divisional reserve, the Borderers suffered their first casualty as a result of an unfortunate incident. Margesson had noted the problems that the Japanese were having in identifying the British soldiers when he had himself been mistaken for a German officer when the Battalion had joined the divisional reserve in late September. The following day, a Japanese sentry opened fire on a small party from D Company assuming that they too, were Germans, and wounded Lance Corporal James Thomas.

> A convoy with one days supplies was following up the force and when passing near Li-tsun came under German shellfire. The carts were galloped out of the way and Lance Coporal Thomas of the 2nd South Wales Borderers ran to the nearest cover. He was mistaken by the Japanese for a German as they thought the Germans were attacking the convoy. He was fired at by the Japanese and shot twice, once in the shoulder and once in the hand. He was not killed.[23]

At the time, it was not considered to be a very serious wound but Thomas was immediately evacuated to Wei-hai-wei where he could receive better treatment. He made good progress in hospital and it appears was well on the way to a full recovery, soon becoming a 'walking wounded'. However, on 2 November, he slipped and fell on his wounded shoulder, causing an aneurism from which he died that day, becoming the battalion's first fatality in the Great War. The incident prompted some action to try to resolve the

N° 3 communication trench – getting the mud off.
[Royal Welsh Museum, Brecon, BRCRM A1959.103]

2/SWB Officers' Mess Table near Yang-Chia-Chung. Rear: Lieut Johnson, Maj Margesson, Lieut Rawle, Lieut Tippetts, 2nd Lieut Behrens, Lieut & Quarter-Master Laman. Front: Lieut Morgan, Lieut Walker, Lieut Cahusac, Capt Dive (MO), Maj Going plus Lieut MacGregor on the end. The helmets carry the white recognition patches which were ordered to be worn by British forces on 28 September 1914.
[Royal Welsh Museum, Brecon, BRCRM A1959.103]

problem of identification. The initial response was that it was decided that every member of the British force was to 'wear a small square patch of white linen on the top of his helmet'. A more permanent solution proved to be equally simple when the British soldiers were issued with a garment described as a 'Japanese smock' which they were to wear over their normal uniform, and which had a hood, so that there could be no mistake by the Japanese sentries in the future.[24] There was a tendency for the Japanese sentries to be a little nervy and inclined to fire first and ask questions after, so that wearing the 'smock' delayed them long enough to allow the Borderers to be identified as allies. It was a simple solution and a sensible precaution but had come too late to help Lance Corporal Thomas.

On 8 October, the South Wales Borderers received orders that they were to move forward to occupy their allotted section of the central part of the line where they were to be known as the Central Force N[o.] 1. The next day, the German big guns opened fire in the morning and continued throughout most of the day:

> The Germans got news of our whereabouts and threw over a heap of shells forcing us to evacuate the position and go into a wood a few hundred yards forward. This wood got a "straffing", but we had left it for an outpost position overlooking Tsingtao Forts. This was a grand view but unpleasant as we were seen at times and came under pom-pom fire from the 6 redoubts.[25]

It may have been no more than chance that the Germans appeared to be searching out the Borderers but the men certainly felt that they were being specifically targeted. It is difficult to understand how the Germans could have known about the specific positions of the Borderers, although there were likely to have been Chinese spies of dubious quality and value, used by both sides. During 9 October, the Germans used a large quantity of ammunition trying to damage the Japanese outposts and reserve positions and, since the Borderers were in that area, it would have seemed as if they were being targeted specifically. However, the Germans were largely unsuccessful in their efforts causing no more than limited damage and, there were no casualties amongst the Borderers.

After this move, the battalion was no longer in the divisional reserve and for the remainder of the siege of Tsingtao, was an integral part of the central part of the line, where as the pace of events began to quicken, they were to become increasingly involved in the active siege operations.

Notes

1. See Plüschow (2003).
2. Margesson Diary.
3. German Dairy, Royal Welsh Museum. Russian land forces played no part in the siege of Tsingtao in spite of the expectations of the diarist.
4. This should be compared with accounts from the Western Front, of which there are many but see Dixon (2000), for instance.
5. German Diary Royal Welsh Museum.
6. Margesson Diary.
7. A number of these cigarettes survived and can still be seen in the Royal Welsh Museum at Brecon; they bear the Chrysanthemum crest of the Japanese Emperor.
8. Simson, Appendix 8.
9. Brigade War Diary (WO32/4996B).
10. Whittaker (1994), 119.
11. Hoyt (1975), 97.
12. Major D. S. Robertson certainly had plenty of experience in the Far East – apart from serving with the Japanese in the Russo-Japanese war, he had also been attached to the Chinese Army during the 1914 troubles along the Yangtse. He was awarded orders from Japan, China and later Russia for his service to each of these countries as well as the Military Cross.
13. Brigade War Diary (WO32/4996B).
14. Plüschow (2003).
15. See Lieutenant Beaumont-Walker's account, Royal Welsh Museum.
16. Captain A. H. J. Ellis, Lieutenant D. H. S. Somerville, 8206 Sergeant S. D. Bean, probably 10085 Lance Corporal Albert Cooke and 10172 Private Arthur Terrill.
17. Captain John Bradstock, Lieutenant R. L. Petre and Lieutenant C. B. Habershon.
18. The Brigade War Diary makes it clear that permission to move the British Hospital ship to the bay was not sought from the Japanese until 10 October.
19. Major H. G. Pringle RA – attached to Staff.
20. This would suggest fifty heavy guns – at the lower end of the estimates for the defences given by various authors.
21. Margesson Diary for 4 October, Royal Welsh Museum.
22. Today this ridge, known as Shuang Shan, is part of a poorer area of the city of Qingdao with its slopes remaining under-developed especially on the southern slopes that would have faced the German positions.
23. Brigade War Diary.
24. It took a few days for the smock to reach the troops in the front line – 1,000 of them were issued by Kamio on 12 October.
25. Walker account Royal Welsh Museum; note there were actually only five redoubts.

Chapter 9

Outpost Line

On 10 October, the South Wales Borderers, acting upon orders received two days earlier from General Kamio's headquarters, organized themselves to begin work on the Outpost Line, the line on Shiboshan Ridge that would place the battalion in a forward position and from which eventually, all the remaining operations would spring. The weather by this time had turned cold and any hopes of really warm days had receded as autumn settled in over north-east China. The weather that had caused so many problems for the battalion's movement to the front in early September, was again conspiring against it as it tried to survive, awaiting the arrival of the winter kit, and got on with the work in hand.

For the work on the Outpost Line, the battalion was divided so that two companies (A and B) were at work within the line, while one company was in reserve and one was with the battalion headquarters, some two miles behind the line. Whilst the British had received clear instructions from their own government on how to behave in the field they were, even at this relatively late stage of the operations, still unsure what the Japanese expected of them. There does not appear to have been an agreed line of communication between the Borderers and the Japanese 67th Regiment on their right and the 48th Regiment on their left, although it can only be guessed at how much this problem resulted from the lack of a simple communication system. Nevertheless, this gave rise to some uncertainty amongst the battalion officers, as not only was there a considerable communication difficulty, but also, there was no desire to upset the Japanese sensitivities by doing the wrong thing. The British officers were very conscious of their very junior position in the campaign and saw the need to perform as best they could alongside their allies whilst, at the same time, recognizing the cultural differences that could make this difficult to achieve. It was not a situation that most of them would have wished to have been in, but at the battalion level, they had to either grasp the difficulties and differences in communication and military culture or gradually become ineffective and unnecessary to the campaign as a whole. At this stage, the wishes of the Japanese were that the British should begin digging the Outpost Line, which they would then occupy in part. But the location of this line had to be agreed with the Japanese, and was an issue that could cause

B Company 2/SWB – men are wearing Japanese smocks. Centre: CSM W. J. Chamberlain, October 1914. [Royal Welsh Museum, Brecon, BRCRM A1959.103]

difficulties. It was not clear whether the Japanese were to give the instructions as to the location or if the battalion officers were to act on their own initiative. It was clear, however, that the Japanese expected the British to push out communication trenches from the Outpost Line to the so-called Artillery Covering Position, which would also need to be prepared, near the crest of the Shiboshan Ridge[1] and then prepare that position for occupation in the near future. There was, however, no clear indication from the Japanese where the Borderers were supposed to start their communication trenches or, indeed, where the Artillery Covering Position was to be located, and according to one of their officers, this information was not easy to obtain:

> They [the Japanese] seemed to be very chary of giving us any information and it usually entailed a tremendous amount of talking to settle even trifling points. Lieutenant Simson was invaluable, in fact it was difficult to say what would have happened if he had not been there. He was imperturbable. We found that we had to dig three communication trenches towards the front running out parallel over the skyline towards our front, each trench being about 50 yards long. As we had only 43 spades and 54 picks and a lot of this work consisted of cutting through solid rock, and had to be done in a very short time, we had rather a strenuous time. A good deal of the work was done with the small entrenching tool. Our own Staff we only saw once during a period of ten days. No orders were received from them, so that the O. C. Outposts had considerable responsibility as not only was he O. C. Outposts but he was also in charge of, and responsible for, the whole work of carrying out the rather extensive siege entrenching work to the front in preparation for the advance.[2]

2/SWB officers, Tsingtao, 1914. Rear: Lieut Morgan, Capt Bradstock, Capt Dive, Lieut Simson (Royal Scots), Capt Johnson, Capt Palmer, Maj Jones, Lieut Petre, Lieut-Col Casson, Capt Greenway, Maj Margesson, Capt Ellis, Lieut MacGregor; Front: Lieut Williams, Lieut (Quarter Master) Laman, Lieut Cahusac, Lieut Tippetts, Lieut Habershon, Lieut Walker. [Royal Welsh Museum, Brecon, BRCRM A1959.103]

Lieutenant Simson, who was acting as interpreter for the battalion, did his best to resolve the issues and in doing so, gained the respect of his fellow officers. However, his opinion of the events of the first night on outpost duty differ somewhat from those of the battalion officers themselves:

> There were two companies on outpost duty under the Senior Company Commander.[3] On the night of the 10th the British dispositions had been made without reference to the Japanese on the right or left, so on the 11th I went round to find the Japanese dispositions and arrangements …
>
> On the British right was a Japanese company and two machine guns and on the left one company. The Japanese line of resistance was on the front slope of the hill just over the crest line. Owing to the shape of SHIBOSHAN and the fact that from it the line to the right was swung back, two sets of arrangements in case of attack were made, one in case of attack from the right, and one from a frontal attack.

Simson goes on to describe the disposition of the British force in the area between Taitung-Chen[4] and the flanks of Shiboshan Ridge. He then relayed this information to the Japanese company commanders in the positions adjacent to the Borderers since they were awaiting the British decisions before they could co-ordinate their work. The Japanese had become somewhat concerned and confused by the British approach to the situation, but not more so than the British themselves.

> The British outpost commander, who had had no orders on the subject was worried with these questions concerning SHIBOSHAN and the main line of defence, the amount of resistance to be offered and what force would occupy

the main line of defence in case of attack, the battalion reserve being quite out of touch away in rear, and no telephone or signal communication existing.

During the course of the day he discussed the matter with other officers and, about 8 pm, told me to go with him and the other company commanders to see the Japanese Company Commanders and let them know that he had decided to go back to his original dispositions – i. e. with the picquet and sentry line behind the crest SHIBOSHAN in the water course; further I was told to ask these officers their opinion on this decision. This, of course, they evaded. In both these interviews it appeared to me that this indecision surprised the Japanese officers, but that they then and there decided to carry on as before without reference to the British. The only request they made was that, as we had decided to hold a line some 200 yards in rear we would strictly define the lines between which we were to fire, so as not to interfere with the action of the Japanese. The limitation of the direction of fire greatly modified the outpost commander's scheme for bringing cross fire to bear on the knolls on the crest of the ridge.

Such was the result of our first opportunity of acting in co-operation with the Japanese. Japanese officers, and even NCOs and men are in the habit of comparing and studying the methods of other troops, and there can be no doubt that they gave considerable attention to the dispositions of the British, who now for the first time appeared in the Outpost Line. These dispositions and this instance of our methods of co-operation must have raised some doubts in their minds.[5]

It would seem from these accounts by British officers that there was an almost complete lack of understanding between the two allies. The Japanese would appear to have failed to give precise orders to the Borderers' officers and the latter therefore, chose a position which caused the Japanese to have a less than favourable view of the British soldiers. Lieutenant Simson's report was submitted to the War Office some time after the event, without reference to the Borderers, and it can be seen that there is a criticism of the battalion for a lack of action and decision during its first joint action with the Japanese. Whilst this may be correct, Simson omitted to mention that he had failed in his job as interpreter, after all it was his responsibility to ensure that these sort of problems did not occur. The British had never acted alongside the Japanese before and it was inevitable that there would be difficulties arising out of the linguistic, not to mention cultural issues, as well as differences in military standards. Furthermore, the British force had accepted, as clearly instructed by its government, a subordinate role and may, therefore, have expected clear direction from the senior partner in the operations. On the basis of the British accounts of this stage of the operations it would seem that this was not forthcoming.

Lieutenant Simson was there to assist in the smooth transfer of ideas and orders and many of his fellow officers appear to have thought highly of him for his work; Lieutenant-Colonel Casson recommended him for a Distinguished Service Order[6] at the end of the operations but before the former's report was sent to the War Office. Eventually, Simson was awarded the Military Cross for his part in the Tsingtao operations. Whilst there should have been a feeling of mutual respect between the battalion and Simson, it would appear that, at least from Simson's standpoint, this was not the case. He took the opportunity of his report to the War Office to present the Borderers in the poorest possible light. It was one thing to have issues with a foreign ally but that difficulties should occur between officers of the same unit was unacceptable. Fortunately, whilst in the line, Simson kept his opinions to himself, but most certainly lost the respect of Lieutenant-Colonel Casson when the report was forwarded to him for comment via the War Office. Casson, understandably, defended the actions of his battalion and there can be little doubt that the battalion was ready and willing to take part in the operations as fully as their limited resources would allow. In that respect, it might be argued that Simson had let down the Borderers by not establishing more clearly the needs and expectations of the Japanese command. The British officers were clearly seeking the advice of the Japanese and their only means of communicating with them appeared to have failed them completely. Some efforts were made to address the communication issues which were becoming problematic for all concerned and a particular irritation to the senior commanders, not least Lieutenant-General Kamio, who saw the potential for the Borderers to cause problems for his carefully worked out siege plans. The Borderers needed to be more integrated into the Japanese scheme, but there was no command structure in place that could achieve this, without the existence of an appropriate communication system – a huge problem where there was such a language barrier. This issue was never addressed to the satisfaction of the senior officers present but there was a tolerable co-operation for most of the remainder of the campaign which relied more upon the individuals co-existing rather than allowing for the full integration of the non-Japanese units. To add to the issue of communications, a further element was about to be added to the British force. Just as the Borderers were beginning their move to the Outpost Line, a telegram was sent from Brigade Headquarters to Colonel Sullivan of the 36th Sikhs, stationed in Wei-hai-wei, that he should get his half battalion ready to leave for Laoshan Bay on 16 October and join the British force in the forward area on Shiboshan Ridge.

On the battalion's first day in the Outpost Line, a Japanese infantry officer, Lieutenant Matsumo, and about thirty men, were attached to it for the purpose of assisting communication with the adjacent Japanese units. These men had been specially selected and some had a slight understanding of English and as such, were able to assist with British patrols, in an attempt to avoid any further unfortunate incidents and mistakes and to calm the nervous Japanese sentries who had caused a few problems up to that time. They were also to act as orderlies carrying messages to adjacent commanders, with the minimum of fuss and delay. Lieutenant Matsumo was soon to show himself a very obliging officer who did all in his power to ensure that the Borderers were aware of the dispositions of the 48th and 67th Regiments, as well as providing general information to assist the battalion in under-

Above: Hill 89 - Field Hospital Mess. Capt A. E. B. Wood and Maj J. A. Hartigan, 10 October 1914. [Royal Welsh Museum, Brecon, BRCRM A1959.103]

Right: Capt G. H. Dive, RAMC, Medical Officer to 2/SWB. [Royal Welsh Museum, Brecon, BRCRM A1959.103]

Below: Capt Dive RAMC on top of the 2/SWB regimental aid post – Japanese medical aid post on the left. [Royal Welsh Museum, Brecon, BRCRM A1959.103]

standing the Japanese methods of soldiering. At the same time, Lieutenant Iba of the 18th Divisional Engineer Battalion, with a platoon of engineers (sappers), was ordered to assist the British force in the preparation of their positions for as long as they were required. To the Borderers, still trying to operate without adequate tools, the arrival of the engineers was most welcome. These Japanese troops, however, remained under the command of the 18th Divisional Engineer Commander and never received orders through the British command structure. This was not an ideal situation as it meant that every request for work by the Borderers had to be transferred to the Japanese Battalion Headquarters and then relayed back to the men in the British sector. Unfortunately, there seemed to have been no inclination on the part of the Japanese to simplify the command structure. Nevertheless, Lieutenant Iba and his engineers proved themselves to be very useful and helped with all kinds of trench work during the period they remained with the Borderers. The men of both groups of Japanese soldiers had a limited command of English but, surprisingly, their officers had no knowledge of the language at all. This meant that responsibility for much of the day-to-day management of the attached troops fell to Lieutenant Simson who, consequently, spent an increasing amount of time in the forward areas which to some extent, prevented him from carrying out a more specific liaison role between the commanders of the operation which should have been his primary duty. It is clear from his final report that before the campaign had finished, he had developed a great respect for the hard-working Japanese engineers. The South Wales Borderers were also very grateful for their help since there had been no resolution to their own problem of the lack of equipment which caused Margesson to comment that 'the lack of picks and shovels is criminal'.[7] However, whilst the assistance of the Japanese was appreciated, it was not always a smooth relationship since the different approaches to soldiering by both groups led to some friction and frustration – particularly over the hours of working – although overall, it must be said that the Japanese engineers in particular had made a useful temporary addition to the ranks of the British force. Another useful outcome of working closely with the Japanese was that the latter were able to identify the British soldiers more readily and not mistake them for Germans, an error which had already happened on a number of occasions.

The Borderers having arrived at the front, now had more pressing issues to concern them than the problems of communication with their allies while dodging the shells of their enemy.

> During the night of the 11/12th the bivouacs were heavily shelled by the Germans. Two men of the South Wales Borderers were wounded by shrapnel bullets. One Transport cart was struck by a shell from one of the German big guns and blown to pieces and 2 ponies were slightly wounded.[8]

The siege preparations were proceeding and the Japanese needed to ensure that everything was in place by the time their siege guns arrived so

Japanese communication trench opposite Nᵒ 2 Redoubt. This photograph could easily be mistaken for the trenches before Sebastopol during the Crimean War.
[Royal Welsh Museum, Brecon, BRCRM A1959.103]

that there was no delay in moving on to the final stages. However, the logistics of the operation and its planning meant that, at least in the early stages of the outposts' duties, the Borderers were less than fully effective. A and B companies, who commenced the battalion forward works, were forced to dig portions of the line and communication trenches with little more than a light entrenching tool which did little to enhance the performance of the battalion as a whole in the eyes of their allies. The first nine days during which the battalion was employed in this work were, perhaps, the most frustrating period of the entire campaign and were not helped by the fact that it was difficult to maintain communications with the Japanese to the left and right of the outposts. The work was carried out mostly at night, sometimes slowly, and it was necessary to borrow tools from the Japanese and rely on their goodwill for even the basics of trench warfare. There can be no doubt that as a force, the British were neither fully prepared nor supplied for the operation, although this should not reflect upon their ability and readiness for action and they were certainly capable of anything that the warfare of the early twentieth century had to offer. During the early weeks of October, more than one battalion officer complained of the inadequacy of equipment, from the light summer-weight uniforms to the lack of sandbags. It was clear to the battalion officers that there had been inadequate staff work carried out to allow the battalion to be put in the field to perform its tasks to the best of its capabilities.[9] There was, however, a stoicism amongst the officers at this time in accepting their lot, sometimes a little grudgingly.

They recognized the fact that by October, the War Office in London had rather more to worry about in France and Flanders (the First Battle of Ypres started on 14 October 1914), and could not concern itself with a relatively small-scale action thousands of miles away. The acceptance of that fact did not make the day-to-day problems in front of Tsingtao any easier to handle and it took considerable determination from both officers and men to achieve anything. Even though the British force was short of nearly everything, it did not stop the War Office, requesting on 12 October that Captain Greenfield, Army Veterinary Corps, and his staff be released to be sent home, presumably in preparation for service in France.[10] The request was declined with a comment that it would be reviewed in ten days when it was considered that the situation in front of Tsingtao would be clearer.

Whilst the land-based preparations continued, the Japanese army had fired very little at the town, wishing to get all their siege pieces in position before beginning the bombardment. The Japanese Navy on the other hand, now over the shock of losing two mine-sweepers, again began to take an active interest. On 14 October, Admiral Kato, under pressure from General Kamio to take some action, used his ships to attack the German forts that faced the sea, particularly Hweichuen Fort (Fort A of the British Intelligence Report). It was reported that the Japanese purposely listed their ships, including their flag ship *Suwo*, to increase the range of their guns as they steamed in line past the forts, shelling as they went.[11] It appears that while the ships were firing at close to the limit of their range, their gunnery was good and the fort was quickly surrounded by exploding shells which set the ground trembling and filled the air with smoke and debris.

> Sometimes the yard long shell splinters flew whirring and hissing weirdly over our heads, without our paying any attention to them, as we were so engrossed by what we saw, which was so stupendous that no words could fittingly describe it.
>
> We thought with deep sorrow of the brave garrison and of their sure destruction, but suddenly in the midst of the heaviest fire, our old 24 centimetre gun fired one shot and our field glasses were immediately fixed on the enemy ships. Suddenly a joyful, triumphant 'Hurrah' burst from our lips for one of our explosive shells had hit the English warship *Triumph* plumb in the middle of her deck. *Triumph* veered at once and ran away for all she was worth, and when our second shell sped after her a little later it was only able to hit the water about 50 metres from her stern.[12]

The *Triumph* had indeed been damaged, and was put out of action until repairs had been effected. With the assistance of the Japanese repair ship, she was made totally seaworthy within twenty-four hours[13] but was not in action again for two weeks. It appears that the 240 mm shell from the fort had smashed through the main mast and had almost destroyed it. There was also considerable damage to the main control-top and to the ship's secondary control system. It was here that one sailor was killed and an officer and

HOLE IN MAST

The foredeck, bridge and main armament of HMS Triumph. Right, an appropriately captioned photograph of the damage to HMS Triumph.

one rating were wounded. The quarterdeck also suffered some splinter damage, but fortunately, there were no casualties there. It was fortunate that such a large shell had caused so little damage and Captain Fitzmaurice had no alternative but to take *Triumph* out of the action temporarily. The warship's 10-inch guns should have been able to out-range the old guns in the forts arranged around the entrance to Kiaochou Bay, but she had clearly strayed within the range of at least one of them. This may have been done to increase the effectiveness of her own fire, although an alternative explanation has been offered. The entrance to the bay had been mined early on in the operation and the outer perimeter of this minefield had been marked with buoys so that a ship rushing onto the forts for a sharp attack could pull out of the engagement before the minefield was reached. According to one source, a second line of buoys had been set 15,000 yards from the coast which was considered to be the maximum range for the shore batteries. It has been suggested[14] that this second line of buoys had been moved closer to the shore, under cover of darkness, by some daring German sailors and this had brought HMS *Triumph* too close to the shore batteries. If this was indeed the case, it only worked on this one occasion since the Japanese warships were not bothered by the forts again. It is difficult to know if this was indeed the truth of the situation; if the Japanese ships were listed slightly for firing, it suggests that they were at their extreme range and should have been in the clear. On the other hand, if the buoys had been moved to draw the ships into the shore, why did the guns in the fort only manage to fire two shells – were they waiting especially for the *Triumph* to steam by? This would seem unlikely, and a far more likely explanation is given by Plüschow who states that the battery commander, *Oberleutnant* Hassagen, had ordered his gunners to raise the gun by no more that a fraction of a degree, which gave it an extra range of between 200 and 800 metres. It appears that the gun crews had simply waited for one of the ships to stray into this zone of added range – it just happened to be the *Triumph*. The success of the bombardment, however, left much to be desired as far as the allies were concerned:

> Still under the impression of a terrible spectacle of the bombardment we were most surprised on our arrival to see the whole garrison merrily tearing around collecting splinters and admiring the huge craters which the enemy shells had dug in the ground. What luck! Not a man wounded, not a gun injured, not a hit on the bomb proof rooms! The whole result of the heavy bombardment amounted to a broken biscuit tin and a soldier's shirt which was hanging out to dry and was torn to shreds! It is strange to think that 51 and $31^1/_2$ centimetre guns were used to such a purpose![15]

One of the heavy shells had, however, pierced the steel turret of one of the guns, but had failed to explode – a lucky escape for the gun crew.

By complete contrast to events off the coast, the allied land-based forces enjoyed a relatively quiet day as they settled into their outpost positions. However, on the morning of 15 October, it started to rain. It was not ordinary rain, but the tail end of one of those huge, peculiarly south-east Asian storms, known as a typhoon. The rain was torrential and lasted for over thirty-six hours.

> Heavy rain all day. Nearly everyone was washed out of their shelters and bivouacs. Large tracks (sic) of the country now under water and rivers and streams in flood. One man of the South Wales Borderers was buried in a shelter which fell in through the earth collapsing but he only sustained a twisted knee.[16]

The area was flooded, everywhere was sodden, all the streams rose rapidly and there was precious little shelter so the men and their kit were wet through. For the Japanese, it was almost a replay of the conditions of early September and it was greeted with some dismay as the flood could cause further delays to the siege preparations – but Kamio had to accept that there was nothing that could be done and all work was effectively suspended. There was nothing that anyone could do but endure the hours of torrential rain. No-one got any sleep as they battled against the rain and flood – there was nowhere dry to sleep anyway. Headquarters, brigade and battalion, were flooded out as the torrential rain rushed off the slopes.

Japanese troops moving through an area devastated by the adverse weather of September and October.

In the Outpost Line, a stream which runs through it rose rapidly and washed away a large bank in which was a dugout containing twelve men of the picquet, one of the men was carried away by the stream for some distance before he recovered himself, and all the arms and equipment of the remainder were buried in the debris of the fallen bank; most of the equipment and all of the rifles but one were recovered.[17]

The ground was turned into a morass; a Japanese supply and ammunition depot was washed away into the bay by the torrent that had been the Litsun stream. The German and Austrian sailors in their ships in Kiaochou Bay thought that the Japanese had floated mines out to them and opened fire on every target, before it was realized that amongst the targets were such harmless, and potentially useful items as casks of beer![18] Soon, throughout the entire area, it was nearly impossible for anyone to move in the mud and water. Mules could no longer stand and many died of exhaustion in their effort to haul equipment. As a consequence, both British and Japanese soldiers were organized into carrying parties, in an attempt to keep both equipment and rations moving to those areas most in need. At Laoshan Bay, the landing area was badly affected by the high seas which accompanied the storm and a number of the landing jetties were washed away and twenty-four Japanese soldiers were drowned.[19] Lieutenant Somerville of the Borderers reserve, lost all his equipment and clothes when his shelter was swept away by the rising flood waters. His sword and empty valise were recovered the following day, and he was left with only the kit he was wearing when the storm broke. This was so severe and its effects so extreme that it brought the work on the preparation for the siege to a standstill for two days – nothing could be achieved while the ground was sodden and the streams ran high. However, it did not prevent three of the Borderers being wounded by shellfire as the German forts continued with their harassing fire to add to the discomfort of the storm. The Germans, holding the high ground, were affected far less, although Plüschow, whose aircraft was kept dry in the hangar, found flying impossible for a number of days, as his airfield was covered with pools of standing water which remained even after the storm had abated.

Perhaps the saddest victims of the storm were the Chinese villagers whose homes were washed away. It is thought that the flooding caused many deaths amongst the civilian population but no-one thought to count how many.[20] The belligerents were all too caught up in their own issues to worry about non-combatant villagers on whose land the battle was being fought.

In spite of the storm, the Germans continued to make every effort to improve their situation by strengthening their defences as best they could. They were, like everyone else, unable to carry out any earthworks, but took the opportunity to ensure that stores were in order and in the right place for the battle they knew was now not far away. Unfortunately, this work did lead to one serious accident on the night of 16 October when a sailor in Redoubt V (the Coastal Redoubt of the Japanese and Redoubt N[o.] 1 of the British)[21] accidentally set off a flare and the fire it caused ran out of control, reportedly leading to the loss of 200,000 rounds of small-arms ammunition and hundreds of grenades.[22] This incident must have made a considerable noise and presented a remarkable sight, but it does not appear to have aroused much interest in the Japanese lines and was not reported by the British, either at battalion or brigade level.

At this stage of the operations, the allies must have begun to feel that things were not going their way. They had effectively lost the *Triumph*, at least in the short-term, from the sea-borne force and the land force was bogged down by the effects of the unusual weather – a storm of this type would not have occurred every year and Major Margesson noted in his diary that the area had been unaffected in 1913.

There was one further incident that must have lowered the spirits even further, particularly for the Japanese. As the allied grip on Tsingtao was tightening, the Germans decided that the old torpedo-boat destroyer, the

The crew of the German torpedo-boat destroyer, S90.

S90, would make a dash for freedom by running the allied blockade of the town as soon as possible. It was confirmed by *Kapitänleutnant* Brunner that an attempt would be made on 17 October, a day considered to be suitable since there would be no moon after 10 p.m., and it was hoped that under the cover of darkness, he would be able to slip through the blockade. Brunner had already taken his vessel out through the minefield to satisfy himself that he could make a run at the blockade. The garrison of Tsingtao was aware of his brave attempt and waited in anticipation as the moon set. It was 11 p.m. before the low profile of the *S90* was glimpsed heading out across Kiaochou Bay and away from Tsingtao for the last time. As it disappeared, those watching were anticipating the piercing shafts of light from the searchlights on the enemy ships, as the Japanese awakened to the threat. It did not happen, and as time ticked slowly by, the defenders of the town became hopeful that the *S90* would succeed. At 1 a.m., the Germans saw a sudden pillar of fire and the noise of a distant explosion out to sea, far to the south of the town. Brunner had launched an attack on a Japanese cruiser with three torpedoes from a range of not more than 500 yards and had destroyed it. It appears that the cruiser had been carrying 120 mines at the time she was struck by the torpedoes, so that within a few moments, the *Takachiho* had been blown apart and disappeared beneath the waves. At 1.30 a.m., the following message reached Tsingtao:

> Have attacked enemy cruiser with three torpedoes, registered three hits. Cruiser blew up at once. Am hunted by torpedo-boat destroyers, return to Tsingtao cut off, trying escape south, and if necessary, shall explode boat. Brunner.[23]

It had been a successful mission for Brunner, he had run the blockade and destroyed a Japanese cruiser, and not just any Japanese cruiser, but the *Takachiho* which had a special place in Japanese naval tradition. She had been built in Britain in 1885 and was, as such, an old ship, somewhat out of keeping with the modern navies of the day and was, by 1914, classified as a second-class cruiser. Nevertheless, she had been the flagship of the Japanese fleet during the Russo-Japanese war and to some extent, the Japanese attached much the same sort of significance to her as the British might have done to Nelson's flagship, *Victory*. The loss of the outdated *Takachiho* was a far more significant blow than the loss of any other cruiser in the fleet blockading Tsingtao. Of the ships complement, only one officer and twelve men survived the attack; twenty-eight officers and 244 men were lost with the ship. As soon as Brunner's torpedoes struck home, the Japanese were aware of an attack but did not admit it to the world for some little time afterwards, insisting that the *Takachiho* had struck a mine.[25] However, they immediately started searching for the culprit, soon realizing that it must have been the German destroyer. As Brunner explained, his return to Tsingtao was cut off and he thought at first that he could make it to Shanghai, but his old destroyer had seen her last action, when the engines began to develop significant problems he realized he could not possibly make it that far and decided to run the destroyer aground on rocks at Sheh sueh-so, some sixty miles south of Kiaochou Bay. By that time, the ship was of no use to anyone and he hoped the crew could escape, to continue the fight for *Kaiser* and Fatherland in some other capacity. However, that was not to be. Brunner and his crew, having violated Chinese neutrality by running the *S90* aground, were arrested by the authorities and interned.[26] It had been a gallant effort which had achieved considerable success and had lifted the spirits of the garrison in Tsingtao. It had also done much to deliver a psychological blow to the Japanese.

By 18 October, the storm had abated and the rain had ceased to lash the countryside. The weather remained unsettled but tending towards the bitter cold of a north-east China winter which was only a short time away. It was time to recommence work on the Outpost Line and to complete the Artillery Covering Position, before the attack could move forward. Communication remained an issue and Lieutenant Simson was of the opinion that neither the battalion nor the brigade headquarters had issued any orders during the period 11–21 October when A and B companies of the South Wales Borderers were in the outpost position. The only communication to the rear, seems to have resulted from Major Margesson, officer commanding the outposts, who requested specific information. This meant that the outposts were not kept fully appraised of the situation immediately around them. Nothing had been forwarded to the outpost commander concerning the future requirements and, according to Simson, the only information A and B companies gained was as a result of his personal conversations with Japan-ese officers, such as the battalion commander and the adjutant of the

Lieut Habershon, Lieut H. J. Simson, Major E. W. Jones, Capt Palmer in front of Captain Dive's dugout, October 1914. [Royal Welsh Museum, Brecon, BRCRM A1959.103]

1st/48th Regiment, on the left of the Borderers. From their divisional orders, information was passed on to the Borderers via Simson who appears to have been kept very busy liaising between the two forces. It is difficult to understand why Simson, who was clearly aware of these communication difficulties, should have been so critical of the Borderers who, effectively, had no guidance as their brigade commander was not issuing orders. Of course, it is very likely that the brigade was in a similar position, simply higher up the chain of command, just as much in the dark about the true wishes of the Japanese. Eventually, it was the Japanese engineer officer who instigated the line to be dug by the Borderers on the night of 13 October. To Margesson, it made little difference which line they were asked to prepare or by whom for without tools, the tasks were all equally difficult. By 16 October, Simson appears to have been approached directly by the Japanese to ensure a position in the Shiboshan Ridge was included in the line ready for occupation by the twentieth of the month. Upon investigation, he realised that:

> This scheme was based on a secret instruction that had been issued to Regimental Commanders and presumably the same instruction was sent to the British Force, but it conveyed quite a different meaning. The difference in the understanding of the course of future operations accounts for most of the difficulties that occurred about this period. (Oct. 15th – 20th).[27]

There was much going on at this time, as Japanese artillery-men were coming forward to prepare gun-pits and observation posts and without a direct, definite command structure, there was room for confusion which could ultimately have led to unnecessary loss of life and prolongation of the campaign. Simson was of the opinion that the orders were unclear but tried to impress on the Japanese engineers and the men of the Borderers working on the outposts, the need to complete such features as communication trenches quickly to allow future operations to proceed as smoothly as possible:

> Men for digging were taken from the picquets and supports as required, but the reserves were not toughened. The Engineers often asked if more men could be produced, but were told no. The two half companies on picquet and support duty were relieved every day by the two half companies in reserve. This arrangement caused a great deal of labour and waste of time. The reserves were looked on as not available for work but they had a good deal to do in the shape of ration fatigues, etc. Work now and for some time to come (to Oct 28th) was terribly hindered by two things (1) lack of tools, (2) the distribution of the battalion.

It was, undoubtedly, a difficult period for the Borderers, as they had some complicated work to complete which they were finding difficult because of the communication problems. Any problems or queries that arose took time to sort out, time that the Borderers did not have if they were to keep to Kamio's timetable. Simson was critical, as indeed was Margesson, of the staff work as it applied to the work of the reliefs in the outposts, but that was in part, the result of their own ignorance of the precise situation. However, unlike Simson, brigade were constrained by operational procedures and the language barrier and so could not simply ask questions of the Japanese officers, and accept verbal responses, as freely as perhaps they would have liked. Added to these problems, the translation of orders and questions in both directions caused further delays. It was not simply a question of digging trenches. There are some indications in Simson's report that suggest that perhaps these difficulties were intentional, particularly when the orders given to Kamio at the start of the operations warned him to keep things away from their ally, were considered necessary to avoid compromising the functioning of their own force.

It eventually became clear that the Artillery Covering Position was to be started by 20 October and the communication trenches pushed forward so that, by 28 October, they could be occupied. Two days later, the 1st Attack Position was also to be ready for the commencement of what the Japanese saw as the final bombardment of Tsingtao. The Japanese had a clear plan for their operations but it had not been sufficiently communicated to the British commanders. However, progress was made:

> This Outpost Line had now been advanced in the centre to the Shiboshan Ridge about a mile from the German redoubts and east of the village if Han-Chia Chuang. It was a clay ridge intersected by ravines which would have given good cover in dry weather, but in heavy rain the loose soil was easily washed away, dugouts in the sides of ravines collapsed, streams carried down

quantities of mud to fill up trenches and reduce roads into quagmires, and a piece of work was no sooner completed than it was washed away and had to be begun afresh. To struggle against such difficulties and in unfavourable conditions was a severe trial. The troops were thinly clad and usually soaked through, much digging was needed and as no wheeled transport was available, rations, ammunition, stores including heavy beams for use in the trenches had to be carried up to the front by hand over a mile and a half across tracks often knee deep in liquid mud.[28]

This account points out that, although the men were in range of the German guns, the battalion suffered more from the bad weather and difficult conditions than they did from the enemy's artillery.

On 21 October, after ten days on the Outpost Line, A and B companies were relieved. At the same time, Lieutenant Matsumo and his men were replaced by Lieutenant Nakamura and about thirty men from the 1st/48th Regiment. Simson asked the Japanese the reason behind the sudden recall of Matsumo since a good working relationship had been established between his party and the South Wales Borderers, but was simply informed that Matsumo was required for divisional duties and that the commander had seen fit to replace him. It was unfortunate, but it was not long before Nakamura had also established a rapport with his European colleagues.

The sudden relief of Lieut. Matsumo and his men, just coinciding, as it did, with our outpost reliefs, was most inconvenient. To replace his men, we got men who did not know our troops or the ground over our front, whereas by now Matumo's N.C.Os and men were thoroughly accustomed to us and everything went smoothly. I saw the Jap. Staff Officer and asked if nothing could be done, but though the Japanese troops had been placed under the orders of the British G.O.C., the Jap. Staff Officer said that the O.C. 48th Regiment had the right to make reliefs when he thought fit and that Lieut. Matsumo was required at Regimental Headquarters to run the Engineering arrangements of the Regiment and act as link between the regimental officers and the engineers allotted to their front. All we required was about 20 men under an N.C.O. to live close to outpost H.Q. and to find men for the standing patrols and be handy in case it was required to send orderlies to Japanese Officer it would be quite a help in keeping touch with troops on R(ight) & L(eft) and with their work, but it would be luxury to have one attached. However, the numbers remained as before and the new officer and his men, acting on orders from the O.C. 1/48th took up quarters on the extreme right of the Company on our immediate left about 10 minutes from outpost H. Q.[29]

From 21 October, the work on the Artillery Covering Position was to occupy a large part of the energies of the South Wales Borderers. C and D companies concerned with the digging, like their predecessors, always sent out covering patrols whilst they were working, to deter any German patrols and warn of a larger-scale attack. This had worked well enough during the first ten days of this type of work and on 22 October, it was decided that a joint patrol with the Japanese should be organized. Lieutenants Simson and

Nakamura went out to look over the ground and soon came across the joint patrol, lost and confused. Nakamura sorted out his NCO quickly and Simson explained the situation to the NCO in charge of the Borderers and the patrol resumed its work.

> Having sent them off we stayed about 5 or 6 minutes in the neighbourhood and then went ENE to the Japanese trenches. The direction taken by the patrol should have been S. Halfway to the trenches a short burst of rifle fire broke out to our right. We stopped and waited a minute or two, thinking it strange, but nothing further happened and so we went to the trenches.
>   Two hours later, a Japanese N.C.O. came up to outpost H.Q. and reported that 1 of our men had been hit by a Japanese patrol and soon after was brought in. The patrol had veered round to ESE and crossed the front of 1 of the Japanese patrols, covering their working parties. The patrol mistook them for Germans and opened fire. The Japanese were very worried and asked that it should be reported as an 'outpost affair', *Sekko no Shototsu*, collision of patrols. They sent an officer to apologise and did all they could for the wounded man. The fault seemed to be entirely ours, though, judging from what I saw during the operations Japanese challenges came simultaneously with the bullets.[30]

The wounded soldier was Private T. Mabbett of D Company who was shot through the lungs. He lingered until the battalion returned to Britain, but eventually succumbed to his wounds in early March 1915. This incident again highlights the inadequate communication and language difficulties between the allies and the general 'jumpiness' of the Japanese sentries. It is interesting to note that the Japanese 'smock' waterproof had been issued on 14 October, in an effort to prevent such an incident and, although it probably helped prevent casualties, it did not entirely prevent the mix-up over identification that dogged the campaign. It is also interesting to note here that while Simson recognized that the Japanese sentries were jumpy, and that there was a breakdown of communications, he was reluctant to accept the same conditions when the Borderes had similar problems.

Unfortunately, it was not only in the business of identification that things were not going as well as they could. Simson was of the opinion that when the Japanese and British soldiers acted together for patrols, there should have been written orders for the British NCO so that he could then take an active part in the running of the patrol. He admits that the reason this did not happen was, at least in part, the result of the scarcity of maps in the British force as a whole, a problem that should have been sorted out by the senior officers. In fact, the Japanese had plenty of maps but they were never issued to the British, apparently because they were never requested – perhaps they were of limited use as they were printed in Japanese. It would seem that on more than one occasion, when Simson was asked directly to arrange for a British NCO to be detailed as senior to the Japanese NCO, he was unable to comply, as the British officers were reluctant to issue written orders for such an undertaking, seeing it as unnecessary. According to

Lieut Habershon, Capt Dive, Capt Bradstock, Maj E. W. Jones, Capt Greenway, Capt Johnson.
[Royal Welsh Museum, Brecon, BRCRM A1959.103]

Simson, this attitude was seen by the Japanese as too casual and did not impress them at all. What Simson had possibly failed to recognize here, was that the Borderers were experienced professionals whose officers had no doubt about the capabilities of the men they commanded. Under different circumstances, there would have been no need to spoon-feed such soldiers as they were at least as capable as their Japanese colleagues. These differences in attitude may also reflect the fact that the British force, as very much the junior partner, could not dictate any specific approach and perhaps should have been done more to accommodate the wishes of the Japanese. Although the Japanese had clear orders to do all they could to assist the British, there were no similar orders for the British command. The War Office had, however, on more than one occasion, made it quite clear to Barnardiston that he was to play a subordinate role to the Japanese commander and it is perhaps here that the root of some of the issues may be found. In the long run, it would have been simple to have issued maps to the ordinary rank and file soldiers (something that did not occur on the Western Front throughout the war), which would have assisted them with their knowledge of the battlefield over which they were about to fight. The passive role adopted on at least some of the patrols did not make the best use of the men involved and gave little opportunity for them to show the Japanese what they were capable of. Although Lieutenant-Colonel Casson certainly thought that Simson's report was completely biased, it does serve to demonstrate that some issues were raised by the Japanese and, perhaps unfortunately, it was then up to Simson to interpret them. However, perhaps

Head of a heavy armour-piercing shell which landed just beyond C Company's position on 13 October. Left to Right: Pte J. J. Wire (Capt Greenway's servant), Pte .J Edwards (C Company Cook) [Royal Welsh Museum, Brecon, BRCRM A1959.103]

if he, being the only person who understood Japanese, had made the point as clearly as he did later in his report, then Casson may have been able to take some action. That this did not happen says as much about Simson as it does about the battalion.

On 22 October, the Borderers were notified that they were to be joined by half a battalion of the 36th Sikhs who had just landed at Laoshan Bay, ready to march towards the Outpost Line in front of Tsingtao. The Sikhs were to follow the same route as the Borderers had taken almost a month earlier, via Puh-li and Tsimo, so it would be a few days before they would be ready for front-line service. For the Borderers, the work continued as it had since 11 October:

> Went out 300 yards in front of Outpost Line last night at 6 pm and commenced to dig fire trench. Each man carried out five sandbags which were filled and put up to form a parapet, also to form cover if we were fired on. Ground very wet and boggy. Covered front of parapet with 'Yam' runners when we had finished work, returned at 12 midnight. German searchlight from the forts and redoubts playing all night (rained all night cleared at 9 this morning). Worked all day on shelters.[31]

This was the start of the work on the Artillery Covering Position which had been hampered by the weather and lack of equipment. Nevertheless, the work proceeded and progress, which may have seemed slow to the Japanese, was made. From the description given by Sergeant Bean, the ground conditions appear to have been poor and rain often managed to damage recently completed work. Generally, the men stuck to the task in good spirits, even though they were on short rations and had little hope of the situation changing very quickly. However, on the night of 24 October, the Battalion's winter kit finally arrived. It is difficult to imagine that, up to this point, the men had been soldiering in summer kit – cotton shirt and shorts, supplemented by anything else they had, including after 14 October, the Japanese 'smock' waterproof. Not only had they been poorly kitted out but for most of the time since they had landed at Laoshan Bay, they had also been on little more than half rations for much of the time. Despite these personal hardships, the Borderers had managed to take over a part of the Outpost Line, which demonstrated their real ability. The assistance of the Japanese engineers had been gratefully accepted and a working relationship established which suggests that perhaps the problems at rank and file level were not as great as those perceived at junior officer level.

By this time, it was clear, to the officers at least, that the siege of Tsingtao was about to enter a new phase. For days, the Japanese had been preparing gun positions for their heavy howitzers and it seemed that these preparations were almost complete. Major Margesson was becoming concerned by the dispositions of the battalion (and of the Sikhs when they arrived), during the bombardment that he knew was not far off. He was told by the staff officers that the Sikhs would occupy part of the front line, but the latter did not seem to grasp the fact that there would be no trenches for them to occupy unless they arrived soon and dug trenches for themselves. Margesson had supervised the construction of positions for two companies, but believed these would only accommodate the two companies of the South Wales Borderers assigned to them.

> Hence all my difficulties. I cannot get anything from Hd Qrs as to the battalion organization when the bombardment begins, which it may any day, nothing has been thought out and the whole thing is being treated both by our Regt. authorities and by the Brigade staff as if we were engaged in field operations and not on a siege. I have asked for biscuit tins in which to store water in the trenches. None have come. We borrow engineers, tools, sandbags, biscuits from the Japanese. It is very humiliating. Simson, Royal Scots, who talks Japanese is our only source of information, which is never sent us from Hd Qrs.

Clearly, at this stage of the operation, Margesson was still concerned about the staff work and the lack of precision in any of the orders which he received. Again, it is not clear whether the blame for this lay solely with the brigade headquarters or whether the Japanese were not disseminating the relvant information to the Borderers.

36th Sikhs in bivouac on arrival, outpost line by Nº 1 communication trench.
[Royal Welsh Museum, Brecon, BRCRM A1959.103]

The weather remained unsettled as the preparations continued and the men were frequently soaked through. Eventually on 28 October, Lieutenant-Colonel Casson and Major Pringle made their first visit to Margesson in the outposts, to settle the problem of which part of the line the two companies of 36th Sikhs were going to hold. Less than two hours later, the Sikhs arrived and Major Iveson, who was senior to Margesson, took over responsibility for the Outpost Line. The Brigade War Diary records that one company of the Sikhs went directly to the Outpost Line while the other went into reserve in a *nullah* about half a mile to the rear. It does not give details of how the additional company was accommodated in the trenches, but it is implied that the Borderers simply moved to accommodate the new arrivals. This would suggest that the Outpost Line was, at least for a time, somewhat overcrowded. Although this was, on the face of it, a very hasty decision, it seems to have worked well enough. It appears that Lieutenant-Colonel Casson was pleased with the preparatory work carried out by his men to that date, but Margesson makes no comment on the presence of too many men in the line which he had made clear the day before that he wished to avoid. His concerns were genuine since over-crowded trenches were about as useful as no trenches when they were bombarded, creating a significant risk to the men holding them. That the Germans did not bombard this trench line owes much to good fortune and very little to military planning.

With the Artillery Covering Position more or less completed, on schedule, despite the bad weather, it was time to consider the position for the next line, the 1st Attack Position, which needed to be constructed and occupied within a day or so of the bombardment of Tsingtao commencing. The decision was made at a staff conference held at 4 p.m. on 29 October.

At 5.30 Pringle, Moore,[32] Simson, Palmer[33] and I walked down the big *nullah* to the open country to see our starting point, which was not settled until 7 pm. Bad staff work; all this should have been settled days ago so that we could have started work as soon as it was dark. The moon is well up now and helps us in our digging and does not slow us up at all. Sent Palmer back to bring down part of C Coy and $^1/_2$ D Coy. Found a convenient *nullah* 35 yards long with running water for a portion of C Coy. Took D Coy out 125 yards to their front in the open and laid out two rows of filled sandbags in a bean field, then started work. Got down easily at first as ground was soft. Search light were turned on us but, but we lay low and men not seen. We could hear Germans hammering in the redoubts and cutting wood. They fired pompoms on our right – on to some Jap working parties. Back by 11.30 pm.[34]

On 30 October, the Brigade War Diary records that the bombardment of Tsingtao was scheduled to start on the following day. It appears that no-one in the British force had previously been aware of this. However, as if to reinforce the imminent bombardment, Captain W. F. Christian, Royal Artillery, arrived at the British headquarters from Wei-hai-wei to act as a forward observation officer for the fleet patrolling the bay and to report on the effectiveness of its fire.[35] The front line, which was at that time the Artillery Covering Position, was to be manned by one company of South Wales Borderers and a double company[36] of the 36th Sikhs in readiness for the assault. As if to confirm that the attack was about to get underway, all the ammunition (350 rounds per man), and twelve days' rations had been brought forward. The Japanese had made similar preparations, although in their case, they had decided that six days' rations would be sufficient. The final phase of the siege was about to begin.

The Japanese had expended a great deal of effort to get to this stage. The large, 280 mm siege guns had been dismantled and, more or less manhandled from the gun park in the landing area, as there was no way that they could be transported any other way. The light railway had helped with this, although the great weight of the gun barrels did, on occasion, cause the track to spread. Perhaps of greatest assistance to the Japanese were the hundreds of 'coolies' who had been drafted in to provide the necessary muscle power. The large guns required a substantial number of men to haul them over the rough terrain even in dry conditions – in the wet conditions that had dogged the campaign, this had become a major undertaking. However, as Kamio had a clear picture as to how the siege would develop, no effort was spared to achieve this; railway lines washed away in the storms were quickly replaced so that there was a minimum loss of momentum in both the general advance and the siege preparations in particular.

Whilst this haulage work proceeded, it was the lot of the engineering units in the forward positions to provide the necessary emplacements ready for the arrival of the modern-day siege engines. Gun emplacements were dug, sandbagged and, in the case of the heavy guns, concrete firing platforms were prepared. This work needed to be carried out well in advance in order for the concrete to cure sufficiently to allow it to bear the heavy weight and the impact loads for the remainder of the siege. Much of this work would have needed to have been carried out a minimum of two weeks before the guns arrived and were assembled. The manhandling of tons of steel under field conditions took a particular kind of expertise, some large timbers and strong backs. Lifting mechanisms, using tripods and blocks and tackles, were used to place the guns in their final firing positions. It must be acknowledged that the Japanese had worked hard to bring everything together, accordig to the requirements of the plan envisaged by their commanding general.

In the days immediately preceding the land bombardment, the Japanese maintained their pressure on the defenders in Tsingtao by ordering their fleet back onto the offensive, assisted once again by a repaired and fully-operational *Triumph*. For much of 29 October, the *Suwo*, *Tango*, *Okinoshima* and *Triumph* shelled the German positions with only a sporadic and ineffective response from Huitschen huk (Fort A). Records show that a total of 197 shells were fired which were believed to have caused significant damage. The Japanese, however, continued the bombardment the next day, firing a further 240 shells from the sea. Now in command of Prince Henry Hill, they were able to observe the fire from their ships, and in doing so, organized a workable communication system between the land and sea forces, enabling the bombardment to be better directed. It was also possible for them, by observing the fire from the Germans in Huitschen Huk, to make an accurate appreciation of the range of those guns, estimated to be 14,130 metres,[37] which allowed the warships to move closer inshore and, thereby, make their fire more effective, without fear of sustaining damage, such as that caused to the *Triumph* two weeks earlier. In actual fact, the damage caused to the German defences was, as from the previous bombardment, relatively small but the psychological effect was great as the vulnerability of their position was continually being made very clear to the defenders as they realized that the final stages of the battle were approaching.

Notes

1. The Shiboshan Ridge is the Japanese name for the low ridge shown as Shuang Shan on the British maps of the area. The Japanese name has been used in the Regimental History of the SWB and in the war diaries at brigade and battalion level and is used here in the same way.
2. Anon. account (possibly that of Major John Going), Royal Welsh Museum.
3. This was Major Margesson at the time in question.
4. Lieutenant Simson seems to be mistaken here since this village was to the south of the Hai-po Ho, although in general, the Borderers' position was in front of the village but north of river.
5. Simson's Report; Royal Welsh Museum.
6. Casson's letter of response to Simson's report, Royal Welsh Museum.
7. See Margesson's Diary.
8. Brigade War Diary.
9. See, for instance, Margesson's Diary.
10. Brigade War Diary.

Archaic heavy artillery is brought up to the siege lines ready for the bombardment of Tsingtao.

Japanese artillery ready to commence the bombardment of the German defences.
Note the telephone operator on the right.

11. Whittaker (1994), 121 and Burdick (1976).
12. Plüschow (2004), 51.
13. Burdick (1975), 144.
14. Hoyt (1975), 105.
15. Plüschow (2004), 52. Note that Plüschow is mistaken about the size of the guns, both *Suwo* and *Triumph* had 10-inch (250 mm) guns. This would seem to be a direct translation of the 1915 German edition.
16. Brigade War Diary (WO32/4996B).
17. Ibid.
18. Burdick (1975), 147.
19. Ibid quoted twenty-five soldiers as being drowned in this incident.
20. Whittaker (1994), 122.
21. The numbering of the redoubts by both the Germans and the British seems to have been from the right to the left. Hence, since they were facing each other the German Redoubt V became the British Redoubt I. The Japanese named them according to their position – hence the same redoubt was known as the Coastal Redoubt by the Japanese.
22. Burdick (1975), 151.
23. Plüschow (2004), 54.
24. Burdick (1975), 153, quotes a figure of 253 officers and men lost and states that ten men had left the cruiser before the attack – this means that of the complement on the night of the attack as few as three survived.
25. For instance, an account published in Great Britain in 1915 (Hilditch) states that the cruiser had sunk as a result of a 'fouled mine' and quotes the total loss as 271 officers and men.
26. The crew of the *S90* eventually spent their war in a camp near Nanking where the régime, at least for the officers, was relaxed.
27. Simson's report Royal Welsh Museum. It should be noted that Simson, writing after the event, remained unclear that the order had ever been issued to the British Force. All he knew for certain was that it had been issued to the Japanese Regimental commanders. This makes the criticisms he raises in his report all the more difficult to understand.
28. Going's account Royal Welsh Museum.
29. Appendix 3 of Simson's Report.
30. See Simson's report.
31. Sergeant Bean Diary, Royal Welsh Museum.
32. Captain C. D. Hamilton-Moore, Royal Warwickshire Regiment. DAA, QMG.
33. Captain R. G. Palmer.
34. Margesson Diary, Royal Welsh Museum.
35. See Brigade War Diary – the fleet had begun a significant bombardment on the day before he arrived and was to continue throughout the coming days.
36. The Sikhs were at this time still organized on the older eight company basis, hence one double company was the approximate equivalent of one company of the SWB.
37. Burdick (1975), 161.

Chapter 10

The Fall of Tsingtao

T he final phase of the siege of Tsingtao began on 31 October, a day that was considered auspicious by the Japanese since it was the Emperor's birthday. Everything in the weeks since their landing had been leading to this point when all their heavy artillery was in place and could commence shelling the German colony. For weeks, the Japanese had been fighting the elements to bring the large guns into position. They had also fought the Germans in a number of sharp skirmishes and had endured shelling from both the forts and the warships in the bay. Now, all that was about to change. The patient preparation and meticulous planning had put the Japanese in a position from which they could strike at Tsingtao itself. At approximately 6.15 a.m., guns of all calibres began firing and did not become completely silent again until the town had fallen. Large calibre guns were directed at the outer defensive earthworks and the Redoubt Line. They were joined by the heavy guns from the warships which were directed at the inner defences, the forts, and the batteries that faced Kiaochou Bay. At first, the German

Breakfast 75 yards in front of the Japanese guns on the first day of the bombardment, 31 October 1914. Smoke from guns firing. L–R: Lieut & QM Laman, Lieut Beherns, Pte Wire.
[Royal Welsh Museum, Brecon, BRCRM A1959.103]

response was very weak, although under the tremendous bombardment from land and sea, perhaps this was hardly surprising. The Brigade War Diary commented that the Germans wasted ammunition trying to shoot down a Japanese aircraft and that their shooting was poor. The Japanese fire that was directed at Iltis Fort was thought to be effective and responsible for the destruction of a number of guns.

The aim of the Japanese, to neutralise the defences as quickly as possible, and more or less simultaneously, was now crystal clear to the Germans. The siege had already been going on for over a month during which time the Japanese had slowly and deliberately prepared themselves for this moment and even the stoutest heart in the German town was feeling the tension:

> Our guns were never silent, but unfortunately we had to go slow on account of our remaining ammunition. The extraordinary length of the siege, the never ceasing artillery fire, and the terrible tension under which we lived, began to tell on us. My own nerves were getting out of hand. I could no longer force myself to eat, and sleep had become impossible. When I shut my eyes at night I immediately saw my map, and below me the Protectorate with its enemy trenches and positions. My head swam and my ears ached from the sound of the propeller.[1]

Plüschow was perhaps under more strain than most, he was in constant danger when he made reconnaissance flights every day that the weather permitted. He was in danger of attack from both the air and the land, and when he landed, his makeshift airfield was under threat from the sea. As the siege developed, the airfield also came within range of the land-based howitzers, thereby increasing the danger still further. Added to this was the danger that his propeller, damaged after the crash-landing in early August and constantly repaired since then, would give out on him during mid-flight. His daily reports were vital for the defence of the town and he had effectively become the eyes of Meyer-Waldeck, giving detailed daily accounts of troop movements and the progress of the enemy's siege preparations. It was a job that was certain to tax even the redoubtable Plüschow, and the great responsibility weighed heavily on his mind. Nevertheless, he continued to give his commander-in-chief useful information throughout the siege and his work was of inestimable value. To the allies, he was a great nuisance as his reports allowed German guns to register new positions almost immediately and their fire harassed them almost to the end of the operations. However, as the siege progressed, Plüschow's job became increasingly difficult as the Japanese made every effort to drive him from the skies and rob Meyer-Waldeck of the last direct observation upon which he could rely. Each time he took off from his small airfield, he knew he would be intercepted by one or more Japanese aeroplanes and, although he had recorded one success against them, the Japanese continued with their efforts to put him out of action for good. Gradually, by his own admission, the Japanese were wearing him down, for he needed to be aware at all times of the enemy below and above him, while he attempted to hold the *Taube*

Japanese howitzer.   [Royal Welsh Museum, Brecon, BRCRM A1959.103]

steady enough to draw the maps and collect the information that was needed by his commander. On more than one occasion, as the siege neared its end, Plüschow was forced to cut his flight short and head directly for the relative safety of the town because of the close attention of the Japanese airmen – although that was a safety which was becoming increasingly precarious as the days passed. It was, however, clear to him and many of his comrades, that the need for his flights was rapidly diminishing as the Japanese were now in close proximity to the town. Plüschow may have been gradually worn down by the Japanese, but he had managed to keep going until his work was completed.

On the other side of the lines, the Japanese and British were eager to be pushing on with the siege and to end the campaign quickly. Major Margesson's diary for 31 October gives an idea of the situation in the British lines:

> At dawn the bombardment of Tsingtao continued. We all put cotton wool in our ears. Very soon the petroleum tanks[2] were set alight and half an hour afterwards a huge column of black smoke rose from other petroleum tanks; at first German artillery replied and tried to knock out the Japanese balloon,[3] but without success. By 9. 30 am only Japanese were firing. Got up on the hill by the motor road with CO to look. Could see Iltis fort being shelled and Bismarck and cruiser lying peacefully in the harbour. There are ships sunk at the entrance of the commercial harbour to block it. 11 am the German guns are beginning to reply again.[4]

2/SWB Officers' Mess during the bombardment: Left to Right: Pte Stuart, Pte Sharpe (cook), Maj Margesson, Maj E. W. Jones, Lieut Petre. [Royal Welsh Museum, Brecon, BRCRM A1959.103]

The bombardment was terrific and there would have been few soldiers, or sailors for that matter, on either side who had witnessed anything like this before:

> The whizzing of the descending howitzer shells, the whistling and explosion of the grenades and their detonation on bursting, the barking of shrapnel and the roar of our own guns resulted in a din as though hell itself had been let loose.[5]

In no time at all, the immediate vicinity of Tsingtao had been turned into an inferno of bursting shells, shrouded in smoke and dust from the detonations. Not until dusk, when the ships began to move away as light failed and their gunnery became more difficult and less effective, was there any let up in the bombardment. For the most part, the Germans were unable to respond, more because of the lack of ammunition than anything else. Even after the massive bombardment of the day, most of their guns remained serviceable, but it was clear to the Germans that their ammunition would not last long if they tried to exchange shell for shell with their enemy. Their gunners needed to conserve ammunition since there was no chance whatsoever of fresh supplies. They did, however, succeed in dropping a number of shells very close to the British headquarters during the night of 31 October but caused no casualties. The German forts suffered direct hits and the hillside soon became pock-marked with shell holes, some so large that a house could have been fitted inside them, in a landscape that would become all too familiar to the Borderers in another theatre of war in the not too distant future. The ground shook as if in an earthquake, and the German defenders could do little but shelter as best they could from the hail of steel, and hope that they might get an opportunity to respond. From the outer defences at the Redoubt Line, to the heart of Tsingtao, the German defences were pummelled by a numerically superior force, and all the time that this was going on, the assaulting infantry was making preparations.

The Japanese 48th and 67th Regiments, together with the 2nd South Wales Borderers and the 36th Sikhs, were working to complete the 1st Attack Position and the communication trenches to link it to the Artillery Covering Position on Shiboshan Ridge. The timetable for the siege was tight and the 1st Attack Position was due to be occupied not later than 2 November, by which time the 2nd Attack Position and its communication trenches, also needed to be under construction. Each line was essentially temporary, since as soon as one forward position was occupied, work commenced on the next and the former forward position became a support line. In this way, the Japanese planned to make a break in the defences of the Redoubt Line and to take the attack right up to the last line of the German defences on Iltis Hill, Bismarck Hill and Moltke Hill. It was an arduous, deliberate approach and, at least for the Japanese, had a proven track record following their successes in the war with Russia some ten years earlier. But to succeed, it required that everything proceeded according to plan, and that each unit completed its part in the work to time, so that the line moved forward uniformly, bringing pressure to bear on all parts of the German line, leaving no exposed flanks as it did so.

On 1 November, the bombardment continued and by the early evening, the Borderers had taken up their pre-arranged position in the Artillery Covering Position, in readiness to move. The sections of the trench to the left and right were also packed with Japanese infantry and, once again, Margesson commented on the insanitary habits of his ally, 'if we escape an epidemic of enteric it will be a marvel.'[6] But, as they waited, they were able to observe the effects of the Japanese guns as they played on and around Redoubt Nᵒ 2 (Daitochin Redoubt),[7] which was several hundred yards away on their left front. It was clear that after two days of shelling, it had sustained considerable damage.

> Nearly the whole of the fire trenches and parapet of the Tai-Tung-Chen (Daitochin Redoubt) were completely destroyed and much of the two wire entanglements in the two ditches. The result on the parapet of Chuo-Horui (Redoubt Nᵒ 3) was equally good but the result on the ditches could not be accurately observed. The trenches and wire entanglements NE of Tai-Tung-Chen were also fired upon. The effect on the trenches seemed good but the wire entanglements do not seem to be much damaged. The shooting on the redoubt on Height 17 just SE of Kaigan-Horui (Redoubt Nᵒ 1) appears very good but actual result could not be seen.[8]

Shortly afterwards, the Borderers were ordered forward to commence their work on the communication trench from the Artillery Covering Position to the 1st Attack Position. This they did from about 8 p.m. until 10.30 p.m. when they were surprised to learn from a Japanese patrol that Redoubt N°. 2 had been abandoned by the Germans – driven out by almost two days of heavy gun fire. Since this redoubt was more or less on the front they were to occupy, a company of Borderers was ordered forward to investigate the situation and, if possible, to occupy the abandoned position. The company had not proceeded far when it became clear that the Japanese information was incorrect, as a machine-gun opened up from the supposedly abandoned redoubt. The company fell back and was lucky not to have sustained casualties. It is interesting to note that this is an early example of a front line being abandoned, or only thinly-manned by the Germans, during heavy bombardment, with the bulk of the troops being held back and called upon in the event of an infantry assault – a tactic that was to be developed further on the Western Front, and eventually reached an advanced stage in the 'strength in depth' policy of 1917. During the night, there was a general move forward by the British force so that the battalion headquarters was moved up much closer to the front on Shiboshan Ridge, thereby reducing the distance which messages and orders needed to travel, and speed up the response times when any difficulties were raised. The Borderers and the Sikhs moved from the support line on the ridge into the Artillery Covering Position and into the communication trenches to the 1st Attack Position which they would occupy the following day. This was effectively the last move forward by the whole of the British force, although there were men working in the forward positions right up to the fall of Tsingtao.

The 1 November also saw the Japanese try their hand at propaganda. Thousands of leaflets were printed and dropped from aircraft over the town,

Hill 89 near Yang-Chia-Chun; 2/SWB officers' sun sheters and bivouacs. Right: Lieut A. E. Williams. [Royal Welsh Museum, Brecon, BRCRM 2005.70.]

Part of D Company's trench in the artillery covering position. Centre: Sgt W. J. Pearce and Sgt Drummer A. W. Matthews. [Royal Welsh Museum, Brecon, BRCRM 2005.70.]

entreating the Germans to recognize their defeat, and not to destroy useful buildings, machinery and weapons of war, 'a most undesirable act against humanity and the will of God'. The Germans did not think much of the message, with its bad grammar and even worse sentiments, and so, almost contemptuously, Meyer-Waldeck had the leaflets passed around the garrison as 'souvenirs'. It was not a successful exercise for the Japanese and it is difficult to understand what they had expected to achieve. They had little reason to expect any assistance from the Germans in this matter, as they themselves had been systematically destroying Tsingtao and its environs, a piece at a time, for almost two months. If anything, the Germans were more determined than ever to give a good account of themselves. Perhaps Kamio was trying to avoid heavy casualties in his own force which would have been in keeping with his reputation for being a rather cautious general.

The early days of November saw the Germans preparing for the inevitable end of the siege as they began to scuttle the remnants of their naval presence. On 29 October, the gunboat *Tiger*, which had been damaged in action, was taken out to the entrance of the harbour and sunk alongside two merchantmen, in the hope that the wrecks would become a hazard to the Japanese and British warships, once the fighting ended. On 1 November, Plüschow recorded that the *Kaiserin Elizabeth* was taken into the channel and likewise scuttled to create an obstacle. She had fired all her ammunition at the approaching Japanese and could serve no other useful purpose, as the siege approached its climax. There seems to be some confusion, however, over the demise of the *Kaiserin Elizabeth* as one source gives 2 November[9] as the day she was scuttled,[9] whilst Major Margesson states in his diary that the

German ships scuttled in the entrance to Tsingtao harbour.

warship was still firing against the Borderers position on 5 November.[10] However, Margesson appears to have mistaken the *Kaiserin Elizabeth* for the gunboat, *Jaguar*, which was still shelling the Borderers' positions as late as 5 November, and was not scuttled until the night of 6/7 November. The Germans were determined that nothing of any use should fall into the hands of the enemy. German naval strength in Tsingtao had been small to begin with, once von Spee had taken the *Scharnhorst* and his squadron away during July and August and, by 1 November, Tsingtao's naval capabilities had all but disappeared. Ironically, on this same day, thousands of miles away to the south-east across the Pacific, von Spee's squadron registered a naval victory when it engaged Sir Christopher Cradock's squadron off Coronel in Chile. Cradock's flagship, the pre-Dreadnought HMS *Good Hope*, was lost with all hands, as was HMS *Monmouth*. Both ships were old and no match for the much more up-to-date *Scharnhorst* and her squadron. The news, when it reached Tsingtao, may have done much to lift the spirits of the beleaguered garrison but von Spee's victory, could do nothing to change the outcome of their battle.

The effects of the first two days of shelling on the forts had been quite marked. Most of the guns in Iltis Fort, the most south-easterly of the forts, had suffered badly, partly because the position of the fort meant that it could be attacked readily from the sea, and big naval guns from the Japanese squadron had caused considerable damage. Bismarck Fort, at the centre of the line of forts, was largely unscathed, and its large guns, up to 280 mm, remained a threat to any attack. Moltke Fort on the north-west of the line had also been knocked about but, although its kitchens and laundry facilities were out of action, it remained largely fully functional after the bombardment. The batteries at Tsaichen and Hweisingchou, on the inner harbour, essentially seaward-facing, had not been targeted at this early stage of the bombardment and so, remained virtually undamaged, although they were not to escape for long. On 2 November, the third day of the bombardment, these batteries received the attentions of the Japanese warships steaming up and down the coast. The *Triumph* was singled out by the Japanese to direct its not inconsiderable fire power against Bismarck Fort. The British ship's 10-inch (250 mm) guns ranged the fort quickly and it was reported that, after an hour's bombardment, one of the large (280 mm) guns was destroyed.[11] It was effectively a battle of attrition as the shells from land and sea gradually wore away at the defences, piece by piece, gun by gun, until the Germans were left with little to defend themselves.

On the night of 1 November, Major Knox and a small party of the 36th Sikhs, went out from their position to reconnoitre the ground they would be working over in the next few days. During the course of the patrol, they were able to locate and render safe a number of charges placed on the bridge over the river. The Germans had clearly hoped to delay the advance by blowing the bridge, perhaps while a column was crossing, but failed in that too.

Parade at 5.30 pm sandbags, picks and shovels and went out to dig a communication trench between N[os.] 1 and 2 attack position, which latter is on the river bank. Germans burst half a dozen shells over us as we walked down the nullah, but we have good cover and only had one man hit, LC Cavalla.[12] The Japs were to take the pumping station tonight; there was a burst of Maxim fire there about 8 pm but I don't know what has happened. Back at 10 pm. The Germans were bursting heavy howitzer shells from behind Bismarck hill all along the front during the night.[13]

Sgt Press, Mess Caterer, 2/SWB with officers' mess table on Shiboshan Ridge.
Regimental Aid Post on left. [Royal Welsh Museum, Brecon, BRCRM 2005.70.]

Stretcher bearers of the 2/SWB removing one of the casuaties of the fighting in early November 1914.
[Royal Welsh Museum, Brecon, BRCRM 2005.70.]

Not for the first time was the question asked as to whether the Germans were actually doing nothing more than expending ammunition. It was, undoubtedly, frustrating for them, trapped and outgunned as they were, but if reports[14] concerning their poor gunnery and wastage of ammunition, are to be believed, then there is an argument to suggest that they were actually hastening their ultimate defeat. However, this is, perhaps, too simple an explanation. It would appear that the Germans had fired off large numbers of heavy calibre shells with the sole purpose of making life as difficult as possible for the Japanese and, if possible, raising an element of doubt in their minds as to the effectiveness of the siege:

> Our heavy artillery fire was not kept up for the purpose of throwing away our shells – it would have been less dangerous to have dropped them in the bay – but solely to do as much damage to the Japanese as possible before the assault on the fortifications could be made. We regulated our fire with the one purpose of covering the country with shells before they had a chance to get under cover. When they attempted to mount their siege guns at the start of the bombardment their forces were exposed to us. We could see their ammunition columns and supply wagons rolling up on open roads, and, by spreading our fire about the valley, we were attempting solely to postpone the fall of Tsingtao as much as possible by hindering the allied forces in their work.[15]

Here a very important point is made that, at the beginning of the siege operations, the Japanese had been clearly observed in their preparations, but as one after another of the observation positions were lost, particularly

Prince Henry Hill, the Germans had become increasingly reliant on an intimate knowledge of the ground and the reports that Plüschow had been able to provide – they were also unable to gauge effectively the disruption, if any, that their shelling was causing. The fact that the siege continued more or less without pause, would suggest that the shelling was not as effective as it could have been. But it should be remembered that the Germans had achieved some measure of success, in forcing the Japanese headquarters to move on at least one occasion and the Borderers to move twice in very short order. Whilst this may not have been the most effective use of the limited ammunition available, it succeeded in keeping the assaulting force on the alert, if nothing else.

Margesson's account for 2 November indicates the Japanese intention to capture the pumping station. This was situated on the north side of the Hai-po Ho and the wire entanglements of the Redoubt Line had been thrown out across the stream at this point, to include the station in the defences of the Redoubt Line. It was covered by the guns of Redoubt N$^{o.}$ 1 (Coastal Redoubt) to the south-west, and on the opposite side of the stream bed. The impor-

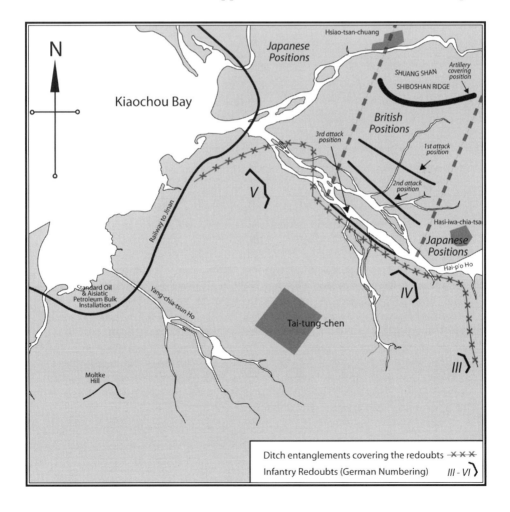

tance of the pumping station lay in the fact that a large portion of the town relied upon this source for its water supply and clearly, its capture would tighten the Japanese grip on the town and increase the discomfort of the defenders. The Germans could do nothing to prevent the determined attack on the pumping station and it soon fell into Japanese hands.

In the siege positions, the attackers were busily preparing the 2nd Attack Position which would soon need to be occupied, to keep to the siege programme drawn up by the Japanese. Unfortunately for the Borderers, the line chosen was in the immediate vicinity of a river bed where there were loose running sands and water just below ground level. Each spadeful removed, either brought the sand back into the hole or the hole filled with water, and digging the line was hard and largely unproductive work. There were even one or two officers in the Borderers who suggested that the 2nd Attack Position could not be dug on the line that had been chosen, and should be abandoned and trenches prepared in another position. Of course, this did not happen and methods were adopted to provide some drainage and cover for the battalion. Sweet potato vines were used to stabilize the trench floor by treading them into the poor soil[16] but these were little more than a temporary expedient which did not stop the water oozing up out of the ground, and it was more or less impossible to occupy the trench permanently. Nevertheless, the working parties were out during the night of 2/3 November, making every effort to complete the task before they could advance to the 3rd Attack Position on the opposite bank of the river, immediately under the guns of the line of redoubts.

Dawn on 3 November revealed a cold rain-swept scene of desolation and destruction but the guns continued their ceaseless work:

> 10 pm. For the last six days Tsingtao has been heavily bombarded from the enemy's land Batteries, most of our land front Batteries as well as most of the guns have been destroyed. This month the sea front Batteries have been sparing ammunition as they expect an attack which does not come. Our Battery has been badly damaged by Howitzers, two of the Howitzers have been damaged – direct hits have gone through the splinter-proof shield, the crews were not wounded as they were all under cover. The chief observation post where I have my war station has been heavily shelled. Large holes have been torn in the concrete roof but the roof is still standing. It is very unpleasant when one has to sit in the position and is unable to protect oneself whilst shells crash into the roof every three minutes. It is better fun in the field where one gets a run for one's money. There is no longer a single Battery here which has not been damaged. Since yesterday the enemy's Artillery has principally bombarded the Redoubts to make it easier for their Infantry to storm them – their attack which was expected today is now expected to take place at three o'clock tomorrow morning.[17]

For the Borderers, their night's toil had not paid off for only 'An indifferent fire trench had been dug'[18] which had not been traversed for much of its length, which meant that it was likely to be enfiladed from the coastal redoubt (*Kaigan* or Redoubt N°. 1) and Redoubt N°. 2 (*Daitochin*). Once again, Lieutenant Simson was critical of the work of the Borderers when he pointed out that the Sikhs had accomplished much more in the same time. Casson pointed out, in defence of his battalion, that the Sikhs were relatively fresh, had arrived better equipped and had not suffered the privations of six weeks on half rations. It was, perhaps, an unfair criticism by Simson, but this keen junior officer wanted to see the work progressing so as to impress the worth of the British force on the Japanese who, by his own admission, were becoming increasingly unimpressed by what they saw as the overall casual attitude of the British soldier. On the night of 3 November, it was decided that the 2nd Attack Position would not be held, and all efforts were focused on the communication trenches. Ground conditions were bad and progress was slow, but by the end of the night, there was a reasonable trench, although not to the liking of Simson:

> The number of sandbags used was, owing to the wet nature of the ground, so great that we were now running very short of them. The trenches built by the Sikhs were very good, deep and well traversed, with earth thrown up in rear as protection from our own shrapnel. The trenches of the SWB were not nearly so good and were almost entirely without traverses. That night the Sikhs lost three officers, but even this did not seem to affect their work, which to the end was better than that of the SWB, and seemed to be more vigorously and willingly done. The Japanese noticed this.[19]

The same night, three Japanese engineer patrols were sent out to reconnoitre the ground where the 3rd Attack Position was to be sited. It appeared that the Borderers had been asked by Simson to put out supporting patrols, but this did not happen, although two officers, Lieutenants Rawle and Cahusac, crossed the river and located the wired entanglements. The outer defence of the Redoubt Line comprised a glacis, sloping up from the southern bank of the Hai-po Ho to a wall beyond which was a ditch. The inside of the wall was whitewashed so as to silhouette any man dropping into the ditch which was twenty feet wide and filled with wire entanglements. The Japanese engineers brought back information on this arrangement which was to prove of great use to the Borderers in the latter stages of their work in the forward area. For their part, the Japanese infantry had worked on their sections of the 2nd Attack Position and had met with rather more success, and were able to occupy the line on the right of the Borderers on 3 November, with a strength of one company per battalion. It is hard to explain the differences in the results obtained by the two different workforces. It is difficult to believe, as Simson would have it, that the Borderers did not work as hard as their Japanese counterparts or that they did not have a similar commitment, as they were experienced, professional soldiers led by equally experienced, professional officers. Part of the answer may have been the ground conditions that prevailed in the area occupied by the battalion. The physical process of a river changing

Japanese observation post outside Tsingtao.

direction and depositing sediments along its length, causes the layers of soil in its vicinity to vary considerably. Similarly, water levels can change very rapidly in such soils, particularly if there are mixed layers of sand and clay. These factors almost certainly played a part in the lack of success of the work, but the fact remains that the Japanese and the Sikhs managed to make better progress. Whatever the reasons behind the Borderers' failings, it is easy to envisage that the Japanese would not have been impressed.

On the German side of the lines, they had their own problems to contend with as their defences came in for more heavy shelling:

> Today many columns can be seen carrying long pieces of wood which they will use for laying on top of the obstacles during the assault. We do not fire at them much as we have got very little ammunition left for the still undamaged guns – this is being saved up for the final attack so that it can kill a few more thousand Japanese. Yesterday two sergeants, four NCOs and thirty two men wer sent from out Battery to reinforce the Redoubts, as also were thirty men from the sea front Batteries, how we should all like to go with them but everyone cannot go.[20]

The conditions for the Germans were, quite clearly, bad and getting worse. By 3 November, it was recorded that '200 case-hardened shells and 150 shrapnel shells'[21] were all that remained in Bismarck Fort which would not last long in the event of an all-out attack. The confined nature of the battery positions inside the forts were also taking their toll on the men, giving them very little chance to move around or go outside. During the day, the defenders sheltered from the large-calibre explosives that were hurled at them, whilst at night, the Japanese used shrapnel to ensure that working parties could not effect any repairs to the damage caused during the day. War weariness was taking its toll; six weeks of siege and setbacks, followed by days of continuous bombardment were, inevitably, having an effect. Every scrap of news that filtered through from the outside world was digested, dissected and discussed. Most of the news from Europe, if not all, told the defenders of German successes only, as their army swept through Belgium and France, but they did not hear of the losses that advance had cost, at places such as Mons and Ypres. For the moment, there were still thoughts of the gallant brotherhood of soldiering:

> If we have an hour's rest in the evenings we find a quiet spot and talk of the beautiful home, our beloved parents and sisters and everything else one loves. These are my happiest hours. I will die happily if I can only die alongside my good friend Rudolf. By tomorrow morning we may be dead or in the hands of the Japanese. With roughly 6,000 men we are opposing a superior force of from 40,000 to 50,000. At any rate we will cause the Japanese the greatest possible loss when they assault – unfortunately we cannot do more – we know that the Kaiser and the Fatherland will look upon us with pride as is evident from the telegram we received last week. I will now lie down for a rest, perhaps for the last time![22]

The next day, 4 November, was a bitterly cold day, but the attacking force still had much work to do on the 2nd Attack Position, which needed to be occupied not later than 5 November, if the siege was to continue according to plan. The work was every bit as difficult as that of the previous night and it was eventually decided that, instead of digging a trench through the poor soils and into the water, it was necessary to construct a breastwork built up from sandbags (such an expedient had already been found necessary by those troops soldiering on the wet plains of Flanders), but this was not without problems for the Borderers who were without a ready supply of sandbags and in some places, the soil was so poor that even filled sandbags sank without trace. It must have seemed that whichever way they turned, they faced failure as they tried to complete the 2nd Attack Position. Progress was being made however, and by the end of the night's work, the 2nd Attack Position and the communication trench back to the 1st Attack Position, were sufficiently well-prepared to be of immediate use. As well as finishing this work, it was necessary to begin pushing out saps immediately, towards the site of the 3rd Attack Position which would involve fording the river, achieved by diverting its flow by using yet more sandbags and making use of sand bars within the channel, to make the distance crossed as short as possible. The success of this part of the operation is not recorded anywhere, but it is known that the Sikhs managed to get their trench well forward into the river bed. The fact that there is no mention of it, (or rather the failure to complete it) in Simson's report, suggests that it was carried out with some success by the South Wales Borderers. It was decided that the site of the 3rd Attack Position should be on top of the glacis which sloped up from the river, putting it immediately in front of the wall which ran along the face of the Redoubt Line. The instructions for the digging of the 3rd Attack Position stated that the trench would only need a low parapet, but that the earth raised from digging, should be thrown behind the trench to form a relatively high parados which would serve to protect the men from their own shrapnel, as this position was now very close to the enemy. This line was to be completed ready for occupation on 6 November. At this stage, it is interesting to note that the work on these attack positions went on almost unhindered by the Germans, and there were few casualties during their construction. It must have become clear to those attacking that, for the Germans to have taken such a casual approach to the enemy creeping nearer to their defences, must mean only one thing – they were very short of ammunition. To have attempted this kind of manoeuvre against a simple redoubt on the Western Front, would have called down a rain of steel on the attackers.

Although the lack of ammunition has been used to explain German inactivity at this stage, it has also been argued that perhaps they were not as interested in the defence of the protectorate as they should have been. If they were, in fact, conserving ammunition, when were they planning to use it? It is difficult to imagine a more crucial time than when the enemy was within yards of the front line. If their inactivity at this point is considered as part of the overall strategy adopted by them, including making no effort whatsoever to prevent the landings at Laoshan Bay, then, perhaps, a casual defensive approach could be argued. However, their resources were extremely limited and, from the outset, their cause was more or less lost. It is understandable, therefore, if their approach was not as vigorous as it could have been. They did use all the weapons that were at their disposal, from ships' guns to old artillery pieces, which would tend to show a high level of commitment. That this was not directed more appropriately was more likely to be down to individuals within the command structure and inadequate communications between the various elements of the defence, rather than to any lack of desire to produce a robust defence.

Preparations in front of the Redoubt Line continued on 5 November. The day was bright and sunny, though cold, which came as something of a pleasant relief, for while dry weather continued, there was some hope of making progress with the siege works to the south of the river. Throughout the day, the Japanese heavy guns were working away at Redoubts N$^{os.}$ 1, 4 and 5 (Kaigain on the north-west coast; Jinzan and Shojinzan on the south-east coast) and Iltis Hill and its fort. The Germans had very little with which they could respond and, for the most of the day, their guns remained silent which gave further hope to the attackers that the siege was almost over. Plüschow was very despondent as he was now forced to destroy the seaplane he had been building, using salvaged parts from Muellerkowski's wrecked *Taube*. This resourceful officer had started building a two-seater biplane that he planned to launch from the sea, having recognized that,

Facing page: Three photographs which clearly show the whitewashed wall in front of all redoubts and the thick wire defences. The lower photograph shows a breach made by the Japanese in front of N° 1 Redoubt with a Japanese trench in foreground. [Royal Welsh Museum, Brecon, BRCRM 2005.70]

sooner or later, he would be unable to take off from the temporary airfield at Iltis Plazt as that came within range of enemy guns. However, he finally realized that his project would not be completed in time to be of any use to him and, with a heavy heart and the help of his engineer, *Leutnant* Clobuczar, a former Austrian pilot, he destroyed the seaplane, an act which indicated that, in his opinion, Tsingtao was lost.[23] He was then summoned to see Governor Meyer-Waldeck who, likewise, had no doubt that the fall of the town was very close.

> We are expecting the Japanese main attack at any hour now. See that you leave the fortress by aeroplane, though I fear the Japanese will give you no time to do. And now God speed you, and may you come through safely. I thank you for the work you did for Tsingtao.[24]

The Governor's words, recorded by Plüschow, came as a surprise to the young airman as he had not anticipated his own escape from the grips of the Japanese. He received a direct order from Meyer-Waldeck to leave the town as soon as possible and to take a 'large bundle of private correspondence' with him. Plüschow did not question the decision and made immediate preparations for his departure.

> At night I went up to the hill top, where my friend *Oberleutnant* Aye had been holding out for weeks, with his small battery, under the most severe shell fire. From there one had a magnificent view of Tsingtao and its surroundings. I sat for some time on the highest peak, fascinated by the panorama at my feet. Below us a sea of fire, with flashes of lightning from the guns thundering across space, and like a golden thread stretched from sea to sea the yellow rifle and machine gun fire. Right over my head screamed, swished and whistled thousands of shells sweeping closely over the hilltop, bent on reaching their targets. Behind me our heavy howitzers roared their last message and in the distance from the farthest southern point of Tsingtao 29 centimetre guns for Fort Hstanniwa poured out their swan song. Harrowed to the depths of my soul I returned to Aye, and after taking a hearty leave of him, carrying with me all his good wishes for my venture, I left him after shaking him warmly by the hand. I was the last officer in Tsingtao to do so for he fell a few hours later in the heroic but unequal fight against the Japanese, he and his gallant little band preferring death to surrender.[25]

Early the next morning, Plüschow had gone, eventually landing his aeroplane at Haichow in neutral China, where he was interned, along with some of his comrades from the *S90* but, after a short stay, he simply walked away from the Chinese guards who did not seem too interested in the German airman, and caught a train to the coast. This remarkable soldier then managed to get a passage to San Francisco and made his way across the United States before crossing the Atlantic to Gibraltar, where he was captured and held by the British, before being sent to Donington Hall prisoner-of-war camp in Britain. He escaped from there and, posing as a merchant seaman in London's docklands, eventually stowed away on a ship back to Germany. He continued to serve the Kaiser in the Baltic Sea Squadron until the end of the war. He was the only German to make a clean escape from Tsingtao, or for that matter from Great Britain, a fact recognized by the Kaiser when he awarded him the Iron Cross, First Class. He was the only German in either world war to escape successfully from the British Isles.[26]

For the Germans in the front line at Tsingtao, the assault preparations that the allies had made, were taking their toll. The commander of Redoubt N⁰ 3 (*Chuo* or Central Redoubt), to the left of the line held by the South Wales Borderers, sent a report to Meyer-Waldeck stating that:

> The entire work is shot to pieces; a hill of fragments without any defences. The entire trench system is demolished; the redoubt is still intact, but everything else, including the explosives depot is destroyed. Only one observation post is usable. I shall hold the redoubt as long as possible.[27]

Conditions had deteriorated rapidly once the large siege pieces had come into use. The Germans were living a subterranean existence, with both food and water in short supply and everyone on the brink of exhaustion and, to add to the problems, dysentery was becoming an increasing problem. Nevertheless, the Germans were still trying to fight back and shelled the allies heavily during the afternoon of 5 November.

In front of the Redoubt Line, the siege preparations were progressing but not without some difficulties. The preparations for the 3rd Attack Position were causing problems as it was very close to the line of the redoubts, only

Postcard issued to commemorate Günther Plüschow's arrival at Haichow on 6 November.

N⁰. 2 Redoubt showing overhead cover completely destroyed by Japanese shell fire. Prinz Heinrich Hill in the distance. [Royal Welsh Museum, Brecon, BRCRM A1959.103]

twenty yards in some places, and the section that the South Wales Borderers and Sikhs were working on was enfiladed from Redoubt N⁰ 1 (Kaigan) to the right and the Redoubt N⁰ 2 (Daitochin) to the left:

> Working 6 –11.30 pm on communication trench between 1 and 2 positions of attack. Heavy rifle and Maxim fire all along line. $^1/_2$ B Company under Bradstock and $^1/_2$ C Company under Johnson were working on a trench on far side of the river enfiladed by fire from Nos 1 and 2 redoubt. B Coy lost 15 out of 50 men. D Coy lost Bettes killed and Stevens wounded. Total casualties 6 killed 18 wounded and 2 missing. The artillery at first kept down the German fire but later on slackened off and practically ceased about 9 pm when German Maxims could fire unopposed. Firing went on practically all night. The river bed was constantly traversed by machine gun fire. Japs lost over 100 Dive[28] says.[29]

It is clear from the accounts in Margesson's diary that he was not entirely convinced by the Japanese approach to dealing with the redoubts. It was not direct enough for this experienced soldier. He believed that, instead of expending great effort trying to ensure that all redoubts were taken almost at the same time, the approach that should be adopted would be to focus on taking out one redoubt quickly, and then bringing pressure to bear on the others from the captured position. His own belief was that the redoubt to capture was Redoubt N⁰ 5 (*Shojinzan*) on the left flank. Once this fell, he was sure the others would follow. The thinking behind this, was that Redoubt N⁰ 5 was the one that could not readily be supported by others, or from the sea, since the Japanese controlled the sea approaches. At least until the *Kaiserin Elizabeth* and the *Jaguar* had been scuttled, Redoubt N⁰ 1 (*Kaigan*) on the north-west coast, could be supported from Kiaochou Bay and, as such, could call upon flanking fire against any attack. Redoubt N⁰ 5 would therefore be the best to attack as it had one flank that was effectively in the air. Margesson believed that the problem with the approach that had been adopted was that, whilst the artillery could easily drive out the German garrisons from the redoubts during the day, there was little that could be done to prevent the line being reoccupied at night, because they were overlooked by the forts (Iltis, Bismarck and Moltke), which created problems for the allied working parties out in exposed positions, trying to prepare the attack line. Hence, shrapnel was used during the night to limit the German activity, although of course, this itself created problems for the allied troops as they got closer to the redoubts. Margesson believed that, if one of the redoubts could be taken, this cycle could be broken which would bring further pressure to bear upon the defenders of the Redoubt Line. This course of action had not been adopted and, as a consequence, the work of 5 November was made particularly difficult. To enable it to be carried out as quickly as possible, B Company the South Wales Borderers, which had been acting as brigade reserve, was sent forward to assist. They were not fully aware of the situation as they had not been in this forward position before, but as many men as possible were needed in the front area to prepare trenches. Experience gained during the night of 4 November showed that there was a German presence in the Redoubt Line immediately in front of the Borderers and B Company was ordered to neutralize this, before C Company could commence digging any trenches on the 3rd Attack Position and D Company could work on its communication trench across the water course. Initially, B Company succeeded in driving back the enemy look-outs, but the firing alerted the line and soon, there were searchlights playing their bright beams all along the positions:

> When B Company was crossing the river bed to go to work, searchlights picked them up and fire was opened on them. The Company swung its right up and opened fire. Then traversing fire from at least two machine guns turned on them from the extreme left of the trench of DAITO CHIN[30] (*Tai Tung Chen*) redoubt. The wounded were sent back to the 2nd Attack Position and the company remained out in the river bed for about an hour and was then withdrawn. After the Company had been brought in, there were still some wounded to be got in. Parties went out and got them all in but two. Several attempts were made to get to the two missing men, but they could not be found in the dark. According to one Officer, they were both dead. At one time the SWB. machine guns which were on the extreme right of the 2nd Attack Position line, opened fire on DAITO CHIN (*Tai Tung Chen*) redoubt. They were answered by a few rounds from the enemy's artillery.[31]

It appears that, as a result of the enfilade fire, at first from their right and from Redoubt N°· 2 on their extreme left, B Company needed to be facing in two directions to reply to the Germans. They moved into position quickly and returned fire, which seemed to work well enough to allow the company to withdraw to safer positions, but there were a number of casualties and some men were left wounded under the German guns. At this point, volunteers were called for, to go and search for the wounded, and Private Herbert Evans stepped forward and managed to bring in one wounded man. Evans went out twice again, each time returning with wounded men. On his fourth sortie, he had just reached another wounded man, when he was caught by a burst of machine-gun fire and killed. Even then, his body protected the wounded man from further injury and he was brought in later. At the end of the night, two of the South Wales Borderers were still missing. Good work had also been done in this rescue mission by Captain D. G. Johnson, Lance Corporal Foley and Privates, Green, Snow and West.[32] According to Captain Bradstock, there had been one good result from the night's work, which gained the Borderers some respect from the Japanese 48th Regiment:

> Having rushed a German Pepper Box[33] the snipers from which made digging impossible as it was actually on the line to be dug by my men, I doubled back from the 3rd to the 2nd Assault Position (distance about 350 yards) to report the situation to my Commanding Officer; having complimented me on taking this post, he told me to take out two platoons (as had previously been arranged) and carry on with the digging; I at once complied and as the men were crawling up the glacis to the 3rd Assault Position they were enfiladed by hostile rifle fire from the direction of N[o.] 2 Redoubt about 2 to 300 yards on my left. I swung one platoon round to face the fire, leaving the other hidden in the rear. Shortly after this the volume of hostile fire increased and came from another position to my left, and well in front of, N[o.] 2 Redoubt; I then brought up my other Platoon on the right and slightly in front of my left Platoon, and personally directed the fire of my men. This new hostile fire was apparently coming from a position some 150 to 200 yards to my front; by the light of a rocket or flare I noticed a small party of Japanese (presumably a patrol) lying down about 40 yards in front of the left of my line. I ordered my men not to fire on them and continued to direct 'SLOW DELIBERATE' fire at the hostile party which I estimated at about 15 rifles; I also ordered every alternate man to prepare to start digging cover for himself; the men were absolutely cool and collected and they fired exactly as ordered by me without signs of excitement.
>
> While my fire was going on the Japanese on my left rapidly disappeared and the Germans shortly afterwards retired or at any rate ceased fire. I recognized that the Japanese, like my own men, were in an awkward position and I deliberately directed my fire upon that I believed at the time to be a small German Advanced Post; I learnt afterwards that it was and, according to the Japanese, a hostile Patrol of 1 Officer and 12 men who were driving back the weaker Japanese patrol lying in front of the left of my men.[34]

In spite of Bradstock's comments about the night's work, Lieutenant Simson seemed to have gained another impression of the contolled fire put down on the German patrol by B Company:

> It appeared that a patrol of the 48th had gone out through the entanglement past the west side of the Daitochin redoubt and was later driven back by a stronger

German patrol. Just at the right moment, the British opened fire on the enemy's patrol, which halted and then drew off. This was an unrehearsed effect by B Company, either when they drove off the look-out sentries, or later when they fired on the machine guns, the shots apparently going over into the enemy's patrol. He asked me to thank the C.O. for this support.[35]

Whilst Simson was not full of praise for the action of the Borderers, seeing it as a complete fluke that their fire had actually helped the Japanese, the fact remains that they had acted well enough to counter the German fire in their own sector and to beat off a fighting patrol in the Japanese sector. The ability of the Borderers to act in this 'unrehearsed' manner should have persuaded Simson that there was a high degree of professionalism within the battalion, but instead, he felt the action demonstrated the inadequacy of the men involved. The Japanese however, had been impressed and grateful for the assistance that Bradstock and his men had been able to offer, but had sustained losses that night:

> When I looked into Lieutenant Nakamura's shelter early in the morning of the 6th, about 1 am, his men were anxious because he was still out and no one seemed to know where he was. They asked me if I had seen him as it was said that he had gone over to see me. Next morning his body was seen near the left of our 2nd Attack Position. He had left his own trenches to come over and see us and report how things were going on when he was killed by a shell. Lieutenant Nakamura had been attached since October 21st and had been of the greatest assistance and took no end of trouble going round getting the disposition of the troops on our flanks and helping generally. As he was killed when attached to the British Force, he was buried in the British section, our troops doing the honours at his funeral.[36]

In spite of the casualties for both the Borderers and the Japanese and the combat success, Brigadier-General Barnardiston reported to the Japanese headquarters the following morning that the 3rd Attack Position was still not ready for occupation. This did not satisfy the Japanese at all and he was told that the plans for the siege required that the 3rd Attack Position was manned that evening, at all costs. To compensate for this shortcoming, picquets were sent out after dark, so that there was a presence in the line. To add to the complexity of the situation that night, there were reports that the Germans had abandoned their trenches in front of the Borderers and, when D Company replaced C Company, Lieutenant Somerville was ordered to take out a patrol to gain information on the situation in front of the battalion. As they moved forward towards the enemy trenches, the Germans opened fire on them and the working party, and they were withdrawn to the relative safety of the 2nd Attack Position.[37] During the course of the night, Simson located the bodies of the two South Wales Borderers who had been missing since the previous night and brought them back to the British lines; it appears that both had been shot through the head.

German howitzers on Bismarck Hill, blown up by the Germans in the final stages of the siege.
[Royal Welsh Museum, Brecon, BRCRM 2005.70]

The work throughout the rest of the night of 6 November was much the same as it had been for the previous days, as the men tried to ensure that the 3rd Attack Position was finished. Margesson and CSM Ross crawled out with a bag of pegs, with paper flags attached, to mark out the line, including the fire bays and traverses, and then six men 'were told off to each bay'.[38] Working during this moonlit, but bitterly cold November night, the men made good progress without any hindrance from the Germans. Then at about 9 p.m., as if suddenly made aware of the work going on in front of them, the Germans opened with heavy machine-gun fire from Redoubts Nos. 1 and 2 (*Kaigan* and *Daitochin*), as a result of which, the company was ordered to spend the rest of the night in the front-line position. There was also heavy firing to the right of the Borderers, and the Germans were making good use of their searchlights. This activity suggested that the Japanese were making a big effort to bring matters to a conclusion as soon as possible, and there were reports that Redoubt No. 3 (*Chuo*) had been captured, but this was not confirmed until much later. The nervousness of the Germans meant that moving around the forward area was difficult, as was contact with the adjacent units as Lieutenant Beaumont-Walker discovered:

> On the night of the 6th November I was given a message to hand to Lieutenant Colonel Sullivan[39] at No. 1 Redoubt on the right flank. It was 10 pm and apart for continually veering a right incline I was not sure of where to locate him. On the journey – about a mile each way, I was 'washed' by searchlights and jumped into a ditch just before small arms fire whizzed past. This ditch was half full of water and after wading about 50 yards in it I jumped out only for a repetition performance of the same thing. On getting

out the second time I heard voices and eventually handed over the message.[40]

The Germans were understandably very jumpy that night, and it would appear that the commanding officer of the Japanese 48th Regiment (to the left of the British force) believed that Redoubt N⁰ 2 (*Daitochin*) was ready to fall, and considered that should an appropriate opportunity arise, it could be rushed and occupied. The Germans, mindful of the heavy shelling, kept only the smallest of garrisons in the front line of the redoubt, preferring to shelter as many men as possible within the redoubt itself. These could be called on should the shelling stop and an assault develop. On the night of 6/7 November, one and a third companies of the 48th Regiment worked themselves forward and dug in on the edge of the outer ditch of the redoubt and, although a considerable fire fight developed, they held their ground. This looked like the opportunity to take the redoubt, but the battalion commander of the 48th Regiment had to wait as Brigadier-General Yamada would not consent to the attack. In fact, his response came as a surprise to the battalion commander who was ordered to retire from the advanced position to the 3rd Attack Position. A short time later, Yamada issued a further order to the effect that the Redoubt N⁰ 2 was to be taken immediately. This rapid change of mind left the 48th Regiment very little time to prepare itself, and orders were issued at about 2 a.m. for an attack which was to take place two hours later. With the help of the engineers who made breaches and ramps within the defences, Redoubt N⁰ 2 fell at 5 a.m. The Japanese casualties were considerable: N⁰ 4 Company of the 48th Regiment lost all its officers and eighty per cent of its men (most to rifle fire from Redoubt N⁰ 1 to their right, and trenches some 200 yards beyond the redoubt). It had been a costly exercise but had resulted in the capture of the first part of the inner defences of Tsingtao. In a similar manner Redoubt N⁰ 3 (*Chuo*) also fell that morning:

> An officer of the regiment that captured the Chuo redoubt gave a short account of how it was done. A subaltern and about 40 men were told off as a forlorn hope (*kesshitai*) to rush into the redoubt and try and surprise the garrison. The Germans kept such a slack look-out that this was considered feasible. The subaltern started operations by addressing his men, lined them up facing east, and presented arms to the Emperor. Then after dark they worked their way up through the ditches and entanglements and dashed into the trench. They were opposed by a small number of the enemy, who were driven right and left along the trench. The subaltern, with a few men, got round to the doors of the underground rooms and stopped the enemy getting out to reinforce. He explained that he was in overwhelming force, and so the Germans (over 200) surrendered. Japanese reinforcements were brought up and the fort taken about 10 pm. Later another officer with about 10 men – this was the officer who told me the story – was sent out to reconnoitre behind the redoubt. He came on 2 sections of Field Artillery one behind the redoubt and the village of Taitung-Chen (Daitochin). In each case he was able to capture the guns and the gunners before the latter could damage the guns. The

gunners were all under cover in bomb proofs and the guns had been run into bomb proof sheds, so that he was able to make the enemy surrender before they could get out to offer any resistance. He could not reconnoitre very far he said, because of the fire of his own artillery.[41]

Unfortunately for the Borderers, the Japanese advance on the redoubts on their left and right had effectively put the battalion out of the action. As the Japanese moved out from the redoubts to cover the captured positions, they fanned out over the front that was to have been the Borderers assault objective. Some officers who were present believed that this action by the Japanese was a deliberate attempt to keep the British force out of the general advance and eventual fall of Tsingtao. Was the capture of the Redoubts on the night of the 6/7 November unplanned and purely fortuitous, or did the Japanese really not want the British force involved? The fact that the Japanese had advanced without warning, suggests the latter, but if it is remembered that the 3rd Attack Position on the British front was not finished, then perhaps the British force might not have been in a position to take part in the general advance against the redoubts anyway. If however, the action was simply opportunistic on the part of the Japanese, then the British could not have been involved. Although Yamada had issued the orders, they do not appear to have been passed on to the British. There would have been delays while any orders were translated and Yamada may have felt that these needed to be avoided. For whatever reason, the British force, Borderers and Sikhs, were excluded from these assaults on the redoubts, and were not even called upon to offer support.

On the morning of 7 November, the outcome of the attacks was not immediately clear to the British. Visibility was poor because of the smoke and dust created by the battle, but it was not long before the Germans were seen evacuating their trenches:

Cannonading heaviest we have ever heard. Furious cannonade up to 7.30 when Japanese began to cheer and a white flag went up. I went up to top of hill and saw Japs on top of Iltis. Others hurrying down all the roads to Tsingtao like children let out of school. An extraordinary sight. At 8.30 am we marched down motor road into Tsingtao took up our quarters in an artillery repairing shed.[42]

On the morning of the 7th November I was looking over the back of my trench and saw on the high ground 500 yards behind that the skyline was covered with Japanese troops with men holding white flags with a large red sun in the centre (Japanese National Flag) and yelling '*Banzai*'. I turned and focussed my field glasses over the front of my trench towards the redoubts and saw pockets of blue and grey of the enemy – German and Austrian sailors and soldiers – behind each of the Redoubts and Japanese flags flying from forts Moltke, Iltis and Bismarck – all fire had ceased. Tsingtao had fallen at dawn and 4,300 prisoners were taken.[43]

During the short, sharp action on Iltis, Plüschow's friend, *Oberleutnant*

Japanese troops inside the Iltis Fort.

Julius Aye, had fallen. He had been in charge of one of the batteries of ships' guns which had seen very little action but had been shelled enough for him to realize that the end of the siege could not be far away. He ordered his men to get what rest they could before the Japanese could mount their final assault, while he and one man mounted guard. It was not long before they were alerted by the noise of someone approaching. This turned out to be a party of Japanese, somewhat earlier than had been anticipated, led by an officer with a drawn sword. Aye, instead of alerting his small garrison to the danger, immediately drew his own sword and attacked the Japanese officer and, in a scene that would perhaps have been more appropriate to earlier wars, the two officers fought. The Japanese officer was a superior swordsman and in no time had wounded Aye in the thigh and right hand, before killing him with a blow to the neck. By that time, the garrison had been alerted and some vicious hand-to-hand combat followed, in which all but one of the German defenders was killed and the position fell as part of the general Japanese advance.[44]

At 7.30 a.m., Barnardiston ordered the general advance of the British troops. It had come as a complete surprise to the Borderers that the siege had ended so quickly and that they had not been involved. Although the flags of surrender had been seen and the Japanese flags fluttered over the key points, the siege ended on a sour note for the battalion as the last shell fired out of the Tsingtao before the official surrender landed on its lines and killed two men:

> The last shell fired before the surrender of the fortress accounted for four of the Borderers, Sergeant Miller was killed outright. Lance Corporal Sydenham was mortally wounded, and two other received injuries. Sydenham showed

rare courage on his way to hospital. Private Gibbons who was one of the stretcher party, recounts that one of Sydenham's legs was blown off, but he sang several songs as he was borne along, two having reference to his parents and home and one to the fact that he would need a wooden leg.

As the bearer party was taking him off Gibbons saw the white flag was hoisted and said 'it's all over Sydenham'. The wounded man replied 'Let's get up and have a look' and his wish gratified he expired.[45]

At 8.30 a.m., the battalion paraded and was marched towards Tsingtao. For Lieutenant Beaumont-Walker, the march was marred by the events of the night before, when he had been soaked through as a result of wading through a water-filled ditch to avoid some rifle fire. Returning to his dugout, he had removed his breeches and thrown them over the side to dry. In the morning, he spent time wrestling with his frozen breeches and was the last officer to appear on parade. As a consequence, instead of his platoon leading the company along the road into Tsingtao, it brought up the rear. According to some, they marched in columns of four and, in lieu of a regimental band, whistled '*Everybody's doing it*'.[46] There is no regimental record of this incident and it would seem to have been unlikely, bearing in mind that on the morning of 7 November, there were orders, issued by Kamio, as to the disposition of the assaulting troops and Barnardiston would have followed these to the letter, in view of the exchanges between him and the War Office.

The battalion's orders were initially to take up a line between Moltke and Bismarck Hills, before eventually moving to a position alongside the main road into town. Later, it was ordered to move across the road to occupy some

Capt Johnson visiting a German battery on Bismarck Hill damaged by Japanese shell fire.
[Royal Welsh Museum, Brecon, BRCRM 2005.70]

buildings that appeared to be German artillery repair sheds, possibly Moltke Huts, where it was billeted briefly. Sentries were posted on all the buildings in the vicinity and orders were received that nothing was to be removed from any of them. During the rest of the day, parties of Germans came to the sheds to claim their kit which they were allowed to take away. From time to time, the Borderers recognized men they had known in Tientsin, seemingly a lifetime ago, and although beaten, some of the prisoners-of-war firmly believed, as a result of the propaganda they had received during the siege, that Paris had fallen and that things were going badly for the allies on the Western Front. It came as a great shock to some of them to realize that they were mistaken and that there was probably no quick end in sight to their status as prisoners-of-war. Tsingtao had fallen and the Germans would eventually be taken off to Japan where they would be held for the duration of the war. For the Borderers, there was still much to do, but after 7 November, their time in Tsingtao was limited as there were to be calls on them to move to other theatres of the war.

Notes

1. Plüschow (2004), 55.
2. It is assumed that Margesson is referring to the Standard Oil and Asiatic Petroleum installation situated on the coast a little to the north of Moltke Hill.
3. It should be noted that, by this stage, the Japanese were using a tethered observation balloon to greater effect than had the Germans.
4. Margesson Diary, Royal Welsh Museum.
5. Plüschow (2004), 57.
6. Margesson's Diary, Royal Welsh Museum.
7. To the British, the redoubts were known as Redoubts 1 to 5 from the west end (right) of the Redoubt Line. To the Japanese, they were known as Kaigan, Daitochin, Chou, Jinzan and Shojinzan respectively. Both are used in contemporary accounts by the British soldiers. To the Germans, the redoubts were numbered 1 to 5 from the east end (right) of the Redoubt Line. Thus, the redoubt known to the British as Nᵒ. 2 was Nᵒ. 4 to the Germans.
8. Brigade War Diary – note the reference to the limited damage to the entanglements.
9. Hoyt (1975), 121.
10. Margesson Diary for 5 November.
11. Hoyt (1975), 118.
12. 9989 Lance Corporal John Cavalla.
13. Margesson Diary, 2 November, Royal Welsh Museum.
14. See, for instance, Margesson's Diary.
15. German officer's account reported by Jefferson Jones and published in *War Illustrated* Nᵒ. 14.
16. Going's account (Royal Welsh Museum) – compare this with the use of geotextiles and geogrids to improve ground conditions for construction purposes today.
17. German Diary, Royal Welsh Museum.
18. Simson's Report.
19. Simson's Report, Section 29.
20. German Dairy, Royal Welsh Museum.
21. Ibid.
22. German Diary, Royal Welsh Museum. Note the figures are as quoted in the diary and are nothing more than the diarist's estimates – see Chapter 2 for a more detailed breakdown of German numbers.
23. It would have been an interesting flight! It should be remembered that Plüschow, although a fine pilot, had never been in an aeroplane until early 1914 and had even less knowledge of design.
24. Plüschow (2004), 59.

25. Plüschow (2004), 59–60.

26. Plüschow continued his life of adventure after the war. He rounded Cape Horn twice on a sailing vessel before going on to explore Tierra del Fuego extensively in a sea plane, aptly named *Tsingtau*. He was killed when this aeroplane crashed on take-off in 1931. A glacier in Tierra del Fuego is named in honour of this redoubtable airman.

27. See Whittaker (1994), 147.

28. Captain Gilbert Henry Dive RAMC, Medical Officer to 2nd SWB.

29. Margesson's Diary, Royal Welsh Museum.

30. N° 4 Redoubt for the Germans.

31. Simson's Report.

32. Captain Johnson was awarded the DSO while Foley, Green, Snow and West received the DCM. Since the award of the DCM was not made posthumously, Pte. Evans was only to receive a Mention in Despatches.

33. Pepper Box refers to one of the concrete strong points created by the Germans intermediate to the redoubts and throughout the Redoubt Line.

34. Captain Bradstock's account of the incident contained in Casson's letter.

35. Simson's Report, Appendix 12.

36. Simson's Report, Appendix 13.

37. Atkinson, 82.

38. See Diary for the date concerned.

39. OC Commanding 36th Sikhs.

40. Beaumont-Walker's account, Royal Welsh Museum.

41. Simson's report.

Chapter 11

Aftermath

The collapse of the German defence and the end of the siege had surprised the allies. It appears that even General Kamio was caught unawares by the abrupt end to his campaign, although based upon the progress the campaign had made to that date, he had been anticipating a German capitulation in a day or so anyway. The Germans themselves were almost as surprised as the allies, but had recognized the futility of any further fighting and the resultant unnecessary bloodshed. They spent what they clearly recognized were the last hours of the siege, destroying anything that might be of use to the enemy, even going as far as burning postage stamps and paper currency amongst the documents they did not want to fall into either Japanese or British hands. When the allied troops entered Tsingtao, the Germans showed a certain disregard or grudging respect for the Japanese, but nothing of the sort for the British; one group of German soldiers supposedly about-faced as the first British soldiers arrived and bared their backsides to them in a mark of disrespect.[1] Lieutenant Beaumont-Walker records that the Germans 'paid us the doubtful courtesy of smacking their backsides at us and spitting as we passed'.[2] Their reaction to defeat, enraged Major Margesson so much, that he added to his diary of 7 November:

> A German officer spat on Pringle's boots and other German prisoners called 'Schwein'. They are a rotten race and don't know how to take a beating like a white man. It is a revelation to me of the German character. No British soldier would behave like that.[3]

The act of baring their backsides would probably have been considered by them to have been a great insult to the British, but it aroused a slightly amused reaction amongst some of the Borderers. It may well have been a disrespectful act, but the Borderers were seasoned, professional soldiers who, as the victors were unlikely to have been greatly upset by it. If the Germans had carried out the performance a little closer, there can be no doubt that they would have provided a perfect target for the British army boot, a suitable reponse suggested by one of the battalion![4] Fortunately, for the sake of law and order in the town, no-one was allowed to fall out to administer the treatment which such an action may have deserved and, in spite of the provocation, the Borderers behaved impeccably. Margesson's anger is perhaps understandable if it is considered in the light of the era in which it occurred; he would have expected nothing more than respect for himself and the battalion under the circumstances. The attitude of the defeated Germans can have done nothing but cause enmity where there had once been friendship and co-operation. There was probably no need for the Germans to have taken the action they did, but they had been stripped of everything and were about to become prisoners-of-war, and were dismayed that the British had fought against them as allies of the Japanese.

Immediately after the surrender, both the Japanese and the British were curious to see the forts and redoubts that had held out against them for so long and this caused a few problems of internal discipline. The Japanese headquarters had issued orders that nothing was to be disturbed or removed in the town and surrounding areas, and had placed guards on the most important sites, presumably to stop any looting. Of course, soldiers' curiosity got the better of them and parties of off-duty Borderers made their way to examine the redoubts. Since the guards had been posted, it can only be assumed that they got to see very little but the officers at least saw the thorough destruction caused by Kamio's artillery on the guns in the batteries and forts. As might be expected, these visits could not go unmentioned in Simson's report to the War Office. It appears that he considered the behaviour of the British soldiers reprehensible and reported that numerous acts of petty pilfering occurred, including the ludicrous accusations that one of the Borderers had stolen the socks of the officer commanding the 48th Regiment. It would be foolish to suggest that soldiers, either Japanese or British, did not help themselves to some mementoes from the battlefield – it simply must have occurred; one officer records the disappearance of a German officer's sword and suggests it was seen as a spoil of war by a colleague.[5] However, bearing in mind that soldiers in any war have a limited ability to carry, store, or transport souvenirs, it is unlikely that any large items could have been removed by anyone. As for the socks, every army is full of opportunists and such an occurrence is not worthy of being made an issue serious enough to be recorded in a report concerning the activities of the British soldiers and destined for the War Office. To some extent, Simson loses his credibility as an accurate chronicler of events in Tsingtao when his report degenerates to this level and there were those who had thoroughly respected his work during the Tsingtao campaign – Lieutenant-Colonel Casson amongst them – but even he was sadly disillusioned when he eventually saw the report that was forwarded to the War Office.[6] It is on record that when the petty pilfering of the Borderers was brought to the attention of their officers, many of the items were returned and an apology made to the Japanese which was graciously accepted, although not without some surprise that the Borderers had gone to such lengths to correct what they had seen as a minor error. The socks, however, remained lost![7]

The debris of war was everywhere and according to Private C. Small,

One of the captured German redoubts, probably Redoubt Nº 2.
[Royal Welsh Museum, Brecon, BRCRM 2005.70]

there were other things with which to be concerned:

> Well we paraded and marched to Tsingtao, and it was a sight I don't want to
> see again. On the road alone there were hundreds of dead and wounded
> Germans. Some must have been there for days. There were broken rifles,
> Maxim guns, bayonets and swords. You could see where some of those brave
> men had tried to get cover but caught it before they got there. One fellow on
> the road still had the rifle up to his shoulder and over 200 spent cartridges
> around him.[8]

The sentiments expressed by Small were echoed by an unnamed British
officer who commented:

> The entry into a place immediately after a bombardment is, to put it mildly,
> not pleasant. There were 26 dead Germans just lying in a ditch on the edge of
> the road as we marched in and the scene of desolation, destruction and ruin
> to buildings and property – shell holes through everything, with books
> clothing papers and what not piled up and hurled in a higgledy-piggledy
> mess – was an extraordinary and pitiable sight.[9]

The destructive effects of the Japanese artillery on the defences of Tsingtao
and of the fabric of the town as a whole, surprised many of the Borderers. It
was the first time that the majority of them had seen anything like it, but for
many, it would not be the last time as the Great War dragged the battalion
first through the destruction of Gallipoli and then the Western Front. An

The damage caused to the German defences by the bombardment is evident in this photograph of one of the reboubts.

account given by Jefferson Jones, an American civilian allowed into the town, gives a very similar picture of the plight of what had been a model German colonial town:

> Giant shells, some three feet long and a foot in diameter, were lying about on side-walk and street still unexploded. Trees, splintered at their bases, lay toppled over the avenues. Windows in the houses were shattered, while gaunt holes in the sides of buildings, where shells had torn their way, made residence blocks appear to be gasping for air.
>
> The whole scene was one of devastation, streets deserted of people, show fronts of stores completely gone as was also the merchandise, harbour deserted of ships, and not even the sign of a rickshaw to remind you of the Orient.[10]

In the forts and amongst the batteries, the Germans' efforts to destroy anything that might be of use to them, had been completed with the utmost thoroughness and effectively finished the job that had been started by the Japanese bombardment.[11] The breach blocks of the large guns had been prepared with nitro-glycerine and the guns tamped with powder so that when detonated, they spilt beyond any possibility of repair. In Bismarck and Moltke forts, the guns had been tamped upon their carriages so that both had been destroyed, and in some cases, the guns blown completely out of the fort. The explosions had been large enough in some instances to crack the concrete of the forts and expose the steel reinforcing bars. The Germans had, however, missed the point, as the thing of greatest value to the Japanese was the foothold in China that the town of Tsingtao gave them and which was now securely in their hands.

As the victorious Japanese soldiers arrived in the town, there was some misbehaviour and drunkeness as the troops celebrated. One or two of their soldiers even ended up in the local hospital, totally paralysed through drink. There were reports that some Japanese soldiers started to enter the private houses where they helped themselves to property and, although these occurrences were not widespread, even isolated incidents were enough to cause nervousness amongst the remaining residents of the town, particularly amongst those business men who had remained to look after their interests. Strict discipline was soon imposed by General Kamio and his staff and off-duty soldiers were not allowed into the town. The British were treated similarly and, even when the rules were relaxed, small groups of soldiers had to be accompanied by an officer. Generally, the civilian population of Tsingtao were treated respectfully since the Japanese did not want to be seen as the villains, and were hoping, not only to win over the residents, but to gain the understanding of the world community. Military hospitals were set up in several of the larger buildings which were partly staffed by soldiers' wives. Now the siege was over, the wounded of both sides were brought to these hospitals where they were cared for, irrespective of nationality, although the hospitals were now under the control of the Japanese Red Cross which issued a proclamation to assure each and every patient that they would be well looked after. This did much to calm things in the town which had been anticipating some harsh treatment at the hands of the Japanese.[12]

During the first few days of the occupation, the Japanese and British were busy gathering together all the weapons of war they could find, to ensure that the Germans were fully disarmed. There were a number of unfortunate incidents and some Japanese engineers were killed and wounded whilst disarming mines and trip-wires in the forward areas, redoubts and forts. There was also the need to make the streets safe again and the unexploded ordnance was cleared by Japanese engineers. The large number of shells that had failed to explode, suggested to one observer that the quality of Japanese ammunition left much to be desired. Overall, the Japanese take-over of the

Medical staff at a Japanese dressing station. [Royal Welsh Museum, Brecon, BRCRM 2005.70]

Japanese strecher bearers at Tsingtao.

town went very smoothly, and they outwardly adopted the stance of mag-
nanimous victors. On 9 November, they allowed the Germans to hold a
collective burial service for those men who had been killed in the action:

> It was an unusually lovely autumn day when great numbers of non-
> combatant German men, women and children swarmed out to the cemetery,
> ideally located at Iltis Platz a few score of metres from Plüschow's still
> smouldering hangar. Golden rays of sun shone onto the graves which were
> decorated with fresh greenery and wreaths. Paster [sic] Winter[13] and Father
> Schopperly[14] presided.
>
> With emotional fervour the minister described the devotion with which
> the brave warriors, true unto death, had given their lives for the Fatherland.
> Never will perish that which German industry and German culture have
> accomplished during years of hard work … Tsingtao is German and remains
> German.[15]

The Germans did not return after the war, but perhaps, the town has never
really lost the German influences of the early years of the twentieth century
and perhaps its later growth and success owes much to the example the
Germans had set in the seventeen years they had been in the area. Today,
over ninety years after the siege ended, there is still plenty to remind the
interested visitor that the town had once been a German outpost.

It was 10 November before Governor Meyer-Waldeck formally
surrendered to General Kamio. The time had been set for 10 a.m. and the
place for the ceremony was to be Moltke Fort. The Emperor of Japan had
given permission for Meyer-Waldeck to retain his sword as a mark of respect
for a defeated enemy and it is presumed that he wore it on this formal
occasion of the hand-over of power in the area. Kamio spoke first:

Maj J. A. Hartigan, RAMC, alongside a damaged machine-gun shield in Nᵒ 2 Redoubt.
[Royal Welsh Museum, Brecon, BRCRM A1959.103]

I regret that inevitable circumstances have brought on the war between Germany and Japan which had been connected by a close friendship, but allow me to state, Colonel Waldeck (sic),[16] that I have the deepest sympathy for the present condition of you and your faithful soldiers, who, being separated so far from your mother country have fought against us so bravely. I hope you will kindly remove your residence to my country and there take a rest awaiting the day of peace. In the event of your coming, I venture to say that the whole nation will welcome you with all their sympathy and respect for your nation.[17]

Kamio was, as ever, the gallant, chivalrous soldier and consummate diplomat, immediately putting the defeated adversary at ease and neither this, nor the nature of the meeting, was lost on Meyer-Waldeck who responded:

I thank you cordially, Lieutenant-General Kamio, for your deep sympathy and for every hospitable wish you have expressed. It is my great regret and sorrow that political relations have led to such closely united nations as the Japanese and the Germans into a terrible war. I had heard of the courage of the Japanese soldiers and this time they truly displayed it before my eyes, and I am really filled with hearty admiration.[18]

This brief exchange of pleasantries finished the formal proceedings and the two men then talked briefly about the terms of the surrender and the forthcoming evacuation of the town and the sojourn of the Germans as prisoners-of-war. It was all conducted in a very amicable atmosphere and finished with a champagne toast. There was no British presence at this meeting – the junior partner to the campaign had not been considered important enough to attend. This was seen by some as a great 'loss of face' for the British[19] but this is overstating the case. Brigadier-General Barnardiston had been ordered to act under Japanese orders and, although it would have been diplomatic for the Japanese to have invited their ally to this meeting, not to have done so would not have been seen as a loss of face. Barnardiston was acting directly on the orders of his government and may have looked upon the omission as 'bad form' on the part of the Japanese. Had the latter understood this, they would have realized that in behaving badly towards their ally, it was they who were in fact 'losing face'. It is easy to make rather too much of the incident since it did very little to affect the already tense situation between the allies, not in the least aided by the accidental shooting of two South Wales Borderers in the early stages of the campaign by the Japanese. There can be no doubt that the behaviour of the Japanese did ruffle a few feathers, and Major Margesson, although certainly considering it as 'humiliating', was equally as upset by the way the battalion had been treated throughout the campaign by its own government. The reality of the situation was that the British politicians had too much on their minds to be greatly concerned about a small-scale side show like Tsingtao. It was far easier for them to let the Japanese control the situation than to try to intervene from a distance of several thousand of miles. If Barnardiston had got the rather larger force that he had originally wanted, and if the British government had been able to adopt a more robust stance, then he might have been in a stronger diplomatic position and would have been able to ask for more recognition for his force's involvement in the siege. As it was, he had not gained the full support of his government for the desired military action, so could expect nothing from the diplomatic discussions that followed. Barnardiston could hardly have expected the Japanese to behave

German howitzer battery below Bismarck Hill destroyed by Japanese shell fire.
L–R: Lieut Cahusac, Capt Palmer, Lieut Morgan. [Royal Welsh Museum, Brecon, BRCRM 2005.70]

Japanese soldiers examining a captured German heavy machine-gun position.

better than his own government and would have recognized this fact and accepted it. However, it is quite wrong to assess this whole affair as a 'loss of face' for Britain[20] who did not leave the region throughout the Great War and continued to play a significant role there until 1997, when Hong Kong was formally handed back to China (when the lease on Kowloon and the New Territories expired). Britain in fact maintained a presence in the area long after other European powers had departed. Tsingtao was a minor event in her involvement in China which, for good or bad, lasted for over 200 years. Britain finally left Weihaiwei in 1922 as part of the outcome of the Washington Conference by which the Japanese were persuaded to return Tsingtao to the Chinese. It is therefore possible to argue that the Japanese, following the agreement which stalled their military and imperial ambitions in China for a decade, eventually lost far more than Britain in relation to the effort that they had expended on the capture of Tsingtao.[21]

Following the conclusion of the meeting, General Kamio allowed Governor Meyer–Waldeck to prepare a message for the Kaiser which he guaranteed would be sent through diplomatic channels to the German head of state as quickly as possible:

> With all my respect I beg to inform your Majesty that in consequence of exhaustion of our ammunition and of the great damage caused to our fortifications by the Japanese shells, our garrison of Kiou-chou was compelled to surrender to the Japanese who had attacked our forts as well as our town, from sea and land, so that it was not possible to check them. But I beg to state with gratitude that the casualties of his Majesty's army were very few considering the heavy damage done to the forts by the Japanese guns.[22]

The news reached the Kaiser who responded quickly through the American Embassy in Berlin and sent news that he had awarded Meyer-Waldeck the

Iron Cross, 1st Class, and promoted him to the rank of admiral in recognition of his gallant service to the Fatherland.

In Germany, the news of the fall of Tsingtao came fast on the heels of the victory at Coronel and was greeted with dismay, even though it cannot have been totally unexpected. In a very jingoistic newspaper article of 8 November, penned by Rear Admiral Schlieper, the sense of outrage can be felt:

> A sudden pang may flash through us when we view so much German blood spilled, but at the same moment our hearts should beat in fervent gratitude for our heroes of Tsingtao …
>
> A dreary, melancholy, grey November day without! Gone is the decoration of flags and rejoicing of the day of Coronel! Everything in its time! Today the throb of our hearts belongs to you heroes out yonder, our whole mood, our whole sentiment; for you have fought as Germans heroes have never been able to do.
>
> But we here at home, we will continually repeat to our children: Do not forget November 7 1914; do not forget to pay back those yellow Asiatics, who learned so much from us, for the great wrong they have done to us, stirred though they were by the petty English mercenary spirit.[23]

There can be no doubt that the loss of Tsingtao was keenly felt in some quarters, not least since it was an important colony for the Germans, and perhaps had it not been for the scale of the fighting in Europe, would have been more clearly remembered, and more keenly felt, by all the nations involved. As it was, Tsingtao would soon be consigned to a small corner of the thoughts of Germans as they struggled with the power of the allies in the west. However, for the moment there was anger that the Japanese had sided

Japanese troops march into Tsingtao.

Joyful Japanese soldiers being driven around in a captured German lorry.

with the British when their army had, to a large extent, been modelled on, and trained by the German army.

However, in spite of all the differences that the action in Tsingtao may have caused between the Germans and the Japanese, the latter treated Meyer-Waldeck with utmost respect and consideration, including getting a message to his mother, although this courtesy was not extended to anyone else captured in Tsingtao. On 14 November, Meyer-Waldeck and his twelve staff officers left Tsingtao on board a Japanese ship which carried them to Kiushu where he was given a European-style mansion, facing the sea of Genkai, where he lived for the duration of the war. The Japanese continued to treat him particularly well and he was allowed to send for his wife and children to join him for his period of enforced captivity.

On the day before the formal German surrender, there had been an opportunity for the officers of the South Wales Borderers to get a closer look at the effect of the Japanese bombardment. Major Margesson recorded the event in some detail in his diary:

> After lunch, Dive, Going, Greenway[24] and I walked over N⁰. 2 Redoubt and our advanced trench. N⁰. 2 was quite flattened out by Jap guns which, however, did not damage the barbed wire entanglements to any appreciable extent. The front face consisted of a wall of reinforced concrete behind which was splinter proofs with patent box loopholes. This concrete wall was knocked down and the front line must have been untenable. The Maxim guns only could fire. The shelters behind were deep down and bomb proof. Here the Germans probably lived by day and only manned the front trench by

night. They must have lost large numbers of the garrison from shell fire ... No forts are proof against heavy artillery. It is only a question of time.[25]

There are a number of features in this account which are worthy of note and perhaps would have helped the planners of future battles on the Western Front had they been aware of them. The first of these points is that artillery did little damage to the barbed wire entanglements – a lesson that had to be learned over and over again as the war in Europe progressed. Secondly, is that the Germans occupied deep, bomb-proof shelters and were thus able to man the line when required in the event of an attack. How depressingly familiar this would become to many of the officers and men who served on the Western Front – the front line may have been untenable, but there would be sufficient men available to defend the ground, with the assistance of machine guns. This situation was to occur when the 2nd South Wales Borderers were attacking Beaumont-Hamel on 1 July 1916 and the battalion suffered heavily as a direct result of this style of defence. The Germans in Tsingtao had already developed some of the defensive tactics which were to become so familiar on the Western Front. Finally, Margesson's comment on the effect of heavy artillery indicated that this weapon was to play an increasingly important part in the war. Many of the Borderers who were present at the siege of Tsingtao would witness the awesome power of artillery in the later battles of the Great War.

The same day that Margesson and his fellow officers made the inspection of Redoubt N°. 2, the battalion also recorded the thanks of the Emperor of Japan:

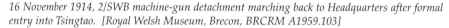

16 November 1914, 2/SWB machine-gun detachment marching back to Headquarters after formal entry into Tsingtao. [Royal Welsh Museum, Brecon, BRCRM A1959.103]

His Majesty, the Commander in Chief of the Forces on land and sea, is filled with admiration for the feat accomplished by the British land and sea Forces, acting in conjunction with the Japanese Forces in the attack on Tsingtao, and for the courageous and intrepid manner in which the enemy's powerful fortifications have been captured and their warships sunk, thereby bringing about the fall of the enemy's citadel and the realization of the final object of the war.[26]

Whether these thanks made Margesson and his comrades feel any better about being left out of both the final assault and the official surrender on 10 November is not recorded – it is to be assumed that they did not. For the Japanese, the war was over and they had been victorious. It had been a short, sharp affair that had required little more than an enlarged division to accomplish. Whether or not the defeat of the Germans in Tsingtao was actually the 'final objective' of their war is a separate question which will be looked at in more detail later.

Meanwhile, arrangements were being made to the get all the Germans out of the town. According to one Japanese source,[27] the Germans, following a lead set by the Kaiser, and perhaps echoed in Schlieper's newspaper article, saw the Japanese as the 'Yellow Peril' and had been prepared for the utmost brutality when the victors arrived in the town. It could not be denied that there had been some looting, but the Japanese soon clamped down on that and, on the whole, the defeated Germans were treated much better than the poor Chinese peasants whose villages had suffered as the Japanese army passed by. There would seem to be no consensus on the number of Germans taken prisoner, the quoted figures varying between 2,300 and 4,000. Many of the men who had been civilian reservists before the siege commenced, simply returned to being civilians as soon as the fighting ceased, and the figure for the total regular military personnel taken prisoner is probably close to the lower figure quoted whilst the total number of those who bore arms is likely to be closer to the higher figure which approximates to the strength of the whole garrison given by contemporary commentators.[28] The treatment of Meyer-Waldeck was not representative of the way the rest of the Germans were treated. For them, life was not as comfortable. The prisoners-of-war were rounded up in small groups, and held in a hastily-prepared camps at the foot of Prince Henry Hill for a few days which, bearing in mind, the deteriorating weather, must have been uncomfortable. Eventually, everyone of military age was placed in the camp so that shop keepers and clerks, who may well have served as reservists, were rubbing shoulders with the regulars of the 3rd *See Battailon*. The prisoners were marched out on 13, 14 and 15 November and embarked on the ships which took them to captivity in Japan. They arrived in Tokyo on 22 November and, according to Japanese sources, were comfortably housed and looked after 'as brave prisoners-of-war should be'.[29] On arrival in Japan, they were divided among twelve prison camps throughout the country where they remained until January 1920. Some of the more seriously wounded, approximately

German naval prisoners of war.

seventy in number, were taken by the British to Hong Kong where they received the best of medical care and were subsequently interned. There, they were joined by about a further 100 German nationals who had been picked up by the British in the Crown Colony businesses or on their way to Tsingtao and had been held on the Stonecutters Island in Hong Kong bay.[30] Both groups were held until the beginning of 1916 in a camp in Kowloon after which they were transported to Liverpool[31] prisoner-of-war camp in Australia, where they remained until March 1919. They were released more than nine months before their comrades held in Japan.

On 16 November, the parade to mark the official entry into Tsingtao took place which included a mixed company of the South Wales Borderers (including the machine-gun section) and a company of Sikhs. The parade also served as an act of remembrance for those lost in the battle. The Shinto service, like the German service held at Iltis Platz, was attended by the staff of both countries and a reported 20,000 troops, and took place around a wooden obelisk that had been specially constructed for the occasion by the Japanese engineers. Kamio led the service reading from a scroll to begin:

> I, the humble General Kamio, Commander-in-Chief of Japanese forces, express my hearty condolences to the souls of the dead who have been killed in battle or have passed away from illness contracted during our days of war ...[32]

When he had finished, he handed the scroll to his aide, and taking a pine branch bowed and placed it at the foot of the obelisk. It was a simple ceremony of respect and remembrance that took only a few minutes to complete, although by the time the march out took place, the whole event had lasted over an hour and a half.

On 15 November, the Borderers had been warned that they would be leaving Tsingtao in the near future. A War Office telegraph, delivered via HMS *Triumph*, standing off in the bay, ordered them to make straight for England in readiness for deployment in the European theatre – most of them would not be returning to Tientsin. They were to embark aboard the hospital ship, *Delta*, which was directed to Hong Kong where they were joined by the details left behind at Tientsin, who had made their way there using locally-hired transport. Major Going and a small party left Tsingtao for Tientsin where he was to settle up affairs and bring all the battalion's heavy kit from the barracks in readiness for their departure for Europe. The garrison in Tientsin was to be significantly reduced for the duration of the war and comprised of no more than one Indian Army battalion which, in 1914, was the 36th Sikhs. Under these circumstances, as soon as the ceremony of remembrance had been completed, Margesson and Captain Palmer took the opportunity of their remaining time in Tsingtao to explore the town a little:

> It is beautifully situated with a magnificent harbour for small ships at any rate … The town is very well laid out with houses with red tiled roofs and white walls – very broad streets. Governor's grounds are well laid out, three cement tennis courts and well wooded, quite like Europe, plane trees, cypress, privet, small oaks and pines with cones in clusters, Spanish chestnuts.[33]

The Germans had worked hard in their time in charge of Tsingtao and Margesson's comments, whilst perhaps limited, do not hide his obvious mild admiration. The following day, work began in preparation for the Borderers' departure, while Brigadier-General Barnardiston and his staff were given an official lunch at the Governor's residence, as guests of

The obelisk erected on Iltis Platz in recognition of the dead.

Lieutenant-General Kamio. The route for their departure was to be via Sha-tzu-kou Bay, south of Laoshan Bay and closer to the town, where they would pick up their transports which included the hospital ship, *Delta*. On 17 November, their heavy baggage began the journey to the embarkation point under the control of Captain Greenway and C Company.

The following day, the battalion left Tsingtao for Sha-tzu-kou Bay which they reached at 5 p.m. that afternoon. The officers were surprised to find Major Going waiting there for them, having been unable to proceed to Tientsin after receiving a War Office telegraph message warning that no-one from the expeditionary force should return for fear that they would be interned by the neutral Chinese government. This would seem to have been a bit of an overreaction from the British authorities as the Japanese had already ignored all neutrality issues, but it did recognize the potential for an unnecessary diplomatic incident and took steps to ensure that it did not happen and probably took into account the fact that German nationals had already been interned in China.

> The Japanese 48th Regiment lined the road with one company near Tai-tung-chen village and cheered '*Banzai*' throwing their hands up. They gave the mounted officers saki and took photographs of us. All Japs on road cheered. At Sha-tzu-kou they did all they could to help us. Hawatashi came on board and made a farewell speech … *Delta* is a fine ship, but only fitted out as a hospital ship, not as a troop ship. Food excellent.[34]

16 November 1914, 2/SWB Battalion baggage leaving Tsingtao at the end of the campaign.
L–R: Capt Johnson, Maj E. W. Jones, Capt Bradstock, Maj Margesson.
[Royal Welsh Museum, Brecon, BRCRM A1959.103]

Lieutentant-Colonel Casson's comments on the departure are much the same, but rather more detailed:

> ... when the Battalion marched out of Tsingtao at very short notice the Japanese soldiers for several miles down the road turned out and cheered ('Banzai') lustily and very heartily, while our men answered equally heartily. They even did the same with out small rear guard which followed about an hour after the Battalion; there was so much cheering that it was difficult to maintain or expect to maintain march discipline, moreover I was especially asked to allow the Mounted officers to fall out while the remainder of the Battalion went on and I felt reluctantly bound to consent; we accordingly did fall out and were invited to drink 'Saki' with the Japanese Officers.
>
> The Colonel of the 48th Regiment came to meet us, lined his men up on the roadside to cheer us, and insisted on our drinking 'Saki' with him and his Officers, made us be photographed together and generally gave us a most hearty and enthusiastic send off; yet this is the Colonel whose socks are said to been 'stolen' ...
>
> Finally, when we had actually embarked for England, the Japanese Staff Officer ... Major Hawatachi (who had ridden all the way from Tsingtao to see us off) came on the ship and asked me if he might see all the Officers together; he then made a most flattering speech to us in English, stated what a great pleasure it had been to him and to all of them to meet the Regiment and thanked us for our most hearty co-operation and kindly help on all occasions. He further expressed to me his very great regret that through no fault of ours or of his, neither we nor he had been in the final rush. He could not possibly have been more complimentary to the Battalion, and I can only say that so far as I am myself concerned all my dealings with him Regimentally and otherwise were of the most friendly nature.

For the South Wales Borderers, the involvement in China was almost over. Four days later, they arrived in Hong Kong having received an unexpected telegraph of congratulations on their recent action from Colonel Lenkovitch of the Russian army who, although not been involved, had watched the developments in China with interest:

> 24th Siberian Rifles on occasion of Regimental Festival send you from Far East best wishes for glorious victory over mutual enemy. Hope meet after crossing enemy's country.[35]

For Brigadier-General Barnardiston, however, the route home was rather different. He was to make a goodwill visit to Japan where he arrived on 9 December. There, he was treated as a hero and his entry into Tokyo was through streets lined with cheering and flag-waving civilians and children from the local schools. He was treated more like visiting royalty than the leader of a small force of British soldiers who had acted in concert with the Japanese, and was granted an audience with the Emperor who decorated him with the Order of the Rising Sun, 2nd Class. Similar awards were made to two members of his staff, Major H. G. Pringle (4th Class) and Captain C.

D. H. Moore (5th Class), during this visit.[36] The Japanese certainly treated Barnardiston with great respect and whilst this may have surprised him, he was comfortable with the situation since he had always been considered a fine, cultured soldier and diplomat, rather happier in the drawing room than on the battlefield. He left Japan on 19 December by which time he had also acquired gifts from the Emperor. However, apart from a hearty send off, the Japanese made no recognition of the work that had been carried out by the South Wales Borderers.

The battalion was temporarily split up at Hong Kong with only A Company going to the camp in Kowloon as originally intended. Rains had flooded part of the camp and, as a result, B and D companies were billeted in the Royal Garrison Artillery Barracks in Kowloon while C Company went to billets on Hong Kong island. They remained in Hong Kong for ten days, just long enough to get beaten at rugby by the Royal Navy, in a match organized in Happy Valley by way of relaxation. From there, they sailed to Singapore, wary of the threat from von Spee's squadron as they had no knowledge of its whereabouts. As soon as the news of the Battle of the Falkland Islands, and the destruction of von Spee's squadron on 8 December, reached the battalion they continued their journey and reached Southampton on 22 January, before moving on to Coventry where they were to be included in the last, and perhaps one of the most famous, regular army divisions to be formed – the Twenty-ninth. In this division, their history was one of epic struggles in titanic battles – Gallipoli, Somme, Arras, Passchendaele, Cambrai and others. At the end of the war, the Battle Nomenclature Committee awarded the 2nd South Wales Borderers, the Battle Honour 'Tsingtao', becoming the only British battalion to gain the distinction. The 36th Sikhs, of the Indian Army, were honoured similarly. The Borderers were the only British regiment to serve alongside the Japanese during the Great War and, perhaps, did not get the recognition they deserved for their part in a very trying campaign that was eclipsed by the later events of a savage and bloody war.

For the Japanese at Tsingtao, the departure of the British and Sikh contingent was simply the beginning of their occupation of the area. It had been suggested that the 36th Sikhs should remain in the Tsingtao to act as support for the Japanese occupation. In reality, Britain wanted to maintain surveillance on her ally in China and thought that the Sikhs were more likely to be accepted by the Japanese who were not in the least impressed by the idea and the British government, with more pressing issues on its mind, did not pursue the possibility. The Japanese were essentially left in charge of this part of the Shandong peninsula. It was the way they had wished things to turn out and it was not long before they did more to assert their war-won rights in Tsingtao, in the form of an ultimatum to the Chinese government, known as the 'Twenty-one Demands',[37] which set out their visions and desires for the former German colony. The ultimatum was divided in to five categories: Group I (four articles or demands) dealt with building better

2/SWB halt on the Japanese light railway near Sha-tzu-kou Bay on leaving Tsingtao, 18 November 1914, prior to embarking. [Royal Welsh Museum, Brecon, BRCRM 1984.64]

friendship between Japan and China; Group II (seven articles) set out the requirement for Chinese recognition of the Japanese predominant position in Manchuria; Group III (two articles) stated that the Chinese had no rights to handle the assets of the Han Yeh Ping Company[38] without the express approval of the Japanese; Group IV (one article) forbade the Chinese from leasing any port to another power (a ridiculous demand considering the British position in Hong Kong); Group V (seven articles) designed to force the Chinese to employ Japanese in influential positions. These demands, unpleasant as they were, were submitted to the Chinese in January 1915, and made it clear that the Japanese had no intention of returning Tsingtao to China, although that had been a stated aim of for the invasion of Chinese neutrality at the beginning of the campaign. China did not want to be coerced into what amounted to another 'unequal treaty' which had so bedevilled the latter days of the Qing dynasty, and they prevaricated for months and attended diplomatic conferences with a view to giving diplomacy, internal and external, time to work upon the Japanese in their favour. Japanese patience lasted only until 7 May 1915, when they issued revised demands and with them, threatened war. China could not consider fighting the Japanese, and on 8 May 1915, acquiesced to all the demands (although the majority of articles in Group V were removed)[39] which gave the Japanese power in the former German territory and the surrounding area. By the time this diplomatic result had been achieved many of the 2nd South Wales Borderers, including Major Margesson, were lying dead on the battlefields of Gallipoli. Their war had moved into a completely different dimension from that experienced by the Japanese during the siege of Tsingtao.

The Great War had given the Japanese the motive and opportunity to move into China, something they had been angling to achieve for decades, and for the remainder of the war, they controlled the region. It was 1922 before Tsingtao was returned to the Chinese, an outcome that was only brought about by diplomatic pressure being exerted by the United States of America, supported by Britain.[40] The Japanese sojourn in Tsingtao had been relatively brief but it was not many years before they returned in larger numbers to treat the Chinese population with a brutal barbarity, especially at Nanking,[41] that was, perhaps, unequalled by even the worst excesses of Nazi Germany.

Notes

1. Whittaker (1994), 161.
2. Beaumont-Walker's account, Royal Welsh Museum.
3. Margesson's Diary, Royal Welsh Museum.
4. See *South Wales Daily News* for January 1915.
5. Beaumont-Walker's account, Royal Welsh Museum.
6. Simson's report reached Casson, via the War Office, as he was about to embark on the troop ship bound for Gallipoli and so, with much more pressing matters to occupy him and without

reference to any of the relevant documents that may have assisted him, he was expected to make an appropriate response to the comments it contained. Needless to say, Casson's response is a fairly robust defence of his battalion. Both can be seen at the Royal Welsh Museum.

7. See Casson's letter of response to Simson's report.

8. Small's (9918 Pte. C. Small) account in the *Daily Chronicle* 1915.

9. The *Cardiff Times* 16.01.1915.

10. Jefferson Jones' account. See Hoyt (1975), 141.

11. See Hoyt (1975), 141 and Burdick (1976), 180 ff.

12. Whittaker (1994), 164.

13. Father Ludwig Winter who had been in Tsingtao since 1905.

14. Father Herman Schopperly, the Catholic priest of the German community.

15. Whittaker (1994), 165.

16. Note the rank given here is incorrect as the town was governed by the German Navy – this is most likely to be a mistake in translation of the original document from the Japanese.

17. Yamada, *USM* (December 1914), 281.

18. Ibid.

19. Whittaker (1994), see also the discussions throughout Burdick (1976).

20. Ibid. the Official Surrender seems to have been so unimportant to the British that it did not even warrant a mention in the Brigade War Diary.

21. Roberts (2003), 354. Here Roberts also points out that as a result of China declaring war on Germany in 1917, she was able to attend both the 1919 Peace Conference and the Washington Conference where her voice was heard independently of the other states.

22. Yamada, *USM* (December 1915) – note slightly different text given in Whittaker (1994).

23. Horne (1923 edn.), posted on First World War. com.

24. Captain T. C. Greenway.

25. Margesson Diary, 09.11.1914.

26. Quoted in Margesson's Diary, 09.11.1914.

27. Yamada, *USM* (December 1914).

28. See von Gottberg (1915).

29. Yamada *USM* (December 1914).

30. See Lucas (1926), 436, and Welsh (1997), 362.

31. Liverpool Camp was the largest internment camp in Australia holding almost 7,000 people for the duration of the war. The majority of these were Germans who had been living in Australia at the start of the war. The camp was situated in Liverpool on the outskirts of Sydney. See www. naa. gov. au. The camp was well-equipped with cafés, restaurants, butchers' shops etc; generally conditions were considered to be good and the internees well looked after. There was also a hospital which took care of the camps needs and included special care for sufferers of tuberculosis and sexually- transmitted diseases.

32. Hoyt (1975), 144.

33. Margesson Diary.

34. Margesson Diary, Royal Welsh Museum.

35. Recorded in Margesson's Diary. Lenkovitch was CO of the 24th Siberian Rifles and by virtue of the regimental number was seen as an associate of the SWB.

36. See Hoyt (1975), 145.

37. These are set out in the appropriate appendix.

38. This company was the largest coal and steel company in Shandong and effectively the Japanese were assuming control, both militarily and economically, of this part of China.

39. Dickinson (1999), 100.

40. Roberts (2003), 354.

41. An excellent account of the capture of Nanking by the Japanese and the treatment of its inhabitants can be found in Chang (1998), 35 ff.

Chapter 12

Tsingtao in Context

T he fact that after more than ninety years, only a few people have heard of the siege of Tsingtao in the context of a military campaign, may suggest that it was either particularly unsuccessful or not very relevant to either the history of the Great War or to belligerents of that war. Closer examination would suggest that neither of these assertions can be sustained.

The success of the campaign for the allies was without doubt due to the Japanese involvement and their ability to throw sufficient weight behind the effort to ensure the capture of the German town. If the situation had been left to the British government alone, it is unlikely that, in 1914, with other more pressing demands in Europe, anything would have been done. Of course, the British had long recognized the tactical importance of the harbour as a place to provide sustenance and shelter for the German Far East Squadron and there can be no doubt they also recognized the folly of giving von Spee's squadron free rein in the Pacific. Von Spee could have probably done more significant damage to the British trade and supply routes had his ships been allowed to roam the Pacific with a safe base to return to at Tsingtao. This would have had a significant effect on Britain's ability to maintain her supplies much earlier in the war, before the introduction of unrestricted submaring warfare.

Knowing there is a problem is only part way to finding a solution for it. The British knew that they could not spare men for the Far East when they had insufficient manpower with which to handle the situation developing in France and Flanders. Britain was drawing men from Canada, Australia, New Zealand and India, to support the mother country, and there were therefore too few soldiers in the Far East. In Hong Kong and Tientsin, these probably amounted to no more than 6,000 men, a pitifully small force to handle a campaign of the scale mounted against Tsingtao by the Japanese. Could a division or two, and all their necessary support mechanism have been found to send to China? If Britain had used a stronger force, the outcome would not have changed – Tsingtao would still have fallen, but perhaps the political balance would not have shifted so much in Japan's favour. However, it was not possible to divert any divisions since the troops from the Empire, particularly those closest to south-east Asia – the

Australians and the New Zealanders – were largely untrained and untested and, whilst very willing and enthusiastic, their use could have been a recipe for disaster. No-one can question the value of these troops later in the war, but in 1914, the problem would have been exacerbated by placing such divisions to fight alongside the very professional Japanese, and against the equally professional Germans. The Indian Army, which also had a presence in China, was preparing for France and could divert few men to Tsingtao. The British also recognized that a blockade of Tsingtao, to restrict its usefulness to Germany, and isolate its garrison was not a viable option, as it would tie up both men and ships for far too long, resources which could be used elsewhere.

Britain had a treaty of friendship with Japan and, as near neighbours to China, it would have seemed logical to ask them for assistance and to oversee the developments in the area as a whole. Of course, in the first few weeks of the war, Britain did not know what sort of assistance would be needed. Nevertheless, asking for support created a very difficult diplomatic problem as Britain could hardly dictate to her ally the nature of the support, which had been unreservedly offered. Japan welcomed the opportunity to assist and entered into the preparations for war with enthusiasm, although within Japan, there was a naval faction that considered it more prudent not to become embroiled in the battles of other nations.[1] Nevertheless by 1914, Japan saw herself as the major player in the Far East, and the apparent British problem presented a golden opportunity to provide proof of that status to two of the major powers in Europe – one as an ally and one as an enemy. Once war had been declared by Japan, the die was cast and there was only one possible outcome to the ensuing campaign in China. As the German diarist quoted in previous chapters commented, there was but one hope for the Germans in Tsingtao and that was that Germany won a quick victory over the allies in Europe and, as victors could then dictate terms to all the allies, including the Japanese. Once it was clear that this quick victory was not going to happen, the Germans in Tsingtao were left largely to their own devices and could only stall the Japanese and the British.

If the outcome of a campaign is seen to be more or less a foregone conclusion, then what criteria should be used to measure its success? Of course, capturing the main objective should be the primary measure, but along with this should be a consideration of the casualties sustained to gain that objective, as well as the logistics and the efficiency of the campaign. The primary objective, the fall of Tsingtao, was gained reasonably quickly, once all the various pieces of the siege were put in place. Therefore, from that point of view, the campaign was a resounding success. In order to meet this declared aim, the Japanese had expended considerable effort, but from the naval point of view, the campaign was perhaps not a total success. Although the naval blockade had successfully kept the Germans confined to their fortress and assisted in the destruction of the forts, it had cost the Japanese one destroyer and one cruiser, as well as several smaller vessels, such as mine-sweepers, which fell victims to the mines they were clearing. This meant that the naval casualties were almost the same as those of the land forces.

Depending on the sources consulted, the Japanese are believed to have put between 40,000 and 60,000 men into the field. The lower figure is probably closer to the truth as this appears to be the approximate equivalent of two divisions, the 18th Independent Division and the attached troops of various types, taking the total to well over 30,000. During the campaign, the Japanese Army was said to have lost 415 men killed and 1,451 men wounded,[2] approximately five per cent casualties which, compared to later battles of the Great War, should be considered as low. From this point of view therefore, the campaign was a great success. The official German losses were 199 killed and 294 wounded, from a much smaller force of around 4,000 men. These casualty figures depend, to a large extent, upon the source used. One Japanese source states that the Japanese had 394 killed and 1,458 wounded[3] and again, there were reports, mainly German, that the Japanese had more than 1,700 killed – but this, even allowing for the naval casualties, would be considerably higher than most estimates, although perhaps it tells something about the full frontal attacks which were popular with the Japanese at this time. Added to these battle casualties, are those men who died from sickness, and it should be remembered that Kamio made special mention of these men in the memorial service in Tsingtao. Perhaps, it is not surprising to learn that there were a substantial number of deaths from dysentery when the comments of the British officers on the Japanese sanitary arrangements are considered. To learn that sickness may have resulted in military losses of as many as 12,000[4] is shocking for such a relatively small and short campaign. If this latter figure, in excess of a quarter of the total force, is correct, then perhaps the success of the campaign should be viewed differently.

From the point of view of bringing both men and guns into action, it must be said that the Japanese had thought through the campaign much more thoroughly than the British. Within hours of landing at Laoshan Bay, the former had started to construct a light railway to get the supplies moving from the depot to the front; they had also organized ammunition and food supplies, but still managed to allow their infantry to travel lighter than the British soldiers. Their men were never short of food and, therefore, never went on to short rations as did the British, for at least part of the time. This suggests that their planning and implementation of the operation had been thorough. Despite this, the Japanese believed was that the British were better off.

> On land, an English transport party was stationed, ready to follow the main body, which had left to join the Japanese force. In the tents of the British troops there were so many electric lights that our soldiers became envious. They envied also the superiority of the English clothes and foodstuffs, the comfortable bedding and the hundreds of cattle, one to be killed every day

and three on a Sunday. 'How luxurious!' cried a Jap: 'the English are beyond us in the matter of food, clothes and living'; and the Japanese had to continue their forced march with only their pickled plums and boiled rice to sustain them.[5]

The Borderers would not have recognized this description of their campaign since their experience was very different, as witnessed by the problems they encountered during their march up from Laoshan Bay and until their transport caught up with them many days later.

The Japanese also had a detailed programme for the siege and capture of Tsingtao, which was flexible in so far as time lost due to storms during their approach to the siege positions, but as far as possible, it was adhered to rigidly – hence some of the difficulties experienced by the South Wales Borderers when preparing the 2nd and 3rd Attack Positions. Nevertheless, the Japanese probably regarded their supply, distribution and timetable deadlines as successes. For the British, even Major Margesson was to comment that there had been bad staff work in the preparations for the campaign. There had been very little consideration given at government level to how the small force was to survive and, at least according to Margesson, even the simplest issues such as a supply train, had been overlooked. However, British involvement was relatively minor which was reflected by casualties of no more than sixteen dead and sixty wounded – about eight percent of the force (these figures included at least two Borderers who died as a result of over-sensitive Japanese sentries). If the campaign is looked at from a purely British perspective, it would probably not be considered a great success, but neither could it be deemed a failure. In hindsight, it was, possibly a waste of effort to send such a small force to achieve what was effectively a political rather than a military end. It was too small, even allowing for the inclusion of the Sikhs, to influence the Japanese in their approach to the siege, or its ultimate outcome. The British had finished on the winning side but that was of little military significance when set against the large effort that was gearing up in France and Flanders. It was, possibly, no more than good field-training for the Borderers in preparation for the rigours of the war in Europe and, at least initially, they did not feel it was something which they should be involved in, believing that they were needed in France.

From the political point of view, the success of the campaign needs to consider the stated goals and the unstated ambitions the Japanese had for the campaign. The goal of capturing Tsingtao and returning it to the Chinese was never met, and the Japanese gained very few friends amongst the powers they had set out to impress. From this standpoint, the Japanese lost more than they gained. Their stated aim in breaching Chinese neutrality at the outset, that is the return of Tsingtao to the Chinese, was not achieved. Their subsequent 'Twenty-one Demands'[6] eventually gave voice to their initially unstated ambitions and set out the framework for their intention of holding power in China and the influence they were to have within the area in the coming years, including a controlling influence in the Han-Yeh-Ping Company. This was important for this Chinese company controlled much of the iron, steel and coal which Japan relied upon for its future military and economic expansion. In the long run, these demands did nothing to improve Japanese credibility in the area, and it took considerable diplomatic pressure to resolve this situation some four years after the Great War ended. The chief, but unstated, war aim of the Japanese was to gain a hold of Chinese territory and from there, be able to influence and where possible control their larger and more populous neighbour. In the short term, this was a success, but in the long term, Japan lost out by alienating those states that might have proved useful to them. The rise in Japanese militarism led them to ignore the need for allies – they had single-handedly beaten the Chinese in 1895, the Russians in 1904–05 and, with only minor assistance from the British, the Germans in 1914. There can be little doubt that the Japanese saw the Tsingtao campaign as a great success which signalled their arrival on the world stage much more than the defeat of Russia had done a decade earlier. They felt that they were now able to treat with the western powers as an equal.

The Chinese were not happy with the Japanese attitude and did all they could via diplomatic means to stall them, but in May 1915, the Japanese government issued an ultimatum which left the Chinese in no doubt of their intentions:

> The reason why the Imperial Government opened the present negotiations with the Chinese Government is first to endeavour to dispose of the complications arising out of the war between Japan and China, and secondly to attempt to solve those various questions which are detrimental to the intimate relations of China and Japan with a view to solidifying the found-ation of cordial friendship subsisting between the two countries to the end that the peace of the Far East may be effectually and permanently preserved.
>
> With this object in view, definite proposals[7] were presented to the Chinese Government in January of this year, and up to today as many as twenty-five conferences have been held with the Chinese Government in perfect sincerity and frankness.
>
> In the course of negotiations the Imperial Government have consistently explained the aims and objects of the proposals in a conciliatory spirit, while on the other hand the proposals of the Chinese Government, whether important or unimportant, have been attended to without any reserve.
>
> It may be stated with confidence that no effort has been spared to arrive at a satisfactory and amicable settlement of those questions.
>
> The discussion of the entire corpus of the proposals was practically at an end at the twenty-fourth conference; that is on the 17th of the last month.
>
> The Imperial Government, taking a broad view of the negotiation and in consideration of the points raised by the Chinese Government, modified the original proposals with considerable concessions and presented to the Chinese Government on the 26th of the same month the revised proposals for agreement, and at the same time it was offered that, on the acceptance of the revised proposals, the Imperial Government would, at a suitable opportunity,

restore, with fair and proper conditions, to the Chinese Government the Kiaochow territory, in the acquisition of which the Imperial Government had made a great sacrifice.

On the first of May, the Chinese Government delivered the reply to the revised proposals of the Japanese Government, which is contrary to the expectations of the Imperial Government. The Chinese Government not only did not give a careful consideration to the revised proposals but even with regard to the offer of the Japanese Government to restore Kiaochow to the Chinese Government the latter did not manifest the least appreciation for Japan's good will and difficulties.

From the commercial and military point of view Kiaochow is an important place, in the acquisition of which the Japanese Empire sacrificed much blood and money, and, after the acquisition the Empire incurs no obligation to restore it to China.

But with the object of increasing the future friendly relations of the two countries, they went to the extent of proposing its restoration, yet to her great regret, the Chinese Government did not take into consideration the good intention of Japan and manifest appreciation of her difficulties.

Furthermore, the Chinese Government not only ignored the friendly feelings of the Imperial Government in offering the restoration of Kiaochow Bay, but also in replying to the revised proposals they even demanded its unconditional restoration; and again China demanded that Japan should bear the responsibility of paying indemnity for all the unavoidable losses and damages resulting from Japan's military operations at Kiaochow; and still further in connection with the territory of Kiaochow China advanced other demands and declared that she has the right of participation at the future peace conference to be held between Japan and Germany.

Although China is fully aware that the unconditional restoration of Kiaochow and Japan's responsibility of indemnification for the unavoidable losses and damages can never be tolerated by Japan, yet she purposely advanced these demands and declared that this reply was final and decisive.

Since Japan could not tolerate such demands the settlement of the other questions, however compromising it may be, would not be to her interest. The consequence is that the present reply of the Chinese Government is, on the whole, vague and meaningless.

Furthermore, in the reply of the Chinese Government to the other proposals in the revised list of the Imperial Government, such as South Manchuria and Eastern Inner Mongolia, where Japan particularly has geographical, commercial, industrial and strategic relations, as recognized by all nations, and made more remarkable in consequence of the two wars in which Japan was engaged, the Chinese Government overlooks these facts and does not respect Japan's position in that place.

The Chinese Government even freely altered those articles which the Imperial Government, in a compromising spirit, have formulated in accordance with the statement of the Chinese Representatives, thereby making the statements of the Representatives an empty talk; and on seeing them conceding with the one hand and withholding with the other it is very difficult to attribute faithfulness and sincerity to the Chinese authorities.

As regards the articles relating to the employment of advisers, the establishment of schools and hospitals, the supply of arms and ammunition and the establishment of arsenals and railway concessions in South China in the revised proposals, they were either proposed with the proviso that the consent of the Power concerned must be obtained, or they are merely to be recorded in the minutes in accordance with the statements of the Chinese delegates, and thus they are not in the least in conflict either with Chinese sovereignty or her treaties with the Foreign Powers, yet the Chinese Government in their reply to the proposals, alleging that these proposals are incompatible with their sovereign rights and treaties with Foreign Powers, defeat the expectations of the Imperial Government.

However, in spite of such attitude of the Chinese Government, the Imperial Government, though regretting to see that there is no room for further negotiations, yet warmly attached to the preservation of the peace of the Far East, is still hoping for a satisfactory settlement in order to avoid the disturbance of the relations.

So in spite of the circumstances which admitted no patience, they have reconsidered the feelings of the Government of their neighbouring country and, with the exception of the article relating to Fukien which is to be the subject of an exchange of notes as has already been agreed upon by the Representatives of both nations, will undertake to detach the Group V from the present negotiations and discuss it separately in the future.

Therefore, the Chinese Government should appreciate the friendly feelings of the Imperial Government by immediately accepting without any alteration all the articles of Groups I, II, III, and IV and the exchange of notes in connection with Fukien province in Group V as contained in the revised proposals presented on the 26th of April.

The Imperial Government hereby again offer their advice and hope that the Chinese Government, upon this advice, will give a satisfactory reply by 6 o'clock p.m. on the 9th day of May. It is hereby declared that if no satisfactory reply is received before or at the specified time, the Imperial Government will take steps they may deem necessary.[8]

The Chinese were left in little doubt as to the intentions of the Japanese and had little room for further diplomatic manoeuvre. The Chinese had employed their favoured diplomatic approach, procrastination and stalling, which would have been familiar to British diplomats of the nineteenth century. The Japanese had raised the stakes and in so doing, made it clear that they never had any intention of returning Tsingtao and that the expenditure of human life and hard cash which they had put into the venture made that inevitable. To this, they also added the losses they had sustained in other campaigns in the area as a justification for their claims. There was no help for the Chinese this time, as those powers who had insisted that the Japanese quit the area previously, were now embroiled in their own problems and could not become involved in the events in the Far East, however unacceptable the situation that had developed may have been to them. There was no alternative for the Chinese other than to accept the wishes of an imperial power stronger than themselves, as they had done throughout the nineteenth century. On 8 May, they responded to the Japanese:

On the 7th of this month, at three o'clock P.M. , the Chinese Government received an Ultimatum from the Japanese Government together with an Explanatory Note of seven articles.

The Ultimatum concluded with the hope that the Chinese Government by six o'clock P.M. on the 9th of May will give a satisfactory reply, and it is hereby declared that if no satisfactory reply is received before or at the specified time, the Japanese Government will take steps she may deem necessary.

The Chinese Government with a view to preserving the peace of the Far East hereby accepts, with the exception of those five articles of Group V postponed for later negotiations, all the articles of Groups I, II, III, and IV and the exchange of notes in connection with Fukien Province in Group V as contained in the revised proposals presented on the 26th of April, and in accordance with the Explanatory Note of seven articles accompanying the Ultimatum of the Japanese Government with the hope that thereby all the outstanding questions are settled, so that the cordial relationship between the two countries may be further consolidated.

The Japanese Minister is hereby requested to appoint a day to call at the Ministry of Foreign Affairs to make the literary improvement of the text and sign the Agreement as soon as possible.

When considering the success of the operations at Tsingtao, a factor that needs closer scrutiny is the relationship that developed between the Japanese and the British forces in the field, and how this impacted on the future attitudes of the two countries. Lieutenant Simson's comments on this issue are illuminating, as he expresses his very direct, personal opinions on the operations as a whole:

The British share in the operations can hardly be called a success. They did nothing to impress the Japanese with the British Army – rather the reverse. The Japanese are a critical people and there can be no doubt that they started out hoping that we would get on well together. I often heard their views on the subject, especially from the NCOs and men, who speak more freely than officers, and speak quite frankly when they discover one knows their language. It is not the least unusual for an NCO or private to speak freely and exchange ideas with an officer 'off parade' in the Japanese army. It seems very difficult for a Britisher, who knows nothing of the Japanese to hit it off with a Japanese who has never had anything to do with us. Both do things which jar on the other – the British rude rough manners and Japanese rude curiosity. Only a very little modification would make things comparatively easy. The British certainly did not give one the impression of being conscious that getting on with the Japanese was one of the problems before them. They did not seem to have a thought about it, whereas there is no doubt that the Japanese did and Japanese of all sorts and ranks. Speaking generally, I am sure that there are many Britishers who went through the operations who, even now, are not aware that they ever had any relations with the Japanese, whereas with the Japanese, even the rough country peasants would be anxious to get on with and be liked by the British. Now from what I saw there must have been very many instances where our men quite unintentionally and quite unthinkingly did things that did not anger and offend the Japanese so much as hurt their feelings, and send them away feeling sorry, but putting it down to our different customs. If a Japanese did something that annoyed or offended the Britisher, the case was entirely different. The Britisher would unmistakably express his disapproval of what the 'native' had done, there the matter would end as far as he was concerned. The above refers more to the relations between the NCOs and men of both nations than to the officers. If they failed to hit it off, the Japanese put it down to different customs, and the British were quite unaware that they had not hit it off, or immediately forgot the fact. These were not things that really mattered very much. There were other incidents which were far more the cause of making our relations with the Japanese which at the beginning stood at zero, as it were, and ready to go either way, slowly and imperceptibly go the wrong way, and, for no obvious reason, end by becoming intolerant dislike. There were cases on the line of march coming up, where our transports would try to gain time by cutting in ahead of Japanese transports and our people shouted at and ordered Japanese NCOs to do things contrary to what they had been told to do by their own officers. Their artillery, manhandling their guns along at night, halted by the road in the early morning, borrowing fire from our reserve and expecting a little help after a long night's work. They put up a shelter for their officer in a place between our troops – there was no other ground available – and our officer, thinking they intended to stay a long time had it pulled down and ordered the Japanese to go away. Japanese fired on our men, mistaking them for Germans, though as often it was our fault as theirs – our officers objected to being stopped by Japanese sentries and forced them, which led to complaints through headquarters. Our officers and men paid no compliments, whereas the Japanese did. Many of our officers started from Tientsin with a strong dislike of the Japanese, which they proceeded to make a hobby of, not taking the trouble to disguise it. But more important than all these things, the Japanese who saw most of us and worked most with us were not impressed with our work. Our action on the 5th and 6th (November) was most unfortunate, and then having taken no action in the final attack, we were the first to rush into permanent barracks.

The Sikhs were only there for a short time, but there is no doubt that those who were in a position to compare their work with the British would say the Sikhs were much better. The Japanese engineers said so, they admired and liked the Sikhs, who were always well turned out on parade and would take any opportunity of washing mud off their boots and puttees, they were obviously keen and worked hard. Their size and bearing on parade impressed the Japanese, with whom their relations seemed to be of the best. Their officers too, seemed to have no difficulty with the Japanese and no prejudice against them.

Much of the above may seem unduly pessimistic and, of course, there were many cases where the British got on excellently with the Japanese. But I do not think they admired us as soldiers, whereas they did admire the Sikhs. I think that the result of the speech and feelings of the Japanese who were at Tsingtao will afterwards tell more against us than for us.[9]

It is quite clear from this that Simson thought the relationship between the allies had been poor to begin with and had steadily worsened throughout the campaign. However, whilst there was undoubtedly some truth in this, Simson has attached a certain bias which has not allowed him to tell the full story of some of the events. For instance, on the line of march, there are comments by British officers on the very poor march discipline practised by the Japanese.[10] Likewise, the comments regarding the fracas over the shelter put up for the Japanese artillery officer, do explain that the Japanese soldiers had seen fit to set this up in the middle of British lines without reference to the British officer involved. As Simson pointed out, a little compromise might have gone a long way to solving most of the problems that had arisen, but compromise is a two-way process and is easily blocked by a lack of understanding – particularly where there are language differences. Nevertheless, Simson's report highlighted the fact that things were not working as well as they could have done between the allies during the campaign.

Another, even more direct appraisal of the British view of the Japanese was given by Colonel Calthorp:

> The British troops brought with them from Tientsin the idea that prevailed in China, with regard to the Japanese. They regarded them as an inferior race, as coolies in uniforms whose good opinion it was quite unnecessary to cultivate. The expedition was unpopular, and it was felt that the units should be preserved as intact as possible for the subsequent operations in Europe.
>
> The most favourable explanation that can be given from the British point of view is that they did not try. British were fired on by mistake for Germans on several occasions.
>
> The position of the British Force was a difficult one, they were largely dependant on the Japanese for transport, their presence was not only unnecessary but a positive inconvenience to the Japanese.[11]

There are a number of interesting issues raised here which reflect the attitude towards the Far East adopted by the British for over a century. The Chinese may have had a poor opinion of the Japanese but the British tended to have a poor opinion of everyone who was not British, so the feeling that they did not need to impress their ally grew out of an imperial association with China. It must be remembered, that the British had been very compli-mentary with regards to the behaviour of the Japanese troops during the siege of the Peking Legations in 1900. Perhaps the comments made by Calthorp are as much his personal views on the Japanese as they are generally British. Nonetheless, there can be little doubt that the ordinary soldier in China at this time felt that his place should have been at the heart of the European war and not in the small-scale side show at Tsingtao, a view reflected in Calthorp's comments. In that context, it is quite possible that, as junior partners in the operation, the British felt no real need to try too hard. Simson's report suggests as much in a number of places. Lieutenant-Colonel Casson, on the other hand, vehemently denies such accusations against his battalion and points out the difficulties they had faced as a result of the lack of equipment and so forth.[12] Furthermore, Calthorp is mistaken in his statement about the British relying on the Japanese for transport. The battalion had reached Tsingtao on troop ships hired in Tientsin for the purpose by the British government – it had brought its own wagons which had caused some problems during their unloading at Laoshan Bay and Captain Knaggs had purchased transport mules which had been difficult to bring ashore during the landings. There were other things that were needed and were supplied by the Japanese. They certainly assisted with transportation, but the biggest item that the British could not provide was artillery – they took no heavy guns with them for an operation that was always going to result in a siege, and perhaps, this reflects the overall lack of interest on the part of the British hierarchy in the campaign as a whole. It may also reflect the simple fact that such large siege pieces were unavailable to the British in China at this time. It is also necessary to consider the lack of such essential items as tools, timber and sandbags, all things needed for the success of an operation that required trench digging and siege works. There can be no doubt that the British force could not have taken to the field in this operation without the help of the Japanese and there was, at least in some quarters, scant recognition of this fact. To some extent, Simson's report may be seen as a British officer trying to redress that balance, but he did it by being critical of the battalion in the field rather than by examining the system that had put it in the field in the first place in such a poor state of preparedness. In that context, his report fails entirely, but he did make it quite clear that he thought very highly of the Japanese and their approach to the siege.

There can be no doubt that the way a British soldier, or for that matter a civilian, thought in 1914 was considerably different to the way he thought after the Great War. In 1914, the British Empire held a virtually unassailable position of power throughout the world, and the British soldier would have thought himself as good as any 'foreigner', never mind the Japanese, which would certainly have given rise to a significant lack of understanding of or lack of interest in, the way the Japanese did things. No-one would have worried much about the way the Japanese did things; nor would they have been too concerned about what the Japanese thought of them. The British considered the Japanese to be rather rude and a bit of a nuisance during the campaign[13]. That they were not invited to the official German surrender would have been in keeping with, and would have reinforced, the British view of the Japanese. Whilst the British staff may not have liked the situation, but they would not have been totally surprised to have been left out. Nevertheless, Lieutenant-Colonel Casson, along with one or two of his officers, recorded that overall, they got on well with the Japanese, and as one observer was to point out:

> There were one or two, hardly more, who embarked on the Expedition with such prejudice against the Japanese that even had the latter proved themselves to be angels there would have been no diminution of the detestation in which they were held. On the other hand, there were a few in

whose eyes the Japanese were the incarnation of superhuman excellence. For these they remained such to the end and the most glaring wrong was absolved with 'It is their custom'. But to the large bulk of the British force the Japanese came on the field with no great racial prejudice against them and with a fair chance to establish their virtues.[14]

This is an important statement which seems to show a fairly balanced approach to the situation since the author, employed during the operations as a civilian interpreter, unlike Simson, had no particular axe to grind. However, it does not alter the fact that there were problems between the two nationalities during the operations, some of which were purely linguistic. There were few Europeans who spoke Japanese and few Japanese who spoke English. The lack of truly competent interpreters has been highlighted as having played an important part in the operation. That there was any cohesion at all between the two forces was remarkable, but that it was not better, was a disappointment to the staff officers of both forces. To a large extent, this again reflects a lack of preparation, particularly by the British, and a mentality that expected everyone to speak English. The British undoubtedly saw themselves as superior in many ways and, although they admired the hardy, courageous Japanese soldiers, they did not get very far along the route of discovering much about them as a cultural group. It was simply accepted that they were different, even Lieutenant-Colonel Casson admits to not understanding the way the Japanese mind worked. The converse was also true – the Japanese demonstrated little understanding of the British during the operations. If Brigadier-General Barnardiston had a larger force at his command, he would only have been in a stronger position to have a say in the running of the siege if he had also had more and better interpreters to link his force more effectively to that of his ally, otherwise it could only have resulted in increased misunderstanding and an eventual lack of trust and co-operation. Perhaps the way the British thought of the Japanese is summed up by Lieutenant Beaumont-Walker's comments:

> We found them tireless automatons, extremely efficient and quite fearless. We felt we were treated as guests and except for the night Nov. 6/7 we never made contact with the enemy while they did.
> They were very helpful but gave us the impression that they were going to seize Tsingtao and we were told just enough to keep us in the picture.[15]

Beaumont-Walker's belief that the Borderer's were 'told just enough' would fit in extremely well with the orders that General Kamio had received concerning his approach to his allies. He was to help all he could as long as it did not compromise the outcome of the operations, as seen from a Japanese perspective. Clearly he had obeyed these instructions and the Borderers were fully aware of this. However, the effects of this on the operations went much further:

> The Japanese opinion of the British may be summed up in a few words: 'In point of number – negligible; in method of warfare – comparatively stupid, on the whole more of a hindrance than a help'.[16]

This attitude was not aided by the fact that the British did not take part in the final assault on Tsingtao which, if one is generous, should be looked upon as an opportunist attack. However, this prejudicial attitude was widespread in the Japanese army. The following extract demonstrates the ill-feeling that had developed amongst some of the British officers at not being included in the final attack:

> I think there is no doubt that we were purposely left in ignorance of the fact that the Japs intended to force a decision on the night Nov. 6/7th. It is impossible to believe that when this operation was decided on, the Japanese GHQ inadvertently forgot that we existed.
>
> I am convinced that this was deliberate, one cannot conceal the fact that the Japanese looked on us with great jealousy. The Japanese fundamental fault is an overwhelming conceit. Their perspective is distorted. All things are a matter of comparison, and their beliefs are founded on the comparison between themselves and their great neighbours, the Chinese, and the Russians, whom they defeated in the campaign of 1905.
>
> Japanese officers went as far as to say that the fact that they came into the war on our side would save the British Empire!!
>
> Their conceit is terrific, and intrigue is a national characteristic. Although the Japanese soldier had the greatest respect for us, and although they were intensely proud to be serving alongside a British regiment, behind it all and superimposed over everything else, was the overwhelming conceit, which in their own estimation, placed them in a position alone.
>
> Bearing this in mind and remembering that our presence was a matter of satisfaction to the Japanese, it is impossible to believe that we were inadvertently omitted from the decisive attack on Tsingtao.
>
> We were waiting, ready, and it is ridiculous to suppose that the Japanese did not know this.[17]

This attitude towards the British was not only held by those Japanese soldiers in the immediate vicinity of the siege operation, who may actually have seen them in action, but also by others who did not come into contact with them:

> What is, however, of greater significance is the fact that the Japanese military officers stationed in Tsinan have been at no pains to conceal their contempt for the British Army as exemplified by the force under General Barnardiston's command. They have freely expressed their opinions to Chinese officials in this place to the effect that the men are not good fighters and that the British officers come from wealthy families and are therefore unfitted for the hardships and dangers of a campaign. The Sikhs and their officers appear not to be included in these strictures.[18]

This would, on the face of it, appear to be an incredible conclusion to be drawn from a limited contact with a small force during a wholly Japanese planned operation. It would appear that the British suffered far more from prejudice during the campaign than did the Japanese and to add to this there seems to have been a very pro-German attitude amongst the latter's officers which no doubt stemmed from the long association between the Germans on the Japanese army.[19]

To some extent, this prejudicial attitude towards the British Army was carried on by historians late into the twentieth century. In trying to show how well the Japanese had performed at Tsingtao, Burdick[20] goes as far as to say that the Japanese had engaged 'a first-rate European power' in Germany. This is close to nonsense as the Japanese had actually engaged one regular battalion and an assortment of reservists and volunteers which they over-whelmed by sheer weight of numbers as much as anything else. It is interesting to speculate how well the Japanese would have performed alongside their allies in the appalling conditions of the Western Front, where they would have really met a first-rate European power on its own terms. As it was, they had won a relatively easy victory at low cost, which was no measure of the real value of the Japanese soldier, let alone the British.

With these respective attitudes, it must be considered that at a diplomatic and political level, the Tsingtao campaign had not been a great success for the British and the relationship between the two nations never really improved, since the aims of the Japanese in the area were soon widely recognized by the Europeans and the impact of this small campaign can be misunderstood because of the later events of the Great War.

The events of Tsingtao were of great importance to the Germans, who lost not only a military base and harbour for her ships, but also brought to an end her imperial aspirations in the Far East. The relevance of Tsingtao's military position has been mentioned already, but it should also be recognized that while it was of importance and had been fortified as a military base, the garrison was essentially isolated once the support from the sea had been removed. Perhaps what surprised the Japanese and the British, was the fact that the Germans were able to continue their defence for so long and, but for their shortage of ammunition, may have maintained it even longer.

The real weakness of the Tsingtao fortress lay in its isolation , particularly after von Spee's squadron had left, as it was bound to do. Had the war remained a totally European affair, there would have been little immediate danger to Tsingtao, as the European allies could have done very little about it. There would have been a need for some kind of action, especially if it was used to harbour warships that could readily disrupt British trade. Britain would have not been in a position to do that in 1914 and would have had to build up a substantial force to counter this eventuality. However, since Britain had a treaty with Japan, the possibility of taking Tsingtao away from the Germans, could be moved up the agenda, and it is perhaps here that the true relevance of the Tsingtao campaign lies. Britain was able to put together a coalition of allies in the Far East which was strong enough to topple their European enemy. However, in doing so, they had encouraged an up and coming power to believe that the time was right for its own expansionism to reach fruition. There can be little doubt that the Japanese took advantage of this situation to further their own foreign policy and there was absolutely nothing that the British could do about it.

In terms of the great conflict that was to take place across Europe over the following years, Tsingtao was of little importance and its fall did not hasten the end of the war. It was far too small a campaign for that. It had, however, set markers out in the Far East which clearly indicated that there could be no return to the pre-war status quo. The events in Tsingtao had changed the balance of power in the region – involving the Japanese had given them the confidence they needed to shout their intentions for the future and for thirty years, the Chinese suffered terribly at their hands. The fall of Tsingtao started a chain of events which culminated in another war some thirty years later. Following Tsingtao, the Europeans more or less disappeared from China. Although the British maintained their hold in Hong Kong, their treaties with China only allowed them a presence elsewhere, while other foreign powers held possessions in the area. When Japan was forced out of China by diplomatic means in 1922, there was no reason for Britain to remain. By the time the Japanese went to war with the Chinese in the 1930s, the world was sliding towards another conflict which brought further great changes to the stability of the region. Whilst it may be too strong to contend that Tsingtao was the root cause of this, it is perhaps true to say that Tsingtao was to play a significant part in the history of the region in the years following 1914.

If events in Europe had worked out differently and Germany had been victorious, then there can be little doubt that she would have returned to Tsingtao and would have had to treat with Japan. As it was, the Tsingtao operation saw the growth of mistrust amongst the allies and Britain was never again as closely linked, either militarily or diplomatically, with the Japanese. Japan certainly wanted a way in to China and Tsingtao offered them an opening, but to believe that they would not have done so at a later date, is perhaps taking a rather naïve approach to their imperial desires. During the years before 1914, Britain had recognized the rise of Japan and signed a suitable treaty of friendship with her but, as demonstrated by the Tsingtao campaign, had no real power to exercise any control over the Japanese who went their own way once the opportunity arose. In 1919, the Treaty of Versailles gave Tsingtao to Japan which was their intended outcome all along and which caused considerable demonstrations in Beijing, including the destruction of the houses of those ministers identified as being pro-Japanese.[21] The situation was not resolved until 1922 when the Treaty of Washington forced Japan to leave the area. This was not something that she was prepared to let rest, looking to the Shandong Peninsula as a desirable entry point for expanding her empire in China and to which she was to return a little over a decade after the treaty had been signed.

Taken in the context of the policitcal situation in the Far East at this time, it is perhaps too simple to dismiss the siege of Tsingtau as an irrelevant sideshow. Admittedly, it may not have formed part of the grand strategy of any of the belligerents, but it certainly demonstrated the interaction of the imperial powers in the early years of the twentieth century and, without question, demonstrated the global nature of the conflict that is still known as the Great War.

Notes

1. Dickinson (1999), 75.
2. Whittaker (1994).
3. Kondo (1991), quoting Fujiwara (1987).
4. Whittaker (1994).
5. Yamada, *USM* (December 1914), 260, describing the British facilites at Laoshan Bay.
6. See appendix.
7. The proposals referred to here are the so called 'Twenty-One Demands'.
8. Great War. com. See appendix for explanatory note that accompanied the ultimatum.
9. Simson's Report, Section 40. Royal Welsh Museum.
10. See, for instance, Casson's response and Margesson's diary, Royal Welsh Museum.
11. WO106/66 Notes by Major E. F. Calthorp, Military Attaché to Tokyo; he was killed in action in December 1915.
12. Casson's response, Royal Welsh Museum.
13. For instance, see Casson's response to Simson.
14. FO371/2381 report by Eckfort quoted in Kondo (1991). Mr R. H. Eckfort was the British Consul in Tsingtao before hostilities began.
15. Beaumont-Walker's account, Royal Welsh Museum.
16. FO371/2381, Eckfort.
17. Note added to Simson's report – apparently by Borderer's officer, possibly Casson.
18. FO371/2381.
19. Kondo (1991).
20. Burdick (1975), 196.
21. Yap and Cotterell (1977), 155.

Appendix 1

The Nominal Roll

The following nominal roll gives the names and ranks of members of the 2nd Battalion the South Wales Borderers who were stationed in Tientsin at the outbreak of the Great War. It has been compiled from the documents held at the Regimental Museum in Brecon (Ref: BRCRM1996.76) and cross referenced with the Medal Index Cards held at the National Archive. Most of those listed served during the siege of Tsingtao and those that did not are clearly indicated in the notes attached to each entry. Soldiers serving in the operations in front of Tsingtao were entitled to the 194/15 Star. It is not certain that all the soldiers that remained in Tientsin were awarded the medal or indeed that submissions were made for the medal. Where there is information on the subsequent service of the soldier concerned this is also indicated in the notes. It will be noticed that the 2nd Battalion the South Wales Borderers suffered heavy casualties in later fighting, notably Gallipoli. It will also be noted that very few of the soldiers who were present with the Battalion in China were with it when the war ended.

The following abbreviations have been used in the roll:

Pte.   Private
Dmr   Drummer
Bdsm   Bandsman
L.Cpl. Lance Corporal
Cpl.   Corporal
L.Sgt. Lance Sergeant
Sgt.   Sergeant
CSM   Company Sergeant-Major
CQMS   Company Quartermaster Sergeant
QMS   (Regimental) Quartermaster Sergeant
AQMS   Armourer Quartermaster Sergeant
BM   Bandmaster (Warrant Officer 1st Class)
RSM   Regimental Sergeant-Major (Warrant Officer 1st Class)
WO2   Warrant Officer 2nd Class
2 Lieut Second Lieutenant
Lieut   Lieutenant
Capt.   Captain
Lt Col Lieutenant-Colonel
QM   Quartermaster

VC   Victoria Cross
DSO   Distinguished Service Order

MC   Military Cross
DCM   Distinguished Conduct Medal
MM   Military Medal
MID   Mentioned in Dispatches
C de G Croix de Guerre (French or Belgian)
MSM   Meritorious Service Medal
LSGCM   Long Service Good Conduct Medal
MBE   Member of the Order of the British Empire
BEM   British Empire Medal
IGSM   India General Service Medal

MGC   Machine Gun Corps
RAMC   Royal Army Medical Corps
RFC   Royal Flying Corps
RAF   Royal Air Force
ACC   Army Cyclists Corps
KSLI   King's Shropshire Light Infantry
RWF   Royal Welsh Fusiliers
RE   Royal Engineers
SWB   South Wales Borderers
NF   Northumberland Fusiliers
KRRC   King's Royal Rifle Corps
KOSB   King's Own Scottish Borderers

Dis   Dis
KinA   Killed in action
DofW   DofW

No.	Rank	Name	Coy	Notes
9522	Pte.	Abbey, Ernest George	B	To British Military Mission to Vladivostock 16.12.21.
10657	Pte.	Abbott, Charles Henry	A	KinA Gallipoli 26.4.15
9688	Pte.	Ackerman, George.	C	Dis 23.10.17
6045	Pte.	Adams, Frank	A	Served Boer War; DofW Egypt 17.6.15
9974	Pte.	Adrian, Louis	D	Served Gallipoli, to hospital 19.6.15; dis 30.5.16
10506	Pte.	Aherne, William	B	Deserted
4977	CQMS	Alabaster, George	B	Served Boer War. Later RSM. MSM; LSCGM.
10625	Pte.	Albone, Arthur	C	Deserted
10123	Pte.	Albone, Thomas	B	Served India with D Coy from 21.9.19; LSGCM; dis 1.10.35
10166	Pte.	Allen, Harry	A	KinA Gallipoli 28.6.15 as corporal
9312	Pte.	Allen, William	D	Served as Pioneer later lance corporal. Real name Albert Perks; MSM. Dis 19.3.22
10897	Pte.	Alline, Charles	A	MM in France; KinA France 11.4.18
9464	Pte.	Allsopp, Charles	B	Later sergeant; MSM; Belgian CdeG; dis 4.11.21
9328	Pte.	Anderson, William	C	Later sergeant; KinA France 1.7.16
10667	Pte.	Andrews, Albert Thomas	C	KinA Gallipoli, 8.5.15
9947	Pte.	Andrews, Ernest Henry		Not at Tsingtao; dis 4.8.16.
10880	L.Cpl.	Andrews, Frederick George	D	KinA Gallipoli, 8.5.15

9539	Pte.	Andrews, William G.	C	Dis 18.1.16
9903	Pte.	Armstrong, G.	B	Wounded, to Hospital Ship *Delta* 9.11.14
9510	Pte.	Ashton, George Henry	C	Later CSM 4(G) RWF; died 12.3.19
10920	Pte.	Atkins, William Denford	A	KinA France 23.4.17
10426	Pte.	Attwater, Bertie	A	KinA France 26.8.18 (attd 10/SWB)
10389	Pte.	Attwood, Arthur George	D	Dis 23.3.22
10404	L.Cpl.	Auger, Richard	D	Wounded in Gallipoli, 8.5.15 and 21.6.15; later lance corporal 3/SWB
10524	Pte.	Bagge, Edward	D	Dis 2.6.16
9331	Pte.	Bailey, Frederick	A	Later sergeant; Dis 29.10.18
9236	Pte.	Bailey, Samuel Henry	B	KinA France 6.4.16
10635	Pte.	Bailey, Thomas	D	Served Gallipoli, to hospital 10.5.15; later served with MGC and RWF
10157	Pte.	Bailey, William Henry	B	Later served with Labour Corps; dis as corporal 28.10.20
10083	Pte.	Baker, Frederick		Not at Tsingtao; Dis 8.8.15
10844	Pte.	Baker, Gabriel	A	Later corporal.
10175	Pte.	Baker, Joseph Henry	A	
10722	Pte.	Baker, Wallace	A	Later served with RE, King's Liverpool Regt. and Labour Corps.
10026	Pte.	Baldock, William Henry	B	Later sergeant; dis 16.9.20.
9517	Pte.	Baldwin, George	B	Later corporal
9747	L.Cpl.	Ball Charles	C	Later corporal KinA Gallipoli 26.4.15
10187	L.Cpl.	Banks, John Benjamin	D	Later WO2; dis 3.11.20; re-enlisted 1/Cambridgeshire Regt, TA
10148	Pte.	Banks, Thomas H.	B	Later served with RWF
10301	Pte.	Barber, Frederick	C	Dis 5.1.16
7770	Sgt.	Barker, Alfred	A	MM, LSGC; Later RSM 2/SWB and 1/Mons
10158	L.Cpl.	Barker, William G.	C	Later sergeant in South Lancs Regt
9304	Pte.	Barnes, Edgar	C	KinA France 29.6.16
9662	Pte.	Barnes, Edward	C	Returned to Weihaiwei 27.10.14, Later sergeant; dis 9.4.29
10750	Pte.	Barnes, Tom.	A	KinA Gallipoli 6.6.15.
5493	Pte.	Barnett, John	B	Later served with Labour Corps
10173	Pte.	Bartlett, James Henry	C	Dis 2.4.19.
10006	Pte.	Barton, Charles	D	Served as medical orderly; later with RWF
10890	Pte.	Bassnett, John James	C	Dis 19.9.19
9539	Bdsm	Bath, Norman	C	KinA France 1.7.16; real name Norman Payne
8206	Sgt.	Bean, Sidney David	D	DCM and wounded at Gallipoli; later RSM; dis 4.7.28, commissioned Indian Army
	2. Lieut.	Behrens, Robert Philip		Died of Wounds Gallipoli 25.4.15
10347	Pte.	Belcher, Stephen	C	Later served with MGC
9871	Pte.	Belford, Colin	A	Wounded at Gallipoli, 14.5.15. Later served with MGC; dis 24.3.30
9271	Sgt.	Bell, Frederick	B	Wounded at Gallipoli, 10.7.15; MM; later CQMS and WO2 with Chinese Labour Corps; dis 20.9.28.
9772	Pte.	Bendall, Thomas	D	Later sergeant. KinA France 21.10.16
9028	Pte.	Bennell, William	B	Later served with RFC and Royal Scots Fusiliers.
9741	Pte.	Bennett, Algernon	D	Later served with RWF and RE
9742	Cpl.	Bennett, William	D	Wounded at Gallipoli 12.5.15 Later sergeant. and WO2 Labour Corps.

11168	Pte.	Bent, Percy Temple	D	Commissioned 1/KOSB; KinA 1.7.16
10019	Pte.	Bettis, Edward James	D	KinA 6.11.14, China
10510	L. Cpl	Biggs, Frederick James	D	Wounded Gallipoli 8.5.15.
10413	L.Cpl.	Biggs, Stephen	D	Later corporal; wounded at Gallipoli 8.5.15; dis 8.10.15
9629	Pte.	Bilby, Albert	B	Later Royal Defence Corps
8265	Sgt.	Bill, Rowland Sidney	A	Later CSM; KinA France 1.7.16
10003	L.Cpl.	Bird, Ernest Owen		Not at Tsingtao. KinA Gallipoli 19.6.15
	Capt.	Birkett, Gerald Halsey.		MID for China 30.5.16 and also 11.12.17 and 20.5.18; wounded Gallipoli 25.4.15. DSO 1918 France
5125	Pte.	Bishop, Charles John		Not at Tsingtao; dis 26.2.15.
9618	Pte.	Bishop, Enoch	B	Later corporal dis 20.12.18
10102	Pte.	Bissender, Sidney	C	Dis 19.10.20
9261	Pte.	Blair, Thomas	B	MM; MID; later sergeant; dis 14.9.18.
10117	Pte.	Blanchard, Ernest William	D	Dis 15.9.16.
7063	Sgt.	Bleasdale, Arthur	A	Wounded Gallipoli 26.4.15 and 21.8.15. LSGCM. Dis 12.8.22; re-enlisted and dis 28.9.26.
10321	Pte.	Blight, Edward J.	A	Later served with RE
9531	L.Cpl.	Blundell, John Thomas	C	KinA Gallipoli 5.6.15 as corporal.
8527	Cpl.	Blunt, Alfred	C	Later sergeant with Labour Corps
10025	Pte.	Bone, William James	A	Dis 5.4.16.
10065	Pte.	Bonner, George		Not at Tsingtao. KinA Gallipoli 25.5.15.
10384	Pte.	Bostock, Frank	B	Dis 21.9.16
10272	Pte.	Botting, Ronald George L.	A	Dis 14.1.16
10464	Pte.	Boucher, John	C	KinA Gallipoli 28.4.15
9711	Pte.	Boultwood, George Henry	B	Dis 17.9.17 later re-enlisted in SWB
9140	Pte	Bourlett, George	C	Later served with RWF
9157	Pte.	Bovill, James H.	D	Served at Gallipoli; later with Lancashire Fusiliers; re-enlisted in SWB 19.2.19; died of malaria in India
9533	Pte.	Bowdler, Lewis	B	Dis 10.1.17
9801	Pte.	Bowen, Bertie	B	MM; Later sergeant with 4/SWB
10796	Pte.	Bower, Ernest William	C	Wounded at Gallipoli 4.9.15; wounded in France 1.7.16; later served Salonika; dis 2.5.32.
10075	Pte.	Bowers, J.	A	Later lance corporal RWF
9679	L.Cpl.	Box, Albert Edward	A	Later sergeant; dis 9.6.16
10740	Pte.	Bracey, Arthur Edward	B	KinA Gallipoli 28.4.15
9005	Pte.	Bradford, William	C	Class Z Army Reserve 16.4.19
	Capt.	Bradstock, John		MID for China 30.5.16 and 5.7.19; MC
10472	Pte.	Brewer, Sidney James	A	Later corporal
10720	Pte.	Bridges, Arthur William	A	Later sergeant; dis 17.12.27
9199	Pte.	Bridges, Walter A.	A	Later served with RWF
9020	Sgt.	Briggs, Frederick	C	MSM and LSGCM; wounded in China; wounded in France 8.6.18; dis 7.1.31
10276	Dmr	Briscombe, Albert	B	Later corporal; dis 17.2.17.
10264	Pte.	Bristol, Albert	A	Real name Bristowe; dis 26.7.21
10683	Pte.	Bristowe, Henry		Not at Tsingtao; dis to commission 30.10.42.
10550	Pte.	Britton, W.	B	
10607	Pte.	Broad, William D.	D	Served at Gallipoli; later with MGC
10383	Pte.	Brooks, Ernest	A	Dis 8.9.15
9481	Pte.	Broom, Henry Edward	B	Remained Laoshan Bay; KinA Gallipoli 21.8.15

9609	L.Cpl.	Brown, James	D	DofW Gallipoli 9.5.15
10160	L.Cpl.	Brown, Launcelot Wake	D	KinA Gallipoli 2.5.15
9751	Pte.	Buchanan, Donald	B	Later corporal; dis as CSM 12.9.28. LSGCM
10498	Pte.	Buckland, John	A	Wounded in France 21.10.16 and 7.10.17; dis 4.5.19.
10329	Pte.	Buckland, William	B	KinA 1.7.16
9827	Pte.	Buckle, Richard	D	Wounded at Gallipoli 2.5.15; dis 2.10.15.
10688	Pte.	Buckley, Yates	C	Later served as corporal with RWF
8996	L.Cpl.	Buckman, Robert A.	A	Later served as corporal Labour Corps
6636	Sgt.	Bunce, George Owen	A	Served Boer War; commissioned 11.2.15; KinA Gallipoli 9.5.15.
9706	Pte.	Burgess, Henry William	A	dis 6.10.16
10002	Pte.	Burgess, Sidney Horace	C	KinA 17.5.15 attached to 1/SWB
9117	Pte.	Burke, James E.	B	Return to Weihaiwei 27.10.14; later served as CSM with NF
9882	Pte.	Burridge, William	B	Dis 14.12.18
10029	Cpl.	Burrows, Alfred Henry	C	Dis 6.6.16.
10781	Pte.	Burrows, Walter George	B	Dis 17.4.24
9868	Pte.	Burton, John Jack	D	To hospital from Gallipoli 19.6.15
9693	Pte.	Burton, W.G.	C	Later served with RAF
10455	Pte.	Burton, William Horace	C	To Army Reserve 16.4.19
10395	Pte.	Busby, Edward Frederick	A	Dis 13.3.17
10701	Pte.	Butcher, William Robert	A	Later corporal KinA France 1.7.16
9133	Pte.	Butler, Charles	D	Later corporal; wounded at Gallipoli 8.5.15; dis 18.1.16
8726	Pte.	Butt, Charles	A	KinA Gallipoli 26.4.15
9727	Pte.	Byford, John	B	Return to Weihaiwei 18.10.14; later served Labour Corps as corporal
9532	Pte.	Cable, George	D	MM for Gallipoli; MID; ater with 1/SWB and R.Tank Regt.
	Lieut.	Cahusac, Arthur Nigel		MC & MID
9660	Pte.	Campion, William	C	KinA Gallipoli 8.5.15
9656	Pte.	Campling, J.	C	
9245	Pte.	Cane, James	A	Later served with RFC
9164	Pte.	Carey, Charles Patrick	A	KinA Gallipoli 26.4.15
10865	Pte.	Carter, Edward	B	Dis 15.1.16
9135	Pte.	Carvell, John Frederick	C	To Class Z Army Reserve 16.2.16
	Lt. Col	Casson, Hugh Gilbert		MID for China; CB; CMG; served Boer War; Order of Karageorge.
9177	Pte.	Castleman, Edward John	C	Remained Laoshan Bay; KinA Gallipoli 6.5.15
9801	Pte.	Castree, Harry	D	Died UK 3.1.16
9989	L.Cpl.	Cavalla, John	D	Wounded in China; later served as Corporal in Gallipoli; dis 24.8.16
6185	CSM	Chamberlain, William	B	Served Boer War; commissioned 11.2.15 served Gallipoli; later captain
9895	Pte.	Chambers, William Henry	B	MM & Bar for Western Front; later sergeant; dis 10.4.29
10189	Pte.	Chandler, John	B	Later served with R. Sussex Regt. and Royal Fusiliers
10199	Pte.	Chandler, Joseph	B	Dis as Sergeant 10.11.20
9956	Pte.	Channing, Arthur	B	KinA France 20.11.17
10432	Pte.	Chant, Edward	C	Later served as sergeant with MGC
9358	Sgt.	Chaplin, John (Jack)	C	Wounded in Gallipoli 9.5.15; wounded France 1.7.16. DCM for Western Front; later RSM

10564	Pte.	Chaplin, Reginald	B	Dis 16.12.17
5258	Sgt.	Chaston, Frederick	D	Served Boer War; later CSM; KinA Gallipoli 22.8.15. LSGCM
10441	L.Cpl.	Cheeseman, Howard George	D	Wounded in China; KinA Gallipoli 28.6.15 as sergeant.
10819	Pte.	Chesterman, Arthur J.	C	
10159	Pte.	Chignall, Albert	B	KinA Gallipoli 25.5.15.
10244	Pte.	Christie, Harry Daniel	B	remained at Laoshan Bay; dis 26.10.20
6755	Pte.	Claffey, Joseph	B	Served Boer War; to Hospital Ship *Delta* 9.11.14; DofW at sea (Gallipoli) 28.10.15.
9654	Pte.	Clapp, John	B	To Hospital Ship *Delta* 9.11.14; DofW 19.12.14.
9719	Pte.	Clargo, Leonard	A	KinA 1.7.16
10843	Pte,	Clarke, Samuel	A	Later served with the RWF
10345	Bdsm	Clarke, Vincent	C	Later served with RGA; dis 21.6.24
10243	Pte,	Clarke, William Tutton	D	KinA Gallipoli 8.5.15
10067	Pte.	Clauson, William	A	Dis 3.7.16
9253	Cpl.	Clements, John	A	DofW at sea 7.7.15 after evacuation from Gallipoli.
10136	Pte.	Cleverley, Frederick John	D	Later L.Cpl. KinA Gallipoli, 21.8.15
10113	Pte.	Clifford, John	B	Dis 1.5.16
10451	Pte.	Clinton, Edwin G	C	Dis 7.7.16
10047	Pte.	Cobb, Frederick	B	KinA France (attd 10 SWB) 13.8.18
9893	Pte.	Cockayne, Henry	A	KinA Gallipoli 11.6.15
9908	Pte.	Cockeram, Herbert	B	Remained at Tientsin; later sergeant; dis 11.6.19
10690	Pte.	Cole, Arthur	A	Later served as Cpl. with RWF
10402	Pte.	Coleman, Patrick	B	Dis 30.3.22
10677	Pte.	Collett, Percy James	A	DofW Germany 4.8.18
10016	Pte.	Collins, Henry	D	Later served MGC as Cpl.
10084	Pte.	Collins, William	D	Company Cook in Gallipoli, dis 10.6.16
10418	Dmr.	Connolly, Frederick P.	C	Wounded at Gallipoli 8.5.15; dis 13.1.17.
10831	Pte.	Connor, James	B	Later L.Cpl. KinA Gallipoli 21.8.15
9288	Pte,	Conway, Arthur	B	KinA Gallipoli 25.4.15
10085	L.Cpl.	Cook, Albert	D	Later corporal; wounded at Gallipoli; dis 3.7.16.
10356	Pte.	Cook, Frederick	D	KinA Gallipoli 8.5.15
9994	Pte.	Cook, George	A	Later served with Cheshire Regt.
10138	Pte.	Cooke, Frederick	C	Later CQMS served with MGC
9666	L.Sgt.	Cooke, William Robert	C	MM and MID for Gallipoli; wounded Gallipoli 21.8.15, served as sergeant RWF and RSM 1/Mons Regt and commissioned to 3/Mons
10129	Pte.	Cooper, Jonathan W.B.	B	Later sergeant served with MGC
10320	Pte.	Cosnett, John H.	C	Wounded to Hospital Ship *Delta* 9.11.14; dis 20.9.16
9945	Pte.	Cottle, Frederick	B	Unfit for operations against Tsingtao; later acting corporal
10205	L.Cpl.	Cotterill, Albert	A	Wounded at Gallipoli 23.6.15; MM for Gallipoli; later sergeant, dis 24.11.30, re-enlisted 2 Mons 7.7.33
8449	L.Cpl.	Cottrell, Arthur	A	Later sergeant drmr; to Class Z Army Reserve 13.3.19.
9142	Pte.	Cox, Charles Domeric	C	Dis 17.5.16
10230	Pte.	Cox, Martin Thomas Frank	A	KinA Gallipoli 29.6.15
10366	Pte.	Cox, P.T.	B	Died in China 30.8.14. No medal
9692	Cpl.	Craker, Thomas William		Not at Tsingtao, wounded at

				Gallipoli; wounded in France, dis as sergeant 9.10.25
9627	Pte.	Cran, William Ernest	A	DofW at sea 7.6.15 after evacuation from Gallipoli
10822	Pte.	Crane, Albert	D	Later corporal Wounded at Gallipoli 28.4.15; DofW attached to 6/SWB
9327	Pte.	Craske, Leslie	C	To Class Z Army Reserve 2.6.19
9330	Pte.	Crawley, Arthur.	A	To Class Z Army Reserve 15.3.19.
10468	L.Cpl.	Crisp, William	A	MM for Gallipoli; Gold Medal of Karageorge (Serbia); wounded in France 3.11.16; dis 12.4.19.
10211	L.Cpl.	Crockett, Edward	D	Later sergeant; dis 31.1.19.
9673	Pte.	Crompton, W.	B	
9805	L.Cpl.	Cruise, Ernest	C	Dis 16.2.15
9557	Pte.	Cussick, William	A	KinA Gallipoli, 2.5.15
9915	Cpl.	Daffurn, O.	A	
10018	Pte.	Dakin, Thomas	D	Wounded at Gallipoli; served as sergeant with Royal Defence Corps
10724	Pte.	Dale, Arthur Leonard	C	KinA China 6.11.14
9708	Cpl	Dale, Henry George	D	Later sergeant; wounded at Gallipoli 25.5.15. Dis 18.9.28.
10024	Pte	Dark, Edwin	A	Later served with Welsh Regiment
10318	Pte.	Dart, Richard	C	Later served with RE
10428	Pte.	Davenport, Leonard	D	Wounded at Gallipoli 29.6.15; KinA France 4.7.17
10574	Pte.	Davies, Albert William	D	KinA Gallipoli, 29.6.15 as L.Cpl.
10669	Pte.	Davies, David	D	Wounded at Gallipoli 8.5.15; later sergeant dis 13.9.23.
10523	Pte.	Davies, David James	A	KinA France 23.4.15
10304	Pte.	Davies, David John	B	KinA Gallipoli, 21.8.15
10238	Pte.	Davies, David Thomas	D	Dis 25.3.16.
10427	Pte.	Davies, David William	C	Dis 1.2.19
10658	Pte.	Davies, E.	A	
10283	Pte.	Davies, Edward	A	Dis 17.8.16
10674	Pte.	Davies, Frederick James	D	DofW Egypt, 13.9.15.
9244	Sgt.	Davies, G.	B	MID for China
10689	L.Sgt.	Davies, Hugh	B	DofW France, 28.6.16
9565	Cpl.	Davies, J.	D	Remained Laoshan Bay
5569	Sgt.	Davies, John	C	Later CSM; to Class Z Army Reserve 19.4.19.
10111	Pte.	Davies, John Rees	C	KinA Gallipoli 8.5.15 as L.Cpl.
10392	Pte.	Davies, Manley	B	Later corporal dis 18.3.18.
9474	Pte.	Davies, Morgan	A	Dis 25.11.15
10486	L.Cpl.	Davies, Spencer Rees	C	Later corporal, to Class B Army Reserve 21.2.19
9777	Pte.	Davies, Stanley	C	DofW Egypt, 10.5.15.
10658	Pte.	Davies, W	C	
10223	Pte	Davies, William	A	Later Transport Sergeant
10641	Pte.	Davies, William J.	C	Later served with South Lancs Regt as lance corporal
10314	Pte.	Davies, William John	A	KinA France 1.7.16
10617	Pte.	Davis, Horace Charles	C	KinA Gallipoli 8.5.15
9786	Pte.	Day, A.	D	
10377	Pte.	Day, A.G.	A	Died in China 10.8.14. No medal issued
10330	Pte.	Day, Francis	A	KinA Gallipoli, 11.6.15
9554	Pte.	Day, Frederick	B	Later served with RWF
9280	Pte.	Day, Harry	B	Served with RWF and London Regt as sergeant.

9574	Pte.	Daye, George J.	C	Later served with the NF.
10239	Pte.	Dean, Joseph	B	Later served with MGC
9935	Pte.	Dearman, Albert	D	Wounded at Gallipoli 28.6.15; served as sergeant with RWF
9179	Pte.	Dignum, Ernest Joseph	B	Later acting sergeant
9196	L.Cpl.	Dilinutt, Albert Edward		Not at Tsingtao. Dis 24.9.17.
10807	Pte.	Ditzel, Harry	D	
	Capt.	Dive, G.H.		Medical Officer attached from RAMC; DSO; MID for China 30.5.16. and three times more
10478	Pte.	Donovan, John	A	Later corporal
10399	Pte.	Donovan, Patrick	B	KinA Salonika (attd. 7/SWB) 18.9.18
9521	Pte.	Donovan, William A.	A	To Class Z Army Reserve 20.3.19
9584	Pte.	Dowse, John	B	Dis 25.3.19
10909	Pte.	Drane, George Edward	C	KinA France 1.7.16
10323	L.Cpl.	Dredge, William George	C	Later Pte. Dis 26.3.16
9620	Pte.	Driscoll, John	C	Wounded at Gallipoli 19.6.15; KinA France (attd. 6/SWB) 25.5.16
10632	Pte.	Dunbar, Trevor Ronald	C	To Weihaiwei; deserted
9849	L.Cpl.	Dunn, Frank James	B	KinA Flanders 21.8.16
10279	Pte.	Dyke, Wilson J.C.	A	To Hospital Ship *Delta* 9.11.14; later served as corporal with RWF, ASC and NF
9998	Pte.	Eastall, Stanley	C	Later lance corporal; KinA France 1.7.16
10260	Pte.	Eckley, Albert Charles	C	Dis 13.7.17
10104	Pte.	Edwards, Alfred S.	C	Later served with RWF
9507	Bdsm	Edwards, Benjamin	C	To Class Z Army Reserve 2.2.19
8065	Pte.	Edwards, Charles E.	A	Dis 21.4.27
9659	Pte.	Edwards, John	C	Army Reserve 7.5.19
10077	Pte.	Edwards, William John	A	Later sergeant; KinA France 1.7.16
9977	Pte.	Elliott, Henry	B	Dis 8.9.20
	Capt.	Ellis, Archibald Horace Joseph		Served in Boer War
10485	Pte.	Ellis, Thomas Stephen	D	Wounded at Gallipoli 8.5.15 and 20.5.15 and France 20.10.16; dis 2.8.30
9547	Sgt.	Ellis, William Henry	D	Wounded at Gallipoli. MSM; dis 12.4.19
10808	Dmr.	Erratt, Alfred Henry Cleveland	A	Later corporal
10893	Pte.	Erry, Thomas Edgar	B	Later served with Labour Corps
10896	Pte.	Espiner, George Samuel	C	dis 28.6.16
9649	L. Cpl.	Evans, Alfred Robert.	B	KinA Flanders 8.2.18
10539	Pte.	Evans, Edward I.	C	Note soldier with same number killed with 1/SWB on 11.11.14 in Belgium
10558	Pte.	Evans, Harry	A	DofW at sea 3.5.15
10654	Pte.	Evans, Harold R.	C	Later corporal Deserted 28.1.19
10614	Pte.	Evans, Herbert	A	MID KinA China 6.11.14
9844	Pte.	Evans, John Allen	B	To Hospital Ship *Delta* 9.11.14; DofW Gallipoli 19.9.15
10624	Pte.	Eve, E.	A	
8885	L.Cpl.	Everett, William	A	Later sergeant; dis 21.8.16
9136	Pte.	Ewens, Albert Henry	B	Dis 25.5.17

10816	Pte.	Eynon, Thomas John	D	Wounded at Gallipoli 30.6.15; later sergeant then commissioned MGC
9189	Sgt.	Fairbrass, Joseph Sydney	B	KinA France 1.7.16 when CSM
10294	Pte.	Farr, Thomas	A	Later served with RWF
9497	Pte.	Farrington, Owen	B	Later served as Driver with RFA
10327	Pte.	Faulkner, James	D	Wounded at Gallipoli 30.4.15; dis 12.12.17.
10371	Pte.	Fenton, Arthur	C	Dis 4.3.22.
10370	Pte.	Field, Frederick	B	Wounded, to Hospital Ship *Delta*, 9.11.14; later corporal dis 28.4.19
10360	Pte.	Field, Thomas George	C	Unfit for operations at Tsingtao; later served with MGC
6053	Sgt.	Finch, Samuel	B	Served Boer War; dis WO2 24.1.20.
10324	L.Cpl.	Fingleton, Joseph	C	Later acting corporal; dis 7.2.22.
8143	Pte.	Fisher, Charles	D	KinA Gallipoli, 28.4.15
10032	Pte.	Fisher, Ernest Alfred	D	Dis 21.11.16.
9640	Pte.	Fisher, James	D	Wounded at Gallipoli 28.4.15; later sergeant, to Class B Army Reserve 20.4.19
10391	Pte.	Fisher, Joseph	D	Wounded at Gallipoli; dis 15.3.22
10501	Pte.	Fitzgerald, Edward	C	Died Gallipoli, 6.6.15
10634	Pte.	Foley, Charles James	A	DCM & MID for China; KinA Gallipoli 26.4.15
9145	Pte.	Foot, George B.	C	Later served with RE.
10629	Pte.	Ford, Francis John	A	KinA Gallipoli 28.6.15
10278	Pte.	Forrest, William	B	To Hospital Ship *Delta* 9.11.14 dis 31.1.19.
9338	Pte.	Foskett, John	D	Wounded at Gallipoli 12.5.15; KinA serving with 1/SWB 2.4.16.
10749	Pte.	Foster, Ivor Llewellyn	B	Later Acting Cpl. dis 10.3.24
8756	Pte.	France, Richard James	A	KinA France 16.8.17
9616	Pte.	Francis, Idwal Wynne	A	DofW Alexandria 22.5.15
10786	Pte.	Francis, Richard Mark.	A	Unfit for operations at Tsingtao; KinA Gallipoli 28.6.15.
9022	Pte.	Friend, Bertie George	D	KinA France 1.7.16
9576	Pte.	Frost, Ernest	A	Later served with RWF as Sergeant.
10307	Pte.	Fry, Arthur E	A	Later L.Cpl. KinA 29.4.16
10240	Pte.	Fuller, Albert	D	Served in Gallipoli as company cook; dis 28.7.16
9698	L.Cpl.	Fuller, Edward	D	Wounded at Gallipoli; later served as sergeant Depot SWB, to Class B Army Reserve 15.2.19
10358	Pte	Fury, Michael	B	Later lance corporal; DofW Gallipoli 1.7.15.
10242	Pte.	Gallaghan, Robert	D	Later sergeant; wounded at Gallipoli 9.5.15; dis 10.1.19
10678	L.Cpl.	Galloway, John Frederick	C	Later sergeant.;
9699	Pte.	Gane, Edmund	A	To Class B Army Reserve 15.2.19
9286	Pte.	Gant, William	A	KinA Gallipoli 25.4.15
9483	Pte.	Gardiner, John	C	KinA (attn 1 SWB) 25.7.16 as acting sergeant
10715	Pte.	Gardner, Edward J.	A	Later served as sergeant with MGC
10403	Pte.	Gardner, Thomas James	A	Dis 19.7.16
10655	Pte.	Garrett, William	C	Dis 4.9.17
9982	Pte.	Pates, Wilfred Richard	B	To Class B Army Reserve 8.9.20
10050	L.Cpl.	Gates, William John	B	Later corporal dis 28.3.16

9979	Pte.	Geoghegen, John	C	DofW Gallipoli 6.7.15
9638	L.Cpl.	George, John Francis	C	To Class B Army Reserve 17.4.19
10945	Pte.	George, Thomas James	A	Later served with 3/SWB; dis 3.6.16
9458	Pte.	Gibbons, Augustus	C	Dis 14.4.19
10768	Sgt.	Gibbs, Stephen	B	Wounded at Gallipoli 7.5.15. and France 29.9.18; dis 20.1.24
10445	L.Cpl.	Giddings, Arthur William	A	KinA Gallipoli 25.4.15
7242	CQMS	Gilby, George William	A	Later CSM. KinA Gallipoli 28.6.15
9491	Pte.	Gillard, Godfrey	B	Later served with Labour Corps
10556	Pte.	Gillespie, John	C	Later served with KSLI and RE
	Major	Going, John		DSO; MID
9544	Pte.	Goldberg, Joseph	C	KinA France 20.10.16
10462	L.Cpl.	Goodenough, Albert Jessie	C	KinA Gallipoli 25.4.15
9665	Pte.	Goodwin, Charles	D	To Class B Army Reserve 4.3.19
10154	Pte.	Goodwin, George	D	Wounded at Gallipoli 2.5.15; dis 6.10.16
9111	Pte.	Gostling, Charles E.	B	Later served as sergeant with Labour Corps
9978	Pte.	Gough, Harry	A	Later sergeant; to Class B Army Reserve 8.3.19
9723	Pte.	Goulston, Henry	D	KinA Gallipoli 25.4.15
9948	Pte.	Gray, Arthur William	B	Later served with MGC. Dis 2.2.19
5777	Pte.	Greatly, Thomas	D	To Hospital Ship *Delta* 9.11.14; to Class Z Army Reserve 2.5.19.
10331	L.Cpl.	Greedy, Ernest	C	Later served with Welsh Regt. as sergeant.
9004	Pte.	Green, Absalom	B	DCM & MID for China; KinA Gallipoli 28.6.15
10599	Pte.	Green, John	A	Later served with Welsh Regt.
10442	Pte.	Green, John Thomas	B	KinA Gallipoli 28.4.15
10576	Pte.	Green, Thomas Edgar	D	Wounded at Gallipoli 22.6.15; dis 2.12.22
8937	L.Cpl.	Greenbury, Joseph	A	Later sergeant; wounded at Gallipoli 9.5.15; LSGCM
	Capt.	Greenway, Thomas Cattell		DSO; MID 5.8.15 & 5.5.16.
9101	L.Sgt.	Gregory, Robert	C	Later sergeant; Class Z Army Reserve 22.3.19
3908	Dmr.	Grey, Ernest William	C	Served Boer War; dis 2.2.19; LSGCM
9635	Pte.	Grey, Frederick	B	Section B Army Reserve 7.3.19
10145	Pte.	Griffin, Thomas J.	D	Later corporal
10642	Pte.	Griffiths, Henry	A	KinA Gallipoli 26.4.15
9792	Pte.	Griffiths, Septimus R.	B	
10726	Pte.	Griffiths, Henry W.	B	Wounded, to Hospital Ship *Delta* 9.11.14; MM; later corporal; dis 7.1.24
9754	Pte.	Groves, S.	C	
9363	Pte.	Gudge, H.	B	
	Lieut.	Habershon, Cyril Bernard		Major 3.6.18
9626	Pte.	Haddon, Henry	B	Later Acting Cpl.
9829	Pte.	Haggarty, William	B	Later corporal Class B Army Reserve 30.3.19
10122	Pte.	Hagger, John Percy	B	Wounded in France 10.11.17; dis as sergeant 19.10.29
9038	Pte.	Hailey, Alfred	A	
8986	Pte.	Haire, James	B	Later served with the MGC

9475	Pte.	Hall, Arthur	A	Class Z Army Reserve 7.5.19
10020	Pte.	Hall, Arthur	D	To Hospital Ship *Delta* 9.11.14; later served with R.Tank Corps.
10652	Pte.	Hall, Herbert T.	A	Later as lance corporal served with Royal Defence Corps and Welsh Regt
10156	Pte.	Hall, James	A	Later served with RAF
9851	L.Cpl.	Hammond, Charles Thomas	B	Dis 20.3.19
10043	Pte.	Hammond, Harry	C	KinA France 1.7.16
10188	L.Sgt.	Hardiman, Joseph T.	C	Later acting sergeant dis 20.7.17
10889	Pte.	Harlow, Nathaniel	B	Later acting sergeant; Class B Army Reserve 12.9.19
9930	Cpl.	Harlow, P. J.	A	Later as acting sergeant served with Military Provost Staff Corps
9837	Sgt.	Harman, Alfred Oscar		Not at Tsingtao. Dis 30.3.17
9535	Pte.	Harper, Thomas Cook	D	Dis 13.3.19
10789	Pte.	Harries, Willie		Not at Tsingtao; drowned aboard RMS *Royal Edward* en route to Gallipoli 13.8.15.
10270	Pte.	Harris, Benjamin Edgar	D	Evacuated to hospital from Gallipoli; dis 27.12.17
9950	Pte.	Harris, James	B	Later served with RWF
10290	Pte.	Harris , John	C	Wounded, to Hospital Ship *Delta* 9.11.14; dis 10.4.17
9125	Pte.	Harris, William	C	MM; MID for Gallipoli. Later corporal KinA 1.7.16
10660	Pte.	Harrison, Ernest Frederick	D	Wounded at Gallipoli; MM for Western Front. Dis 15.10.18
10812	Pte.	Harrod, Leopold	A	Commissioned 3.3.16
9519	Pte.	Hart, Daniel	D	To Weihaiwei 27.10.14; later served with RWF
10313	Pte.	Hart, Nelson	B	KinA Gallipoli, 25.4.15
10316	Pte.	Hatfield, Thomas Charles	A	Dis 5.2.22; later served with Mons Regt
9320	Pte.	Havelock, Frederick J.	B	Later served with Nigeria Regt as corporal; to Class Z Army Reserve 18.4.19
9667	L.Cpl.	Hawkins, Edward	B	To Hospital Ship *Delta* 9.11.14; later served with Labour Corps
6517	Sgt.	Hayes, Thomas	C	Served in Boer War; later as CSM to MGC
9364	Pte.	Hayward, Thomas W.	B	To Hospital Ship *Delta* 6.11.14; later served with Welsh Regt
5006	CSM	Heal, Charles Henry	C	Commissioned 11.2.15. KinA Gallipoli 9.5.15. as second lieutenant
10249	Cpl.	Heath, Clement Frederick Percy.	C	Wounded at Gallipoli 5.7.15; later CSM; dis 23.11.18.
11027	Boy	Henderson, John	D	Not at Tsingtao; discharged as c corporal, 24.11.23
8978	Pte.	Hendy, John	C	Later served as L.Cpl. with MGC
9929	Pte.	Hendy, Percy J.	C	DCM for Gallipoli; later served with Labour Corps
10565	Pte.	Hennessey, Maurice	D	Deserted

9709	Pte.	Herbert, Thomas John	C	KinA Gallipoli 21.8.15
10892	Pte.	Hester, George Joseph	A	KinA Gallipoli 26.4.15
9524	Pte.	Hewitt, John	D	DCM for Gallipoli; Later sergeant with Worcestershire Regt
10608	Pte.	Hicksom, Morgan	A	Served as L.Cpl with RWF
10225	L.Cpl.	Higgins, James Bartholomew	A	Later sergeant; dis as CSM 4.1.21
10665	Pte.	Hill, Joseph	C	Later served as sergeant with MGC
9697	Pte.	Hill, Frederick	A	Wounded Tsingtao; later corporal DofW France 4.7.16
10687	Pte.	Hillier, Frederick	C	Later CSM; wounded at Gallipoli 29.6.15. DCM for Western Front; dis 4.6.21
9394	Pte.	Hillier, William	C	Later served with Labour Corps
10368	Pte.	Hobby, John	A	Later sergeant; KinA France 23.4.17.
10143	Pte.	Hodge, Sidney Jabez	C	KinA Gallipoli 11.5.15.
10857	Pte.	Hodges, William Henry	D	Unfit for operations in Tsingtao; KinA France (attd 1/SWB) 10.11.17
9983	Pte.	Hogg, Henry	B	Remained at Laoshan Bay; drowned aboard SS *Manitoba* en route to Gallipoli 16.4.15
10259	Pte.	Holbrook, Charles	D	Later served with RWF; to Class B Army Reserve 7.5.19.
9240	Pte.	Holloway, Arthur Frederick	A	MM; KinA France 6.10.17
9859	Pte.	Holloway, Frank	B	Later served with Welsh Regt.
10246	Pte.	Holmes, Charles	B	Later served with RWF
10548	Pte.	Honeybun, George	D	Wounded and evacuated to hospital from Gallipoli 8.5.15; to Class B Army Reserve 7.2.19
8679	Pte.	Hook, Frederick Herbert	B	KinA Gallipoli 2.5.15
9168	Pte.	Hook, Joseph	B	Dis 17.11.17
9725	Bdsm	Hooker, Thomas		Not at Tsingtao; KinA Gallipoli 15.5.15.
9886	Pte.	Hopkins, William Henry	C	Died China 13.9.14. No medal issued
9681	Pte.	Horan, Harry	D	Later served with Welsh Regt
9501	Pte.	Hoskins, William	D	Wounded at Gallipoli 28.6.15; dis 9.1.19
9838	Pte.	Howard, Arthur William	B	Later served with Welsh Regt
10027	L.Cpl.	Howard, John	D	KinA Gallipoli 28.5.15
10072	Pte.	Howe, Reginald James	B	Unfit for Tsingtao operations; KinA Gallipoli 28.6.15.
7125	Sgt.	Howse, Edward		Remained at Tientsin; dis 3.10.33.
8148	Pte.	Hughes, John William	A	Wounded at Gallipoli 28.6.15; KinA 19.8.18
5748	CSM	Hulbert, Lewis Edwin	A	Served Boer War; DofW (self inflicted) France as RQMS 25.6.17; LSGCM
10375	Pte.	Humphreys, Thomas.	D	Later served with Labour Corps and King's Liverpool Regt
9378	Pte.	Hunt, Edward A.	A	To Weihaiwei 18.10.14; later served with RWF
9725	L.Cpl.	Hunt, Richard Henry	C	KinA Gallipoli 21.6.15
10365	Pte.	Husselbee, James	D	Wounded at Gallipoli 8.5.15.
9923	Pte.	Hutchings, Albert George	D	Wounded at Gallipoli 28.6.15; dis 16.8.20

10224	Pte.	Ifold, William Frederick	B	Later corporal dis 30.1.19
6073	Sgt.	Iggleden, Charles F.	B	Served in Boer War as Andrews, C.F. Later served as private with Labour Corps.
10521	L.Cpl.	Jackson, William	B	DCM for Gallipoli; later sergeant; dis 13.3.19
10400	Pte.	Jackson, William Scott	B	To Hospital Ship *Delta* 9.11.14; died UK 12.11.19
6823	Sgt.	James, George Herbert	D	Served Boer War; not at Tsingtao; KinA Gallipoli 28.5.15
9714	Pte.	James, Lewis John	B	Dis 2.10.17
7131	Sgt.	Jamieson, Robert	D	RSM with ACC; MSM & LSGCM; dis 18.2.22
9695	Pte.	Jarrett, Frank Edward	D	Later corporal Dis 25.2.27
9960	Pte.	Jenkins, Edward	D	Dis 24.9.17
10605	Pte.	Jenkins, Evan Richard	C	Wounded at Gallipoli 4.5.15; later lance sergeant served with Gold Coast Regt; dis 31.5.32
9287	Bdsm.	Jenkins, John	B	LSGCM; to India 19.10.19; dis 15.7.24
9831	Pte.	Jenkins, William	B	Dis 9.6.22.
10684	Pte.	Jenkins, Walter	A	Later served as sergeant with Labour Corps
9980	Pte.	Jenkinson, Thomas	B	MID for China; KinA France 26.2.17
6083	Pte.	Jenner, Thomas Charles	B	Served Boer War, MID; KinA Mesopotamia 11.4.17 serving with 4/SWB
10303	Cpl.	Jennings, John R.	D	DofW Gallipoli 19.5.15
10545	Pte.	Jennings, Philip William	C	Wounded at Gallipoli 16.5.15.Attached as sergeant to KAR; dis 7.8.22
10126	Pte.	Jessen, Herman P.	D	Later served with MGC
10668	Pte.	Jinks, William James.		Not at Tsingtao; KinA Gallipoli 8.5.15
9737	Pte.	John, Daniel	C	Died Gibraltar 8.9.15
10484	L.Cpl.	Johns, Ernest Cyril	D	Wounded at Gallipoli 28.6.15, later sergeant; dis 30.9.16
9971	Pte.	Johnson, Alfred	C	Unfit for operation at Tsingtao; KinA France 2.9.18
	Capt.	Johnson, Dudley Graham		VC; CB; DSO & MID (for China); DSO Bar; MC; MID 3 times; served Boer War; later Lieutenant-Colonel North Staffs; retired as a major-general 1944; Hon Colonel SWB
5417	Sgt.	Johnson, Frederick Edmund	A	Served Boer War; died UK 1.3.19 LSGCM
10231	Pte.	Johnson, Frederick	C	Later L.Cpl.; dis A/Sgt. 4.1.21
9881	L. Cpl.	Johnson, George Aaron	A	To Hospital Ship *Delta* 9.11.14; DofW 15.11.14
10845	Pte.	Johnson, J	D	Served in Gallipoli; later served with King's Liverpool Regt
9760	Pte.	Jones, Arthur	D	Later served with Labour Corps
9999	Cpl.	Jones, Alfred William	B	Wounded in China; KinA Gallipoli 28.6.15
10489	Pte.	Jones, Charles	A	Later served with MGC

10560	L. Cpl.	Jones, Charles	A	KinA Gallipoli 29.6.15
9513	Pte.	Jones, Daniel Thomas	C	Later sergeant; dis 23.12.18 (also shown as David)
10757	Pte.	Jones, David Charles	B	Wounded Tsingtao and to Hospital Ship *Delta* 9.11.14; dis 23.3.15
10586	Pte.	Jones, Ernest	D	Wounded at Gallipoli 8.5.15; dis 20.8.17
	Major	Jones, Ernest Whitmore		Served Boer War and with 4/SWB in Mesopotamia
10691	Pte.	Jones, Frederick	D	Wounded at Gallipoli 28.6.15. To Class B Army Reserve 18.1.19
10335	Pte.	Jones, Frederick J.	B	Later served with RWF
9793	Pte.	Jones, George	D	To Hospital 14.9.14; KinA France (attd 1/SWB) 25.7.16
10710	L. Cpl.	Jones, George	A	Wounded at Gallipoli 24.7.15. Wounded France 1.7.16 and 30.5.18. Later corporal and dis as sergeant 29.1.31
10508	Pte.	Jones, George Thomas	C	Wounded in China; KinA Gallipoli 28.5.15
9764	Pte.	Jones, Harry John	C	Dis 14.6.19.
10015	Pte.	Jones, Harry F.	D	
10280	L. Cpl.	Jones, Henry	D	KinA France 6.4.16
10295	Pte.	Jones, Henry James	D	Wounded at Gallipoli 26.5.15 and 28.6.15. KinA Belgium 11.4.18
10182	Cpl.	Jones, Herbert	D	KinA Gallipoli 8.5.15
10308	Pte.	Jones, Robert	B	Later sergeant; Class B Army Reserve 13.5.19.
10448	Pte.	Jones, Walter Leonard	D	Wounded at Gallipoli 28.6.15. Class B Army Reserve 21.1.19
9509	Pte.	Jones, William	C	KinA 11.4.18
9450	Pte.	Jones, William	D	DofW Gallipoli 5.7.15
10220	Pte.	Jones, William E.	A	Later served with South Lancs Regt
10378	Pte.	Jones, William	B	Later served with RE
9811	Pte.	Jones, William Henry	A	To Weihaiwei 18.10.14 KinA Gallipoli 28.6.15
10171	Dmr.	Jones, William Isaac	B	MID for China; KinA Gallipoli 28.4.15
10542	Pte.	Jones, Wyndham	D	Wounded Gallipoli 8.5.15; KinA Gallipoli 12.6.15
10702	Pte.	Joseph, John		Not at Tsingtao; wounded at Gallipoli 23.8.15; dis 14.11.29
10126	Pte.	Keating, Timothy	D	Dis 12.2.16
9866	Dmr.	Keefe, Ellis John	D	KinA Gallipoli 8.5.15
9424	Dmr.	Keefe, William George	A	KinA Gallipoli 26.4.15
10338	Pte.	Keeling, Samuel	D	KinA Gallipoli 21.8.15
10589	Pte.	Keirle, Albert	D	Wounded 28.4.15; DofW Alexandria 15.8.15
9138	L. Cpl.	Kelly, Burham	C	MM and Bar; Later Pioneer sergeant; dis 20.1.19
10222	Pte.	Kelly, Edward Alexander	C	Wounded Tsingtao; MSM& LSGCM; later sergeant; dis 4.12.34.
9105	Cpl.	Kelly, Francis John	B	Later sergeant; Class Z Army Reserve 13.3.19
8876	Pte.	Kelly, William John	B	MM for Western Front. KinA France 23.4.17

10107	Pte.	Kent, Charles	B	KinA France 6.4.16
9934	Pte.	King, Harry	B	Later sergeant; dis 16.11.18
10132	Pte.	King, Robert H.	B	Later served with MGC
10438	Pte.	King, Walter Phillip	C	KinA France 1.7.17
10466	Pte.	Kingstone, Albert Edward		Not at Tsingtao; dis 29.4.16.
10526	Pte.	Kinnock, Willfred Hayman		Not at Tsingtao; KinA France attd 10/SWB 8.10.18.
10181	Pte.	Knatt, James L.	C	Dis 1.11.20
9224	Pte.	Knight, Charles F.	D	Later served with RE
9082	L.Sgt.	Knight, Frederick John	A	Later sergeant; dis 17.10.17
10134	Pte.	Knowles, Henry	D	Wounded in China. Later corporal with ACC; dis 23.10.20
10961	Pte.	Knowlson, William		Not at Tsingtao, DofW Gallipoli 18.8.15.
10793	Pte.	Lacey, Ernest J.	A	Later served with Cheshire Regt.
	Lt.& QM	Laman, Eric Kirkland		MBE, MC.
10194	Pte.	Lane, A.	A	
10300	Pte.	Lane, Cecil Henry	A	Later corporal MM and Bar while serving with 10/SWB; dis 30.6.18
10185	Pte.	Lane, J. D		
9710	Pte.	Langley, John	C	Remained Laoshan Bay. Class B Army Reserve 16.2.19
6379	Sgt.	Larley, Alfred G.	C	Served with South Lancs Regt as QMS
10662	Pte.	Lawrence, Sidney	A	Later served with RE
7309	Sgt.	Leach, Harold	B	MID for China; DofW at sea 6.6.15.
9988	Pte.	Lee, Alfred P.	B	Later served with ASC
10594	Pte.	Lees, Robert		Not at Tsingtao. Dis 14.6.19
9677	Pte.	Lewis, Alfred Henry	D	DofW Gallipoli 30.6.15
4528	Dmr	Lewis, Charles William	B	MID for China
10805	Pte.	Lewis, Henry Frank	C	Dis 12.5.28
10604	Pte.	Lewis, James	A	Later served at Depot Brecon. Dis 26.11.15.
9158	Pte.	Lewis, John Watkin	C	Dis 31.8.17. Died UK 31.1.20
9561	Pte.	Lewis, Lewis	A	Later served with the Middlesex Regt
9743	L. Cpl	Lewis, Reginald	C	Later corporal dis 30.1.16
9733	Pte.	Lewis, Samuel Thomas	C	Later corporal dis 6.8.17
10640	Pte.	Lewis, Thomas	C	KinA at Gallipoli 25.4.15
10511	Pte.	Linton, Charles		Not at Tsingtao; wounded Gallipoli 9.5.15 MID; Died in UK while on Army Reserve 9.11.20.
10407	Pte.	Lippett, Henry Theobald Ernest	A	Dis 5.4.22
10268	L.Cpl.	Lloyd, Frederick	D	Wounded at Gallipoli; Later sergeant. KinA France 1.7.16
10735	Pte.	Lloyd, George	A	Later sergeant; dis 19.8.19; died UK 9.3.19
10463	Pte.	Lloyd, John	B	KinA in France (attd 1 SWB) 27.3.16
10606	Pte.	Lloyd, John	A	KinA France 6.4.16
9781	L.Cpl.	Lloyd, Thomas	A	Later sergeant; dis 16.3.19.
10578	Pte.	Lloyd, William John	C	Wounded at Gallipoli 15.5.15; Later acting sergeant; dis 1.12.22
10411	L.Cpl.	Lockyer, E.	C	
9675	Pte.	Lofthouse, William	A	KinA Gallipoli 1.6.15
10100	Pte.	Long, Charles	C	Unfit for operations against

				Tsingtao; later served with RWF and RAMC
10461	Pte.	Long, Nelson	D	Dis 22.8.16
9962	Pte.	Longley, Arthur	D	Wounded at Gallipoli 28.4.15; later corporal, KinA France (attd 1/SWB) 15.4.18
10491	Pte.	Louch, George	D	Wounded at Gallipoli, 16.5.15, and France 1.7.16. Dis 2.3.19
9283	Dmr.	Lovegrove, George	D	Wounded at Gallipoli; later lance corporal; dis 8.12.17
9861	Pte.	Loveridge, Ernest Reuben	C	Wounded in China to Hospital Ship *Delta* 9.11.14 dis 11.12.15
10340	Cpl.	Lowe, James	D	Wounded at Gallipoli; dis 10.11.16
8866	Sgt.	Lucas, Ernest	A	C.deG. (France); commissioned; KinA (attd 7 SWB) 19.9.18. in Salonika
9815	L.Cpl.	Lyons, James J.	D	Wounded in Gallipoli; later as corporal served with the Labour Corps.
10470	Pte.	Mabbett, Trevor	D	Wounded in China: to Hospital Ship *Delta* 6.11.14; died UK 5.3.15
10311	Pte.	McFarlane, Alfred Henry Stuart	D	MM; wounded at Gallipoli; later CSM; dis 30.8.39
9628	Pte.	McFarren, Frederick	C	KinA 1.7.16
	Lieut.	MacGregor, Cortlandt Richard		KinA Gallipoli, 5.5.15.
9356	Pte.	MacKay, James D.	B	Served with Tank Corps as sergeant
10709	Pte.	Maddox, George	D	Dis 21.3.21.
9572	Pte.	Mahoney, Garrett	D	To Class Z Army Reserve 3.8.19
9987	Pte.	Mahoney, Oscar	C	Dis 16.2.19
10584	Pte.	Mahoney, Thomas	A	Dis 2.4.17
9395	Pte.	Maidment, Frank.		Not at Tsingtao; died in China 28.10.14
9035	Pte.	Mandell, John	D	Wounded in Gallipoli; later KinA Gallipoli 25.12.15
9645	Pte.	Manning, Will Frederick	C	
10450	Pte.	Manns, Frank	A	KinA Gallipoli 26.4.15
	Major	Margesson, Edward Cunningham.		MID for China; KinA Gallipoli 25.4.15
9175	Pte.	Marks, William Robert	B	Later sergeant; dis 28.4.25
9788	Pte.	Marsden, Edward J.	A	Later served with Labour Corps
8647	L.Sgt.	Marsh, Samuel S.	C	Later sergeant; dis as CQMS 21.1.31.
9113	Pte.	Martin, William	D	Served as company cook in Gallipoli; later sergeant.
10419	Pte.	Mason, Harry, Randolph	A	Later corporal dis 11.4.22
6026	Sgt.	Mason, John Alexander	B	Served Boer War; wounded at Gallipoli 7.5.15; later RSM; LSGC MSM and BEM
8125	Pte.	Mason, James	D	Wounded in China evacuated to Weihaiwei 27.10.14; KinA Gallipoli 28.5.15
9753	Pte.	Mason, Thomas Henry	B	Class B Army Reserve 1.3.19;

				brother of Mason, John
10078	Pte.	Mason, William Henry	C	DofW at sea 11.5.15.
10601	Pte.	Masters, John T.S.	D	Wounded at Gallipoli; later served with Norfolk Regt and King's Liverpool Regt.
9841	Sgt.Dmr.	Matthews, Archibald William	D	Wounded at Gallipoli 21.8.15; later WO2; dis 19.2.22. re-enlisted 1/Mons
10630	Pte.	Matthews, Edwin	B	Wounded in China; to Hospital Ship *Delta* 6.11.14; later served as sergeant with Welsh Regt and RWF
8602	Pte.	Matthews, Thomas	B	MM - Deserted
10876	Pte.	McBain, William Alexander	B	KinA France 1.7.16
10092	Pte.	McCarthy, Charles	A	Dis 18.10.20
10814	Pte.	McCarthy, D.	D	
10653	Pte.	McCarthy, Michael	A	Later Acting Sergeant; Class B Army Reserve 1.4.19.
10537	Pte.	McCarthy, William	C	KinA Gallipoli 8.5.15
8593	Cpl.	McGiff, William	C	To Weihaiwei, 27.10.14; later corporal with RFC
9820	Pte.	McGowan, Leslie O.	B	Remained Laoshan Bay; later served with Army Pay Corps and Wiltshire Regt.
10535	Pte.	Meredith, Walter J.	C	Wounded in China; later served with Labour Corps
10299	Pte.	Mesquitta, Percy Everitt	D	KinA Gallipoli 8.5.15
6294	Pte.	Milburn, Thomas J. H.	C	Served Boer War; later served with King's Liverpool Regt.
8994	Pte.	Miller, Herbert Robert Gladstone	C	Later sergeant. KinA France 18.9.18
8436	Sgt.	Miller, William	C	KinA China 7.11.14
9885	Cpl.	Miller, William	D	Wounded at Gallipoli; later as acting sergeant served with West Yorkshire Regt.
10791	Pte.	Miller, William Kinchella	C	Wounded at Gallipoli 14.5.15; later sergeant and commissioned QM. MSM and LSGCM
6475	Sgt.	Millichamp, Albert Harbridge	C	Served Boer War; KinA Gallipoli 8.5.15 as CSM
10322	Pte.	Milling, Thomas George Henry	A	Dis 25.6.15.
10052	Pte.	Millington, Edward Richard	B	KinA Belgium 11.4.18
9143	L.Cpl.	Millman, Francis William	C	Wounded at Gallipoli 14.6.15; later WO2; dis 8.4.27; LSGCM
9919	Pte.	Mills, Albert James	B	Wounded in China; to Hospital Ship *Delta* 9.11.14; later corporal; KinA 1.7.16
9600	Pte.	Millward, Thomas	C	DCM; KinA Gallipoli 8.5.15.
10169	L.Cpl.	Millward, William Churchill	C	MM and MID for Gallipoli; KinA France 1.7.16.
10088	Cpl.	Milne, Alexander Gordon	B	KinA Belgium 11.4.18 when CSM
9153	Pte.	Milson, Frank	C	Later sergeant; Class Z Army

				Reserve 10.4.19
9612	Pte.	Mitchell, Albert	C	Dis 1.11.18
10033	L.Sgt.	Mitchell, Harry Francis	A	MM; Later CQMS; dis 17.6.18.
9094	Pte.	Mitchell, James J.	D	Unfit for operation against Tsingtao; later to hospital in Gallipoli; served with Welsh Regt and RWF
10004	Cpl.	Moody, George M.	B	Served as sergeant with Labour Corps.
9623	Pte.	Moon, William	C	Class B Army Reserve 3.2.19
9973	Pte.	Morgan, Alfred Harry	B	Dis 29.12.17
10675	Pte.	Morgan, Charles	C	DofW Alexandria 24.5.15
10573	Pte.	Morgan, David	B	Later served with Labour Corps
9732	L.Cpl.	Morgan, David John	B	Later corporal dis 8.9.15.
7430	Pte.	Morgan, Joseph	D	Wounded at Gallipoli 25.4.15; dis 20.1.16.
	Lieut.	Morgan, Morgan Cyril		MC; MID (4 times); C de G (France); Cavalier Crown of Italy.
9550	Pte.	Morgan, Thomas Henry	A	Later sergeant; dis 19.4.19
9547	Pte.	Morgan, William	C	DofW (self inflicted) France 23.7.16
9615	Pte.	Morgan, William John	C	Wounded in Gallipoli 16.5.15. MM; MID; later corporal; wounded in France 21.10.18; dis 18.3.27.
10170	Pte.	Morris, Charles	B	KinA Gallipoli 21.8.15
9796	Sgt.	Morris, Frederick	A	Wounded and evacuated to Weihaiwei 18.10.14; wounded at Gallipoli 8.5.15; later CSM; dis 7.3.19.
9759	Pte.	Morris, Thomas	D	KinA in France when serving as lance corporal in 10/SWB 13.3.18.
11055	Pte.	Morris, William Edward	A	Not at Tsingtao; DofW France 14.11.16
9494	Pte.	Morris, William Hopkin	A	To Class Z Army Reserve 16.4.19.
10382	Pte.	Morris, William Hopkin	D	Wounded at Gallipoli; later served with KSLI and RWF; to Class Z Army Reserve 16.4.19
8293	Pte.	Morrison, Alexander R.	D	Wounded at Gallipoli; later served with Royal Defence Corps.
10041	Pte.	Moseley, Albert	A	Dis as sergeant 27.9.20.
6021	Sgt.	Moses, George		Served Boer War; not at Tsingtao; later RSM; MID, LSGCM
10522	Pte.	Munnings, William D.	D	Wounded at Gallipoli; later served as colour sergeant with RWF.
9586	Pte.	Murphy, Charles J.	C	Later served with Labour Corps; to Class B Army Reserve 22.2.19
10496	Pte.	Murrin, Archibald	B	Dis as corporal 22.2.19
9809	Pte.	Napper, Llewellyn	A	KinA Gallipoli 14.5.15
10302	Pte.	Nash, Frank Albert	A	Wounded in China, to Hospital Ship *Delta* 9.11.14; dis 16.5.15.
9624	Pte.	Nash, Walter	D	Remained at Laoshan Bay; wounded at Gallipoli 25.4.15.; dis 19.11.18.
10373	L.Cpl.	Noble, Joseph	D	Wounded at Gallipoli 8.9.15; wounded in France 29.1.17; later sergeant; dis 29.5.29
10547	Dmr.	Norgrove, William Henry	A	Wounded at Gallipoli 7.5.15; later

				served with Labour Corps; dis as corporal 21.10.22.
10390	Pte.	Norman, Charles	B	Dis 25.9.18.
10458	L.Cpl.	Norman, Christopher Albert	B	DCM; later RSM with 10 SWB; LSGCM; retired 2.8.35.
10087	L.Cpl.	Norris, Claude Rupert Dudley	D	KinA Gallipoli 8.5.15
10179	Cpl.	Nunn, Frederick Walter	D	Drowned aboard RMS *Royal Edward* 13.8.15
10780	Pte.	O'Brien, David	D	KinA Gallipoli 8.5.15
9235	Cpl.	O'Brien, Patrick	C	DofW at sea 7.5.15
10553	Pte.	O'Brien, William	C	Wounded in France; 1.7.16; later sergeant; dis 31.11.22.
10725	Pte.	O'Connell, Terence J.	A	KinA Gallipoli 25.4.15
11028	Boy	Organ, George Albert		Not at Tsingtao; dis 31.10.26.
9936	Pte.	Osborn, George William Edward	C	Later sergeant; LSGCM; dis 29.3.33.
10682	Pte.	Osborne, Frederick	A	MM; dis 31.3.21.
10500	Pte.	Owens, William	C	Later acting sergeant; dis 31.1.19
10717	Dmr.	Page, Charles Herbert	C	KinA France 1.7.16
	Capt.	Palmer, Roland Gaskell		Served Boer War, MID; KinA Gallipoli 25.4.15
9045	Pte.	Palmer, Frederick A.	C	To Class Z Army Reserve 20.2.19.
9860	Pte.	Pargetter, William	C	Wounded in China; later acting sergeant. KinA (attd 1/SWB 10.11.17)
10647	Pte.	Parish, Frank	D	Wounded at Gallipoli; dis 11.7.17.
9955	Pte.	Parker, William	A	To Class B Army Reserve 22.2.19.
10202	Pte.	Parkes, George	B	KinA China 6.11.14
10167	Pte.	Parsons, Lewis Samuel	C	Wounded in China; KinA Gallipoli, 21.8.15
10527	Pte.	Partridge, James	A	Remained at Laoshan Bay; KinA Gallipoli 28.6.15
9982	Pte.	Pates, Wilfred Richard	B	To Class B Army Reserve 8.9.20
10035	Pte.	Paul, Albert Thomas	A	Dis 20.3.17
10273	Pte.	Pavett, Charles William Walter	B	KinA China 6.11.14
9995	Bdsm	Payne, Arthur Frank	C	Dis 10.9.20.
7235	Sgt.	Payne, Arthur George	C	KinA China 6.11.14
9699	Pte.	Payne, Henry	C	KinA Gallipoli 26.4.15
9996	Pte.	Payne, Walter Guy		Not at Tsingtao; KinA with 10/SWB 11.3.18.
10342	Pte.	Peacock, Harry	B	MM; dis 13.2.22.
9566	Pte.	Pearce, Job	B	Dis 27.3.19
8916	Sgt.	Pearce, William Joseph	D	Later CSM; KinA France 6.4.16
10098	Pte.	Pears, Walter G.	B	Later served with RWF.
9294	Pte.	Pearson, Frederick	D	Dis 20.2.18
9984	Pte.	Penfare, George Charles	C	Wounded in China; to Hospital Ship *Delta* 9.11.14; dis 23.5.16.
10853	Pte.	Pennington, Arthur	C	Dis 15.2.15. Died UK 9.7.20
10443	Pte.	Perkins, Frederick John	D	Wounded Gallipoli 28.4.15; 15.5.15; 17.6.15; dis as lance corporal 30.1.19.
	Lieut.	Petre, Roderick Loraine		Wounded in China; CB; DSO; MC; MID for China; later major; MID

				seven times.
8998	Dmr.	Pewtner, William H.	A	Wounded in China; later served as sergeant with Military Provost Staff Corps and RWF.
10079	L.Sgt.	Phillips, Albert.	A	To hospital in China; KinA Gallipoli, 26.4.15
10603	Pte.	Phillips, Edgar	C	Wounded at Gallipoli 16.5.15; dis 14.6.19.
9911	L.Cpl.	Phillips, Walter		Not at Tsingtao; Class B Army Reserve 15.4.19.
10503	Pte.	Phillips, William George	B	Wounded at Gallipoli 5.5.15; dis 8.2.19.
10262	Pte.	Phipps, Charles	C	Dis 18.3.16.
10895	Pte.	Pickering, Charles	D	Wounded in Gallipoli; later corporal; DofW (attd 4 /SWB) 21.1.17.
9126	Pte.	Pickering, Charles, Frederick	C	KinA France (attd 1/SWB) 15.10.15
10337	L.Cpl.	Pickering, Samuel	C	Dis as sergeant 13.2.22.
9570	Pte.	Pine, Frederick Thomas	B	MM; KinA France 11.4.18
10074	Pte.	Pook, Edgar John James	B	Later served RAF; dis 5.10.20.
9598	Pte.	Poole, Richard William	C	MM; MID; KinA France 14.4.17
10274	Pte.	Pople, C.	C	Later served with RFC
10969	Pte.	Pople, Thomas	D	Wounded at Gallipoli; later served with Somerset Light Infantry
10520	Pte.	Popp, Henry	D	Dis 14.9.22
10730	Pte.	Porter, Francis	D	Later served at Depot SWB, Brecon
9608	L.Cpl.	Porter, Harold Arthur	B	DofW at sea 2.5.15
9901	Pte.	Porter, Stanley	D	MM; later served with ASC; dis 15.6.16.
9478	Pte.	Pounds, Charles Powell	A	KinA Gallipoli 26.5.15
10549	Pte.	Powell, Aaron	D	Served as CQMS with RWF
10444	Dmr.	Powell, Arthur Edwin	D	Wounded at Gallipoli 14.5.15; later sergeant; dis 3.2.26; later Indian Army; IGSM
10966	Pte.	Powell, Charles E.	B	Later corporal served with Royal West Kent Regt
10483	Pte.	Powell, James H.	C	Later served with Mon Regt and RWF as corporal
8963	Pte.	Powell, William	D	DofW Belgium 21.3.18
10233	Pte.	Powell, William	A	deserted 25.7.15
10591	Pte.	Powell, William	C	Dis 22.3.16.
10367	Pte.	Power, Robert J.	A	Wounded in China; to Hospital Ship *Delta* 9.11.14; later served with Labour Corps.
9734	Pte.	Powley, P.	C	
9875	Pte.	Poynter, Henry	B	Class Z Army Reserve 15.3.19
10217	Pte.	Preece, Albert James	B	Later served with KAR
10218	Pte.	Preece, J.	B	
3692	Sgt.	Press, Thomas Richard	D	Served Boer War; MID, LSGCM, MSM; Officers' Mess Sergeant Tsingtao
10978	Pte.	Price, E	B	
10670	Pte.	Price, Edward Sydney	C	KinA Gallipoli 6.7.15
9825	Pte.	Price, Frederick	C	Later sergeant; Class B Army Reserve 17.1.19

8477	Pte.	Price, William	D	Wounded at Gallipoli; dis 8.1.17
9816	Pte.	Price, William Henry	D	KinA Gallipoli 25.4.15
10797	Bdsm.	Price, William Thomas	D	Dis as sergeant 31.3.36.
10651	Pte.	Pring, Frederick Charles	B	Dis 3.3.16
10784	Pte.	Pyne, Edward E.	C	Remained at Laoshan Bay; later served with RAMC
10577	Pte.	Rackham, G.	C	
9671	Pte.	Raftery, Charles	A	Dis 8.9.19
	Lieut.	Rawle, William		To Grenadier Guards 28.4.15; retired 5.8.18
10048	Pte.	Rawlinson, Richardson E.	B	Later served with Hampshire Regt.
9803	Pte.	Reed, James		Not at Tsingtao; dis 1.11.17
10285	L.Cpl.	Rees, Thomas	B	Dis 11.8.16
6414	Pte.	Remnant, George.	D	Served Boer War; later sergeant; MSM, LSGCM; retired as sergeant 22.11.22
10317	Pte.	Reveley, Charles	A	Remained Laoshan Bay; KinA Gallipoli 26.4.15
10727	Pte.	Reynolds, William	A	To Hospital Ship *Delta* 9.11.14; KinA (attd 1/SWB) 8.9.16
9964	Pte.	Rice, John Richard	C	MM, MID; KinA France 11.4.18
9776	Pte.	Richards, Arthur J.	C	Later served with ASC and RWF
9740	Cpl.	Richards, Ferdinand James	D	Wounded at Gallipoli; later sergeant; dis 11.8.16.
10248	L.Cpl.	Richards, Thomas	D	KinA Gallipoli 21.8.15
10060	Pte.	Richardson, Arthur James	D	KinA Gallipoli 2.5.15
10178	Pte.	Richardson, James Sivui	C	Dis 18.1.15
10705	Pte.	Richardson, John	D	Later served with 1/SWB and Labour Corps; died UK 2.10.17
10012	Pte.	Riches, John	B	Dis 13.9.20
9151	Pte.	Rickward, Albert Victor	A	Deserted 1915
10583	Pte.	Rider, Charles	D	Wounded at Gallipoli; Later served with RWF as lance corporal
10142	Pte.	Ridgewell, Wilfred George	D	Served Gallipoli as signaller and later as lance sergeant SWB Depot Brecon; dis 10.7.17
9563	Pte.	Riley, James Alexander	A	Later corporal; dis 1.5.19
10361	Pte.	Roberts, Bertie	A	Later served with Manchester Regt
10422	Pte.	Roberts, James.	C	DofW in Gallipoli 25.4.15
10541	L.Cpl.	Roberts, J.	C	
9484	BM	Roberts, John Charles		Not at Tsingtao; dis 24.9.15
9131	Dmr	Robinson, James Henry	B	KinA Gallipoli 2.5.15
11045	Boy	Robinson, Stephen William		Not at Tsingtao; dis 8.4.19
10209	L.Cpl.	Rogers, Joseph Henry	A	Later acting sergeant; dis 22.7.27
8636	L.Sgt.	Rogers, William	A	KinA Gallipoli 12.6.15
10965	Pte.	Rose, James John	B	MM; dis 15.12.28
10249	Cpl.	Rosier, William Samuel	B	MID for China; later commissioned SWB; resigned commission 1.4.19.
6082	CSM	Ross, Willie	D	Served Boer War; commissioned 11.2.15; KinA 16.8.17 as acting captain
8236	Pte.	Rothenbaugh	C	
9393	Pte.	Rousell, Llewellyn	B	Later served SWB Depot, Brecon; dis 13.6.16.
9688	Pte.	Rowe, Thomas W.	A	Later served with RE
9602	Pte.	Sadler, F.	A	

10711	Pte.	Sage, Charles	A	To Weihaiwei 27.10.14; wounded at Gallipoli 7.6.15; dis 3.12.23.
8750	Sgt.	Saggers, George William E.	A	Dis 11.10.15; later re-enlisted SWB; dis as sergeant 4.12.34
10007	L.Cpl.	Sale, Harry	C	Dis 13.9.20
9329	L.Cpl.	Sanderson, George Stanley	A	KinA France 1.7.16 serving as sergeant
9241	Pte.	Saunderson, Frederick	A	Later served with Labour Corps and Royal Fusiliers.
9798	Pte.	Saunderson, William	B	KinA Gallipoli 17.5.15
10119	L.Cpl.	Sawkins, Stephen	D	Wounded at Gallipoli 28.6.15; later as CQMS served with RWF
9567	Sgt.	Sawyer, Charles Benjamin	C	KinA Gallipoli 21.8.15
9104	Pte.	Scantlebury, Edgar	C	Later acting corporal Class Z Army Reserve 19.1.19
10415	Pte.	Scarborough, Ernest Arthur	C	DCM serving with 5/SWB as sergeant; dis 8.4.22.
9689	Pte.	Sear, Sidney George	A	
10040	Pte.	Seth, William Robert	D	Wounded at Gallipoli; MM; dis 28.9.20
10203	Pte.	Sewell, Archibald	D	Later served with RAMC and RWF as acting sergeant
7000	Pte.	Sewell, Harry		Not at Tsingtao; DofW Gallipoli 4.5.15.
9243	Pte.	Sewell, John Rowland	C	KinA China 6.11.14
10919	Pte.	Sharpe, Albert William	A	KinA Gallipoli 28.6.15
9951	Pte.	Sharpe, Frederick William	B	Dis 17.2.17.
9543	Pte.	Sharp, Thomas	C	Dis 5.4.19
10344	Pte.	Sheppard, George	B	Wounded in China; to Hospital Ship *Delta* 9.11.14; KinA Gallipoli, 14.5.15.
10343	Pte.	Shore, John	D	DofW Gallipoli, 3.5.15
9633	Pte.	Sibley, Samuel	D	DofW Alexandria 20.5.15.
9170	Pte.	Silk, George	D	KinA Gallipoli 2.5.15
9477	Pte.	Simmonds, Thomas Joseph	B	KinA Gallipoli 1.7.15
9588	L.Cpl.	Simpson, Thomas	C	Dis 12.2.19
10076	Pte.	Sims, Frederick	C	Later served with KSLI and RWF
9229	L.Cpl.	Skeggs, Charles	B	Later WO2. Class Z Army Reserve 12.4.19
9663	Pte.	Sladden, Edward James	A	
10210	Pte.	Slater, Harold	A	MM for Gallipoli; dis 9.10.17
10934	Pte.	Sly, Frank	C	Dis 28.3.16
10131	Pte.	Slyde, Albert	B	To Hospital 15.9.14; dis 12.2.15
9918	Pte.	Small, C.	D	Wounded at Gallipoli; later served with 3/SWB and Military Foot Police
8074	L.Cpl.	Smart, James	C	To Hospital Ship *Delta* 9.11.14; later colour sergeant; dis 26.9.22
10195	Pte.	Smith, Arthur John		Not at Tsingtao; later served Bedfordshire Regt; dis 28.12.22
10386	Pte.	Smith, Evan	D	Later served with Bedfordshire Regt
9797	Pte.	Smith, Frederick	B	Later served with Labour Corps
9274	Pte.	Smith, George	C	KinA Gallipoli 28.4.15
9029	Pte.	Smith, Henry	C	Dis 28.6.15
9118	Pte.	Smith, John E.	D	Wounded in China; later served

				with Labour Corps
10777	Pte.	Smith, Henry	D	Wounded at Gallipoli; dis 22.6.16
10531	Pte.	Smith, James	B	Unfit for operations against Tsingtao; KinA Gallipoli 28.6.15
9917	Pte.	Smith, Joseph Richard	B	DofW Belgium 1.4.18
10833	Pte.	Smith, Oliver Charles	D	Died UK 12.2.17
5827	CQMS	Smith, Robert	C	Served Boer War; later acting RSM with RWF; dis 6.8.19; MSM
9767	Pte.	Smith, Thomas	B	KinA Gallipoli 2.5.15
10950	Pte.	Smith, Thomas	C	Wounded at Gallipoli 3.7.15; dis 6.10.20
9042	Pte.	Smith, James	A	Dis 15.8.17
10023	Cpl.	Smith, Walter	B	KinA France 1.7.16
9981	Pte.	Smith, William Walter	B	Later corporal; KinA France 6.4.16.
10417	Pte.	Smith, William Harvey	A	KinA Gallipoli 24.5.15
9661	Pte.	Smith, William Henry	A	Served with Depot SWB; dis 16.5.18.
10296	Pte.	Smyth, Patrick	B	KinA Gallipoli 29.6.15
9972	Pte.	Snow, George	B	DCM & MID for China; dis 2.9.20
	Capt.	Somerville, Desmond Harry Sykes		CBE, MC & Bar MID (twice); retired as a major-general 4.8.45
9986	Pte.	Sparrowhawk, Albert Leonard	D	Wounded at Gallipoli 2.5.15; later lance coporal; dis 24.2.19
10743	Dmr	Spicer, Edwin	A	Wounded at Gallipoli 9.5.15; dis as coporal 23.6.28
9121	Pte.	Spinks, Alfred Richard	C	Wounded in China; DCM (Gallipoli); KinA France 13.7.16
9735	Pte.	Squires, Charles Frederick	D	Class B Army Reserve 8.5.19
8329	Pte.	Stagg, Robert	A	Died of influenza 1.11.18
9795	Cpl.	Stagg, Sydney L.J.	A	Remained Laoshan Bay; later sergeant; dis 28.6.18
4187	QMS	Stanborough, Walter Thomas		Served Boer War, wounded; commissioned 11.2.15; DofW Gallipoli 13.5.15; LSGCM
3828	Pte.	Stephens, Robert	D	Served Boer War; wounded in Gallipoli; served as lance corporal with Labour Corps; dis 23.3.19 (name also shown as Stevens)
9993	Pte.	Stevens, Herbert	D	Wounded, to Hospital Ship *Delta* 9.11.14; wounded at Gallipoli; MM
10091	Pte.	Stevens, Thomas	D	Wounded at Gallipoli; dis 15.1.16
9169	Pte.	Stock, Isaac	A	Later sergeant; KinA France (attd 1/SWB) 27.8.16
10518	L.Cpl.	Stokes, Percy	D	Dis 19.6.16
9784	Pte.	Stone, Walter	D	Wounded at Gallipoli, dis 13.5.16
9291	Pte.	Stoner, Edward Thomas	B	Died of disease, China 3.11.14
9642	Pte.	Storer, William	B	Wounded in China, to Hospital Ship *Delta* 9.11.14
10229	Pte.	Straney, George C.	A	KinA Gallipoli 28.6.15 when lance corporal
5555	Sgt.	Stratford, Thomas William V.	C	Served Boer War; later WO2; dis 22.5.17; LSGCM

8898	Cpl.	Stuart, David Lyall	D	MID; later as CSM; KinA Belgium 11.4.18
9949	Pte.	Stuart, James Harold	D	Later served with Labour Corps; dis 7.8.20
9912	Pte.	Sturgess, Ivan Arthur	A	KinA Gallipoli, 11.6.15 when lance corporal
9696	Pte.	Suggett, William	B	Wounded in China; to Hospital Ship *Delta* 9.11.14; later corporal; dis 11.3.19.
10828	Pte.	Sullivan, Daniel		Not at Tsingtao; dis 22.9.16.
9967	Pte.	Sullivan, Patrick	B	Dis 23.1.19
10228	Dmr.	Sutterfield, William	D	Wounded at Gallipoli; later served with Labour Corps
9900	Pte.	Sutton, Harold		Not at Tsingtao
9678	Pte.	Swaine, Richard	A	Dis 22.2.19
6040	Pte.	Swift, Asher	B	
10056	Pte.	Swinfield, William	D	Wounded in China; to Weihaiwei 18.10.14; later wounded at Gallipoli; dis 27.8.15.
9880	L.Cpl.	Sydenham, Albert George	C	KinA China 7.11.14
9064	Pte.	Taffs, A.	A	Later as CQMS served with Tank Corps; MM; commissioned KSLI 14.4.18
10405	Pte.	Tanner, Harry G.	C	KinA France 28.4.16
10856	Pte.	Taylor, Herbert Claude	A	KinA Gallipoli 1.7.15
10437	Pte.	Teece, Alfred	D	Wounded at Gallipoli; KinA (attd 1/SWB) 7.9.16
9887	Pte.	Terrett, Frederick	B	Class B Army Reserve 11.3.19
9505	Cpl.	Terrett, William Charles	A	MM; MID; later RSM, Class Z Army Reserve 8.3.19.
10172	Pte.	Terrill, Arthur	C	KinA Gallipoli 8.5.15
9865	Pte.	Theobald, Oscar Francis	C	LSGCM; later RSM 1 SWB
10387	Pte.	Thomas, Abraham	B	Later sergeant with RWF and SWB; LSGCM; dis 30.4.42
10770	Pte.	Thomas, Arthur	B	Wounded in China, to Hospital Ship *Delta* 9.11.14; wounded at Gallipoli 14.5.15; dis 15.4.28
10401	Pte.	Thomas, Caleb John		Not at Tsingtao; KinA Gallipoli 8.5.15.
10902	Pte.	Thomas, Charles William	A	KinA in France 1.7.16
10645	Pte.	Thomas, E.	D	
10336	Pte.	Thomas, George	D	DofW at sea 2.5.15
10406	L.Cpl.	Thomas, James	D	DofW China 3.11.14
9778	Pte.	Thomas, John Henry	A	Later corporal Dis 9.4.18.
8226	Pte.	Thomas, Levi	C	KinA Gallipoli 25.4.15
10579	Pte.	Thomas, Stanley	A	Wounded at Gallipoli 22.6.15 and in France 6.8.17; dis 12.12.22
10326	Pte.	Thompson, Walter	C	KinA Gallipoli 21.8.15
10481	Pte.	Thompson, William	D	Unfit for operations against Tsingtao; dis 21.7.22.
10312	Pte.	Thomson, Hugh Arthur		Not at Tsingtao; dis 9.6.16.
9685	Pte.	Thornton, Percy	C	Later served with RE
8737	Cpl.	Thornington, Alfred Daniel		Not at Tsingtao. To Class Z Army Reserve 15.3.19
10269	L.Cpl.	Tiley, Ernest	B	Wounded in China, to Hospital Ship *Delta* 9.11.14 Dis 30.3.18

10932	Pte.	Tiley, Thomas Norman	C	Dis 26.4.17.Later served with 3/Mons Regt. as lance sergeant
	Lieut.	Tippetts, Cecil Malpas		MID (twice); retired as major 4.3.33
10306	Pte.	Tolley, Albert	B	Later sergeant; dis 23.1.22
8488	Pte.	Tomkins, Geoffrey Charles	A	Dis 9.8.16.
9836	L.Sgt.	Tootill, William	B	MM, MID (twice); later WO2 2/Mons; dis 2.10.21
10633	Pte.	Townsley, William	A	Served as Jones, William; wounded at Gallipoli 14.5.15; dis 31.3.21
10247	Pte.	Trickey, Arthur	D	Dis 25.1.21.
6296	CQMS	Tring, Henry	D	Served Boer War; DCM; wounded at Gallipoli 6.8.15; later RSM; MSM, LSGCM
9722	Pte.	Trowsdale, William Henry	B	
9853	Pte.	Tucker, John	C	Later served with South Lancs Regt
9921	L.Cpl.	Tudor, Harrison	A	KinA Gallipoli 25.6.15 as corporal
10906	Pte.	Turner, Charles Thomas	A	Wounded at Gallipoli 6.7.15; dis 28.8.24
9888	Pte.	Turner, Clifford George	A	KinA 31.10.18
9713	Pte.	Turner, James	D	Wounded at Gallipoli; KinA France 1.7.16
9762	Pte.	Turner, Thomas George	A	Dis 1.7.16
10582	Pte.	Turrell, James	C	MID; later lance corporal with RWF
10460	Pte.	Urch, Enoch	A	Wounded in Gallipoli; dis 21.9.16
9622	Pte.	Vass, George H.	A	Served with NF as acting sergeant
10504	Pte.	Venn, Albert Edward	B	Later lance corporal; KinA France (attd 1/SWB) 26.9.15
10741	Pte.	Verrin, Ernest Albert	A	To ACC 636421 – name shown as Verren
10121	Pte.	Vickery, William	D	Later served with MGC
9899	Pte.	Vinall, Alfred	A	KinA Gallipoli 25.4.15
10628	Pte.	Vizard, Richard		Not at Tsingtao; KinA Gallipoli 25.4.15
10364	Pte.	Vousden, Cyril	D	Remained at Laoshan Bay; later served as sergeant with MGC
9299	Pte.	Waddington, John William	D	Wounded at Gallipoli; KinA France (attd 1/SWB) 8.9.16
9579	Pte.	Walke, Alfred	D	Evacuated from Gallipoli to hospital 28.6.15; dis 13.6.16
9922	Pte.	Walker, Reginald James	B	DofW at sea 7.7.15
	Lieut.	Walker, Robert Konoma Beaumont		Later served in Gallipoli and with Egyptian Army. MC MID Khedive Sudan Medal, Order of the Nile.
9726	Pte.	Wall, Edgar William	C	Dis 18.10.16
10372	Pte.	Wallace, Ernest	D	Wounded at Gallipoli 28.6.15; later served with Worcestershire Regt.
9744	Pte.	Wallbank, John	A	Later served as Cpl. with RWF
9682	Pte.	Waller, William	B	Wounded in China to Hospital Ship *Delta* 9.11.14. DofW, Belgium 6.10.17
9892	Pte.	Waller, Samuel	A	KinA 15.9.28. as corporal
10227	Pte.	Walliker, Arthur	B	KinA in Iraq (attd 4/SWB) 16.2.17 as lance sergeant
9546	Cpl.	Walters, John	B	Later sergeant; Class Z Army Reserve 6.4.19
9345	Pte.	Walton, George Henry Alfred	A	KinA Gallipoli 26.4.15

9292	L.Cpl.	Warchus, William	C	Later served Depot SWB as lance corporal; dis 28.5.16
9932	Pte.	Ward, James	A	Dis 28.3.16
10153	Pte.	Ward, John J.	B	Later served with Cheshire Regt. and Training Reserve Bn
10423	Cpl.	Ward, John James	B	DCM & MID for China; KinA 28.6.15 at Gallipoli when sergeant
9690	Pte.	Warner, George Edward	A	Dis 18.1.19
9504	Pte.	Wassley, Edgar	B	Wounded at Gallipoli 19.6.15; MM for Western Front
10080	Pte.	Waters, Charles	B	To Weihaiwei 27.10.14; KinA Gallipoli 25.4.15
9751	Pte.	Watkins, G.	D	
10646	L. Cpl.	Watson, Thomas	D	Wounded at Gallipoli 30.6.15; KinA France 6.4.16
10341	Pte.	Webb, Edward Henry	D	Later served with Labour Corps
8744	Pte.	Wells, George Alfred	B	KinA Gallipoli 28.4.15
9952	Pte.	West, James	A	DCM & MID for China; DofW Gallipoli 25.4.15
10039	Pte.	West, John	A	
4961	RSM	Westlake, Henry		Served Boer War; RSM; MBE, DCM, MID, LSGCM, Medaille Militaire; later commissioned
9053	Pte.	Weyman, Frederick	B	Later served with RE
8993	L.Sgt.	White, Frank	B	DCM France; MID. Served with MGC as CSM
9943	Pte.	White, James	D	Dis 25.8. 20
9985	Cpl.	White, Tom Roland	C	Wounded in China. Wounded Gallipoli 16.5.15; wounded France 11.11.17. Later, as Sergeant served with the Indian Army.
10802	L.Cpl.	Whitehead, Edwin	C	Wounded Gallipoli 21.8.15; Later corporal Dis 9.5.32
10515	Pte.	Whitehouse, Albert	D	Dis 13.4.19.
A/873	AQMS	Whitehouse, Sydney	C	Army Ordnance Corps Armourer. Dis as WO2 24.10.18
9267	Pte.	Whyle, James	D	DofW at sea 27.4.15
9492	Pte.	Wilks, Albert A.	D	Wounded at Gallipoli 8.5.15; dis 23.5.15
	Lieut.	Williams, Aubrey Ellis		Wounded in China; CBE, DSO & Bar, MC, MID (5 times), C de G (France); retired as a major-general 1.4.41; as temp major CO 2/SWB September 1915
9637	Pte.	Williams, David	C	Dis 16.3.19
9875	Pte.	Williams, David Watkin	A	DofW France 2.5.16
10207	Pte.	Williams, Ernest	B	Later served with RWF
9766	Pte.	Williams, Frederick,	A	KinA Gallipoli 26.4.15
10059	Pte.	Williams, Frank	D	KinA Gallipoli 8.5.15
10219	Pte.	Williams, Herbert J.	A	
10631	Pte.	Williams, James H	B	Later served with MGC
9601	Pte.	Williams, John Henry	B	Unfit for operations against Tsingtao; later sergeant; Class B Army Reserve 14.3.19.
10873	Pte.	Williams, John Owen	D	KinA Gallipoli 8.5.15
10263	L.Cpl.	Williams, Jonah	B	Later corporal; dis 26.3.18.

9763	Pte	Williams, Joseph	B	KinA China 6.11.14
9341	L.Cpl.	Williams, Owen C.	C	Later served with Labour Corps as acting sergeant
10875	Pte.	Williams, O.	B	Later served with RFC
10408	L.Cpl.	Williams, Reginald	B	DofW France 17.7.17
10566	L.Cpl.	Williams, Wallace	A	KinA Gallipoli 26.4.15
9506	L.Cpl.	Williams, William		Not at Tsingtao; dis 15.2.19.
9975	Pte.	Wills, Thomas Ernest	A	KinA France 23.4.17
10922	L.Cpl.	Wilson, Arthur	B	Dis 16.6.16.
8062	Sgt.	Wilson, Joseph	A	Remained at Laoshan Bay
8616	Pte.	Winch, Henry J.	D	Later CSM with MGC
10490	Pte.	Winkworth, Shadwick		Not at Tsingtao; dis 19.8.16
10505	Pte.	Winter, George	D	Dis 2.9.19
9676	Pte.	Wire, James J.	C	Dis 18.1.16
9821	Pte.	Woffenden, Albert	D	Wounded at Gallipoli 7.5.15; KinA France 1.7.16
10081	L.Cpl.	Wood, Edward	C	Later served with RWF
10042	Pte.	Wood, Harry	B	Later served with Labour Corps
9941	Pte.	Wood, William Edward	B	Later served with Western Command Depot; dis 11.8.16
9911	L.Cpl.	Woods, A.	D	
9596	Pte.	Woods, Charles	A	Dis 29.11.21
10354	Pte.	Woods, John	A	KinA Gallipoli 26.4.15
10493	Pte.	Woods, John	A	Later served with RE
7091	QMS	Woods, John Alexander Inglis		Remained at Laoshan Bay; MBE, MSM, LSGCM; dis 8.9.22
9813	Pte.	Woods, Thomas	D	DCM for Gallipoli, KinA Gallipoli 21.8.15
10103	Pte.	Woolley, Edward Needham	C	Died Egypt 12.12.15
10475	Pte.	Wright, John	D	Wounded at Gallipoli 30.6.15
10609	Pte.	Wright, Sidney	A	Later served KRRC as corporal
10355	Pte.	Wymark, Frank E.	C	Later served with RE

Appendix 2

British Roll of Honour

Casualties of HMS *Triumph*, Tsingtao.

Sai Wan (China) Memorial, China, (including Hong Kong)
> SWORDS, Edward, Able Seaman, 216794, HMS *Triumph*, Royal Navy. Killed in Action, 14 October 1914.

Casualties of HMS *Kennet*, Tsingtao.

Sai Wan (China) Memorial, China, (including Hong Kong)
> SHUTE, A., Stoker 1st Class, K/8282, HMS *Kennett*, Royal Navy. 25 August 1914.

Chatham Naval Memorial, United Kingdom
> ARMSTRONG, John, Able Seaman, J/3996, HMS *Kennet*, Royal Navy. Killed in action with destroyer, off Tsingtao, 22 August 1914.
> RYAN, John James, Able Seaman, SS/3609, HMS *Kennet*, Royal Navy. Killed in action with destroyer, off Tsingtao, 22 August 1914.

Plymouth Naval Memorial, United Kingdom
> JAMES, David, Petty Officer, 183045, HMS *Kennett*, Royal Navy. Killed in action with destroyer, off Tsingtao, 22 August 1914. Age 38.

Casualties of the 2nd Battalion the South Wales Borderers, China.

Sai Wan (China) Memorial, China, (including Hong Kong)
> BETTIS, Edward James, Private, 10019, killed in action 6 November 1914.
> COX, P. T., Private, 10366, died in China 10 August 1914.
> DALE, Arthur Leonard, Private, 10742, killed in action 6 November 1914.
> DAY, A. G., Private, 10377, died in China 30 August 1914.
> EVANS, Herbert, Private, 10614, killed in action 6 November 1914.
> HOPKINS, William Henry, Private, 9886, died 13 September 1914.
> JOHNSON, George Aaron, Lance Corporal, 9881, died of wounds 15 November 1914.
> MABBETT, Trevor, Private, 10470, died of wounds, UK, 5 March 1915.
> MAIDMENT, Frank, Private, 9395, died 28 November 1914.
> MILLER, William, Sergeant, 8436, killed in action 7 November 1914.
> PARKES, George, Private, 10202, killed in action 6 November 1914.

PAVETT, Charles William Walter, Private, 10273, killed in action 6 November 1914.

PAYNE, Arthur George, Sergeant, 7235, killed in action 6 November 1914.

SEWELL, John Rowland, Private, 9243, died of wounds 6 November 1914.

STONER, Edward Thomas, Private, 9291, died of sickness 3 November 1914.

SYDENHAM, Albert George, Lance Corporal, 9880, killed in action 7 November 1914.

THOMAS, James, Lance Corporal, died of wounds 2 November 1914.

WILLIAMS, Joseph, Private, 9763, killed in action 6 November 1914.

Hong Kong (Protestant) Cemetery
SINGH, John, Private, 9654, died of wounds 19 December 1914.

Casualties of the 36th Sikhs, Tsingtao.
Sai Wan (China) Memorial, China, (including Hong Kong)
SINGH, Bishan, Lance Naik, 2919, killed in action 6 November 1914.

SINGH, Udham, Sepoy, 2806, killed in action 6 November 1914.

Appendix 3

2nd Battalion, The South Wales Borderers, Honours and Awards

Companion of the Distinguished Service Order (DSO)
> JOHNSON, D. G., Captain

Military Cross (MC)
> BRADSTOCK, J., Captain

Distinguished Conduct Medal (DCM)
> FOLEY, C. J., Lance Corporal, 10634 (A Company)
> GREEN, A., Private, 9004 (B Company) later died of wounds
> SNOW, G., Private, 9972 (B Company)
> WARD, J. J., Private, 10423 (B Company)
> WEST, J., 10039, Private (A Company)

Mentioned in Despatches
> BIRKETT, G. H., Captain (Adjutant)
> BRADSTOCK, J., Captain
> CASSON, H. G., Lieutenant-Colonel (Commanding)
> DIVE, G. H., Captain, RAMC (Medical Officer)
> JOHNSON, D. G., Captain
> MARGESSON, E. C., Major
> PETRE, R. L., Lieutenant
> SIMSON, H. J., Lieutenant, Royal Scots, attached as Japanese interpreter
> DAVIES, G. A., Company Sergeant-Major, 9244
> EVANS, H., Private, 10614 (killed)
> FOLEY, C. J., Lance Corporal, 10634
> GREEN, A., Private, 9004
> JENKINSON, T., Private, 9980
> JONES, W. I., Drummer, 10171 (killed)
> LEACH, H., Sergeant, 7309 (died of wounds)
> LEWIS, C. W., Drummer, 4528
> ROSIER, W. S., Acting Sergeant, 10249
> SNOW, G. C., Private, 9972
> WARD, J. J., Sergeant, 10423 (killed)
> WEST, J., Private, 9952 (died of wounds)

Appendix 4

Agreement between the British and Japanese armies for the capture of Tsingtao

As the Governments of Great Britain and Japan have decided to cooperate in the capture of the military and naval Forces of Germany in Tsingtao China, in order to accomplish the object of the Anglo-Japanese Convention concluded in London on the 13th July, 1911, the Military Authorities have agreed upon the following Articles in accordance with the Article Five of the said Convention.

Article 1. The Command of the Allied Forces shall be vested in the Commander in Chief of the Japanese Force. The said Command will date from the moment when the British Force begins its disembarkation in the theatre of operations.

Article 2. Each Force, Japanese and British, will make its own arrangements for the supply of military stores accompanying the troops and required subsequently. However, under special conditions when the military necessities of the British Force should become deficient the Japanese Army will give assistance as far s possible.

Article 3. The transport of the Forces of both High Contracting parties to the place of disembarkation will be conducted by the respective Forces, however, in the transport by sea of the British troops and stores the Japanese Army will give assistance if required.

Article 4. The transport of ammunition, supplies and other military necessities and also of the wounded and sick may be conducted by the Japanese line of communication; however when the line of communication of the two Forces do not coincide this article will be void.

Article 5. The purchase and hire in the theatre of operations will be conducted by the Japanese Force and the articles needed will be delivered to the British. The British Force will despatch Officers necessary to transact this work to the Japanese Force. However, direct purchase and hire may be made by the troops of both Forces.

The standard price of articles purchased will be determined by consultation with both Forces.

Article 6. The War Notes issued by the Japanese Force will be used in payment of the purchase and hire of the British Force in the theatre of operations.

Article 7. The Medical Establishment of the Japanese Army (both in the theatre of operations and at home) will endeavour to attend the sick and wounded of the British Force.

Article 8. Despatches to be sent to places outside the theatre of operations by the British Force may be entrusted to the Signal establishment of the Japanese Force. In that case telegrams sent should be written in Japanese and this will apply to the district from the theatre of operations to Dairen. However, from the point of disembarkation of the Japanese Force to Dairen, telegrams may be written in English.

Article 9. The Japanese Field Postal Establishment may handle the mails of the British Force, but this applies only to the district from the theatre of operations to Nagasaki or Yokohama.

Article 10. An exchange of officers for purposes of intercommunications will be made by the headquarters of each Force.

The British Force will further send necessary officers to the Japanese Line of Communication Department for the purpose of conduction the British line of communications work.

Article 11. Communications between the two Forces will be written as a rule in the language of the Force from which the messages originate.

Article 12. The control of foreign officer spectators and Press correspondents permitted to accompany the Forces of the High Contracting Parties and the censorship of their correspondence will be carried out by the headquarters of the Japanese Army.

For this the British Force will despatch the officers needed to the headquarters of the Japanese Army.

The avoidance of leakage of military secrets from correspondence other that that mentioned above, sent outside the field of operations will be entrusted to the honour of the person responsible.

Article 13. The Japanese Army will pay for articles supplied, purchased or hired for the use of the British Force. Such payments will be repaid by the British at a later and convenient date.

Article 14. Any matters besides those mentioned in this Agreement which may arise in the field of operations will be settled and put into effect after consultation by the Commanders of the Forces of the two High Contracting Parties.

Signed by Brigadier-General N. W. Barnardiston and Lieutenant-General M. Kamio. 16th day of the 9th month of the 3rd Year of Taishio.

Appendix 5

Japanese Documents relating to the Tsingtao Campaign

a) Japanese Minister for Foreign Affairs, Baron Kato's, explanation of Japan's decision to go to war with Germany

Early in August the British Government asked the Imperial Government for assistance under the terms of the Anglo-Japanese Alliance. German men-of-war and armed vessels were prowling around the seas of Eastern Asia, menacing our commerce and that of our ally, while Kiao-Chau was carrying out operations apparently for the purpose of constituting abase for warlike operations in Eastern Asia. Grave anxiety was thus felt for the maintenance of peace in the Far East.

As all are aware, the agreement and alliance between Japan and Great Britain has for its object the consolidation and maintenance of general peace in Eastern Asia and the maintenance of the independence and integrity of China as well as the principle of equal opportunities for commerce and industry for all nations in that country, and the maintenance and defence respectively of territorial rights and special interests of contracting parties in Eastern Asia.

Therefore, inasmuch as we were asked by our ally for assistance at a time when commerce in Eastern Asia, which Japan and Great Britain regard alike as one of their special interests, is subjected to a constant menace, Japan, who regards that alliance as a guiding principle of her foreign policy, could not but comply to the request to do her part.

Germany's possession of a base for powerful activities in one corner of the Far East was not only a serious obstacle to the maintenance of permanent peace but also threatened the immediate interests of the Japanese Empire.

The Japanese Government therefore resolved to comply with the British request and if necessary to open hostilities against Germany. After the Imperial sanction had been obtained I communicated this resolution to the British Government and a full and frank exchange of views between the two governments followed and it was finally agreed between them to take such measures as were necessary to protect the general interests contemplated in the agreement and the alliance.

Japan had no desire or inclination to become involved in the present conflict, only she believed she owed it to herself to be faithful to the alliance and to strengthen its foundation by insuring permanent peace in the East and protecting the special interests of the two allied Powers.

Desiring, however, to solve the situation by pacific means, the Imperial Government on August 15th gave the following advice to the German Government. (Here the Japanese Minister quoted the text of the ultimatum to the Germans included in the main text.) Until the last moment of the time allowed, namely, until August 23rd, the Imperial Government received no answer and in consequence the Imperial rescript declaring war was issued the next day.

With Austria-Hungary, as she had only the most limited interests in the Far East, Japan desired to maintain peaceful relations as long as possible. At the same time it appeared that Austria-Hungary also desired to avoid complications. In fact, as soon as Japan and Germany entered into a state of war, Austria-Hungary asked for the consent and good offices of the Imperial Government to permit the Kaiserin Elizabeth, the only Austrian man-of-war in the Far East likely to force a state of war, to go to Shanghai and there to disarm.

I was about to communicate to the Austrian Ambassador the fact that Great Britain and Japan did not entertain any objections to the disarming of the Kaiserin Elizabeth, when suddenly on August 27th the Austrian Ambassador informed me that in consideration of Japan's action against Germany his Government instructed him to leave his post, and diplomatic relations were broken off.

When the relations of Japan and Germany reached the point of rupture the Imperial Government asked the American Government if in case of need it would be good enough to undertake the protection of Japanese subjects and interests in Germany.

This request the American Government promptly complied with and subsequently upon the rupture of diplomatic relations between Japan and Austria-Hungary the Imperial Government again appealed for American protection for Japanese subjects and interests in Austria-Hungary, when the American Government gave the same willing consent.

I desire to avail myself of this opportunity to give expression to the sincere appreciation of the Imperial Government of the courtesy so kindly extended by the American Government.

While regretting that Japan has been compelled to take up arms against Germany, I am happy to believe that the army and navy of our illustrious sovereign will not fail to show the same loyalty and valour which distinguished them in the past, so that all may be blessed by early restoration of peace.

b) The Twenty One Demands

The following document gives the so called Twenty One Demands presented by the Japanese to the Chinese Government during January 1915. The document resulted in much diplomatic activity between the two governments but ultimately the Japanese got their wishes on nearly all the points but not before there had been a threat of war. This was one of the immediate effects of the fall of Tsingtao.

GROUP 1

The Japanese Government and the Chinese Government, being desirous to maintain the general peace in the Far East and to strengthen the relations of amity and good neighbourhood existing between the two countries, agree to the following articles:

Article 1

The Chinese Government engage to give full assent to all matters that the Japanese Government may hereafter agree with the German Government respecting the disposition of all the rights, interests and concessions, which, in virtue of treaties or otherwise, Germany possesses vis-a-vis China in relation to the province of Shantung.

Article 2

The Chinese Government engage that, within the province of Shantung or along its coast, no territory or island will be ceded or leased to any other Power, under any pretext whatever.

Article 3

The Chinese Government agree to Japan's building a railway connecting Chefoo or Lungkow with the Kiaochou Tsinanfu Railway.

Article 4

The Chinese Government engage to open of their own accord, as soon as possible, certain important cities and towns in the Province of Shantung for the residence and commerce of foreigners. The places to be so opened shall be decided upon in a separate agreement.

GROUP II

The Japanese Government and the Chinese Government, in view of the fact that the Chinese Government has always recognized the predominant position of Japan in South Manchuria and Eastern Inner Mongolia, agree to the following articles:

Article 1

The two contracting Parties mutually agree that the term of the lease of Port Arthur and Dairen and the term respecting the South Manchuria Railway and the Antung-Mukden Railway shall be extended to a further period of 99 years respectively.

Article 2

The Japanese subjects shall be permitted in South Manchuria and Eastern Inner Mongolia to lease or own land required either for erecting buildings for various commercial and industrial uses or for farming.

Article 3

The Japanese subjects shall have liberty to enter, reside, and travel in

South Manchuria and Eastern Inner Mongolia, and to carry on business of various kinds commercial, industrial, and otherwise.

Article 4

The Chinese Government grant to the Japanese subjects the right of mining in South Manchuria and Eastern Inner Mongolia. As regards the mines to be worked, they shall be decided upon in a separate agreement.

Article 5

The Chinese Government agree that the consent of the Japanese Government shall be obtained in advance:

1) whenever it is proposed to grant to other nationals the right of constructing a railway or to obtain from other nationals the supply of funds for constructing a railway in South Manchuria and Eastern Inner Mongolia, and

2) whenever a loan is to be made with any other Power, under security of the taxes of South Manchuria and Eastern Inner Mongolia.

Article 6

The Chinese Government engage that whenever the Chinese Government need the service of political, financial, or military advisers or instructors in South Manchuria or in Eastern Inner Mongolia, Japan shall first be consulted.

Article 7

The Chinese Government agree that the control and management of the Kirin-Chungchun Railway shall be handed over to Japan for a term of 99 years dating from the signing of this treaty.

GROUP III

The Japanese Government and the Chinese Government, having regard to the close relations existing between Japanese capitalists and the Han-Yeh-Ping Company and desiring to promote the common interests of the two nations, agree to the following articles:

Article 1

The two Contracting Parties mutually agree that when the opportune moment arrives the Han-Yeh-Ping Company shall be made a joint concern of the two nations, and that, without the consent of the Japanese Government, the Chinese Government shall not dispose or permit the Company to dispose of any right or property of the Company.

Article 2

The Chinese Government engage that, as a necessary measure for protection of the invested interests of Japanese capitalists, no mines in the neighbourhood of those owned by the Han-Yeh-Ping Company shall be permitted, without the consent of the said Company, to be worked by anyone other than the said Company; and further that whenever it is proposed to take any other measure which may likely affect the interests of the said Company directly or indirectly, the consent of the said Company shall first be obtained.

GROUP IV

The Japanese Government and the Chinese Government, with the object of effectively preserving the territorial integrity of China, agree to the following article: The Chinese Government engage not to cede or lease to any other Power any harbour or bay on or any island along the coast of China.

GROUP V

Article 1

The Chinese Central Government to engage influential Japanese as political, financial, and military advisers;

Article 2

The Chinese Government to grant the Japanese hospitals, temples, and schools in the interior of China the right to own land;

Article 3

In the face of many police disputes which have hitherto arisen between Japan and China, causing no little annoyance the police in localities (in China), where such arrangement: are necessary, to be placed under joint Japanese and Chinese administration, or Japanese to be employed in police office in such localities, so as to help at the same time the improvement of the Chinese Police Service;

Article 4

China to obtain from Japan supply of a certain quantity of arms, or to establish an arsenal in China under joint Japanese and Chinese management and to be supplied with experts and materials from Japan;

Article 5

In order to help the development of the Nanchang-Kiukiang Railway, with which Japanese capitalists are so closely identified, and with due regard to the negotiations which have been pending between Japan and China in relation to the railway question in South China, China to agree to give to Japan the right of constructing a railway to connect Wuchang with the Kiukiang-Nanchang and Hangchou and between Nanchang and Chaochou;

Article 6

In view of the relations between the Province of Fukien and Formosa and of the agreement respecting the non-alienation of that province, Japan to be consulted first when- ever foreign capital is needed in connection with the railways, mines, and harbour works (including dockyards) in the Province of Fukien;

Article 7
China to grant to Japanese subjects the right of preaching in China.

c) Japanese ultimatum to China, 7 May 1915

The reason why the Imperial Government opened the present negotiations with the Chinese Government is first to endeavour to dispose of the complications arising out of the war between Japan and China, and secondly to attempt to solve those various questions which are detrimental to the intimate relations of China and Japan with a view to solidifying the foundation of cordial friendship subsisting between the two countries to the end that the peace of the Far East may be effectually and permanently preserved.

With this object in view, definite proposals were presented to the Chinese Government in January of this year, and up to today as many as twenty-five conferences have been held with the Chinese Government in perfect sincerity and frankness.

In the course of negotiations the Imperial Government have consistently explained the aims and objects of the proposals in a conciliatory spirit, while on the other hand the proposals of the Chinese Government, whether important or unimportant, have been attended to without any reserve.

It may be stated with confidence that no effort has been spared to arrive at a satisfactory and amicable settlement of those questions.

The discussion of the entire corpus of the proposals was practically at an end at the twenty-fourth conference; that is on the 17th of the last month.

The Imperial Government, taking a broad view of the negotiation and in consideration of the points raised by the Chinese Government, modified the original proposals with considerable concessions and presented to the Chinese Government on the 26th of the same month the revised proposals for agreement, and at the same time it was offered that, on the acceptance of the revised proposals, the Imperial Government would, at a suitable opportunity, restore, with fair and proper conditions, to the Chinese Government the Kiaochow territory, in the acquisition of which the Imperial Government had made a great sacrifice.

On the first of May, the Chinese Government delivered the reply to the revised proposals of the Japanese Government, which is contrary to the expectations of the Imperial Government.† The Chinese Government not only did not give a careful consideration to the revised proposals but even with regard to the offer of the Japanese Government to restore Kiaochow to the Chinese Government the latter did not manifest the least appreciation for Japan's good will and difficulties.

From the commercial and military point of view Kiaochow is an important place, in the acquisition of which the Japanese Empire sacrificed much blood and money, and, after the acquisition the Empire incurs no obligation to restore it to China.

But with the object of increasing the future friendly relations of the two countries, they went to the extent of proposing its restoration, yet to her great regret, the Chinese Government did not take into consideration the good intention of Japan and manifest appreciation of her difficulties.

Furthermore, the Chinese Government not only ignored the friendly feelings of the Imperial Government in offering the restoration of Kiaochow Bay, but also in replying to the revised proposals they even demanded its unconditional restoration; and again China demanded that Japan should bear the responsibility of paying indemnity for all the unavoidable losses and damages resulting from Japan's military operations at Kiaochow; and still further in connection with the territory of Kiaochow China advanced other demands and declared that she has the right of participation at the future peace conference to be held between Japan and Germany.

Although China is fully aware that the unconditional restoration of Kiaochow and Japan's responsibility of indemnification for the unavoidable losses and damages can never be tolerated by Japan, yet she purposely advanced these demands and declared that this reply was final and decisive.

Since Japan could not tolerate such demands the settlement of the other questions, however compromising it may be, would not be to her interest.† The consequence is that the present reply of the Chinese Government is, on the whole, vague and meaningless.

Furthermore, in the reply of the Chinese Government to the other proposals in the revised list of the Imperial Government, such as South Manchuria and Eastern Inner Mongolia, where Japan particularly has geographical, commercial, industrial and strategic relations, as recognized by all nations, and made more remarkable in consequence of the two wars in which Japan was engaged, the Chinese Government overlooks these facts and does not respect Japan's position in that place.

The Chinese Government even freely altered those articles which the Imperial Government, in a compromising spirit, have formulated in accordance with the statement of the Chinese Representatives, thereby making the statements of the Representatives an empty talk; and on seeing them conceding with the one hand and withholding with the other it is very difficult to attribute faithfulness and sincerity to the Chinese authorities.

As regards the articles relating to the employment of advisers, the establishment of schools and hospitals, the supply of arms and ammunition and the establishment of arsenals and railway concessions in South China in the revised proposals, they were either proposed with the proviso that the consent of the Power concerned must be obtained, or they are merely to be recorded in the minutes in accordance with the statements of the Chinese delegates, and thus they are not in the least in conflict either with Chinese sovereignty or her treaties with the Foreign Powers, yet the Chinese Government in their reply to the proposals, alleging that these proposals are incompatible with their sovereign rights and treaties with Foreign Powers, defeat the expectations of the Imperial Government.

However, in spite of such attitude of the Chinese Government, the Imperial Government, though regretting to see that there is no room for further negotiations, yet warmly attached to the preservation of the peace of the Far East, is still hoping for a satisfactory settlement in order to avoid the disturbance of the relations.

So, in spite of the circumstances which admitted no patience, they have reconsidered the feelings of the Government of their neighbouring country and, with the exception of the article relating to Fukien which is to be the subject of an exchange of notes as has already been agreed upon by the Representatives of both nations, will undertake to detach the Group V from the present negotiations and discuss it separately in the future.

Therefore, the Chinese Government should appreciate the friendly feelings of the Imperial Government by immediately accepting without any alteration all the articles of Groups I, II, III, and IV and the exchange of notes in connection with Fukien province in Group V as contained in the revised proposals presented on the 26th of April.

The Imperial Government hereby again offer their advice and hope that the Chinese Government, upon this advice, will give a satisfactory reply by 6 o'clock p.m. on the 9th day of May. It is hereby declared that if no satisfactory reply is received before or at the specified time, the Imperial Government will take steps they may deem necessary.

Explanatory Note
Accompanying Ultimatum delivered to the Minister of Foreign Affairs by the Japanese Minister, May 7th, 1915.

1. With the exception of the question of Fukien to be arranged by an exchange of notes, the five articles postponed for later negotiation refer to (a) the employment of advisers, (b) the establishment of schools and hospitals, (c) the railway concessions in South China, (d) the supply of arms and ammunition and the establishment of arsenals and (e) right of missionary propaganda.
2. The acceptance by the Chinese Government of the article relating to Fukien may be either in the form as proposed by the Japanese Minister on the 26th of April or in that contained in the Reply of the Chinese Government of May 1st. Although the Ultimatum calls for the immediate acceptance by China of the modified proposals presented on April 26th, without alteration, but it should be noted that it merely states the principle and does not apply to this article and articles 4 and 5 of this note.
3. If the Chinese Government accept all the articles as demanded in the Ultimatum the offer of the Japanese Government to restore Kiaochow to China, made on the 26th of April, will still hold good.
4. Article 2 of Group II relating to the lease or purchase of land, the terms 'lease' and 'purchase' may be replaced by the terms 'temporary lease' and 'perpetual lease' or 'lease on consultation,' which means a long-term lease with its unconditional renewal.
   Article IV of Group II relating to the approval of police laws and ordinances and local taxes by the Japanese Council may form the subject of a secret agreement.
5. The phrase 'to consult with the Japanese Government' in connection with questions of pledging the local taxes for raising loans and the loans for the construction of railways, in Eastern Inner Mongolia, which is similar to the agreement in Manchuria relating to the matters of the same kind, may be replaced by the phrase 'to consult with the Japanese capitalists.'

The article relating to the opening of trade marts in Eastern Inner Mongolia in respect to location and regulations, may, following their precedent set in Shantung, be the subject of an exchange of notes.

6. From the phrase 'those interested in the Company' in Group III of the revised list of demands, the words 'those interested in' may be deleted.

7. The Japanese version of the Formal Agreement and its annexes shall be the official text or both the Chinese and Japanese shall be the official texts.

Chinese Reply to Japanese Ultimatum, 8 May 1915

On the 7th of this month, at three o'clock p.m., the Chinese Government received an Ultimatum from the Japanese Government together with an Explanatory Note of seven articles.

The Ultimatum concluded with the hope that the Chinese Government by six o'clock p.m. on the 9th of May will give a satisfactory reply, and it is hereby declared that if no satisfactory reply is received before or at the specified time, the Japanese Government will take steps she may deem necessary.

The Chinese Government with a view to preserving the peace of the Far East hereby accepts, with the exception of those five articles of Group V postponed for later negotiations, all the articles of Groups I, II, III, and IV and the exchange of notes in connection with Fukien Province in Group V as contained in the revised proposals presented on the 26th of April, and in accordance with the Explanatory Note of seven articles accompanying the Ultimatum of the Japanese Government with the hope that thereby all the outstanding questions are settled, so that the cordial relationship between the two countries may be further consolidated.

The Japanese Minister is hereby requested to appoint a day to call at the Ministry of Foreign Affairs to make the literary improvement of the text and sign the Agreement as soon as possible.

Appendix 6

Treaty Between Germany and China for the lease of Kiao-chau

Extracted from the Reichsanzeiger of 29 April 1898
The following is the text of the Treaty between the German Empire and China respecting the lease of Kiao-chau, which was received in Berlin on 28 April 1898:

The incidents connected with the Mission in the Prefecture of Ts'ao-chou Fu, in Shan-tung, being now closed, the Imperial Chinese Government consider it advisable to give a special proof of their grateful appreciation of the friendship shown to them by Germany. The Imperial German and Imperial Chinese Governments, therefore, inspired by the equal and mutual wish to strengthen the bands of friendship which unite the two countries, and to develop the economic and commercial relations between the subjects of the two States, have concluded the following separate convention:

Article I
His Majesty the Emperor of China, guided but the intention to strengthen the friendly relations between China and Germany, and at the same time to increase the military readiness of the Chinese Empire, engages, while reserving to himself all right and sovereignty in a zone of 50 kilometres (100 Chinese li) surrounding the Bay of Kiao-chau at high water, to permit the free passage of German troops within this zone at any time, as also to abstain from taking any measures or issuing any ordinances therein, without the previous consent of the German Government, and especially to place no obstacle in the way of any regulation of the watercourses which may prove to be necessary. His Majesty the Emperor of China at the same time, reserves to himself the right to station troops within that zone, in agreement with the German Government, and to take other military measures.

Article II
Within the intention of meeting the legitimate desire of His Majesty the German Emperor that Germany, like other Powers, should hold a place on the Chinese coast for the repair and equipment of her ships, for the storage of materials and provisions for the same, and for other arrangements connected therewith, His Majesty the Emperor of China cedes to Germany on lease, provisionally for 99 years, both sides of the entrance to the Bay of Kiao-chau. Germany engages to construct, at suitable moment, on the territory thus ceded, fortifications for the

protection of the buildings to be constructed there, and of the entrance to the harbour.

Article III

In order to avoid the possibility of conflicts, the Imperial Chinese Government will abstain from exercising rights of sovereignty in the ceded territory during the term of the lease, and leaves the exercise of the same to Germany, within the following limits:

1. On the northern side of the entrance to the bay:
   The peninsula bounded to the north-east by a line drawn from the north-eastern corner of Potato Island (Yin-Tao) to Lao Shan Harbour.
2. On the southern side of the entrance to the bat:
   The peninsula bounded to the south-west by a line drawn from the south-westernmost point of the bay lying to the south-south-west of Huang-tao (Chi-po-san) Island to the direction of Ling-shan-tao (Telosan) Island.
3. The Island of Haung-tao (Chi-po-san) and Potato Island (Yin-tao).
4. The whole water area of the bay up to the highest water mark at present known.
5. All islands lying seaward from Kiao-chau Bay which may be of importance for its defence, such as Ling-shan-tao (Telosan), Cha-lien-tao, and others.

The high contracting parties reserve the right to themselves to delimitate more accurately, in accordance with local traditions, the boundaries of the territory leased to Germany and of the 50 kilometres zone round the bay, by means of Commissioners to be appointed by both sides.

Chinese ships of war and merchant vessels shall enjoy the same privileges in the Bay of Kiao-chau as the ships of other nations on friendly terms with Germany; and the entrance; departure and sojourn of Chinese ships in the bay shall not be subject to any restrictions other than those which the Imperial German Government, in virtue of the rights of sovereignty over the whole of the water area of the bay transferred to Germany, may at any time fine it necessary to impose with regard to the ships of other nations.

Article IV

Germany engages to construct the necessary navigation signals on the islands and shallows at the entrance to the bay.

No dues shall be demanded from Chinese ships-of-war and merchant vessels in the Bay of Kiao-chau, except those which may be levied upon other vessels for the purpose of maintaining the necessary harbour arrangements and quays.

Article V

Should Germany at some future time express the wish to return Kaio-chau Bay to China before the expiration of the lease. China engages to refund to Germany the expenditure she has incurred at Kiao-chau, and cede to Germany a more suitable place.

Germany engages at no time to sublet the territory leased from China to another Power.

The Chinese population dwelling in the ceded territory shall at all times enjoy the protection of the German Government, provided that they behave in conformity with law and order; unless their land is required for other purposes they may remain there.

If land belonging to Chinese owners is required for any other purpose, the owner will receive compensation.

As regards the re-establishment of Chines customs stations, which formerly existed outside the ceded territory but within the 50 kilometre zone, the Imperial German Government intends to come to an agreement with the Chinese Government for the definite regulation of the customs frontier, and the mode of collecting the customs duties, in a manner which will safeguard all the interests of China, and proposes to enter into further negotiations on the subject.

The above agreement shall be ratified by the Sovereigns of both Contracting States, and the ratification exchanged in such a manner that, after the receipt in Berlin of the Treaty ratified in China, the copy ratified by Germany shall be handed to the Chinese Minister in Berlin.

The foregoing Treaty has been drawn up in four copies – two in German and two in Chinese – and was signed by the representatives of the Contracting States on the 6th March 1898, equal to the 14th day of the second month of the 24th year Kuang-hsü.

Signed by The Imperial German Minister
Baron von Heyking
Li Hung-Chang

Imperial Chinese Grand Secretary, Minister of the Tsung-li Yamen
Weng Tung-ho

Imperial German Grand Secretary, Member of the Council of State, Minister of the Tsung-li Yamen

Appendix 7

German Roll of Honour

The following roll has been compiled from the information contained on the internet site www. tsingtau. info. The source gives the names and units of those killed and often contains biographic information, this is not included here for the sake of brevity and because it is beyond the scope of this work. The ranks and spellings shown are those given in the German source material and in most cases it will be clear what is meant.

Acs, Josef, Matrose auf k.u.k. Kreuzer *Kaiserin Elisabeth*; kia 31.10.1914 Tsingtau.

ALBRECHT, August Hermann Friedrich, Obermatrose auf Fluflkanonenboot *Otter*; kia 07.11.1914 Tsingtau.

ANABECK, Wilhelm; Seesoldat in der 2. Kompanie des Ostasiatischen Marine-Detachements; kia 09.10.1914 Tsingtau.

ANDERNACH, Jakob; Seesoldat in der 2. Kompanie des Ostasiatischen Marine-Detachements; kia 02.10.1914 Tsingtau.

AYE, Julius; Kompanieoffizier bei der 3. Kompanie der Matrosen-Artillerie-Abteilung, kia 07.11.1914 Tsingtau.

BAUER, Karl B.; Seesoldat in der 2. Kompanie des III. Seebataillons kia 07.11.1914 Tsingtau.

BAUER, Wilhelm Otto; Seesoldat der Reserve in der 1. Kompanie des III. Seebataillons, dow 23.01.1915 Tsingtau.

BAUMANN, Christoph; Seesoldat in der 1. Kompanie des III. Seebataillon; kia 07.11.1914 Tsingtau.

BECKER, Arthur; Unteroffizier der Reserve in der 1. Kompanie des III. Seebataillons; kia 07.11.1914 Tsingtau.

BEHRENS, August, Torpedo-Obermatrose in der Matrosen-Artillerie-Abteilung Kiautschou, dow 07.01.1915 Tsingtau.

BENNECKE, Karl, Oberartilleristenmaat in der 3. Kompanie der Matrosen-Artillerie-Abteilung Kiautschou; kia 07.11.1914 Tsingtau.

BERGER, Albert, Seesoldat in der 1. Kompanie des Ostasiatischen Marine-Detachements; kia 13.08.1914 Tientsin.

BERKENHOFF, Johann W.; Seesoldat in der 1. Kompanie des Ostasiatischen Marine-Detachements; kia 07.11.1914 Tsingtau.

BERNER, August; Matrosenartillerist in der 1. Kompanie der Matrosen-Artillerie-Abteilung Kiautschou; kia 07.11.1914 Tsingtau.

BIELER, Ernst, Obermatrosenartillerist in der 4. Kompanie der Matrosen-Artillerie-Abteilung Kiautschou; kia 07.09.1914 Tsingtau.

Bofl, Leo; Seesoldat in der 1. Kompanie des Ostasiatischen Marine-Detachements; kia 02.10.1914 Tsingtau.

BÖTTCHER, Ewald; Seesoldat in der 1. Kompanie des Ostasiatischen Marine-Detachements; kia 02.10.1914 Tsingtau.

BRAUN, Albert; Obermatrose auf Kanonenboot Iltis, kia 06.11.1914 Tsingtau.

BREUER, Edmund; Seesoldat in der 3. Kompanie des Ostasiatischen Marine-Detachements; died 04.09.1914 Tsingtau.

BROCKSTEDT, Walter; 1914 Matrose auf Fluflkanonenboot Vaterland, kia 07.11.1914 Tsingtau.

BROHL, Jakob; Matrosenartillerist in der 1. Kompanie der Matrosen-Artillerie-Abteilung Kiautschou; kia 05.11.1914 Tsingtau.

BRUCKHAUS, Otto Julius August; Artilleristenmaat in der 3. Kompanie der Matrosen-Artillerie-Abteilung Kiautschou; kia 07.11.1914 Tsingtau.

BÜCKER, Wilhelm; Seesoldat in der 2. Kompanie des Ostasiatischen Marine-Detachements; kai 07.11.1914 Tsingtau.

BURKHARDT, Friedrich; Seesoldat in der 2. Kompanie des III. Seebataillons; kia 13.10.1914 Tsingtau.

CHARRIÈRE, Georg *Oberleutnant*; kia 07.11.1914 Tsingtau.

DAWID, Engelbert; Gefreiter in der 2. Kompanie des III. SB; kia 22.10.1914 Tsingtau.

DECKER, Emil; Seesoldat in der 2. Kompanie des III. SB.; kia 22.10.1914 Tsingtau.

DETLEFS, Wilhelm; Seesoldat in der 3. Kompanie des OMD; kia 07.11.1914 Tsingtau.

DIEHL, Wilhelm; Unteroffizier in der 1. Kompanie des III. SB; kia 22.10.1914 Tsingtau.

DOBERT, Paul Dietrich; Seesoldat in der 7. Kompanie des III. SB.; kia 17.10.1914 Tsingtau.

DRESSEL, Josef; Seesoldat in der 1. Kompanie des OMD; kia 07.11.1914 Tsingtau.

DUCKE, Johann; Steuergast auf k. u. k. Kreuzer Kaiserin Elisabeth; dow 08.11.1914.

ECKERT, Walter Matrosenartillerist in der 3. Kompanie der MAK; kai 07.11.1914 Tsingtau.

EGLSAER, Rudolf; Matrose 1. Kl. auf k.u.k. Kreuzer *Kaiserin Elisabeth*, kia 05.11.1914 Tsingtau.

ELTZE, Theodor Willy; Unteroffizier in der 2. Kompanie des III. SB.; kia 07.11.1914 Tsingtau.

ENDERLEIN, Paul; Seesoldat in der 2. Kompanie des III. SB.; kia 07.11.1914 Tsingtau.

ENGELBRECHT, Willy; Artilleristenmaat in der 2. Kompanie der MAK; kia 07.11.1914 Tsingtau.

FABIAN, Kurt; Matrosenartillerist in der 2. Kompanie der MAK; kia 07.11.1914 Tsingtau.

FELLINGHAUER, Anton; Matrose 3. Kl. auf k.u.k. Kreuzer *Kaiserin Elisabeth* kia 07.11.1914 Tsingtau.

FEY, Damian; Obermatrosenartillerist in der 3. Kompanie der MAK; kai 07.11.1914 Tsingtau.

FLÖTER, Leo; Seesoldat in der 3. Kompanie des OMD; kia 01.11.1914 Tsingtau.

FORBRICH, Erwin; Matrosenartillerist in der 1. Kompanie der MAK; kia 07.11.1914 Tsingtau.

FREISSMUTH, Ludwig; Obermatrosenartillerist in der 2. Kompanie der MAK; kia 07.11.1914 Tsingtau.

FRIES, Wolfgang von, Leutnant der Reserve in der 5. Kompanie des III. SB.; kia 28.09.1914 Tsingtau.

FROMM, Franz; Sergeant in der 1. Kompanie des OMD; 02.10.1914 Tsingtau.

GÄRTNER, Nicolaus; Seesoldat in der 5. Kompanie des III. SB.; kia 05.11.1914 Tsingtau.

GEIGER, Franz Josef; Obermatrosenartillerist in der 1. Kompanie der MAK; kia 07.11.1914 Tsingtau.

GERBER, Max; Marinefeldartillerist in der MFB des III. SB.; kia 07.11.1914 Tsingtau.

GERHARDS, Franz K. H.; Seesoldat in der 1. Kompanie des OMD; kia 07.11.1914 Tsingtau.

GERHOLD, Karl, Marine-Ingenieur der Seewehr I in der 1. Kompanie der MAK; kia 07.11.1914 Tsingtau.

GERKEN, Wilhelm Hajo; Artilleristenmaat der Reserve in der 1. Kompanie der MAK; kia 07.11.1914 Tsingtau.

GOHRBANDT, Reinhold; Oberfeuerwerker in der 4. Kompanie der MAK; kia 07.11.1914 Tsingtau.

GOTTHARDT, Jakob; Matrosenartillerist in der 1. Kompanie der MAK; kia 28.09.1914 Tsingtau.

GOTTSCHLICH, Wilhelm; Seesoldat in der 3. Kompanie des III. SB.; kia 02.10.1914 Tsingtau.

GROSSKLAUS, Gottfried, Obermatrosenartillerist in der 2. Kompanie der MAK; kia 07.11.1914 Tsingtau.

HAARS, Erich; Unteroffizier der Landwehr II in der 5. Kompanie der MAK; kia 06.11.1914 Tsingtau.

HAAS, Hermann, Seesoldat in der MGK des III. Seebataillons; kia 07.11.1914 Tsingtau.

HAASE, Kurt Hermann, Heizer auf Fluflkanonenboot Otter; kia 07.11.1914 Tsingtau.

HAFFNER, Alois; Obermatrosenartillerist in der 3. Kompanie der MAK; kai 07.11.1914 Tsingtau.

HAGMANN, Gustav; Unteroffizier der Reserve in der 7. Kompanie des III. Seebataillons; kia 05.11.1914 Tsingtau.

HALAMA, Alfred; Marinefeldartillerist in der MFB des III. Seebataillons; kia 07.11.1914 Tsingtau.

HALBLEIB, Karl; Seesoldat in der 1. Kompanie des OMD; kia 02.10.1914 Tsingtau.

HALLER, Friedrich; Obermatrosenartillerist in der 2. Kompanie der MAK; kia 07.11.1914 Tsingtau.

HANDROCK, Richard; Seesoldat in der 1. Kompanie des OMD; kia 02.10.1914 Tsingtau.

HARDING-KLIMANEK; Kriegsfreiwilliger beim Österreichischen Landungszug; kia 30.10.1914 Tsingtau.

HARRY, Karl; Heizer in der 1. Kompanie der MAK; kia 07.11.1914 Tsingtau.

HASENCLEVER, Alfred; Artilleristenmaat der Reserve in der 2. Kompanie der MAK; kia 07.11.1914 Tsingtau.

HASER, Jakob; Seesoldat und Trompeter in der 1. Kompanie des OMD; kia 02.10.1914 Tsingtau.

HAUTEL, Wilhelm; Seesoldat in der 1. Kompanie des OMD; kia 31.10.1914 Tsingtau.

HEESEN, Johann; Obermatrosenartillerist in der 2. Kompanie der MAK; kia 07.11.1914 Tsingtau.

HEIN, Wilhelm; Matrosenartillerist in der 4. Kompanie der MAK; kia 07.11.1914 Tsingtau.

HEMELING, Wilhelm, Dr. Leutnant der Reserve im III. SB.; kai 21.10.1914 Tsingtau.

HERTZBERG, Graf von, Klaus, Führer der 1. Kompanie des OMD; kia 02.10.1914 Tsingtau.

HINDERKS, Elderikus; Artilleristenmaat in der 1. Kompanie der MAK; kia 05.11.1914 Tsingtau.

HINZMANN, Joseph; Sergeant in der 4. Kompanie des III. Seebataillons; kia 07.11.1914 Tsingtau.

HOFFMANN, Leopold; Pionier in der 1. Kompanie des OMD; kai 07.11.1914 Tsingtau.

HOLMES, Karl; Artilleristenmaat in der 1. Kompanie der MAK; kia 05.11.1914 Tsingtau.

HOPPE, Joseph; Gefreiter in der 4. Kompanie des III. Seebataillons; kia 07.11.1914 Tsingtau.

HORMES, Hugo; Seesoldat in der 1. Kompanie des III. Seebataillons; kia 03.11.1914 Tsingtau.

HÜGEL, Franz; Seesoldat in der 5. Kompanie des III. Seebataillons; kia 05.11.1914 Tsingtau.

HURNICKI, Karl; Seesoldat in der 3. Kompanie des OMD; kia 04.09.1914 Tsingtau.

ILGENER, Wilhelm Karl; Gefreiter in der 3. Kompanie des III. SB. Died 13.11.1914 Tsingtau.

IMHOFF, Leopold; Gefreiter in der 3. Kompanie des OMD; died 04.09.1914 Tsingtau.

IMHOLT, Josef; Gefreiter in der 1. Kompanie des OMD; kia 02.10.1914 Tsingtau.

JANSEN, (Jensen), Wilhelm; Pionier der Landwehr in der MPK des III. SB. 07.11.1914 Tsingtau.

JESSE, Johann; Seesoldat in der 4. Kompanie des III. SB.; kia 10.11.1914 Tsingtau.

JOCKERS, Karl; Seesoldat in der 1. Kompanie des OMD; kia 02.10.1914 Tsingtau.

JOST, Wilhelm, Gefreiter in der 3. Kompanie des III. SB.; kia 31.10.1914 Tsingtau.

KANTZ, Wilhelm; Unteroffizier auf k.u.k. Kreuzer *Kaiserin Elisabeth*; kia 30.10.1914 Tsingtau.

KEUTHEN, Lorenz; Matrosenartillerist in der 4. Kompanie des III. SB.; kia 05.11.1914 Tsingtau.

KLAEBER, Berthold Karl; Seesoldat der Reserve in der 2. Kompanie des III. SB.; kai 07.11.1914 Tsingtau.

KLAUS, Paul Karl Sergeant in der MPK des III. SB.; dow 14.09.1914 Tsingtau.

KLEINKE, Kurt J. W.; Seesoldat in der 1. Kompanie des OMD; kia 07.11.1914 Tsingtau.

KLINKSIEK, August; Seesoldat in der 1. Kompanie des III. SB.; kia 28.09.1914 Tsingtau.

KOHNKE, Karl; Seesoldat in der 1. Kompanie des OMD; kia 07.11.1914 Tsingtau.

KOITEK, Johann; Sergeant in der 1. Kompanie des OMD; kia 07.11.1914 Tsingtau.

KOPECNY, Ladislaus; Steuermatrose auf k.u.k. Kreuzer *Kaiserin Elisabeth*; kia 07.11.1914 Tsingtau.

KÖTTER, Erich (?); Seesoldat der Reserve in der 3. Kompanie des III. SB.; kia 02.10.1914 Tsingtau.

KÖTTING, Anton; Matrosenartillerist in der 5. Kompanie der Matrosen-Artillerie-Abteilung Kiautschou; kia 03.11.1914 Tsingtau.

KÜFER, Max Engelbert; Gefreiter in der 4. Kompanie des III. SB.; dow 21.10.1914 Tsingtau.

LAUNSPACH, Friedrich; Seesoldat in der 1. Kompanie des OMD; kia 02.10.1914 Tsingtau.

LEHMANN, Ernst Walter; Gefreiter der Landwehr in der Reserve-Feldbatterie des III. Seebataillons; kia 07.11.1914 Tsingtau.

LINDEMANN, Albert; Seesoldat in der 1. Kompanie des OMD; kia 02.10.1914 Tsingtau.

LÜDEMANN, Gustav Ewald; Matrosenartillerist in der 1. Kompanie der MAK; kia 07.11.1914 Tsingtau.

LUTHER, Karl; Artilleristenmaat in der 4. Kompanie der MAK; kia 07.11.1914 Tsingtau.

MALITZ, Franz; Seesoldat der Reserve in der 2. Kompanie des III. SB.; kia 28.09.1914 Tsingtau.

MEINHOLD, Max Richard; Matrose auf Fluflkanonenboot Vaterland; kia 08.1914.

MEISE, Paul Johann; Seesoldat in der 3. Kompanie des III. SB.; kia 28.10.1914 Tsingtau.

MELCHER, Wilhelm K. F. ; Marinefeldartillerist in der MFB des III. SB.; kia 07.11.1914 Tsingtau.

MENGERINGHAUSEN, Heinrich; Unteroffizier in der 2. Kompanie des III. SB.; kia 07.02.1915 Tsingtau.

MEYER, Willy; Matrose auf Kanonenboot Iltis; kia 1914 Tsingtau.

MEYER-COHN, Johann, Unteroffizier der Reserve in der MFB des III. SB.; kia 07.11.1914 Tsingtau.

MICHELS, Sigismund; Kriegshilfsgeistlicher'beim Gouvernement, died 08.11.1914 Tsingtau.

MOERSCH, Wilhelm; Seesoldat in der 1. Kompanie des III. SB.; kia 07.11.1914 Tsingtau.

MÜLLER, Otto Friedrich; Gefreiter der Landwehr in der 4. Kompanie des III. SB.; kia 27.12.1914 Tsingtau.

MÜLLER, Wilhelm; Vizewachtmeister der Landwehr; died 02.1915 Mandschurei.

Müller, Willy; Seesoldat in der MGK des III. SB.; kia 03.11.1914 Tsingtau.

MÜNNICH, Ferdinand, Obermatrose auf Fluflkanonenboot Tsingtau; kia 07.11.1914 Tsingtau.

NEUL, Reinhold; Unteroffizier in der 3. Kompanie des III. SB.; kia 16.10.1914 Tsingtau.

NIEMEYER, Wilhelm Heinrich; Seesoldat in der MGK des III. SB.; kia 07.11.1914 Tsingtau.

NUNINGER, Emil; Seesoldat in der 2. Kompanie des III. SB.; kia 07.11.1914 Tsingtau.

PERTHEL, Johannes; Gefreiter in der 1. Kompanie des OMD; kia 02.10.1914 Tsingtau.

PFÄFFLE, Georg; Matrose der Seewehr II in der 5. Kompanie der MAK; kia 03.11.1914 Tsingtau.

PLUME, Hans; Artilleristenmaat in der 2. Kompanie der MAK; dow 19.11.1914 Tsingtau.

POKORNY, Franz; Steuermatrose auf k.u.k. Kreuzer *Kaiserin Elisabeth*; kia 30.10.1914 Tsingtau.

POLTE, Alfred; Oberartilleristenmaat in der 1. Kompanie der MAK; kia 07.11.1914 Tsingtau.

QUABECK, Wilhelm; Seesoldat in der 2. Kompanie des OMD; kia 09.10.1914 Tsingtau.

RADECKE, Heinrich; Obermatrosenartillerist in der 3. Kompanie der MAK; kia 07.11.1914 Tsingtau.

RAEGENER, Hermann; Unteroffizier der Reserve in der 2. Kompanie des III. SB.; kia 07.11.1914 Tsingtau.

RAMMLING, Johann; Vizefeldwebel in der 1. Kompanie des OMD; kia 07.11.1914 Tsingtau.

RAUH, Hans; Obermatrosenartillerist in der 5. Kompanie der MAK; kia 08.12.1914 Tsingtau.

REBHAN, Georg Pionier in der MPK des III. SB.; kia 03.11.1914 Tsingtau.

REHM, Max; Seesoldat in der 1. Kompanie des OMD; kia 02.10.1914 Tsingtau.

REILARD, Joseph (?); Seesoldat in der 4. Kompanie des III. SB.; kia 28.09.1914 Tsingtau.

RETSCH, Heinrich; Gefreiter in der 1. Kompanie des III. SB.; kia 28.09.1914 Tsingtau.

RIEDESEL FREIHERR ZU EISENBACH, Gottfried; Leutnant der Reserve in der 5. Kompanie des III. SB.; kia 18.09.1914 Tsingtau.

RÖNNSPIESS, Otto; Matrosenartillerist in der 2. Kompanie der MAK; kia 01.11.1914 Tsingtau.

ROSSBACH, Adam; Obermatrosenartillerist in der 1. Kompanie der MAK; kia 05.11.1914 Tsingtau.

RÜGER, Johann Christoph; Seesoldat der Reserve in der 2. Kompanie des III. SB.; kia 06.11.1914 Tsingtau.

SAMBERG, Arno; Matrose der Reserve beim Gouvernement; kia 07.11.1914 Tsingtau.

SAUER, Martin Gustav; Unteroffizier in der 5. Kompanie des III. SB.; kia 07.11.1914 Tsingtau Seevers, Hermann Dietrich; Gefreiter des Landsturms in der 4. Kompanie des III. SB.; kia 27.09.1914 Tsingtau.

SELKE, Paul; Gefreiter in der 1. Kompanie des OMD; kia 07.11.1914 Tsingtau.

SIEBERT, Fritz; Obermatrosenartillerist in der 2. Kompanie der MAK; kia 07.11.1914 Tsingtau.

SOMMER, Rudolf, Gefreiter in der MPK des III. SB.; kia 16.09.1914 Tsingtau.

SONNABEND, Hans W.; Unteroffizier der Reserve in der 7. Kompanie des III. SB.; kia 02.11.1914 Tsingtau.

SÖTEBIER, Karl August; Seesoldat in der 1. Kompanie des OMD; kia 07.11.1914 Tsingtau.

SÜSSENBACH, Wilhelm Karl; Unteroffizier der Landwehr in der MPK des III. SB kia 07.11.1914 Tsingtau.

SCHALL, Georg; Seesoldat in der MGK des III. SB.; kia 07.11.1914 Tsingtau.

SCHEIB, Anton; Seesoldat in der 2. Kompanie des III. SB.; kia 28.09.1914 Tsingtau.

SCHELENZ, Karl; Seesoldat in der 1. Kompanie des OMD; kia 07.11.1914 Tsingtau.

SCHIKORA, Paul; Matrosenartillerist in der 1. Kompanie der MAK; kai 05.11.1914.

SCHLAADT, Josef, Seesoldat in der 1. Kompanie des OMD; kia 07.11.1914 Tsingtau.

SCHMIDT, Georg Eugen; Matrosenartillerist in der 3. Kompanie der MAK; kia 07.11.1914 Tsingtau.

SCHNEIDER, Bruno, Seesoldat in der 1. Kompanie des III. SB.; kia 24.08.1914 Tsingtau.

SCHNEIDER, Max; Unteroffizier in der 2. Kompanie des III. SB.; kia 06.11.1914 Tsingtau.

SCHOLZ, Paul; Seesoldat in der 2. Kompanie des III. SB.; kia 07.11.1914 Tsingtau.

SCHÖNKNECHT, Willy; Obermatrosenartillerist der Reserve in der 5. Kompanie der MAK; kia 07.11.1914 Tsingtau.

SCHRAMM, Friedrich; Kanonier in der SHB des III. SB.; kai 07.11.1914 Tsingtau.

SCHRENK, Alois Matrosenartillerist in der 1. Kompanie der MAK; kia 05.11.1914 Tsingtau.

SCHUBACH, Karl; Gefreiter in der 1. Kompanie des III. SB.; kia 07.11.1914 Tsingtau.

SCHÜLER, Gustav Emil; Seesoldat in der 1. Kompanie des OMD; kai 07.11.1914 Tsingtau.

SCHULTZ, Rudolf [?]; Seesoldat in der 5. Kompanie des III. SB.; kia 27.09.1914 Tsingtau.

SCHULZ, Karl; Seesoldat ['Schulz II'] in der 2. Kompanie des III. SB.; kia 07.11.1914 Tsingtau.

SCHULZE, Adolf; Matrosenartillerist in der 1. Kompanie der MAK; kia 05.11.1914 Tsingtau.

SCHULZE, Walter; Seesoldat in der 1. Kompanie des OMD; kia 02.10.1914 Tsingtau.

SCHURHECK, Winand; Seesoldat in der 1. Kompanie des OMD; kia 22.09.1914 Tsingtau.

SCHUSTER, Ludwig; Seesoldat in der 2. Kompanie des III. SB.; kia 13.09.1914 Tsingtau.

SCHWAMM, Hans; Marinefeldartillerist in der MFB des III. SB; kia 07.11.1914 Tsingtau.

STEINBORN, Bernhard; Marinefeldartillerist in der MFB des III. SB.; kia 07.11.1914 Tsingtau.

STEINBORN, Peter; Obermatrosenartillerist in der 2. Kompanie der MAK; kia 07.11.1914 Tsingtau.

TAUCHMANN, Franz; Steuermatrose auf k.u.k. Kreuzer *Kaiserin Elisabeth*; kia 03.11.1914 Tsingtau.

THAMM, Eduard; Seesoldat in der 2. Kompanie des OMD; dow 30.09.1914 Tsingtau.

TREDE, Hans; Matrose auf Kanonenboot Iltis, kia 07.11.1914 Tsingtau.

UEBELBACHER, Robert; Matrose auf k.u.k. Kreuzer *Kaiserin Elisabeth*; kia 30.10.1914 Tsingtau.

UFERMANN, Hermann, Heizer in der 1. Kompanie der MAK; kia 13.10.1914 Tsingtau.

ULLRICHS, Friedrich; Sergeant in der MFB des III. SB.; kia 07.11.1914 Tsingtau.

VALTER, Peter; Seesoldat in der 1. Kompanie des OMD; kia 07.11.1914 Tsingtau.

VOIGT, Heinrich; Obermatrosenartillerist in der 1. Kompanie der MAK; kia 01.11.1914 Tsingtau.

VOSKAMP, Gerhard; Einjährigfreiwilliger in der 7. Kompanie des III. SB., kia 04.11.1914 Tsingtau.

VOSPOHL, Hermann; Seesoldat in der 1. Kompanie des OMD; kia 02.10.1914 Tsingtau.

WAGNER, Christoph 1914 Obermatrosenartillerist in der 3. Kompanie der Matrosen-Artillerie-Abteilung Kiautschou; kai 07.11.1914 Tsingtau.

WAGNER, Peter; Unteroffizier in der 1. Kompanie des OMD; kia 02.10.1914 Tsingtau.

WALTER, Georg; Vizefeldwebel der Reserve in der 4. Kompanie des III. Seebataillons; kia 28.09.1914 Tsingtau.

WALTER, Hermann; Matrosenartillerist in der 1. Kompanie der Matrosen-Artillerie-Abteilung Kiautschou; kia 05.11.1914 Tsingtau.

WEBER, Friedrich; Seesoldat im III. SB; kia 07.11.1914 Tsingtau.

WEIHRAUCH, Wilhelm; Seesoldat in der MGK des III. Seebataillons; kia 07.11.1914 Tsingtau.

WERLICH, Kurt; Obermatrosenartillerist in der 1. Kompanie der Matrosen-Artillerie-Abteilung Kiautschou; kia 05.11.1914 Tsingtau.

WIELÄNDER, Robert Richard; Obermatrosenartillerist in der 1. Kompanie der Matrosen-Artillerie-Abteilung Kiautschou; kia 07.11.1914 Tsingtau.

WILLERS, Alois; Seesoldat in der 1. Kompanie des OMD; kia 02.10.1914 Tsingta.

WUTHKE, Karl Goldberg[?], Ersatzreservist in der 5. Kompanie der Matrosen - Artillerie-Abteilung Kiautschou; kia 17.09.1914 Tsingtau.

ZIELINSKI, Franz; Seesoldat in der 2. Kompanie des III. SB.; kia 06.11.1914 Tsingtau.

German Prisoners of War who died in captivity

The following is list of those Germans taken prisoner at Tsingtao who died while in captivity. The largest number in any given year was in 1919 – after the armistice had been signed – and it appears that many of these men died as a result of the Spanish Influenza pandemic that swept the world at that time causing more deaths than the Great War itself. It will also be noticed that some deaths are recorded into 1920 and that the Germans were held in captivity in Japan long after the fighting had ceased – most prisoners of war had been released months before this and the captives from Tsingtao who had ended up in Liverpool Camp in Australia had been released in March 1919. The details for this table have been taken from the German language Tsingtau Information web site (www.tsingtau.info).

Died	Name	Number	Camp
1914 (3)			
25.10	Koch, Heinrich	562	Kurume
08.12	Rauh, Hans	4660	Tsingtau
27.12	Müller, Otto Friedrich	4661	Tsingtau

Died	Name	Number	Camp
1915 (10			
07.01	Behrens, August	4662	Tsingtau
15.01	Welter, Heinrich	1645	Fukuoka
23.01	Bauer, Wilhelm Otto	4663	Tsingtao
07.02	Mengeringhausen, Heinrich	4664	Tsingtao
13.02	Jansen, Gustav Adolf	2576	Nagoya
13.04	Matheis, Gustav	1753	Shizuoka
15.04	Schilling, Karl	3733	Kumamoto
06.06	Temme, Ammandus	2094	Marugame
22.07	Emoan, Max	3268	Kurume
07.09	Goll, Hermann	4509	Osaka
1916 11			
19.03	Simon, Robert	3645	Kurume
06.04	Klein, Richard	4383	Oita
17.04	Boesler, Ernst	356	Kurume
21.04	Sanz, Josef	3742	Kurume
25.05	Vita, Janos	2442	Aonogahara
31.05	Schmidt, Karl Friedrich	2713	Nagoya
04.06	Stertz, Fritz	255	Narashino
17.06	Gomolka, Theofil	2204	Aonogahara
18.06	Schmidt, Willy	2691	Nagoya
07.09	Hellmuth, Jean	4182	Tokushima
06.11	Lauenstein, Arthur	2995	Matsuyama
1917 10			
10.02	Nowak, Karl	168	Narashino
01.03	Saldern, von, Siegfried	1461	Fukuoka
01.03	Kraft, Diederich	4542	Osaka
09.05	Kiesewetter, J. Paul	4382	Oita
12.08	Laengner, Martin	2297	Aonogahara
17.08	Grallert, Hans	4518	Ninoshima
29.08	Suran, Franz	247	Narashino
04.12	Kühne, Karl	3424	Bando
06.12	Riedel, Georg Erich	3072	Bando
09.12	Gomille, Paul	1890	Bando
1918 20			
02.01	Cravatzo, Peter	1856	Bando
10.02	Nowak, Stefan	173	Narashino
13.03	Schlund, Alfred	1489	Kurume
19.03	Pape, Otto	4647	Ninoshima
26.03	Pauly, Karl	3567	Kurume
08.05	Werner, Alfred	3804	Kurume
27.05	Luczeck, Franz	1277	Narashino
21.07	Hubbe, Fritz	4179	Bando
29.07	Schlotfeldt, Hans	2389	Aonogahara
31.07	Rockser, Alexander	4580	Ninoshima
14.11	Jakob, Johann	2574	Nagoya
17.11	Schulze, Robert	2712	Nagoya

Died	Name	Number	Camp
23.11	Oppel, Wilhelm	2641	Nagoya
23.11	Flögel, Wilhelm	3313	Nagoya
25.11	Philipps, Lorenz	2653	Nagoya
26.11	Puchert, Wilhelm	1407	Nagoya
26.11	Georgi, Paul	2542	Nagoya
30.11	Seeger, Hermann	2056	Bando
Died	*Name*	*Number*	*Camp*
01.12	Kardinal, Herrmann	2593	Nagoya
05.12	Schulze, Gustav	1465	Narashino
1919 36			
?	Schürmann, Fritz	4038	Ninoshima
?	Zeffler, Albert	1692	Ninoshima
26.01	Kraus, Simon	139	Narashino
26.01	Becker, Hermann	34	Narashino
28.01	Noppeney, Philipp	1369	Narashino
29.01	Focken, Charly	4351	Narashino
29.01	Spöler, Heinrich	4445	Narashino
29.01	Stauch, Karl	228	Narashino
31.01	Mehlis, Peter	157	Narashino
31.01	Körner, Peter	1187	Narashino
31.01	Schütze, Julius	1513	Narashino
31.01	Rosenberger, Heinz	1776	Narashino
31.01	Johannes, Hugo	1164	Narashino
31.01	Berndt, Alfons	876	Narashino
01.02	Agethen, Heinrich	1	Narashino
02.02	Böhmer, Wilhelm	28	Narashino
02.02	Thönes, Fritz	4447	Narashino
02.02	Siebel, Robert	1482	Narashino
02.02	Hagemann, Harald	1105	Narashino
04.02	Glasmacher, Hans	1059	Narashino
04.02	Teller, Herbert	1798	Narashino
04.02	Linel, Leo	152	Narashino
06.02	Seng, Karl	1486	Narashino
07.02	Dörr, Christian	50	Narashino
07.02	Böcher, Karl	3201	Narashino
11.02	Bauch, Johann	914	Narashino
11.02	Krämer, Hermann	1194	Narashino
02.03	Kettgen, Johann	3443	Kurume
06.03	Schmiedel, August	3686	Bando
03.07	Pötter, Karl	4695	Ninoshima
08.07	Lehmann, Hugo K. A.	1282	
02.08	Pönitz, Erich	3578	Narashino
09.09	Jellovcic, Anton	2254	Kurume
19.09	Onodi, Michael	2138	Aonogahar
07.11	Bauer, Joseph	3212	Aonogahar
18.12	Knell, Friedrich	3458	Nagoya
1920 3			
05.01	Hildebrandt, Reinhold	2901	Bando
16.01	Brilmayer, Joseph	3841	Ninoshima
21.01	Halbritter, Robert	4527	Ninoshima

Appendix 8

The Despatches of
Brigadier-General N. W. Barnardiston
Printed in the Supplement to the *London Gazette* of 30 May 1916

Despatch N$^{o.}$ 1

From Brigadier-General N. W. Barnardiston, M.V.O., to the War Office.

Investing Line before Tsingtau, 9th October, 1914.

I have the honour to report that the force under my command embarked at Tientsin on the 19th September in the hired transports *Kwang Ping, Shao Shing* and *Shuntien*, and, escorted from Taku Bar by HMS *Triumph* and the torpedo-boat destroyer *Usk*, arrived at Wei-hai-wei at 2.15 p.m. on 20th September [1914].

The number of mules necessary to complete our requirements in transport, which had been purchased by Captain Knaggs, Indian Army, were there embarked, that officer offering valuable assistance both there and also on disembarkation at Lao Shan Bay. The SS *Shenking*, chartered by the Naval Authorities as a hospital carrier, for conveyance of sick and wounded to Wei-haiwei, joined us, and the whole left at 4.0 p.m. on 21st September.

Before leaving, I inspected the arrangements made by Captain House, RN, and Fleet-Surgeon Clarke, on the hospital carrier, and also on shore for the reception of the sick and wounded. These two officers, especially the last named, deserve the greatest credit for the excellent arrangements made to meet all our requirements.

Lao Shan Bay was reached at 2 p.m. on 22nd September, and arrangements were made with HMS *Triumph*, the Japanese Navy and the Military Disembarkation Authorities for the disembarkation of the Force on the following day. Accordingly, on 23rd September, the 2nd Bn. South Wales Borderers disembarked at 8 a.m., followed by stores, ponies, mules and carts, &c. The men worked hard and cheerfully at landing and stacking stores, &c. , and the entire disembarkation was accomplished by 6 a.m. on 24th September, with the exception of Base stores not immediately required, which were left on board the SS *Kwang Ping* in anticipation of a change of Base, to Sha-tzukou Bay, within about 10 miles of the lines of investment.

The 24th September was spent in transferring stores from landing place to Base Supply Depot. I sent Major H. G. Pringle, General Staff, Japanese Commander-in-Chief, who, I was informed, had just arrived at that place. I despatched Captain C. D. Hamilton Moore, D.A.A. and Q.M.G., to reconnoitre two roads over the Lao Shan Range, by which I thought I could move the force towards the left of the line of investment, which would be the most convenient position for purposes of supply, as my transport was only sufficient to carry 4 days' rations. One of these roads was found to be quite unsuitable and the other only possible with a complete re-organization of the transport, using pack mules or coolies over the worst parts of the Pass, and man-handling such carts as were necessary for use on the further side. I was prepared to make this re-organization if necessary.

On arrival, however, on the 25th, at Pu-li, about six miles from Lao Shan Bay, I learned that the Japanese Commander wished to use the Force under my command in the centre of the line, and he desired me, therefore, to march via Chimo and Liuting towards Litsun. I also gathered that the Japanese plan of operations was to advance south from Chimo on 27th and 28th, and to attack on 29th and 30th the German advanced line, extending from Prince Henry Hill to Ku Shan, in order that siege material might be brought up to bombard the main position in front of Tsingtau. To comply with the wishes of the Japanese Commander implied a very heavy strain on my transport, and probably very short rations, as it implied a line of communications nearly 40 miles in length, over a single, bad, narrow and congested road, or rather track. It was essential, however, to make the effort, and I decided to do so, even if we had to exist on half rations.

On the 26th September the Force marched to Chimo, about 13 miles, where it arrived at 11.30 a.m., the transport arriving later in the afternoon, and a convoy of supplies from the Base about 11 p.m., after experiencing the greatest difficulties, owing to the blocked roads. I consider that the officers and others concerned deserve the greatest credit for accomplishing what seemed an almost insuperable task, and I desire specially to bring to notice the excellent services rendered by Captain Don, Indian Supply and Transport Corps. To the men, the marches, although not long, were very trying, owing to the constant halts and checks owing to the road being blocked by Japanese artillery and transport, but, with the exception of a few cases of fever, no men fell out. On arrival at Chimo my supply difficulties were greatly lessened by the offer of the Japanese military authorities to use their transport for the purpose of establishing an advanced supply depot at Chimo, from which point our own transport would be able to work forward to the refilling point.

On the 27th the force moved on about 9 miles to Liuting and halted. I rode on to Divisional Headquarters, where I was received very cordially by Lieut-General Kamio, the Japanese Commander-in-Chief, who gave me an outline of the following day's operations, in which we were to take part.

On the 28th, in accordance with his orders, the force proceeded towards Litsun with a view of participating in the attack on the German advanced position, which was then being reconnoitred by the Japanese troops. The Germans holding the position retired, however, before the Japanese advanced troops, who occupied the position which it was General Kamio's intention to have assaulted on the following night and morning. The force under my command was therefore not engaged, and marched on to a village about 2 miles in rear of the Japanese line, where it bivouacked. This position, however, proved to be unsuitable, as we were exposed to the enemy's artillery fire, luckily without suffering any casualties; but on the 30th September I moved the force to the reverse slopes of a hill about 1 mile to the eastward of our former position, where the men were under cover, and were able to make splinter proof shelters.

Despatch N⁰· 2

From Brigadier-General N. W. Barnardiston, M.V.O., to the War Office.
Investing Lines before Tsingtau, 29th October, 1914.
In continuation of my despatch dated 9th instant, I have the honour to report
that on the 10th instant I received orders from the Japanese Commander to the
effect that the Force under my command was to take its place in the front line of
the investing force, a front of about 600 yards being assigned to us. Accordingly,
on the 11th instant I directed the Officer Commanding 2nd Bn. South Wales
Borderers to take up, with 2 companies a line running approximately north-west
and southwest through a point a little north of Point 177 on Shuang Shan,
furnishing two piquets with their supports and a local reserve. The remaining
companies of the 2nd Bn. South Wales Borderers were distributed in such
nullahs, south of Huang-Chia-Ching, as afforded the best cover from shell fire.

2. The range of heights forming the position of the line of investment south
of that village, with their under-features, is intersected by numerous deep
ravines of clay, excellent for protection and accommodation in dry weather. In
wet weather, however, such as we have been unfortunately experiencing, the
loose soil is washed away, the sides of the nullahs fall in, carrying with them the
shelters for the troops; every valley becomes a torrent and every road or track a
mass of deep mud. Cover for the men both from fire and weather becomes
impossible. The men have been soaked through and through for as much as 48
hours, and equipment has been buried by falls of earth, and ammunition has
rusted, but in spite of all hardships and privations the spirits and health of the
troops have been excellent, and they have worked continuously at digging and
at the heavy fatigue work of carrying rations and ammunition and heavy beams
for head cover 1¹/2 miles to the front where wheeled traffic has been impossible
– often in liquid mud halfway up to the knees.

3. By degrees, and as I can obtain space, I am moving the rear companies up
towards the front line preparatory to the attack on the fortress. Considerable
delay has taken place in the preparations of the Japanese owing to heavy rains,
but I learned yesterday that the bombardment will commence on the 31st
instant. The health of the troops, notwithstanding the hard work and trying
weather, is most satisfactory.

5 [sic – no paragraph 4]. The line of investment we now hold extends from
Kiao-Chau Bay to the sea, running approximately through Kushan, 119 degrees
21 minutes, 36 degrees 8 minutes (Lat. 36⁰ 8′ N., Long. 119⁰ 21′ E.), the high
ground south of Chia-Lien-Kow to Foushan (Prince Henry's Hill). The following
is a summary of the order for the attack on the fortress, so far as concerns the
British Force – The whole of the enemy's main line of defence will constitute the
front of attack. All arrangements are calculated for a deliberate advance, but any
opportunity of attacking which presents itself will be seized upon. The front of
attack is divided into four sections, the right central section being assigned to the
force under my command. One front of about 600 yards is roughly bounded by
two parallel lines running north-east and south-west – the right flank line
passing through Tashaii, 119 degrees 22 minutes, 36 degrees 7 minutes (36⁰ 7′ N.
, 119⁰ 22′ E.) , village and Point 375, 372 the left, the north-west corner of Ho-Hsi
and the eastern corner of Tiu-Tung-Chien (T'ai Tung Chen). Tomorrow the line
of investment will be advanced to a line running through Kushan, Shvang-Shan,

119 degrees, 6 minutes, 36 degrees 6 minutes (36° 6' N., 119° 6' E.), Tung-Wu-Chia-Tsun, Tien-Chia-Tsun, Hsin-Chia-Chiang in the construction of which working parties from each section are employed daily and nightly. When the bombardment begins, the Infantry and Engineers of the front line will prepare for the subsequent advance, and during the night of the 1st November will occupy a line through the high ground west of Han-Chla-Chuang, and south of Tung-Wu-Chia-Teun, and north of Fou-Shan-So – also that village. The first position of attack will be prepared on this line, and during the first two or three nights will, be strengthened, communicating trenches completed, and preparations made for the next advance. The second position of attack will be strongly constructed, approximately on the line Pump Stratton, Hsi-Wu-Chla-T'sun, the high ground east of Kang-Chla-Chuang and the ridge west of Fou-Shan-So, and in this position preparations will be made for the destruction of obstacles and the subsequent approach. The main portion of the siege artillery will first fix on the enemy's forts and the remainder against his war vessels. Subsequently, as the first line advances, this portion of the artillery will fire on the enemy's redoubts. Co-operation with the Navy is arranged for.

6. I am collecting 12 days' supplies at a suitable place in rear of the advanced position to provide against the eventuality of its being found impossible, in this very difficult country, to bring them up during the bombardment. A suitable place for my Brigade Ammunition Reserve, about 2 miles in rear of the first position of attack; has been selected. The Field Hospital has been established at Che-Chla-Hsia-Chuang, about half-way between Litsun-Erh-Shan and Prince Henry Hill, and dressing-stations have been arranged for in nullahs in rear of the front-line.

7. The half battalion of the 36th Sikhs, under command of Lieut-Colonel E. L. Sullivan disembarked at Lao-Shan-Bay on the 22nd instant and arrived yesterday at the front.

Despatch Nᵒ· 3
From Brigadier-General N. W. Barnardiston, M.V.O. , to the War Office.
Tsingtau, 10th November 1914,
I have the honour to report the successful conclusion of this Expedition in the surrender of Tsingtau on the 7th instant. The operations in which the force under my command have taken part proceeded as outlined in my Despatch No. 2, dated 29th October. The advanced position indicated in that despatch was occupied on the 30th October. The bombardment commenced on the 31st, the enemy not replying to any great extent. During the first day some oil tanks and coal stores near the dockyard were burnt, and the forts and redoubts suffered severely. Throughout the bombardment the practice of the Japanese artillery was surprisingly good, and the accuracy of their fire and their numerical superiority in guns no doubt proved the principal factor in compelling the enemy's surrender. It is stated that the Germans expended all their gun ammunition. The bombardment continued with slight intermissions until the fall of the place.

On the 1st November the First Position of attack (see my Despatch No. 2) was occupied, and the preparation of the Second Position commenced. This position was ready for, occupation on the 3rd instant, but, owing to its location in the immediate vicinity of the bed of the river, it was impossible to drain it or to occupy it permanently, and as it was everywhere under close infantry fire from the First Position, I merely held it during the night with piquets.

On the night of the 4th November somewhat heavy artillery fire was directed on our trenches, the 36th Sikhs losing 2 Sepoys killed and 2 officers wounded, while the 2nd Bn. South Wales Borderers had also several casualties.

On the 5th November I was ordered to prepare a Third Position of attack on the left bank of the river. This line was to a great extent enfiladed on both flanks by No. 1 and 2 Redoubts, especially the latter, from which annoying machine-gun fire was experienced. The bed of the river (a small stream running over a broad bed of sand) had also to be crossed, and in doing so the working parties of the 2nd Bn. South Wales Borderers suffered somewhat severely, losing 8 non-commissioned officers and men killed and 24 wounded. The 36th Sikhs had only slight losses. Notwithstanding this a good deal of work was done, especially on the right flank. I considered it my duty to represent to the Japanese Commander-in-Chief the untenable nature, for permanent occupation, of the portion of the Third Position in my front, but received a reply that it was necessary for it to be held in order to fit in with the general scheme of assault.

On the evening of the 6th, accordingly, I occupied it with piquets, and the working parties continued to improve it. During the night, on hearing rumours of the evacuation of one or more of the redoubts, I sent out officer's patrols to ascertain if the enemy were still holding the trenches in front of us, and prepared to advance should the front be clear. They were met, however, with rifles and machine-gun fire, and reported that No. 2 Redoubt, on our left, was still held. Between 5 and 6 a.m. on the morning of the 7th, the enemy started a further cannonade for field, artillery and an occasional shot from their heavy guns, and I issued preparatory orders for an advance as soon as I knew the redoubts were captured. At 7 a.m. all firing ceased, and I was informed that the enemy had sent out a flag of truce. About 7. 30 a.m. I received orders to advance, and, the enemy along the whole of our front having then retired, I marched into Tsingtau. The troops under my command have behaved extremely well under trying conditions of weather and those inseparable from siege warfare, and all ranks have worked loyally and hard.

I propose in a subsequent despatch to bring to your notice those who have merited special mention. The total casualties in the force up to the present date are given in the annexure to this despatch.

Despatch No. 4
From Brigadier-General N. W. Barnardiston, M.V.O., to the War Office.

Tsingtau, 13th November, 1914.
In continuation of my Despatch No. 3, dated 10th instant, I have-the honour to forward the names of the following, officers, non-commissioned officers and men of the force under my command whom I consider deserving of special notice for their services.

These names are in addition to those mentioned in my despatch, dated 9th October.

Staff

    Major H. G. Pringle, Royal Artillery.

General Staff

    Captain C. D. H. Moore, R. Warwick Regt., Deputy-Assistant Adjutant and Quartermaster-General.

    Captain J. Gray, 36th Sikhs (attached).

    Captain J. A. Hamilton, Army Service Corps, Base Commandant.

    Major J. A. Hartigan, M.B., Royal Army Medical Corps, Senior Medical Officer.

2nd Bn South Wales Borderers

    Lieutenant-Colonel H. G. Casson, Commanding.

    Major E. C. Margesson.

    Captain J. Bradstock.

    Captain and Adjutant G. H. Birkett.

    Captain D. G. Johnson.

    Lieutenant R. L. Petre.

    Lieutenant H. J. Simson, Royal Scots (Japanese interpreter), attached.

    Captain G. H. Dive, Royal Army Medical Corps, attached.

    2/10423, Serjeant J. J. Ward (killed).

2/9972	Private G. C. Snow.
2/9004	Private A. Green.
2/9980	Private T. Jenkinson.
10171	Drummer W. I. Jones (killed).
10634	Private (Lce -Corpl.) C. J. Foley.
10614	Private H. Evans (killed).
2/9952	Private J. West (died of wounds).
2/4528	Drummer C. W. Lewis.
2/9244	Co. Serjeant-Major G. A. Davies.
7309	Serjeant H. Leach (died of wounds).
3/10249	Corporal (Actg. Serjeant) W. S. Rosier.

Army Service Corps

    1st Class Staff-Serjeant-Major S. C. Warner (now Quartermaster and Hony. Lieutenant).

    1st Class Staff-Serjeant-Major A. Goodwin (now Quartermaster and Hony. Lieutenant).

Royal Army Medical Corps

17933	Quartermaster – Serjeant D. E. Dean (now Serjeant-Major).
11313	Corporal A. Bateman (now Serjeant).
19823	Corporal T. J. Kilyon.
1884	Corporal E. S. Gaughan (now Serjeant).

36th Sikhs

    Lieutenant-Colonel E. L. Sullivan, Commanding.

    Major E. F. Knox.

    Captain A. D. Martin.

    Lieutenant and Adjutant S. des Voeux.

Subadar Gurmukh Singh, I.O.M.
Jemadar Sundar Singh.
Jemadar Jaimal Singh.
1707   Havildar Massa Singh.
271   Lance-Naik Bhagat Singh.
2757   Lance-Naik Harman Singh.
2829   Lance-Naik Hari Singh.
3126   Sepoy Fakir Singh.
3785   Sepoy Ram Singh.
3782   Sepoy Bant Singh.

Appendix 9

A Note on the British Cemetery
in Tsingtao

The soldiers who died on the battlefield were buried near to the British field hospital situated near Shang-Hsiao-Tsun Chang, some six miles north of Tsingtao. This is in the rear of the area that was the main position of the South Wales Borderers throughout the siege. The cemetery, on a narrow strip of agricultural land, originally contained only the bodies of the Borderers who had been killed in the action. In 1915, funds were raised by the British community in Tsingtao so that the land could be bought and in November of that year, ten marble crosses were erected to mark the graves. It appears that, at quite an early stage, there was the intention to use the plot of land for burials other than those killed in action and in April 1917, Mr P. S. Thornton, who was working with the Chinese Labour Corps, died and was buried alongside the Borderers.

During 1918, a committee was formed and charged with the responsibility for the upkeep and maintenance of the cemetery. Funds were available from the British community and augmented by donations of the friends of Mr Thornton in Tientsin. The first action of the committee was to

SWB Cemetery at Tsingtao. [Royal Welsh Museum, Brecon, BRCRM A1937.7]

Graves – L–R: 9763, Pte Joseph Williams; 8436, Sgt William Miller; 7235, Sgt Arthur Payne.
[Royal Welsh Museum, Brecon, BRCRM A1937.7]

repair areas of the cemetery where erosion, caused by the periodic storms, not unlike those experienced by the Borderers in 1914, had become a problem. The problem of erosion of the ground around and within the cemetery was to remain a problem for a number of years and was a continual maintenance issue for which the committee took full responsibility. In 1919, in an attempt to limit the erosion, the cemetery was enclosed by a wall for the first time.

A further addition to the cemetery was made in 1924 when it was decided that a suitable memorial to the South Wales Borderers should be erected. This took the form of a cenotaph made from local Loashan granite. By this time also, the upkeep of the graves was assisted by the Imperial (later Commonwealth) War Graves Commission which donated a sum of thirty pounds towards the maintenance of the cemetery. Monies were also received from the Shanghai Race Club which was based upon the income raised from debentures at the rate of 6.5%.

Although much had been done to ensure the future of the cemetery and to look after its fabric, nothing could be done during the extraordinary heavy rains of 1925 to prevent two graves being washed away. These graves were immediately reinstated and work to repair a retaining wall to prevent future similar events was also completed.

In 1928, a pair of entry gates in bronze and bearing the embossed badge of the South Wales Borderers was erected and the cost was met by the returns on the debentures of the Shanghai Race Club.

Further burials of servicemen took place: in 1933, Engine Room Artificer Hornbury of HMS *Caradoc* was buried in the cemetery; in 1936, Major Stockwell and Leading Signalman Moulton of HMS *Medway* were also buried in the cemetery. The policy of burying civilians in the cemetery

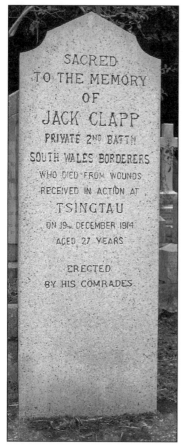

The grave of Pte John Clapp in the Sai Wan Military Cemetery, Hong Kong.

continued when Mr A. R. T. Finch, one of the men who worked to ensure the upkeep of the cemetery, was also buried there. Also in that year, it was thought to be appropriate that a special memorial stone should be raised to Pte. E. T. Stoner of the South Wales Borderers who had died of disease during the campaign but, inexplicably, had no known grave.

It appears that, at this time, the committee had significant funds to maintain the cemetery and, although there was a clear and stated policy to use the plot for civilian burials, there does not seem to have been any burials there between 1936 and the end of the Second World War. In 1949, the area was taken over by the Communist Regime and upkeep of the cemetery by the Commonwealth War Graves Commission appears to have ceased as a result of the difficult political situation and the poor relationship between the west as a whole and the communist regime. It was, perhaps, inevitable that in 1967 during the Cultural Revolution that the cemetery was reported to have been destroyed along with those of the Germans in Tsingtao and the Japanese near Prince Henry Hill (Fu Shan). There has been no attempt to re-establish the cemetery in recent years and

The memorial in the Sai Wan Military Cemetery, Hong Kong.

it appears that the exact location is now lost and the site redeveloped. Those soldiers who died in China during the war years are now commem-orated on a memorial at the entry to the Sai Wan Military Cemetery in Hong Kong.

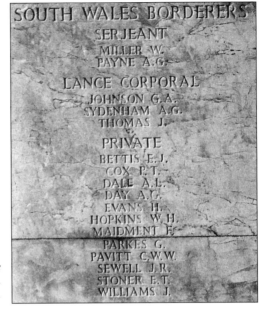

One of the commemorative plaques on the memorial at the Sai Wan Military Cemetery, Hong Kong.

Appendix 10

Embarkation Orders
Tiensin, 18 September 1914

The Embarkation of the Field Force will take place tomorrow as under the detail for each ship being given on attached order of Embarkation.

1. All the Chinese employ will be on board their respective ships by 6.30 am except the 160 for the SS *Shaoshing* who will be on the Quay at the end of the Brompton Road by 7 am.

    The *Shaoshing* will be tied up on this Quay by then.

    They must all be on board by 7.30 am.

    Captain Don, Indian Supply and Transport Corps will Superintendent the Embarkation of all Chinese.

2. Troops for the *Kwangping* will be on board by 7.50 am.

3. The troops for the *Shaoshing* will be on the Quay at the end of Brompton Road by 7.45 am and must be on board by 8.35 am.

    The gangways will be withdrawn at 8.25 am.

4. Troops for the SS *Shuntien*, which will belying in her present berth, will be on board by 9.15 am.

5. The OC South Wales Borderers will arrange for Signallers (Flag and Lamp) to be on board each transport.

Postal Arrangements

6. All letters for troops from Tientsin or elsewhere should be addressed as follows:

    Rank   Name
    Unit
    C/O Base Commandant
    Wei-hai-Wei

The letters should be posted at the Base Post Office and stamped with a 1 anna CEF Stamp (per oz).

Letters from the front to Tientsin will require no stamps. For other places stamps will be required and Units or individuals should arrange accordingly.

The Mails from Tientsin to Wei-hai-Wei will close at the Base Post Office as under:

Tientsin Peking

Monday	- 4 pm
Tuesday	10 am -
Wednesday	- 4 pm

Thursday	10 am -
Friday	- 4 pm
Saturday	10 am -

Censorship

7. Letters liable to censorship may cause delay.

In no circumstances is specific reference to be made to plans of operations, whether rumoured, surmised, or known; to organization, numbers, or movements of troops; to their armament or moral or physical condition; to defensive or other works; to casualties, prior to the publication of the official lists; to the service of maintenance, or the effects of hostile fire.

Criticism of operations is forbidden, as are statements calculated to bring either of the allied forces or individuals into contempt.

C. D. Hamilton Moore, Captain
DAA & QMG, NCG

Order of Embarkation of
NORTH CHINA FIELD FORCE

SS *Shuntien*

Officers

Staff Major Hartigan RAMC
GOC Dr Shaw, Civil Surgeon
GSO Captain Don, Transport
DAA & QMG Reverend Walker, Chaplain
Captain Gray
Captain Colyer
Major Hiwatashi

2nd Battalion South Wales Borderers

Major Going; Lieutenant Cahusac
Captain Palmer; Lieutenant Walker
Captain Greenway; 2nd Lieutenant Behrens
Lieutenant Habershon
Mr Eckford, Interpreter
Captain Christian, Base Commandant Wei-hai-Wei
Captain Hamilton, OC ASC

NCOs and Men

A Company, 2nd Battalion South Wales Borderers,			210
No 9 and 10 Platoons C Company	"	"	107
		Total	317

RAMC		12
AVC		1
Staff Clerk		1
ASC		5
	Total	336

Chinese: on aft 'tween deck, 50 Drivers
Mules: on aft 'tween deck, 64
Carts: In main lower hold, 40 carts and harness.
Regimental Stores: In aft hold, Company Stores.
Wood ASC: In fore hold
Hospital: 3 Chinese cabins on starboard side, forward.
Hospital Stores: (Other than those for base) in Mail Room on main deck.
Total Accommodation 20 officers, 336 NCOs and men, 50 Chinese, 64 Mules, 40
    Carts.

SS *Shaoshing*
Officers 2nd Battalion South Wales Borderers
    Major Jones; 2nd Lieutenant MacGregor
    Captain Bradstock; 2nd Lieutenant Morgan
    Lieutenant Petre
    Lieutenant Heselwood, APD
    Captain Wood, RAMC
    Captain Knaggs, Indian Army
    Captain Greenfield, AVC

NCOs and Men
B Company, 2nd Battalion South Wales Borderers		202
MI		10
RAMC		2
AOC		2
ASC		6
	Total	222

Chinese:	On fore 'tween deck		50
	On Main 'tween deck		80
	On aft 'tween deck		30
		Total	160

Ponies:	On fore 'tween deck		24
	On aft 'tween deck		29
		Total	53

Mules:	On fore 'tween deck		36
	On Main 'tween deck		116
	On aft 'tween deck		86
		Total	238

Baggage: Fore hold - Forage, Company Stores etc.
Carts: Main hold - 81 Carts and harness
        Aft hold - ASC supplies.
Ammunition: Brigade Reserve and Base Supply in Mail Room on aft 'tween
    deck.
Hospital: 3 Chinese cabins.

Total: 8   Officers and 1 Officer from Wei-hai-Wei.
222   NCOs and Men
160   Chinese
53   Ponies
238   Mules
81   Carts.

SS *Kwangping*

Officers 2nd Battalion South Wales Borderers

Colonel Casson; Lieutenant Tippets
Major Margesson; Lieutenant Williams
Captain and Adjutant Birkett; Lieutenant Somerville
Captain Ellis; Lieutenant Rawle
Captain Johnson; Lieutenant & QM Laman
Lieutenant Moore; SLI Captain Dive, RAMC

NCOs and Men

D Company, 2nd Battalion South Wales Borderers	217
Nos 11 &12 Platoons C Company, South Wales Bordrers	103
Total	320

RAMC	2
AOC	2
ASC	3
Total	327

Chinese: In aft 'tween deck and bunks behind aft 'tween deck	82
Cattle: In aft 'tween deck	50

Hospital: 3 Chinese cabins, starboard side, forward.
Regimental Stores: Aft hold.
AOD Stores: Fore hold.

Total   12   Officers
327   NCOs and Men
82   Chinese
50   Cattle

APPENDIX XI

Order of Battle

Japanese Navy

Dreadnoughts
Kawachi (Left early September)
Settsu (Left early September)

Battle Cruiser
Kongo (Left early September)

Pre-Dreadnoughts[1]
Note that these ships were old and had been captured by the Japanese Navy
from the Russians during the war of 1904-05.

Suwo (ex *Pobieda*) (Flagship)
Tango (ex *Poltava*)
Okinoshima (ex *Apraksin*)
Iwami (ex *Orel*)
Mishima (*Seniavin*)

Note that these ships were old and had been captured by the Japanese Navy
from the Russians during the war of 1904-05.

Armoured Cruisers
Chiotose
Akashi
Akitoushim
Ghiveda
Iwate (Left 2 October)
Yakumo (Left 2 October)
Tokiwa (Left 2 October)

Light Cruisers
Tone
Megami
Yedo
Takachiho

Gunboats
Seven took part in the blockade

Destroyers
Shirotai and thirteen others

Seaplane Carrier
Wakamiya Maru

Repair Ship
Kwanto Maru

ROYAL NAVY

Pre-Dreadnought
HMS *Triumph*

Destroyers
HMS *Kennet*
HMS *Usk*

GERMAN NAVY

Light Cruiser
Cormoran

Gunboats
Tiger
Luchs
Iltis
Jaguar

Destroyers
Taku
S-90

Minelayer
Lauting

River Gunboats
Otter
Vaterland

AUSTRIAN NAVY

Protected Cruiser
Kaiserin Elizabeth

Japanese Army
18TH INDEPENDENT DIVISION *(Lieutenant-General Kamio)*
34th Infantry Regiment
46th Infantry Regiment
48th Infantry Regiment
67th Infantry Regiment
22nd Cavalry Regiment
1st Independent Engineer Battalion
18th Battalion of Engineers
24th Regiment Field Artillery
1st Battalion 3rd Heavy Field Artillery
2nd Regiment Heavy Field Artillery
3rd Regiment Heavy Field Artillery
Light Short Range Mortar Sections
1st Battalion Independent Siege Artillery
2nd Battalion Independent Siege Artillery
3rd Battalion Independent Siege Artillery
4th Battalion Independent Siege Artillery
Independent Siege Artillery Battery
Naval Heavy Artillery
Regimental Ammunition Train
Ammunition Train Heavy Field Artillery (two)
Field Searchlight Company

Special Troops
Flying Corps
Divisional Telephone Company
Field Telegraph Corps
Wireless Telegraph Corps
1st, 2nd, 3rd, 4th Field Hospitals

British Army
(Brigadier-General N.W. Barnardiston)
2nd Battalion South Wales Borderers
36th Sikhs (Indian Army) (half battalion)
and personnel of:
Royal Army Medical Corps
Army Service Corps

German Army
(Captain Meyer Waldeck)
3rd *See Bataillon*
Pioneer company
One field battery
Sailors from Kiaochou in 5 companies
Other personnel (initially unattached)
Marine Detachment
Men from German Warships
Volunteers at outbreak of war
Men from *Kaiserin Elisabeth*

Bibliography

ANON., 'The Borderers at Tsingtao. Thrilling Stories of the Siege', *China Mail* (25, 28 and 30 November, 1914).

ANON., 'The Investment of Tsingtao – Progress of the Japanese Attacks', *The Far East*, 6, No. 133, 61, see also 59 and 60, (1914).

ANON., 'The Naval Fighting off Tsing-Tau. The Damage to a British Battleship', *The Sphere*, 80 (16 January, 1915).

ANON., 'Naval Operations Against Tsingtau. Professional Notes', *Journal of the United States Artillery*, 89–92 (May-June, 1916).

ANON., *Tsingtao British Cemetery. A Short History 1914–1936* (Publisher unknown and undated but see: The Museum of the Royal Regiment of Wales, Brecon).

ATKINSON, C. T., *The History of the South Wales Borderers 1914 -1918* (The Medici Society, London, 1931).

ATKINSON, C. T., 'The British in Tsingtao', *History of the First World War*,1, 330–3 (Purnell, 1969).

BAKER, A., *Battle Honours of the British and Commonwealth Armies* (Ian Allan Limited, Shepperton, 1986).

BEECHING, J., *The Chinese Opium Wars* (Harvest/HBJ Books, London, 1975).

BICKERS, R. and TIEDEMANN, R. G., *The Boxers, China and the World.* (Rowman and Littlefield, Plymouth, 2007).

BLANE, W., 'Tsingtao and its Significance', *United Services Magazine*, 1213–26 (1914).

BURDICK, C. B., 'The Japanese Siege of Tsingtau', *World War I in Asia* (Archon Books, Hamden, Connecticut, 1976).

CARY, A. D. L. and McCANCE, S., *Regimental Records of the Royal Welch Fusiliers (Formerly 23rd Foot)* (Royal Welch Fusiliers, Wrexham, 1923).

CHANG, C. S., *The Making of China* (Engelwood Cliffs, 1975).

CHURCHILL, W. S., *The World Crisis 1911–1918*, 1 (Odhams Press Limited, London, 1938).

CLUTTERBUCK, COL. L. A., (Reprint of 1915 Edn.), *The Bond Of Sacrifice*, 2, (Naval and Military Press Ltd., Dallington, 1992).

COLLIS, M., *Foreign Mud: An account of the Opium War* (Faber, London, 1946).

CONNAUGHTON, R., 2003. Rising Sun and Tumbling Bear: Russia's War with Japan (Cassell, London, 1946).

CORBETT, J. S. SIR., 'A Naval History of the Great War Based on Official Documents', *Naval Operations, 1. To The Battle of The Falklands December 1914* (Longman's Green and Company, London, 1920).

COTTRELL, A., *China: A History* (Pimlico, London, 1990).

DICKINSON, F. R., 'War and National Reinvention', *Japan in the Great War, 1914–1919* (Harvard University Asia Centre, 1999).

DIXON, J., *Out Since '14. A History of the 1/2nd Monmouthshire Regiment, 1914–1919* (Old Bakehouse Press, Abertillery, 2000).

DE RUVIGNY, THE MARQUIS, *The Roll of Honour* (Naval and Military Press Limited, Dallongton).

GELBER, H. G., 'Opium, Soldiers and Evangelicals', *England's 1840–42 War with China, and its Aftermath* (Palgrave MacMillan, Basingstoke, 2004).

GORST, H. E., 'History of China: Political, Commercial and Social', *The Imperial Interest Library* (Sands and Company, London, 1899).

GOTTBERG, O. von, *Die Helden Von Tsingtau* (Ullstein and Company, Berlin, 1915).

GRIFFITHS, J., *Tea: The Drink that Changed the World* (André Deutsch, London, 2007).

HALPERN, P. G., *A Naval History of World War I* (UCL Press, 1994).

HANES, W. J. and SANELLO, F., *The Opium Wars: The Addicition of One Empire and the Corruption of another* (Robson Books, London, 2003).

HARRISON, H., 'Village Politics and National Politics', in Bickers, R. and Tiedemann, R. G., *The Boxers, China and the World*, 1–15 (Rowman and Littlefield, Plymouth, 2007).

HERNON, I., 'Britain's Forgotten Wars', *Colonial Campaigns of the Nineteenth Century* (Sutton Publishing, Stroud, Gloucestershire, 2003).

HORNE, C. F., *Source Records of the Great War Volume III* (National Alumni, 1923).

HOYT, E., *The Fall of Tsingtao* (Barker, London, 1975).

HSÜ, I. C. Y., *The Rise of Modern China* (Oxford University Press, Oxford, 1990).

HURD, D., *The Arrow War: An Anglo-Chinese Confusion 1856–1860* (Collins, London, 1967).

INGLIS, B., *The Opium War* (Hodder and Stoughton, London, 1976).

JARVIS, S. D. and JARVIS, D. B., *The Cross of Sacrifice, Volume IV* (Naval and Military Press Limited, Dallington, 2001).

KEAY, J., *The Honourable Company* (Harper Collins, London, 1991).

KIRCHOFF, VIZEADMIRAL Z. D., *Der Krieg in den Kolonien; Der Krieg 1914–15 in Wort und Bild, 30 (1915).*

KNOX, MAJOR E. F., 'The Siege of Tsingtao', *The Journal of the United Service Institution of India*, XLIV, No. 200, 267–91 (1915).

LUCAS, SIR C., *The Empire at War* (Oxford University Press, London, 1926).

MACDONALD, SIR C., 'Despatches and Report Relating to the Boxer Rebellion', *The Siege Collection* (The Stationary Office, London, 2001).

MASSIE, R. K., *Dreadnought: Britain, Germany and the Coming of the Great War* (Jonathan Cape, London, 1992).

MASSIE. R. K., *Castles of Steel* (Jonathan Cape, London, 2003).

MOXHAM, R., *Tea, Addiction, Exploitation and Empire* (Robinson, London, 2003).

NISH, I., 'Japan Declares War', *History of the First World War*, 1, No. 12, 313–9 (Purnell, 1969).

NISH, I., 'Admiral Jerram and the German Pacific Fleet 1913–1915', *Mariners Mirror*, 56, 411–21 (1970).

OLIPHANT, L., reprint, *Narrative of the Earl of Elgin's mission to China and Japan in the Years 1857/58/59* (Praeger Publishers, London, 1970).

OUCHERLONY, LIEUTENANT J., reprint, *The Chinese War,* 522 *(*Naval and Military Press, Uckfield, 1843).

PAINE, S. C. M., *The Sino-Japanese War of 1894-1895. Perceptions, Power and Primacy* (Cambridge University Press, Cambridge, 2003).

PARKER, E. H., *Chinese Account of the Opium War* (Kelly and Walsh Limited, Shanghai, 1888).

PLÜSCHOW, G., 'Escape From England'. *Ripping Yarns*, 154 (Findon 2004). PRESTON, D., *The Boxer Rebellion. China's War on Foreigners, 1900* (Robinson, London, 2002).

ROBERTS, J. A. G., *The Complete History of China* (Sutton Publishing, Stroud, Gloucestershire, 2003).

SOUTHEY, S., *British Roll of Honour* (Published for Private Circulation, undated).

STRACHAN, H., *The First World War, I: To Arms* (Oxford University Press, London, 2001).

Supplement to the London Gazette for 30th May 1916. 'The Despatches of Brigadier-General N. W. Barnardiston to the War Office'.

TIEDEMANN, R. G., 'The Church Militant. Armed Conflicts Between Boxers and Christians in North China' in Bickers, R. and Tiedemann, R. G. *The Boxers, China and the World*, 17–41 (Rowman and Littlefield, Plymouth, 2007).

WALEY, A., *The Opium War through Chinese Eyes* (George Allen and Unwin, London, 1958).

WELSH, F., *A History of Hong Kong* (Harper Collins, London, 1997).

WHEELER, W. R., *China and the World War* (MacMillan, New York, 1919).

WHITTAKER, R. E., *Dragon Master. The Kaiser's One-Man Airforce in Tsingtao, China, 1914* (Compass Books, Cleveland, Ohio, 1994).

WISE, T., *Tsingtao. History of the First World War*, I, 12, 320–9 (Purnell Partworks, 1969).

WONG, J. Y., *Deadly Dreams. Opium and the Arrow War (1856–1860) in China* (Cambridge University Press, Cambridge, 1999).

XU, G., *China and the Great War*. 'China's Pursuit of a New National Identity and Internationalism' (Cambridge University Press, Cambridge, 2005).

YAMADA, N., *The Capture of Tsingtao*, 266–84 (United Services Magazine, 1915).

YAP, Y. AND COTTERELL, A. *Chinese Civilization. From the Ming Revivial to Chairman Mao* (Book Club Associates, London, 1977).

Unpublished Documents

Agreement between the British and Japanese Armies for the Capture of Tsingtao (The National Archives, WO32/4996B H122312).

ANON., Translation of German Diary found at Observation Station Fort Bismarck, Tsingtao. (Believed to have been written by a soldier named Pauer of the 3rd Company Marine Artillery). Unpublished personal account. The Museum of the Royal Regiment of Wales, Brecon.

BEAN, SGT. S.D., Diary of the Tsingtao Campaign. The Museum of the Royal Regiment of Wales, Brecon.

BEAUMONT-WALKER, LIEUT. R. K., Tsingtao Campaign 1914. Unpublished personal account. The Museum of the Royal Regiment of Wales, Brecon.

BRADSTOCK, MAJOR J., Diary - Tsingtao. Unpublished personal account. The Museum of the Royal Regiment of Wales, Brecon.

BRADSTOCK, MAJOR J., 1915, Report by Captain J. Bradstock, B Company, 2nd BATTALION SOUTH WALES BORDERERS, on part of the Operations on the night of the 5/6 November, 1914, before Tsingtao. (Included as Appendix 12A in Casson's reponse letter - see reference below).

BRIGADE WAR DIARY, The National Archives. WO32/4996B H122312.

BUCHANAN, SGT. D., Tsingtao. Unpublished personal account. The Museum of the Royal Regiment of Wales, Brecon.

CASSON, LIEUT. COL. H. G., Response to the Report Made on the Action at Tsingtao by Lieutenant Simson. The Museum of the Royal Regiment of Wales, Brecon.

GOING, LIEUT. J., Tsingtao. Unpublished personal account. The Museum of the Royal Regiment of Wales, Brecon.

KONDO, T., 1993. Anglo-Japanese Relations During the Siege of Tsingtao in 1914. Unpublished M.Phil. Thesis. University of Cambridge.

MARGESSON, MAJOR E. C., Diary for 1913 and 1914. Unpublished personal account. The Museum of the Royal Regiment of Wales, Brecon.

General Staff War Office. 1906 Military Report on Kiao-Chau.

Japanese Plan of Attack. National Archive. WO32/4996B H122312

Orders - Brigadier N H. Barnardiston, September 22nd 1914 (and subsequent days). The National Archives. WO32/4996B H122312.

SIMSON, LIEUT. H. J., Report on the Action at Tsingtao. The National Archives (MO 3(c) 9554).

Standing Orders. H.B.M. Legation Guard Peking 1913. Printing Section 1st K.G.O. Sappers and Miners - Tientsin. The Museum of the Royal Regiment of Wales, Brecon.

War Diary of the 2nd Battalion the South Wales Borderers September - November 1914.

The Museum of the Royal Regiment of Wales, Brecon.

War Dairy of the 36th Sikhs October 22nd 1914 to November 7th 1914. National Archives. WO32/4996B H122312.

WATANABE, MAJOR-GENERAL. Note to Barnardiston indicating Japanese artillery fire plan. The National Archives. WO32/4996B H122312.

Web Pages

DENIS, C., 'Tsingtao Campaign', *Japan in the Great War: Diplomacy and Internal Politics* (2000), www.gwpda.org/naval/tsingtao
www.jadu.de/jaduland/kolonien/asien/kiautschou/japan/index
www.tsingtau.info
www. vlib.us/medical/pow/consul

Index

(Page numbers in italics indicate a reference to a photograph)